Old Testament Times

Text first published in the U.S.A. by
Wm. B. Eerdmans Pub. Co.
255 Jefferson Ave. S.E.
Grand Rapids
Michigan 49503
U.S.A.

Published 2005 in the U.S.A.
by Baker Books,
a division of
Baker Publishing Group
PO Box 6287, Grand Rapids
MI 49516-6287 USA

ISBN 0-8010-1286-4

Design by Peter Wyart,
Three's Company

Worldwide co-edition produced by
Lion Hudson plc, Mayfield House,
256 Banbury Road, Oxford OX2 7DH,
England
Tel: +44 (0) 1865 302750
Fax +44 (0) 1865 302757
Email: coed@lionhudson.com.
www.lionhudson.com

Printed in Singapore

Picture acknowledgments

Photographs
British Museum: pp. 29, 71, 81, 87, 89, 93,
105, 107, 113, 115, 135, 247, 248, 250, 255,
261
Karen Demuth: p. 14
Tim Dowley: pp. 5, 109, 141, 149, 165, 169,
176, 185, 199, 202, 298, 299, 303, 313, 315,
317, 318, 319, 323, 327
Illustrated London News: p. 209
Hanan Issachar: pp. 138, 139
Zev Radovan: pp. 1, 48, 51, 57, 159, 288
Jamie Simson: pp. 267, 271
Peter Wyart: 3, 19, 21, 25, 59, 73, 101, 103,
125, 150, 151, 195, 201, 207, 214, 222, 223,
225, 235, 241, 242, 243, 245, 244, 251, 275,
285, 301, 321, 329, 330, 331

Illustrations
Brian Bartles: pp. 192-93
Jeremy Gower: pp. 210-11
James MacDonald: pp. 11, 53, 203
Alan Parry: p. 306

Maps
Hardlines & Jeremy Gower

Charts
Peter Wyart

OLD TESTAMENT
TIMES

A SOCIAL, POLITICAL, AND CULTURAL CONTEXT

BY

R. K. HARRISON

BakerBooks

Preface

THE STUDY OF ANCIENT NEAR EASTERN HISTORY IN general has become a highly complex matter involving unfamiliar original languages, a long series of important archaeological discoveries, and an appreciation of the characteristics that distinguish the Oriental outlook on life from its Western counterpart. Because the Hebrews drew to a large extent upon the contemporary cultural patterns of Near Eastern life, the history of the Israelites can best be understood by placing the narratives of the Old Testament against a background of what is known about the culture and archaeology of the period covered.

The present work is an attempt to trace the outline of this history and to bring such cultural, archaeological, and sociological discoveries to bear upon the Old Testament narratives as will illumine some of the more obscure events, and place others firmly within the framework of ancient Near Eastern life. There are numerous unanswered questions connected with the history of Old Testament times, of course, and while modern archaeological discoveries have done much to clarify and resolve certain difficulties, they have as yet been unable to provide a final answer to some of the more pressing problems with which the student of Old Testament times is confronted. The author has endeavored to outline these difficulties when they occur as fairly as possible without imposing an undue burden of detail upon the text.

For permission to reproduce short quotations from copyright works the author wishes to express his grateful thanks to the following: to the University of Chicago Press for permission to reprint sections from A. Heidel, *The Gilgamesh Epic and Old Testament Parallels* (second edition, 1949), A. Heidel, *The Babylonian Genesis* (second edition, 1951), and D. D. Luckenbill, *Ancient Records of Assyria and Babylonia* (two volumes, 1926); to Princeton University Press for permission to quote from J. Finegan, *Light From the Ancient Past* (1949), and J. B. Pritchard (Ed.), *Ancient Near Eastern Texts Relating to the Old Testament* (1950); to the American Philosophical Society for their kindness in allowing the use

Excavations at Hazor in northern Israel.

of copyright material in S. N. Kramer, *Sumerian Mythology* (1947 edition), originally published in Volume 21 of the *Memoirs* of the Society, and to Dr. Kramer himself for his ready consent; to Dr. G. E. Wright for permission to use material contained in various numbers of *The Biblical Archaeologist;* to the Clarendon Press of Oxford for their kindness in permitting the use of material in S. L. Caiger, *Bible and Spade* (1936); to Ventnor Publishers Inc. for their readiness to allow quotations from C. H. Gordon, *Introduction to Old Testament Times* (1953); and to Messrs. Ernest Benn Ltd. for permission to quote from C. L. Woolley, *Ur of the Chaldees* (1950 edition).

I wish to express my gratitude to Principal Leslie Hunt of Wycliffe College for his encouragement during the preparation of this work, and to Mrs. W. A. Holmes, who came so willingly to my aid and typed out the manuscript with great speed and accuracy. I wish to express my gratitude to Mr. Bruce A. Easson and his associates for so generously supplying me with photographs of artifacts in the Royal Ontario Museum, and to Mr. Cornelius Lambregtse and the staff of the Wm. B. Eerdmans Publishing Company for the care taken in the production of this book. Finally my thanks are due to the Rev. Norman Green, Assistant Director of the McLaughlin Planetarium, Toronto, for his skill and patience in correcting the proofs.

R. K. Harrison
Wycliffe College, University of Toronto

Contents

1. Recovering Near Eastern Antiquity

The Old Testament Cultural Context

AT ALL PERIODS OF OLD TESTAMENT HISTORY THE ANCIENT Hebrews were brought into contact with other nations in the Near East. Abraham moved with his family and possessions from Mesopotamia to Canaan during the second millennium B.C., and visited Egypt briefly before settling down in the land that was to become the home of his descendants. In the days of Moses, the Israelites who had settled some two centuries earlier in the Goshen region of the Nile delta found themselves living under conditions of bondage in Egypt, and before they occupied the Promised Land they came into conflict with the nations of Transjordan and with the pagan inhabitants of Canaan itself.

During the time of David the Philistines, who had migrated earlier to southwest Palestine from the Aegean, presented a grave threat to the existence of the Israelite nation, and were only subdued after a prolonged struggle. In the days of King Solomon there was a great degree of cultural and commercial contact with the Phoenicians of northwest Palestine, and their influence was particularly evident in the constructional activity of the time. Scarcely had the northern kingdom of Israel become an independent entity after the death of Solomon when the rising power of the Syrian regime began to challenge its existence, while to the south Judah became the unwilling victim of Egyptian military aggression.

As time passed, the Syrian empire yielded to the menacing power of the Assyrians, and this turn of events ultimately brought about the destruction of the northern kingdom. The kingdom of Judah, though rather more remote geographically than Israel, also had periodic contacts with the Syrian rulers of

Damascus and, like Israel, was invaded occasionally by the armies of the Assyrians. Partly as the result of Egyptian intrigues the southern kingdom came to a calamitous end at the hand of Babylonian and Chaldean forces, and its most prominent citizens were carried off in captivity to Babylonia. After nearly seventy years a remnant returned to Palestine under Persian rule to begin life again among largely unsympathetic neighbors, of whom the Arabs were the most troublesome. The rise of Alexander the Great saw the rapid spread of Greek culture across the ancient Near East, and with it came a great many customs and traditions that affected all parts of the Greek empire, including Judea. This situation persisted until the Romans assimilated the Greek provinces of Syria and Egypt into their own empire, and in the process brought the Jews under imperial rule.

In point of fact, however, it was by no means accidental that the Hebrews encountered these and other, smaller, nations during their long and varied history, for the land God gave to them was actually an important land bridge, linking the various cultural areas of the Near East. To the northwest in Anatolia was the locale of the ancient Hittite empire, while to the southwest stretched the fertile land of Egypt. Further to the east, between the Tigris and Euphrates rivers, lay the bustling territory of Babylonia, while to the north and east were situated most of the important cities in the Assyrian empire.

Caravan trading routes extended in antiquity from northern India to the Sumerian cities of southern Mesopotamia, and from there wended their way along the length of the meandering River Euphrates to Syria, northern Palestine, and the land of the Hittites, or else traversed the Arabian desert westward and then passed to the north through southern Canaan or to the southwest into Egypt. In the busy, thriving world of Old Testament times the Israelites were placed in a fundamentally important, strategic geographical position. Any travelers who wanted to pass from one part of the Near East to another generally found that their journey took them within easy reach of Palestine if not actually through Israelite territory.

Citizens of the land of Palestine were thus members of a vigorous Near Eastern life whether they were always aware of it or not, for there was a constant interchange of cultural forms in one way or another. For example, certain fundamental building techniques developed by the Sumerians were utilized by the Egyptians in the construction of the pyramids in the Old Kingdom period. The pottery of the Minoan Age in Crete was widely circulated among Near Eastern nations in the second millennium B.C., a fact that enabled Sir Flinders Petrie, the eminent archaeologist, to formulate a system of ceramic dating for given periods of Near Eastern history. Again, the discovery by the Hittites of Anatolia of techniques for the smelting of iron ore introduced the Iron Age to Israel and her neighbors, and this eventuality brought with it a great many advances in commerce, warfare, and daily life.

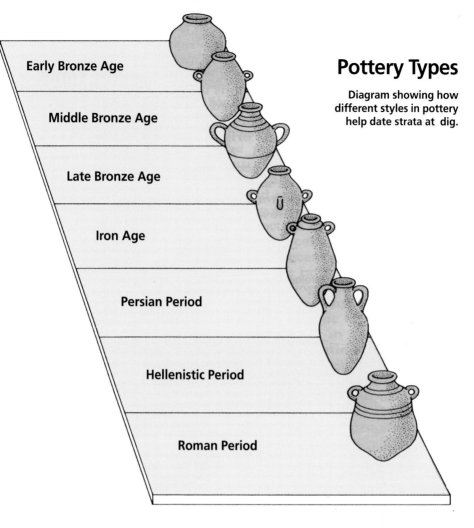

Pottery Types

Diagram showing how different styles in pottery help date strata at dig.

Early Bronze Age

Middle Bronze Age

Late Bronze Age

Iron Age

Persian Period

Hellenistic Period

Roman Period

From at least the seventh century B.C. the Greeks had supplied mercenary soldiers in varying degrees for the armies of the Babylonians, Egyptians, and Persians, and the traditions they brought with them were quick to bear fruit when the victorious forces of Alexander the Great swept so dramatically across the Near East in the fourth century B.C. These and many other instances of cultural and political interdependence make it clear that from the standpoint of geography, history, and life in general the world of the Old Testament was coextensive with that of the ancient Near East. Because of this situation it has now become evident that the people and times of the Old Testament cannot and must not be studied in isolation from the larger Near Eastern background. Whatever information can be discovered about the history, religion, languages, literatures, and cultures of the ancient Oriental peoples will necessarily have an important bearing upon comparable aspects of the Old Testament.

While many facets of the cultural background were only of rather incidental interest to the various writers whose works have been preserved or reflected

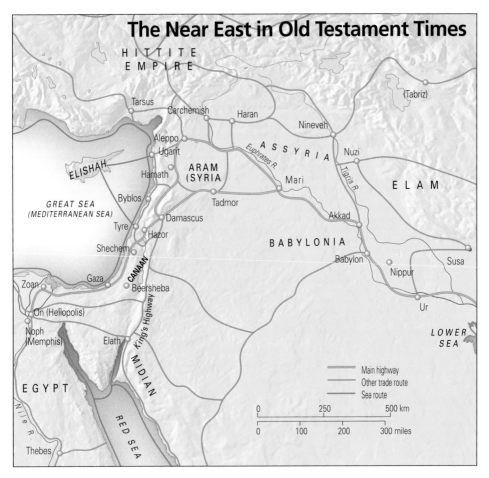

The Near East in Old Testament Times

HITTITE
EMPIRE

Tarsus

Carchemish

Haran

Nineveh

(Tabriz)

Aleppo
Ugarit

ASSYRIA

Nuzi

ELISHAH

Hamath

ARAM
(SYRIA)

Euphrates R.

Mari

ELAM

GREAT SEA
(MEDITERRANEAN SEA)

Byblos

Tadmor

Tigris R.

Akkad

Tyre

Damascus

Hazor

BABYLONIA

Shechem

Babylon

Susa

Gaza

Nippur

Zoan

Beersheba

CANAAN

Ur

On (Heliopolis)

LOWER
SEA

Noph
(Memphis)

Elath

King's Highway

MIDIAN

EGYPT

Nile R.

RED SEA

Main highway
Other trade route
Sea route

0   250   500 km

0   100   200   300 miles

Thebes

in the Old Testament, the Scriptural narratives can nevertheless be illumined with profit at a great many points by being set appropriately in the full context of all the related ancient Near Eastern material available. Such a procedure has the undeniable advantage of enabling the modern reader to contemplate the Old Testament scene in a manner that was not possible until comparatively recent years, and in consequence it will give him a sense of participation in the labors, aspirations, trials, and triumphs of the men and women whose lives formed part of the stream of Old Testament history.

Records of the Past

Because the vast majority of the ancient Near Eastern peoples were busily engaged in writing history as well as in making it, there are a great many written sources of various kinds that have survived to furnish an interesting and authoritative picture of the ancient past. These materials emerge from many

An Assyrian cylinder seal and its impression. The Babylonians and Assyrians signed their documents by rolling such a seal over the surface of a clay tablet while the clay was still wet.

different situations, and while some of them are only of a local nature, others have a bearing upon much wider aspects of ancient Near Eastern life.

Literary Records

The high degree of literacy that obtained in Mesopotamia and Palestine from the beginning of the second millennium B.C. resulted in a vast assortment of written compositions, many of which are no longer extant. Some of these were records in the best sense, whether of domestic, personal, national, or international affairs. Others, however, were literary products in their own right, and varied from the religious epic poetry of Sumeria and Babylonia to the carefully written medical texts of the Egyptian Old Kingdom period. Not uncommon throughout Near Eastern lands were *stelae,* or large upright monuments generally made of diorite, limestone, granite, or some other durable stone, on which was engraved an inscription commemorating specific persons and events. Thus when Meneptah of Egypt (c. 1224–1215 B.C.) defeated an invasion of Sea Peoples and Libyans in the fifth year of his reign, he recorded his noteworthy achievement in a series of hymns inscribed on the back of a black granite *stele* that had originally been erected almost one hundred and fifty years earlier by Amenhotep III. This monument was then set up in his mortuary temple at Thebes, while at the same time a duplicate of the inscription was engraved on the walls of the massive temple at Karnak, and has unfortunately only survived the passing of the centuries in fragmentary form.

Biographies as such were also commissioned from time to time, and were generally executed within the lifetime of the individual concerned. For example, the redoubtable general Uni, who commanded the Egyptian armies of the

Part of the approach to the Karnak Temple, Luxor, Egypt.

Sixth Dynasty about 2300 B.C., ordered his biography to be carved in stone so as to publicize his military exploits in Canaan. This work, which was conceived, composed, and completed within a few months at the most, dealt with various phases of his career, one important aspect of which was the recognition of his successes by the pharaoh, and included the victory paean he and his forces chanted during their return from Palestine.

A great many inscriptions have been found on buildings of all kinds throughout the Near East, and in nature and content they frequently resemble their more modern counterparts. The Sumerians were the first people to place inscriptions on the cornerstones or foundation stones of temples, palaces, and other structures. When excavated, many of these are of considerable help in clarifying problems of dating and general chronology, since they invariably contain the names of contemporary rulers, and in consequence are eagerly sought after by archaeologists. When Sir Leonard Woolley was excavating at the al Ubaid levels on the outskirts of Ur of the Chaldees, the traditional home of Abraham, he unearthed a small oblong tablet of white limestone bearing an inscription. On being deciphered it disclosed that the building had been erected by a certain Sumerian ruler named A-anne-pad-da, the son of the founder of the First Dynasty of Ur. This contemporary source at once established the historical factuality of the ancient Sumerian king lists, and also preserved the name of A-anne-pad-da, which had somehow fallen out of all the other surviving ancient records of royal rule in Sumeria.

Inscriptions were sometimes placed on sacrificial altars to commemorate the deity who was being worshiped or to designate the function of the particular altar. In this latter connection a rather minor problem of Hebrew translation was clarified by the discovery at Palmyra in northern Syria of a limestone altar with projections or "horns" at each corner. On it was inscribed the hitherto obscure word *hammanim* or "altar of incense," and this must now be accepted as the correct rendering for the "images" (K.J.V.) or "sun image" (R.V.) of Leviticus 26:30; II Chronicles 14:5; 34:4, 7; Isaiah 17:8; 27:9; and Ezekiel 6:4, 6.

Unlike the Egyptians, the ancient Mesopotamians made extensive collections of laws, which are fundamentally important both for a modern understanding of the contemporary social structure and also for the task of reconstructing a history of jurisprudence. The most celebrated Mesopotamian legal code was that of Hammurabi, the last great ruler of the First Dynasty of Babylon. This corpus drew upon earlier Sumerian legislative material such as the codes of Eshnunna and Lipit-Ishtar, and several copies of it were made in the form of *stelae* so as to bring its contents to the notice of the general public. While the precise date of Hammurabi is still rather uncertain at the time of writing, there can be no doubt that the code itself reflected, and legislated for, the social conditions that obtained at the beginning of the second millennium B.C., if not earlier.

Medical and scientific texts from both Babylonia and Egypt go as far back as the late third millennium B.C. at the least. Tablets that have been unearthed from sites in ancient Sumeria have been found to contain important material relating to such scientific topics as astronomy, mathematics, geography, pharmacy, and medicine, demonstrating clearly how advanced Sumerian culture actually was. The medical traditions of ancient Egypt seem to have arisen at the end of the third millennium B.C. for the most part, and were copied out at a later period with some additions and modifications to assume the form of medical and surgical textbooks or case histories.

The most important of these Egyptian papyrus documents were discovered from 1862, and include the Edwin Smith surgical papyrus from Thebes; the Ebers papyrus dealing with pharmacy and medicine, also found at Thebes about 1862; the Hearst papyrus, which was recovered from Upper Egypt in 1899 and which was found to constitute a fairly close copy of the Ebers scroll; and the Kahun medical papyri found in 1889 by Sir Flinders Petrie in the Egyptian Fayyum. To this impressive list of documents can be added the Greater Berlin papyrus, which, although it is later in date than the Ebers papyrus, is apparently derived from even more venerable sources.

King lists were compiled from a very early period in Mesopotamia, and those from Sumeria in particular are of great value in helping to establish proper chronological sequences. Some of these documents present rather unexpected problems with regard to the length of the reigns attributed to the various kings. One of these, the so-called Weld-Blundell prism, preserved a king list that had evidently been compiled during the prosperous Third Dynasty of Ur, and while it furnished a list of eight rulers of Sumerian cities in chronological order, it assigned reigns of completely unrealistic length to each of them. From ancient Egyptian sources came a small ivory tablet that listed the rulers of the first two dynasties, and because of its nature it is extremely valuable for the information it furnishes about that remote period of Egyptian history. The first six Egyptian dynasties were described more fully in the form of annals in the celebrated Palermo Stone, which can be dated with reasonable accuracy at about 2400 B.C.

Subsequent to this time the recording of events after the fashion of annals became widespread in the ancient Near East. Consequently anything that was of importance in the reigns of particular monarchs was either engraved on the walls of palaces, mortuary temples, pyramids, and *stelae,* or was preserved for posterity in some other equally appropriate manner. This practice had the undeniable benefit of giving a special kind of permanence to written records, and has made available to the modern student the achievements of such renowned Near Eastern rulers as Thotmes III, Ramses II and III, Shishak, Shalmaneser III, Sennacherib, Sargon II, Esarhaddon, Cyrus the Great, and Darius the Great.

Religious epics were common in Mesopotamia, and these compositions furnish a great deal of information concerning the superstitious beliefs and practices of antiquity. A great epic of creation, based upon earlier Sumerian mythological material, was compiled during the First Dynasty of Babylon, and originally comprised seven tablets of an average length of 150 lines each. It dealt with the story of the origin of the gods; the battle between Marduk, patron deity of Babylon, and Tiamat, the salt-water ocean; and the creation of man in a divinely ordered universe. Yet another celebrated literary cycle of the First Babylonian Dynasty was the Epic of Gilgamesh, which also depended upon earlier Sumerian mythological traditions that described the adventures of the legendary Gilgamesh, who was ruler of Uruk towards the end of the fourth millennium B.C. The eleventh tablet of this composition is important in that it preserved the Babylonian tradition of a devastating flood, the details of which have numerous features in common with the corresponding account in Genesis.

Other sources of information concerning the beliefs of the ancient Mesopotamians included hymns to the deities, pantheons or lists of gods along with their relationships and functions, and a wide variety of texts containing the rituals that were to be followed in the different forms of worship. From Egypt came works such as the celebrated *Book of the Dead,* a haphazard collection of magical spells that were thought to be of value to the deceased when he confronted Osiris, the judge and ruler of the realm of the dead.

This material was in fact the accumulation of the Coffin Texts that from the Middle Kingdom period onwards had been written on papyrus strips and placed in the coffin alongside the body of the dead person. The Coffin Texts actually comprised a number of potent magical spells that were recited during funeral services in ancient Egypt, and they received their name because they were also written on the walls of coffins so as to be within easy reach of the departed individual should he need them at any moment in the afterlife.

The Coffin Texts in turn were part of a larger body of magical spells and incantations known as the Pyramid Texts. These inscriptions were written on inside walls of pyramids for the benefit of the dead who occupied these funerary monuments, and they make it abundantly clear that the departed were thought of as being in need of the assistance of magic to an even greater extent than the gods or living human beings. From this type of material it becomes evident that in ancient Egypt any "religious" acts such as attempts on the part of worshipers to contact their gods were in fact of a magical nature. Indeed, the Egyptian language had no specific word for "religion" any more than that of the Hebrews had, and as a result the nearest that the Egyptians could come to the idea was through the use of the term *hike,* "magic" or "magical power."

Of a rather different nature were the ancient Egyptian Execration Texts, which originated in the Middle Kingdom period, perhaps about the Twelfth Dynasty. They comprised the means by which the reigning pharaohs ceremonially and magically cursed all their actual and potential enemies. The texts have been recovered in two forms, either as red pottery bowls or as roughly fashioned human figurines in clay, all of which were inscribed with specific cursings and then smashed ceremonially in accordance with the principles of sympathetic magic that indicated how all opposition to the pharaohs ought to be shattered. The texts have an important bearing upon the geography and topography of the ancient Near East, since in the Asiatic lists there are names of towns whose identification is still far from certain. The personal names are also interesting, since they show among other things that the settled inhabitants of Palestine and Syria were having to accommodate strange national groups in their midst in the Egyptian Middle Kingdom period.

Literary compositions as such from the Near East also throw a great deal of incidental light upon the political and social conditions of the time, as can be illustrated by reference to the *Tale of Sinuhe.* This interesting Egyptian story narrated the fortunes of a nobleman of the twentieth century B.C. who had to flee to Palestine to seek political asylum when the aged pharaoh Amenhemet I died. Very much the same considerations apply to a later age of Egyptian history as reflected in the narrative describing the *Travels of Wen-Amun.* This composition shows the low esteem into which Egyptian power had fallen in the eyes of surrounding nations by 1100 B.C. by describing the frustrations and humiliations an Egyptian priest encountered on his mission to Phoenicia to obtain cedar for the sacred boat of the god Re.

Other valuable sources of information about Near Eastern antiquity include diplomatic correspondence, whether of the kind recovered from the days of Hammurabi or the more familiar Tell el-Amarna letters of the fourteenth century B.C. Business documents of all kinds have been unearthed at a great many

Mesopotamian sites, and have provided an unexpected picture of advanced social development in the third and second millenniums B.C. Discoveries of such sources as lists of names are of great importance in establishing connections between geographical areas in different periods of history, and in showing, to some extent at least, the general trend of migratory movements in the Near East.

Particularly significant for the Mesopotamians were genealogies and family trees, of which a great many examples have been found at Mari and Nuzu. Although there were both civil and religious calendars in use in the Near East by at least the beginning of the second millennium B.C., from which reckonings could be made, the favorite method of recording the rather personal histories of individual families was independent of calendrical usage and involved instead the formulation of a genealogy or a family tree. In these lists there were no references to the reigns of kings or other objective features of calendars or chronologies, apart from attempts at scribal dating in the colophon or concluding section of the tablet, and instead the lists concentrated upon prominent individuals of the various families and their descendants. For a great many people this delineating of the different generations in order of descent was the only history with which they ever came into contact, and this same situation will be readily observed in the Old Testament, where the genealogical lists are in fact one form of ancient historical composition. Aside from purely personal considerations, however, the family trees recovered from Mari and Nuzu are significant for the nature of the information they furnish concerning certain contemporary social customs, notably that of adoption, a matter that will be dealt with subsequently.

Archaeological Sources

It will be evident from the foregoing outline of available records of Near Eastern antiquity that much of what constitutes literary material is actually of an archaeological nature also. While some of the sources of information mentioned previously were in existence long before the rise of modern archaeology as a scientific discipline, a great many have come within the reach of scholars as the result of fairly recent excavations at widely separated locations in the Near East. Some of these materials are pictorial in nature, as with the sculptured bas-reliefs of Babylonian and Assyrian palaces and temples, or the beautifully executed paintings that decorated the interior of Egyptian palaces, temples, pyramids, and mortuary chambers.

Yet there are many others of a nonpictorial nature that have only been recovered after painstaking work amidst the ruins of long-buried cultures. Here the skill of the archaeologist counts for a very great deal, since he is frequently faced not only with the delicate and exacting task of excavating damaged artifacts, but also with the responsibility of attempting to reconstruct them to some extent before any significant evaluation of the discoveries can be made. While the professional archaeologist now has such spectacular aids as electromagnetic detection devices and radiocarbon dating machines to assist him in his work, much of the skill of archaeology continues to depend upon the patient removal and sifting of sand or soil, the accurate assembling of broken pottery artifacts, the correct decipherment of badly weathered inscriptions that in the first instance may have been indifferently inscribed in an obscure language, the establishing of proper chronological sequences based upon ceramic and other evidence, and the correlating of the information gleaned from the site under excavation with what is already known of the general period from other related locations or sources.

There is obviously a point at which all this activity begins to transcend the strict functions of the archaeologist, whose primary task after all is to recover the material remains of the human past, and to move into the realm of the Near Eastern scholar, who has the responsibility of evaluating the material that has been recovered and of estimating its significance in and for the life of the ancient Near East as a whole. Because of the continuous contacts the various nations had with one another, specific archaeological discoveries not infrequently prove to have a wider bearing upon Near Eastern culture generally than might appear at first sight.

Thus the discovery of the Tell el-Amarna letters provided scholars with the

A death boat carries the deceased to the underworld to await judgment. Model of a familiar theme in Egyptian thought.

first major example of international diplomatic correspondence written in cuneiform, and demonstrated among other things the extent to which Akkadian had come to be recognized as the language of diplomacy in the second millennium B.C. Hittite treaties from the same general period that were recovered from ruined Boghazköy demonstrated the classical structure of international suzerain-vassal and parity treaties, the first of which is of great importance for a correct understanding of the literary form and theological significance of the book of Deuteronomy. The cuneiform tablets from Mari and Nuzu furnish a great deal of information about the conditions of life in the period of the Hebrew Patriarchs, and this has been supplemented by the excavations at Alalakh, where the texts are actually considerably closer in matters of chronology and geography to the Patriarchal age than the materials from Mari and Nuzu.

The archaeologist is particularly fortunate when he happens to uncover the archives of a royal palace or a temple, particularly if, as at Mari and elsewhere, this turn of events takes place fairly near the beginning of an expedition. Equally auspicious is the recovery of a library that had been built up painstakingly by some ruler of antiquarian tastes, such as was the case in 1853 with the excavations at Nineveh by Rassam, where the library of Ashurbanipal was unearthed from the ruins of the royal palace.

This enormous and valuable collection of approximately one hundred thousand tablets had been amassed during the reign of the cultured and erudite monarch who was the last great ruler of the Assyrian empire. From the nature of the excavations it became apparent that Ashurbanipal had ordered his scribes to collect and copy a vast range of material in such diverse fields as history, grammar, law, literature, medicine, and astrology. In addition to all this, Ashurbanipal had managed to acquire a great many letters, poems, hymns, incantations, dictionaries, and business contracts of all kinds, along with hundreds of other tablets that dealt with topics of general and more particular interest.

Subsequent to this discovery several other important cuneiform archives were unearthed at various sites, and these have added enormously to the material resources of ancient Near Eastern studies. The excavation of the library of Ashurbanipal and its related artifacts at Nineveh from 1853 was followed by the discovery of the Tell el-Amarna tablets in 1887, the collection of cuneiform texts from Nippur in 1889 that are still in process of being evaluated by scholars, the recovery of the Hittite archives at Boghazköy from 1906, the group of tablets at Nuzu found from 1925, the important literary texts from Ugarit that were first uncovered in 1929, the vast archives from Mari excavated since 1936, and the amazing discovery of the Dead Sea scrolls since 1947. To these can be added hundreds of subsidiary artifacts ranging from cuneiform cylinders and prisms to inscribed bricks, scarabs, seals of various kinds, ostraca, *stelae,* papyrus documents, sculptures, and the less spectacular items of everyday life.

The enormous antiquity of the site of Jericho (Tell es-Sultan) was demonstrated in 1952 by Dame Kathleen Kenyon, whose work there showed that Jericho had an occupational history that reached back to the fifth millennium B.C.

21

On certain notable occasions the archaeologist is able to extend the horizon of ancient history in a surprising manner. For example, the enormous antiquity of the site of Jericho (Tell es-Sultan) was demonstrated in 1952 by Kathleen M. Kenyon, whose work there has shown that Jericho was one of the oldest locations in the Near East and had an occupational history that reached back to the fifth millennium B.C. The nature of the prepottery phase at Jericho was made clear by the excavations, which revealed among other things the presence of a huge defensive ditch some thirty feet wide. The primitive inhabitants of the site had dug this fosse down into the bed rock to a depth of eight feet by means of primitive hand tools, and had surrounded it with an eighteen-foot wall. A circular stone bastion was mounted on the top of this structure, and proved to be the earliest known example of a city fortification in the ancient Near East. Discoveries of this kind push back the frontiers of knowledge concerning the origins of Near Eastern culture and demand a revision not merely of current ideas of prehistory, but also of the chronological considerations involved.

Just as important as the manner in which archaeological excavations have served to illumine the contemporary scene in the Near East is the fact that many discoveries have helped to confirm, directly or indirectly, the historicity of certain events mentioned in the Old Testament, the nature of which will become evident in subsequent chapters. The reader should beware of the temptation of assuming that all that is necessary for the historicity of given sections of the Old Testament to be made evident to all is for the archaeologist to put his spade into the ground. This view is as ill advised as it is unfortunate, since it is merely a matter of record that the historical picture has, on occasions, become more confused than was the case previously as a consequence of archaeological activity at specific sites. Thus the various excavations at ancient Jericho have combined to make it almost impossible for the modern scholar to say anything with absolute certainty about the nature of the city in the time of Joshua, a result that was naturally far removed from the intentions of those who worked at the site.

Despite this and other problems, such as the divergent interpretations of the same archaeological material, there can be no question but that the general tenor of the discoveries serves to confirm the historicity of the Biblical accounts rather than to depreciate or disparage them, in the manner adopted by a former generation of liberal scholars. Thus the Moabite Stone, discovered at Dibon in 1868, furnished independent confirmation from Moabite sources of the fact that Omri, king of Israel (885/4–874/3 B.C.), gained control of northern Moab and exacted heavy tribute from the country throughout his reign.

Again, four additional tablets of the Babylonian Chronicle that were first published by D. J. Wiseman in 1956 not merely substantiated the Old Testament tradition relating to the fall of Jerusalem in 597 B.C., but also contained an account of a previously unrecorded battle between the Babylonians and Egyptians in 601 B.C., in which both sides suffered heavy losses of men and equipment. These and other similar examples of the way in which our knowledge of the ancient past has been enriched show that it is legitimate to expect archaeological discoveries to shed at least some light on the purely historical aspects of the Old Testament, as well as on the social, political, and religious elements of Hebrew life.

Biblical Writings

Yet it has to be recognized that archaeology by itself cannot and ought not to be expected or required to prove the "truth" of the Old Testament. The real function of the sources under consideration is to provide such information about the life and structure of ancient Near Eastern society as will enable the modern student of Scripture to see the sacred record in proper cultural and historical perspective. Only from this point onwards can the concern of the archaeologist or the Near Eastern scholar be transformed into a theological one, for by then there will be to hand some of the more important material information necessary for a correct understanding and interpretation of the inspired Scriptures.

Again it must be emphasized that it is no longer legitimate or desirable to study the contents of the Old Testament in isolation from other aspects of ancient life in the Near East, if only because, as observed previously, the world of the Old Testament was coextensive at all periods with that of the Near East. Viewing the Hebrew Scriptures against the appropriate cultural background in which God spoke to men will also serve another important purpose, namely, that of establishing in the mind of the student of Near Eastern antiquity a proper chronological sense in relation to the Divine revelation. This will then prevent the expositor of Scripture from applying inappropriate categories of Christian morality or interpretation to settings or events that were governed by a widely different ethos, and will ground his explanations in a legitimate historical sequence.

In the light of what is now known about the high degree of literacy that obtained in the ancient Near East during the second millennium B.C., it is possible to assign written Biblical material with confidence to a much earlier phase of cultural development than was formerly the case. Because of the fact that important events were invariably recorded by the scribes of antiquity at the time when they actually occurred, or very shortly thereafter, it is now unnecessary to propose a prolonged degree of oral transmission of material before it assumed a written form. In fact, it is now realized that the chief function of oral transmission in the Near East was to disseminate the material in contemporary society, and not primarily to preserve it for posterity, since written records of important occurrences would already be in existence in any event.

That the bulk of the source material of some of the earlier Old Testament books is of great antiquity is beyond serious question. Many of the records of ante- and postdiluvian life in Genesis were most probably of a contemporary nature, or nearly so, and appear to have been brought from Mesopotamia, where they seem to have originated for the most part, to Canaan as a result of the Patriarchal migrations. The narratives concerning Joseph fit naturally into a clearly defined historical period of ancient Egyptian life, namely, that of the Hyksos pharaohs, who ruled from about 1720 B.C. to about 1570 B.C.

Again, much of the source material that underlies the books of Exodus, Leviticus, and Numbers reflects a specific wilderness milieu such as obtained for a generation following the Exodus from Egypt. Allusions to ancient literary sources that have not survived the centuries are seen in the mention of the *Book of Jashar* in Joshua and Samuel, while another document known as the *Book of the Wars of the Lord* is cited in Numbers. The objectivity and selectivity of the Hebrew historians is made evident by the controlled manner in which they handled the sources available to them for the compilation of such works as the books of Kings and Chronicles. Since a great deal more is known at the present about their principles of compilation than was the case formerly, their writings are now seen to be historically reliable and trustworthy.

The wide range of literature that existed in the ancient Near East is amply reflected in the stories, poems, collections of proverbs, anthologies of prophetic utterances, and chronicles of events that can be found in the Old Testament. Indeed, this collection of writings mirrors its background with such fidelity that one can assert quite safely that the Old Testament compositions are in fact a microcosm of Near Eastern life and literary activity. There is, however, one significant difference, and that involves the spiritual ethos of the various Biblical authors. Whereas the scribes of all neighboring countries lived and wrote against a profoundly polytheistic background, the writers of Israel were essentially monotheistic in outlook, worshiping one God alone and denying both the existence and authority popularly attributed to the images of wood and stone that were venerated by pagan peoples.

Furthermore, the vocation of the Israelites as the Chosen People carried with it the responsibility of witnessing to the surrounding nations concerning the ethical and moral nature of God and His will for mankind. The fact that the Israelites never attained to this evangelistic ideal in no way diminished the importance of the task to which they had been called in their covenant relationship with God. In the end most of the prophetic figures of Old Testament times found themselves fully occupied with the internal problem of attempting to recall the Israelites to the demands of their vocation, and as the pre-exilic prophetic oracles show, the endeavor was greatly prejudiced from the very beginning. It was only after the sin of the nation had been punished by exile

Panels from the quadrangular prism known as the Black Obelisk of Shalmaneser III.
The scenes depict captive Israelites bringing tribute.

in a foreign land that the Jews began to make some attempt to meet their spiritual responsibilities, but the witness thus engendered was largely of a passive order and seems to have made no attempt to convert pagan nations to the worship of the God of Israel. The sources that deal with this prolonged phase of Hebrew history reflect with great fidelity the difficulties the servants of God encountered in different generations as they endeavored to promote the ideals of the Sinai covenant in Israelite life, and at the same time they demonstrate clearly the uniqueness of the Divine revelation given by God to the Hebrew Patriarchs and their spiritual successors.

Describing the Near Eastern Past

When the writers of Mesopotamian antiquity compiled their king lists, genealogies, and other historical accounts, they were attempting, as responsible historiographers, to set down the data as they knew them. Yet at the same time they were frequently concerned to present their information in such a manner as to preserve a proper relative internal balance of factuality. This principle, which by no means died with the passing of Near Eastern antiquity, meant that, for example, unimportant individuals in genealogical lists or family trees could be omitted if it was thought desirable by the compiler. It also allowed a degree of latitude in the use of such terms of descent as "son" or "daughter," which among the Semites were frequently employed to mean "grandson" and "granddaughter" when the occasion required, a practice that has led many an unwary student astray. It meant, too, that numbers could be used not merely to signify concrete factual data but also to indicate value judgments on the part of the ancient history writers.

Thus it seems probable that the compilers, in attributing what appear to modern Occidental readers to be impossibly long reigns to individuals named in some Mesopotamian king lists, were actually commenting on the significance or importance of specific individuals by means of the symbolic use of numbers, a custom that is by no means unknown in different connections in the Western world. It seems clear from cuneiform and other annals that the ancient scribes felt at liberty to describe momentous events in the kind of terms that were appropriate to the occasions under discussion. One method in common usage was to employ large numbers, as with the computation of those Hebrews who left Egypt at the time of the Exodus. Still another symbolic use of numbers can be seen with respect to Joseph and Joshua, both of whom are said to have died at the age of one hundred and ten years (Gen. 50:26; Josh. 24:29; Judg. 2:8). This apparent coincidence becomes completely understandable when it is realized that, in ancient Egypt, the highest accolade that could be bestowed upon a prosperous, productive, and beneficial life was the epitaph, "He died aged one hundred and ten years."

A great many incautious remarks have been made by scholars in days gone by about the chronologies of rulers in the books of Kings and Chronicles. Attempts to correlate the various reigns on the basis of Western methodology proved consistently fruitless, and it was left to Edwin Thiele to demonstrate the nature of the underlying principles of computation and compilation that the ancient Hebrew scribes, following certain attestable Near Eastern traditions, had employed in their chronologies. It now appears evident that the scribes of Israel and Judah used both an accession-year system of dating such as that found in Assyria, Babylonia, and Persia, and also the non-accession method favored by the Egyptians. The accession-year or "postdating" system regarded the year in which the new monarch ascended the throne of his kingdom as his "accession year," and his first year of rule only commenced on the first day of the first month of the following new year. By contrast, in non-accession systems the king's rule was counted from the time he ascended the throne.

What is complicated about the records of the kings of Israel and Judah is the fact that the scribes occasionally changed the system of chronological reckoning without warning, and to make things even more difficult for the modern student there were times when the scribes of each kingdom employed different methods of chronological computation. The picture is made more complex still by the use of such devices as synchronisms or the presence of coregencies. However, once the basic pattern is understood, the chronologies of Kings and Chronicles become clear, and can be used as reliable historical source material accordingly.

In attempting to understand how the Near Eastern past was described it is important to remember that the ancient professional writers followed certain well-established traditions. The training scribes underwent was of a very exacting nature, generally involving proficiency in several languages as well as a broad knowledge of the most important areas of national culture. Scribes usually came from middle- and upper-class families, and when qualified they occupied an important place in the community. Accurate transmission of material was basic to ancient scribal ideals, as can be illustrated by an Egyptian funerary papyrus of about 1400 B.C. whose colophon included this certification: "The work is complete from beginning to end, having been copied, revised, compared, and verified sign by sign."

Accurate copying of texts was emphasized consistently in Mesopotamia, especially in Sumeria, where the ancient epics and other venerated materials were copied out without any significant modification by generations of scribes. Editing or revising of any kind was discouraged in Sumeria, so that the texts that were copied out passed down the centuries virtually unchanged. By contrast, Egyptian scribes regularly revised earlier literature, substituting contemporary grammatical and orthographic forms for more archaic ones, bringing ancient names up to date, and introducing more modern vocabulary without at the same time impairing the genuineness or authority of the original composition.

In the same way the Israelite scribes took the greatest of care in the transmission of their sacred writings, as is now evident from the manuscript discoveries at Qumran. However, they were by no means as conservative in their approach as the Sumerians, and as a result they felt at liberty to employ such techniques as explanatory glosses and certain other forms of revision in order to bring ancient material up to date. In the light of Egyptian scribal practices, therefore, it would be perfectly legitimate for the Hebrew scribes to adopt such procedures as the insertion of certain material into a work such as the Pentateuch in order to revise or update it without altering in the slightest degree the Mosaicity of the work as a whole.

When attempting to understand the Near Eastern past it is thus important to bear in mind the differences of approach the ancient writers employed in their task of composition and transmission. Yet because the Biblical authors were in every sense responsible individuals who brought a profound sense of vocation to bear upon their activities, it is not too much to expect that the historians among them collected, evaluated, and interpreted the frequently incomplete and conflicting records of the past with the same general degree of conscientiousness as that which characterizes the modern Western historian.

Recent archaeological discoveries have made it plain that the Hebrews, along with the Hittites of Anatolia, were by far the best technical writers of history in Near Eastern antiquity. The Egyptians by contrast seem to have had very little interest in history writing, despite the abundance of source material, since no histories have survived from the Dynastic period. Because of the comparative objectivity of the Hebrew records it is possible to employ them as control material in appropriate instances as a means of scaling down the inflated claims of such sources as the Assyrian and Babylonian annals and the occasional Egyptian inscription.

Since it was the regular practice in the Near East to exaggerate victories but to ignore defeats completely, it is important for the modern student to be wary of possible bias, whether accidental or deliberate, in his ancient sources. It need hardly be said that, for this purpose, objective control data such as that produced regularly within the traditions of the Hittite and Hebrew writers is of incalculable value in assessing the ancient past. Similarly it is important to avoid the kind of embarrassment caused in some scholarly circles by the assumption that the Egyptian historical sources were as reliable factually as they appeared to be at first sight. It is now known that the bulk of such material is propaganda

The celebrated Rosetta Stone, whose trilingual inscription in hieroglyphics, demotic Egyptian, and Greek enabled the ancient tongue of Egypt to be deciphered. The black basalt stone stands nearly four feet (1.3 meters) high.

rather than history, and that it was composed in order to present to future generations a "correct" view of what happened. Thus it is far less reliable as a description of events than had formerly been supposed.

In evaluating ancient Near Eastern records that purport to be historical, the reader must also bear in mind that the facts may possibly have been modified somewhat, or even falsified, in order to accomplish some specific purpose. Again, in the interests of a proper critical methodology, it is necessary to inquire if the original writer was dependent upon primary or secondary sources, and to ascertain if possible whether his material was authentic, mistaken, or even falsified. Equally important is the question as to whether the account is actually as objective as it purports to be, or whether in fact it has been governed by some hidden subjective consideration. In this latter connection, however, the moral presuppositions of the writer need have no particular bearing upon the objectivity of the narrative, since moral distinctions or evaluations are a quite legitimate concern of a discipline such as history, which deals with events in the lives of moral beings.

Far more serious problems are raised by the presence of apparent discrepancies in historical records. In this connection it is important to emphasize the principle of determining the basic measure of agreement underlying the extant records, in the realization that, throughout all ancient history, the surviving sources are necessarily incomplete, and on some occasions even elliptical. Moreover, in original records it is still possible for apparent discrepancies to have been caused by the presence of factual error at the time the material was composed, although there are clearly other instances where the supposed discrepancy was actually found to have resulted from an unusual kind of scribal compositional technique. In the latter connection the various inscriptions from the reign of Sargon II seem to present contradictory accounts of his rule, both as regards specific events and their dates. But when all the relevant texts are studied together in order to obtain a total picture of the situation, the apparent discrepancies are seen to be the product of a particular kind of scribal reckoning and composition.

The Near East and the Old Testament

Because of the consonance between the ancient Near East and the world of the Old Testament, it is obvious that discoveries that have a bearing upon the former will also be of some importance for an understanding of the Old Testament. In the following chapters some attempt will be made to correlate the more significant findings of Near Eastern studies with the appropriate phases of Old Testament history. This procedure can be expected to serve the twofold purpose of illumining the Old Testament scene generally, and confirming certain specific details of the history and culture of Israel. This is not to imply, of course, that no credence ought to be given to any one section of the Old Testament until it has been authenticated beyond doubt by means of archaeological, linguistic, or other discoveries. The approach under consideration does, however, guarantee an important degree of control over the kind of unbridled speculation that has marred Old Testament scholarship for too many generations by demanding a closer relationship between theory and fact.

One of the greatest mistakes that resulted from the isolating of Old Testament scholarship from Near Eastern studies generally was the insistence upon the primacy of theory in the absence of a proper methodological approach. No longer is it either permissible or desirable for scholars to formulate some concept of development, whether of a biological order or not, and then attempt to fit the facts into such a structure regardless of the outcome. Instead, all the relevant factual material, of which at present there is an abundance, must be considered first, and on this basis some cautious conclusions may then be adopted with the proviso that they will be subjected to change in the light of whatever appropriate material evidence is subsequently discovered. Linguistic, archaeological, historical, and other studies will have a fundamentally important part to play in the methodological approach, which will have as its objective the fullest understanding of the life and times from which the Old Testament writings came.

While there are still a great many gaps in our knowledge of Near Eastern antiquity, there is also an increasing amount of material becoming available for study by scholars, and some of this often sheds quite unexpected light on the Biblical narratives. Not the least benefit of understanding the Old Testament writings against their contemporary Near Eastern background will be the awareness that the sacred Hebrew Scriptures were given by God to men and women who were caught up in the struggle of making headway against the problems presented by the society of their day. The Word of God thus met its hearers in their life situation, and in speaking to them in contemporary intelligible terms brought its own vitality to bear upon theirs in process of unfolding the message of eternal salvation through Divine grace. The general historical background of this revelation will now be considered in the following chapters.

2. Ancient Mesopotamia

Outline of Geography

WHAT IS GENERALLY ACKNOWLEDGED TO BE THE CRADLE of human civilization consists of a huge tract of land that in modern terminology is styled the Near East. A brief geographical survey of this region shows that it is bounded on the north by the Caucasus mountains and Asia proper, while to the east stretch the Zagros ranges of Persia, leading to Afghanistan and Baluchistan. On the southeast corner of this quadrangle of territory is the Persian Gulf, and to the south are to be found the enormous desert wastes of Arabia. The Sinai peninsula forms the southwestern land bridge with Africa, and the western boundaries are completed by the Mediterranean Sea and the mountainous terrain of Asia Minor.

For some centuries, historians and geographers alike have called attention to the existence in the Near East of what has been named the "Fertile Crescent." The extent of this territory will be appreciated if an imaginary line is drawn northward and westward from the Persian Gulf along the course of the Tigris and Euphrates rivers, then southward through Syria and Canaan, with its termination in Egypt. This rich tract of land saw the development of human activity in the New Stone Age (c. 6000–4500 B.C.), and from this traditional home of *homo sapiens* emerged the whole range of ancient civilization until the fifth century B.C., when the flowering of the Greek Golden Age marked the rise of a specifically European culture.

The eastern arch of the Fertile Crescent was known as Mesopotamia, a designation which it acquired after the time of Alexander the Great, and which to the geographers of the Greek and Roman empires indicated broadly the extent of land lying between the meandering Tigris and Euphrates rivers. Ancient Mesopotamia did not include the mountainous regions to the north and east, where the sources of these two rivers were to be found, nor were the wide expanses of the Syro-Arabian desert to the southwest ever regarded as coming within its area. The Hebrews spoke of the northern part of this territory as Aram-naharaim, or "Syria of the two rivers" (Gen. 24:10), which included most of the territorial expanse of the ancient Assyrian empire. To the south of Aram-naharaim stretched the rich alluvial lowlands of what was later to be known as Babylonia.

Near Eastern Prehistory

The earliest inhabitants of the Near East apparently flourished during the Ice Age, but to what extent they occupied any part of ancient Mesopotamia is uncertain, since their fossil deposits have to date been restricted to Palestine. Human skeletons that are thought to belong to the Middle Paleolithic period have been discovered in the caves of Mount Carmel and in the vicinity of Nazareth. From an anthropological standpoint they represent a stage of development intermediate between Neanderthal man and *homo sapiens*.[1] The fact that the bones were discovered in caves has encouraged the belief that during the Ice Age the inhabitants of Canaan were forced to live at least for some of the time each year in mountain caverns, owing to the damp, inclement weather. This need not necessarily be the most acceptable or even probable explanation of the cave deposits, since the Levalloiso-Mousterian period, in which the skeletons are dated, was marked climatically by dry, warm intervals, especially at the beginning.

Furthermore, the caves offered protection from wild animals as well as the weather, and they may even have been used as primitive burial grounds. The age of these bones, which is held to be upwards of one hundred thousand years, raises considerations of dating that will need some revision if recent studies dealing with the antiquity of the earth are successful in reducing its age from estimates as high as five billion years. If the artifacts have been interpreted correctly by the archaeologists, it would appear that Palestine was a racial melting pot during the Ice Age, and that neanthropic man crossed the intercontinental land bridge of Palestine into Europe from his original home to the southeast.

Ancient Mesopotamia

B L A C K   S E A

A S I A   M I N O R

HITTITE KINGDOM

LYCIA

CILICIA

KITTIM
(CYPRUS)

H

H
Mt. Lebar

PHOENICIA

Jordan R.

AM

CANAAN

DEAD

MOA

G R E A T   S E A
(MEDITERRANEAN SEA)

MIZRAIM

Memphis

Nile R.

LOWER SEA
(THE GULF)

Mt Sinai

E G Y P T

PATHROS
(Upper Egypt)

*R E D
S E A*

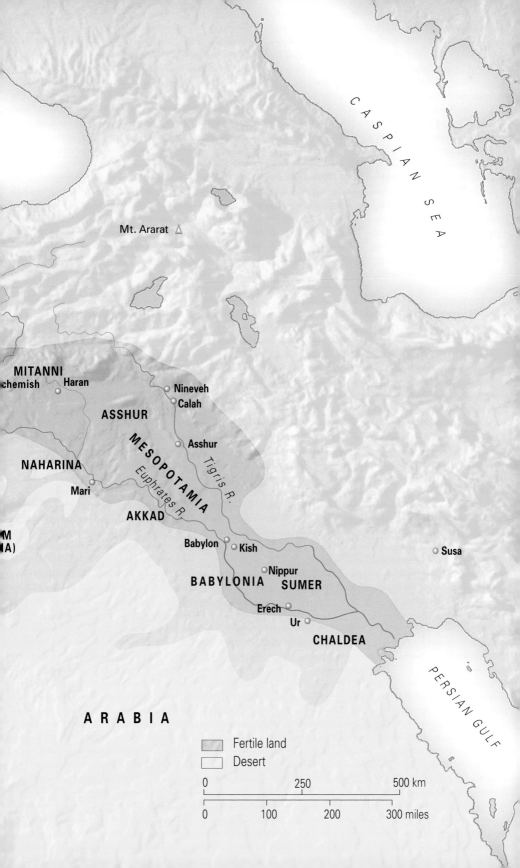

C A S P I A N   S E A

Mt. Ararat △

MITANNI
chemish ● Haran

ASSHUR
● Nineveh
● Calah

MESOPOTAMIA
● Asshur

NAHARINA
Tigris R.

Euphrates R.
● Mari

AKKAD

Babylon ● Kish

BABYLONIA Nippur ● SUMER

● Susa

Erech ●
Ur ●

CHALDEA

PERSIAN GULF

ARABIA

Fertile land
Desert

0 ———— 250 ———— 500 km

0 —— 100 —— 200 —— 300 miles

The Natufians

The Mesolithic period is represented in the Near East by further deposits in Palestine, belonging to a culture which has been named "Natufian," and which flourished about 8000 B.C. From skeletons that have been recovered it is apparent that the Natufians were slender in build and little more than five feet in height. They have certain things in common with the predynastic Egyptians, and they probably belonged to the ancestors of the Semito-Hamitic stock. The Natufians are usually credited with instituting the first phases of agricultural activity in the Near East, and the discovery of a wide range of flint artifacts has shown that they derived some of their food from the cultivation of crops such as millet, which they harvested by means of flint sickles and ground in stone mortars. Their artistic talents extended to the fashioning of animal bones and the carving of small images, though they did not make pottery. The position of the skeletons shows that they normally buried their dead in the contracted fashion of the predynastic Egyptians, with the knees drawn up under the chin and the arms folded across the chest.[2]

The Neolithic Period

During the Old Stone Age that portion of the Fertile Crescent which lay to the north of the Persian Gulf consisted entirely of swamp- and marshland. How far to the north these conditions prevailed is uncertain, but from available evidence it would appear that few if any links with the Stone Age are to be expected in this part of the Near East. But in the northern reaches of Mesopotamia, Neolithic culture (c. 6000–4500 B.C.) is represented by a number of village settlements, notably those which have been unearthed at Tell Hassuna, a site somewhat south of modern Mosul, at ancient Nineveh, and at Tepe Gawra, twelve miles northeast of Nineveh.

These sites are all in the same general area, and indicate that the primitive villages probably grew up side by side for economic reasons. The excavations of Professor M. E. L. Mallowan at Nineveh in 1931 penetrated the mound to a depth of ninety feet, where it was found that the lowest levels of Assyrian culture gave place to the remains of prehistoric villages. The wooden huts of this early period had been reduced to fragments, and mingled with this debris were found broken pieces of crude, hand-made pottery, bearing roughly devised patterns by way of markings.

The lowest levels of the mound at Tepe Gawra disclosed the existence of decorated ceramic ware of delicate structure, and some of this was found in a pit that contained the skeletons of the Neolithic settlers. In Syria this type of early village culture was represented in the plain of Antioch by the lowest levels at Tell-ej-Judeideh, while in Palestine the excavations of Garstang at Jericho revealed the existence of Neolithic levels that on examination showed that the site was once the location of one of the oldest communities in the Near

East. Like other prepottery villages in the early Neolithic period, a religious shrine was a prominent feature of the community. The houses were built of beaten earth or small mud bricks, while the shrine had an outer and inner chamber of considerable dimensions. Cult objects of a sexual nature were unearthed, along with molded marl statues of human beings, the purpose and significance of which are unknown.

The Neolithic culture of northern Mesopotamia and the Assyrian uplands is probably earlier than the beginning of the fifth millennium B.C., which makes the construction of houses and the introduction of pottery a matter of great antiquity, and shows that the people of the Stone Age were far from being uncivilized.[3]

The Chalcolithic Period: Halafian Phase

The "Copper-stone" or Chalcolithic period (c. 4500–3000 B.C.) succeeded the Neolithic, and with it came the increasing use of metal for implements and utensils. This period is characterized by an advanced degree of culture that is often regarded as marking the transition from primitive life to the great civilizations of antiquity. The best representative of the Chalcolithic in northwestern Mesopotamia is the site of Tell Halaf, which has given its name to this phase of Assyrian civilization. It should be noted in passing that archaeologists have found it convenient to classify the different stages of development in the predynastic cultures in terms of the sites where they have been originally unearthed, and this is now a well-established procedure.

The antiquity of Tell Halaf was revealed through the work of an enterprising German archaeologist, Baron Von Oppenheim, who spent two years at the site just prior to the First World War, and continued his excavations in 1927 and 1929. Here he found a culture that was far superior to that of the Neolithic settlements encountered in other parts of Assyria. Halafian occupational deposits have been found in a number of other sites scattered through Mesopotamia and Syria, notably at Tell Chagar Bazar, some fifty miles to the east of Tell Halaf, at Tell Arpachiyah near Nineveh, at Carchemish, and elsewhere.

The houses that characterized this period were built mainly on stone foundations, and were rectangular in shape. Excavators discovered that later edifices, constructed on a more circular plan, were prominent in the Chalcolithic villages, and these buildings proved to be religious shrines. The earliest varieties consisted of a single circular chamber, but later ones, reflecting the prepottery Neolithic phase of Jericho, had a rectangular anteroom added to the structure. The shrines were found to contain rough models of domestic animals as well as a number of human figurines, which generally depicted the nude female body with exaggerated sexual characteristics, in a manner reminiscent of earlier Aurignacian practice.[4]

The domestic art of weaving had attained a high level at this time, and the manufacture of rugs was well established. Carpet-weaving originated in Mesopotamia at a remote period of human history, and the characteristic Sehna and Ghiordes knots of subsequent Persian carpets reach back to hoar antiquity. From the westward reaches of the old Hittite empire in Asia Minor to the broad expanses of China, the same methods were employed to prepare the materials and weave them into widely divergent patterns characteristic of Oriental rugs. Even to the present day, the "Persian" variety of knot is predominant in the basic weaving of Chinese rugs, and reflects the long history of Mesopotamian influence on what is one of the oldest of human crafts.

But the most characteristic feature of Halafian culture was the beautiful and distinctive painted pottery that was unearthed at the lowest levels. In style it was not unlike the geometrical polychrome frescoes from Chalcolithic Ghassul in Palestine, which is of approximately the same date. The pottery itself was of a fine, rather fragile nature, made by hand and fired in closed kilns that produced an intense, readily controlled heat. The resulting ceramic ware had a well-glazed finish and was adorned with a variety of patterns and designs of a geometrical order. Bowls were often decorated on the inside with representations of plants, animals, and human beings. What is of special interest to the archaeologist is the representation of a wheeled vehicle, probably a chariot, found on one of the Halafian vases. The wheel is of the spoked variety, and its portrayal under such circumstances attests to the great antiquity of wheeled conveyances. Scholars have been unanimous in their verdict that the standard of manufacture and design of Halafian pottery is unsurpassed in antiquity.[5] As has been observed above, the date of this ancient culture is approximately that of the Ghassulian of Palestine, and must be considered well in advance of 4000 B.C.

The Chalcolithic Period: al Ubaid Phase

During this period, the southern reaches of Babylonia terminated in the swamps of the Tigris-Euphrates delta, and in consequence they felt the impact of human habitation somewhat later than the uplands of Assyria, where the Halafian culture was so strongly represented. The first task that confronted the prehistoric village settlers of southern Mesopotamia, therefore, was the draining and irrigating of the land so that the cultivation of crops might be undertaken. This was a formidable enterprise, for sudden inundations were common, and the courses of the meandering rivers were apt to change from time to time. Huge deposits of alluvial mud from the Babylonian plain gradually altered the shape of the coastline in the Persian Gulf, with the result that sites such as Ur and Eridu were considerably nearer to the sea in antiquity than they are now. When the rich alluvial soil had been drained and the land irrigated by means of canals and dams, the great wealth of the lower Mesopotamian plains attracted a succession of cultures that formed the basis of historical civilization in the Near East.

The most clearly defined culture of the prehistoric period in Babylonia is found at al Ubaid, a low mound situated four miles northwest of Ur.[6] The site was first investigated by Campbell Thompson in 1918, excavated the following winter by H. R. Hall, and subsequently by C. L. Woolley from 1923 on. The culture that came to light was found to be that of the earliest settlers in the Euphrates delta, and has been dated about 4000 B.C. Deposits of the al Ubaid variety have been reported from a number of other ancient Mesopotamian sites, including those of Eridu, Erech, Ur, and Uruk, which at this time were small village communities. Because of the absence of stone, all the houses in these primitive marsh settlements were constructed either of reeds plastered with mud, or, at a somewhat later period, of sun-baked mud bricks.

Though these buildings were far from substantial, they were made virtually waterproof by the application of decorative clay mosaics to the plastered walls, a custom that was still in vogue several centuries later.[7] The end of this period, however, produced more substantial edifices in Assyria, and a late stratum (XIII) of the al Ubaid as excavated by Speiser at Tepe Gawra in 1936 revealed the existence of three well-planned rectangular temples, arranged on three sides of a courtyard. A series of niches recessed vertically into the walls marked a type of construction that began at the close of the fifth millennium B.C., and dominated the architecture of Mesopotamian temples for many centuries.

Specimens of al Ubaid pottery have been recovered in quantity, and show considerable affinity in style and design with the ceramic ware excavated from the lowest levels of the mound at Susa in Persia, which is roughly contemporary. The al Ubaid potters produced quantities of bowls, vases, and other containers, which they decorated with geometrical patterns in dark-colored paint. The texture of the pottery is quite fine and the wheel seems to have been employed to some extent in its production. By comparison with the earlier Halafian stage, however, the ceramic ware of the al Ubaid period is definitely inferior, both in design and aesthetic appeal. Weapons and implements made from flint have been found in deposits of this period, and the presence of beads made from lapis lazuli and amazonite points to contact with central Asia and India, where these decorative stones were in use as ornaments at this time.[8]

The Chalcolithic Period: Uruk Phase

A dramatic forward step in civilization characterized the next cultural phase, known as the Uruk period, which is usually dated towards the end of the fourth millennium B.C. The site of ancient Uruk, the Erech of Genesis 10:10, was excavated by German archaeologists, who uncovered evidences of the earliest *ziggurat* in Babylonia. The *ziggurat* consisted of a low hill or mound, formed artificially by the accumulation of clay and debris, on which stood a religious shrine. The term *ziggurat* actually describes the tiered or staged towers that comprised the temples built on these mounds, but it is often used in a wider sense to include the mound also. This type of construction reflected the desire of the builders to safeguard the temples of their patron deities from inundation when sudden floods threatened the community. The *ziggurat* at Erech was about forty-five yards square and approximately ten yards in height, while the temple buildings were erected around a narrow courtyard, after the manner of the Tepe Gawra structures, and occupied a total area of approximately three hundred and fifty square yards. The inner walls and columns of the building were decorated in geometrical patterns with colored clay cones inserted into the soft plaster, after the fashion of those found in the al Ubaid period.[9]

A number of clay tablets were unearthed at Erech, on which a rough pictographic script had been imprinted by means of a stylus. The pictographs, as the name implies, were crudely drawn representations of the form of the object under consideration. Such picture-writing was gradually simplified into equivalent groups of lines, and when the triangular stylus was introduced the pictographs assumed the form of wedge-shaped or *cuneiform* characters. The development of writing, however, was preceded at Uruk by the invention of the stone cylinder seal, which was used originally to establish the ownership of goods or property. This device, which in late Uruk times gradually replaced the decorated stamp seals of the al Ubaid period, consisted of a stone cylinder on which a distinctive pattern had been engraved. When it was rolled across a soft surface such as moist clay, it left a design which was clearly recognizable.

As writing developed, cuneiform inscriptions appeared as part of the pattern, along with other decorations, certain of which are still unexplained. Once the principle of the seal had been established, there was no limit to the artistry that could be employed in its design and manufacture. Seals that date from the early Dynastic period are rather primitive in nature, and are generally marked by undulant lines grouped into a rough pattern. But seals that have emerged from later periods depict complex motifs of humans and animals, and are remarkable for the beauty and detail of their design. Such seals were widely used in business transactions, and their popularity spread to Egypt and India, where they were used for many centuries.[10]

The Uruk phase was continued towards the end of the fourth millennium at the site of Jemdet Nasr in northern Mesopotamia. The artifacts that have been recovered indicate that civilization was becoming increasingly complex. Metals, notably bronze, came into use, while sculpture made its first appearance at a number of Babylonian sites. Jemdet Nasr painted pottery is generally regarded as being inferior to that of earlier stages of the Chalcolithic period. The ancient sites of Kish and Shuruppak were founded at this time, and it is from here, as well as from contemporary levels at Ur and Uruk, that the culture of the late Mesopotamian Chalcolithic has been recovered.

The Growth of Sumerian Culture

The proto-literate period of southern Mesopotamia was in every sense an irrigation culture. The lower reaches of the plain of Shinar were formed by the consistent deposits of mud and silt from the Tigris and Euphrates. This process is still in operation today, with the result that cities such as Ur that were once on the sea coast are now a considerable distance from the Persian Gulf. Only when canals had been dug to drain the rich alluvial soil, and dams built to control the ever-present floods, could the agricultural wealth of Sumeria be developed. This was achieved with such success that by the end of the fourth millennium the peoples of southern Mesopotamia enjoyed a wide range of cereals, fruits, and vegetables, including wheat, millet, sesame, onions, beans, dates, olives, grapes, and figs.

The small villages that had characterized the al Ubaid period were developed into a comparatively small number of city-states, which exercised a monopoly over surrounding territory. Each of these city-states was dedicated to a patron deity, who was venerated as the absentee owner of the land. His temple was the dominant building in the community, and the priests were his servants, to whom was committed the responsibility of caring for the land. In the al Ubaid period the priests had already ushered in the beginnings of an urban revolution by their minute organization of community labor for the draining and cultivation of the land. At this time the temple became the center of the local economy, and the chief priest or *ensi* was recognized as a civil governor who was generally styled *ishakku* or "tenant-farmer."

This arrangement represented an advance on patriarchal rule, for it gave sanction to a theocratic state, and enabled the priests to become organized in such a way that they could administer the lands of the deity effectively, and also supervise the development of community life. These responsibilities necessitated the keeping of records and accounts, which could be preserved in the temple archives for future reference. This is regarded by archaeologists as the beginning of a system of expression that developed into writing,[11] and may have been prompted by the symbolic designs on the stamp seals of the al Ubaid period. Tablets recovered from the Uruk levels at Erech have proved to consist of primitive accounts drawn up by the temple priests as part of their administrative duties.

The relationship that existed between the city and the religious shrine was one of interdependence. As a state, the city comprised the political unit, whereas the temple provided the material and religious impetus for the functioning of the state. During the Dynastic period, some cities had several temples, each of which claimed a certain amount of land as its own, part of which was cultivated by the temple community for its own use. The temples also exercised other functions in addition to those of a cultic or religious nature, for they were the storehouses and workshops of the whole community. Priestly corporations were created to manage the affairs of a developing society and to regulate the type and amount of work that had to be done in and around the city. Dikes and irrigation channels needed constant repair, and it was necessary to apportion such work among members of the community, and to supervise the workers at their tasks. A proportion of the agricultural produce was donated each year to the temple, and according to early Dynastic tablets that have been recovered, the storehouses contained a wide variety of staple crops and other commodities, of which a detailed record was kept. The temple appears to have been the regulating factor of social life in the city-states, and thus it exercised an important influence over all facets of community living.

The peoples who entered the marshy delta region about 4000 B.C. formed the first historical civilized communities of southern Mesopotamia. They were known as the Sumerians, after the name of their capital city Sumer, and they ushered in the classical Sumerian age, which was to exert a far-reaching influence over all subsequent cultural development. The Sumerians were a mixed, non-Semitic, non-Indo-European race, who spoke an agglutinative language. In appearance they were swarthy, with dark wavy hair and full beards that amply justified their own description of themselves as the "black-headed ones." But they were people of superior intellectual caliber, and this enabled them to rise to cultural dominance in the Near East from a very early period.

It is thought that they arrived in the fertile plain of Shinar from the mountainous regions to the east, though some scholars are of the opinion that they originated in the Caucasus. With the Sumerians were included another non-Semitic group, the Elamites, who may have constituted part of the pre-Sumerian population of southeastern Mesopotamia. This conjecture is based in part on the fact that early Elamite pottery excavated from Susa their capital city is older than the Sumerian al Ubaid decorated ware. The Elamites came from beyond the Zagros mountains, and their occupancy of the Mesopotamian plain was for long a matter of dispute by the Sumerians. They were generally regarded as invaders, and at an early point in the historical period the Sumerians began to push them back towards their original home. Retaliatory raids characterized Sumerian-Elamite relations for some centuries, and there were periods of Sumerian history when an Elamite dynasty was in military control of the plain of Shinar. But whatever the political importance of the Elamites, it is evident that their culture made very little impression upon the Sumerians, who were in every respect superior to any contemporary form of civilization.

The Sumerians took over and enlarged the system of city-states that had been in existence since the al Ubaid period. Each community claimed a particular patron deity or deities, and followed its own pattern of cultic worship. The local god was acknowledged as the supreme ruler of a theocratic society, and from him alone was derived lordship and authority. In the early Dynastic period, which is generally regarded as the first half of the third millennium B.C., the gods of Sumeria were organized into a pantheon that was recognized throughout the entire country. Great importance was attached to religious activities, and a considerable amount of time was devoted to the formation of theological concepts and cultic traditions. Temples increased in size, and were constructed according to patterns the Sumerians believed had been revealed to men in visions. Community lands were divided up among the local deities, and a proportion of the produce was returned to the temple in the form of rent. The overall size of the city-states tended to increase also, and at this period Ur occupied an area of well over two hundred acres, while the population of Lagash was somewhat under twenty thousand.

One result of the development of city temples was that a wide variety of specialist craftsmen came into being. The wealth of urban Sumeria made it possible for imports to be made of all those materials which were not native to the alluvial plain. Semiprecious stones such as lapis lazuli and obsidian were being used prior to the Jemdet Nasr phase, and in the third millennium there was an increase in Sumerian trade with the surrounding nations. Copper was imported from Anatolia, the Iranian highlands, and probably from western India.[12] Stone was transported from Oman on the Persian Gulf, while tin was obtained from Iran, Asia Minor, and Syria. Silver, gold, and pinewood had all been used in the Uruk phase, and the coppersmiths of that period had become proficient in casting an alloy of copper and lead. New implements were designed for agricultural work, and they were widely acclaimed beyond the borders of Sumeria. Craftsmen in gold and silver turned their attention to the manufacture of a wide range of toilet articles and personal ornaments. Pins, earrings, toilet sets, and other articles of delicate artistry and execution were in great demand in the early Dynastic period, and the tastes of rich and poor alike were catered for by means of products of different quality.[13] Metal containers gradually replaced the decorated pottery of an earlier age, which was now regarded as suitable only for the poor. Magnificent vessels fashioned from gold, silver, bronze, and semiprecious stone were produced in quantity in a wide variety of shapes and sizes. The artistry displayed in the decoration of these articles reflects the skill and craftsmanship of the fourth millennium, when Sumerian art was at its height.

The Rise of Kingship

The city temples of the early Dynastic period were not left unscathed by the development of society, for their own authority underwent a degree of modification by the transfer of power from the assembly of elders to the personage of an individual. The elders were not replaced in the process, however, for the original idea of single jurisdiction arose from the need for one member of the assembly to take responsibility for leadership in an emergency. The office of ruler or *lugal* was temporary by definition, but in certain instances a succession of local crises tended to give it a more permanent form. Originally there was nothing of an hereditary nature connected with the function of a king or ruler, for he was acting on behalf of the assembly of elders, and ultimately as a deputy of the patron deity of the city, since kingship was in any event a matter of divine election.[14] If a son succeeded his father as *lugal*, it could only be understood as an indication of divine approbation, since the Sumerians believed that the gods could withdraw the blessings and privileges of kingship at any time.

As society became more complex in nature, the organization of the temple communities tended to expand also. An executive priest, known as the *ensi*, was made responsible for organizing and integrating the work of the community, and his headquarters were located in the main temple of the city. He delegated certain of his powers to other members of the priestly class, and when war threatened he became the responsible authority for the disposition of the local military units and the mobilizing of the people. Such a position was open to considerable abuse, for when community welfare was subordinated to personal ambition, as happened on occasions, the weakness of the entire system became apparent.

The accumulation of wealth by individuals was not precluded by the theocratic socialism of the early Dynastic period. Once the specified quota of goods had been delivered to the temple, the individual was at liberty to dispose of any surpluses as he thought fit. Some took advantage of the way in which the *ensi* organized the flow of commodities to and from the country to acquire a wide range of imported goods, many of which came from the Iranian valley. Remains of these imports have been found at Ur, Susa, and Mari, including stamp seals of the Indus variety and stone vases of the type that issued from the Bronze Age Kulli cultures of western India. In the main, however, imports consisted of the raw materials from which the Sumerian craftsmen manufactured articles destined for export as well as for the domestic market. The delicacy and beauty of some of these products is evident from the excavations at the cemeteries of Ur and Kish, affording eloquent testimony to the dominance the Sumerians exercised over all other cultures.

Towards the end of the Jemdet Nasr period, the office of *lugal* was stabilized by the development of a regal succession or dynasty. According to the religious traditions of later times, kingship was "lowered from heaven" and was established in Eridu. The Weld-Blundell prism, whose contents were published in 1923 by Professor Langdon, preserved an almost complete text of an ancient Sumerian king list,[15] which appears to have been drawn up during the prosperous Third Dynasty of Ur. The list furnished the names of eight kings in chronological sequence, and attributed to them reigns of grossly exaggerated length in the cities of Eridu, Badtibira, Larak, Sippar, and Shuruppak.[16] Berossus, a priest of Marduk in Babylon in the third century B.C., extended the list of kings to ten, and more than doubled the sum of their individual reigns. It is possible that the same tradition underlies the ten antediluvian kings of Berossus and the ten patriarchs that existed from Adam to the time of Noah, but how far there is a genuine connection between them is difficult to say.[17]

The Sumerian Flood Tradition

This early kingship was brought to an abrupt end by a devastating flood that apparently inundated Shuruppak and neighboring cities, including Kish. That the deluge formed an important part of early Sumerian tradition is evident from the statement which immediately follows the list of the antediluvian monarchs, and which noted that "after the flood came, kingship was lowered from on high" and was reestablished in Kish. The crisis this deluge occasioned found expression in a number of other literary forms, and it became a popular part of Sumerian religious tradition. Some versions even mentioned Shuruppak as the actual city upon which the deluge descended, and a fragmentary Sumerian tablet found at Nippur, almost midway between Kish and Shuruppak, and dated in the third millenium, described the background of the event.

After they had created animals and men, and had established the five ante-diluvian cities, the gods apparently regretted their action. The third column of the tablet then introduced the idea of a deluge that would engulf humanity. The pious king-priest Ziusudra, the Sumerian counterpart of Noah, was advised of the plan by Enki the powerful water deity:

> Ziusudra, standing . . . heard (a voice) . . .
> "I will speak a word to thee. . . .
> By our hand a rainflood (. . .) will be (sent);
> To destroy the seed of mankind . . .
> Is the decision, the word of the assembly."[18]

The fifth column described the terrible storm that arose after Ziusudra had built a large boat:

> All the windstorms, exceedingly powerful, attacked as one. . . .
> After, for seven days and seven nights,
> The deluge had raged in the land,
> And the huge boat had been tossed about on the great waters,
> Utu came forth, who sheds light on heaven and earth.
> Ziusudra opened *a window* of the huge boat. . . .
> Before Utu prostrated himself
> The king kills an ox, slaughters a sheep.[19]

After the storm, the pious king had the blessing of immortality bestowed upon him, and was transferred to the mount of Dilmun, a paradiselike abode that is now identified with the island of Bahrain in the Persian Gulf.

The Flood thus commemorated in religious tradition must have been considerably more devastating than the majority of inundations that were prevalent in antiquity in the Tigris-Euphrates valley. The late Jemdet Nasr phase at Shuruppak was found to contain an alluvial deposit indicating that a flood of considerable magnitude once swept over the area. A similar layer of some eighteen inches in depth, lying just above the Jemdet Nasr levels at Kish, marked the deposit left by a later flood.[20] This alluvial stratum was uncovered by Langdon, who interpreted it as the deposit of the Biblical Deluge, while a similar conclusion was reached by Woolley, who found an eight-foot stratum of clean alluvial clay when excavating the middle al Ubaid levels at Ur.[21]

Scholars of widely differing schools of thought now recognize that the identification of these flood deposits with the Noachian Deluge of Genesis is both mistaken and improbable. In the first place, the alluvial levels at Ur and Kish are not contemporary, a fact Woolley recognized when he urged the former as being the true Flood deposit. When Kish was subsequently excavated by Watelin, it was discovered that there were several such layers of silt, two important ones being separated by a nineteen-foot layer of debris. Furthermore, Woolley failed to find any water-laid strata when he excavated Tell el-Obeid, which is only four miles distant from Ur. Discoveries of alluvial deposits at the sites of Kish, Uruk, Shuruppak, and Lagash show that none of them is contemporary with the flood stratum at Ur.[22]

An indication that the Flood tradition was already known in Kish was afforded by the discovery of cylinder impressions of Gilgamesh, the legendary hero of Babylonian epic literature, at levels lower than the one that Langdon held to be identical with the Flood of Genesis.[23] Probably the most satisfactory explanation of this situation is that Ur, Kish, and other cities suffered periodic inundation of varying degrees whenever the courses of the rivers in the delta were changed through silt obstructions and flooding. Watelin regarded torrential rains as the cause of inundation at Kish rather than a tidal wave, while Parrot thought that floods were a major factor, combining with the characteristic violence of Mesopotamian rainstorms to produce large deposits of mud.

Following the catastrophic deluge that overtook Sumeria, kingship was resumed with the First Dynasty of Kish, according to the king list, and was continued in other dynasties, some of them probably contemporary, in the cities of Uruk, Ur, Mari, and elsewhere. The legendary shepherd-king Etana was one of the early rulers of Kish, and the story of his ascent to heaven in search of the "plant of birth" was preserved in Sumerian mythology.[24]

Dynastic Rule at Ur

The early stages of the growth of kingship in this important Sumerian cultural center culminated in the First Dynasty of Ur, during which four kings reigned for a total period of one hundred and seventy-seven years, according to the king list. A small limestone tablet unearthed by Woolley at Tell el-Obeid and dated c. 2700 B.C. proved to be contemporary with the First Dynasty of Ur. It read, "A-Anne-pad-da, king of Ur, son of Mes-Anne-pad-da king of Ur, has built this for his Lady Nin-kharsag," and at once confirmed the claim of the Sumerian king list that Mes-Anne-pad-da was the founder of the First Dynasty.[25]

The temple in whose foundations the tablet was discovered had long been in ruins, but it yielded graphic evidence of the heights to which culture had attained in the First Dynasty of Ur. Copper bulls were excavated in fragmentary form, along with decorated columns and mosaic friezes depicting rural life.[26] An even more impressive indication of the splendor of this period resulted from the excavation of a cemetery at Ur, which at its lower level contained what appeared to be the graves of royal personages. The tombs were constructed from blocks of limestone, which had probably been brought from the desert some thirty miles away. When the surface earth had been removed, the tombs were found to contain two chambers, vaulted with stone. Although some of these burial places had been plundered, one which had been undisturbed contained the remains of a woman identified as Queen Shub-ad. She had been buried in ceremonial attire, which included an elaborate headdress of gold ornaments and lapis lazuli.[27] Near her bier were found some vessels of gold, decorated with fluting and other ornamentation.

Beneath the grave of Shub-ad lay that of A-bar-gi, identified from a cylinder seal found in the burial chamber. Woolley thought that A-bar-gi was the husband of Queen Shub-ad, and the subsequent discovery of a large burial pit adjacent to the grave indicated that the two personages were of more than ordinary importance. Excavation of the pit disclosed that upwards of sixty people had been buried with A-bar-gi, while Queen Shub-ad claimed a more modest retinue of some twenty-five persons. From the appearance of the remains it was evident that the attendants had gone to their death voluntarily, for there were no special signs of violence observable on the skeletons. They seemed to have been ceremonially attired for the occasion, and to have been accompanied in death by a procession of oxen and chariots. The bodies were laid out in an orderly fashion, with their clothing and jewelry neatly arranged. Woolley concluded that the grim sacrificial rite must have been one of considerable color and splendor, and restricted to the honoring of deceased royal personages.[28]

A number of interesting artifacts were recovered from the death pit, including a magnificent harp elaborately decorated with mosaic work, a wide variety of vessels in metal and stone, intricately designed ornaments of gold and

Standard of Ur, dating from 2600 B.C. An elaborately decorated artwork inlaid with shell and lapis lazuli. This section depicts the triumph of the king following a victory in battle.

silver, and some articles inlaid with lapis lazuli, obsidian, and other semiprecious stones. The standard of workmanship attained in the execution of the articles in silver and gold is as advanced as anything the world has known, as is well illustrated by the superb craftsmanship exhibited in the celebrated golden helmet from Ur. This magnificent specimen of metallurgical artistry was recovered from a tomb whose occupant, according to the inscriptions, was "Meskalam-dug, Hero of the Good Land." It was made of beaten gold, and fashioned in the form of a wig, with the separate locks of hair standing symmetrically in relief, while individual hairs were represented on it by means of precisely engraved lines.[29]

Skillful restoration of a mosaic panel found in a royal tomb at Ur provided further illustration of Sumerian artistic taste and workmanship, while at the same time it portrayed the nature of Sumerian military equipment in the early dynasties. The panel is the "Standard" of Ur,[30] so called because it was probably carried as a banner in processions. Two main panels depict the themes of

War and Peace by means of three rows of shell figures on lapis lazuli. The bottom row of the side that represented war contained several four-wheeled chariots, each drawn by four asses and carrying the charioteer and a warrior, both of whom were armed with light javelins. The middle panel depicting fully armed infantry in close order showed soldiers wearing heavy kilts and cloaks. They carried axes in their hands and had copper helmets on their heads. Preceding them were lightly armed infantrymen carrying scimitars, daggers, axes, and short spears.

The upper panel showed a royal personage standing in front of his chariot to receive prisoners, while the reverse of the Standard used the scene of a sumptuous royal banquet to illustrate the theme of Peace. The restored panel indicates that the high degree of intelligence the Sumerians possessed was applied to military as well as to cultural pursuits, and this was probably the reason why the Sumerians were able to survive for so long as a military power. Their use of chariotry in warfare set the pattern for other nations, while the existence of the phalanx indicates an appreciable degree of tactical knowledge and skill. Sumerian graves have yielded many types of flint arrowheads, leading scholars to suppose that companies of archers formed part of early Dynastic military strength.

One of the city-states that made war on Ur at this time was Lagash (Tello), which was situated some fifty miles to the north. Its ruler Eannatum fought against Kish, Mari, Ur, Umma, and Uruk, and depicted his victories on stone monuments. But when Lugalzaggesi became governor of Umma, he retrieved the honor of the city by conquering Urukagina, king of Lagash, and later extended his conquests to Uruk and Ur. The king list records that his reign formed the Third Dynasty of Uruk, and he was without question one of the most prominent figures of Sumerian history.

The Rise of Akkad

About this time, Sumerian power began to be challenged by the Semitic inhabitants of the northern part of the plain of Shinar. During the middle of the fourth millennium B.C., the upper reaches of the plain had been the home of a group of seminomadic Semitic tribes, who consolidated their position during the first half of the third millennium and established trade with Sumeria. The tribesmen were distinguished by their language, which belonged to the eastern branch of the great Semitic linguistic family. Although they had not constituted a pronounced military threat to Sumeria prior to the latter part of the third millennium, they had been gradually increasing in power, and some Semitic names had already found their way into the Sumerian king list. In the twenty-fourth century B.C. they rose to prominence under a dynasty of Semitic rulers founded by Sargon. He was a man of humble birth, probably an illegitimate child, and, like the baby Moses, was placed as an infant in an ark of bulrushes. He was set adrift on the Euphrates, but was rescued and according to the Sumerian legend was reared by "Akki the irrigator."

Sargon established the city of Agade, which in the form Akkad gave its name to the surrounding territory and its inhabitants, who became known as Akkadians. Sargon organized his forces carefully, and about the year 2355 B.C., which is the beginning of the Old Akkadian period, he defeated the powerful Lugalzaggesi of Sumeria, and occupied the country. His daughter was made chief priestess of Nanna, the moon god, who was the patron deity of Ur, while he himself set about transforming his newly acquired territory into a Semitic realm. This aim was pursued with such success that his Babylonian empire ultimately extended from Elam in the east to Syria and the Mediterranean coast, exceeding by far his original expectations.

The Akkadians were quick to appreciate the value and attainments of Sumerian culture, although they instituted a major change by replacing the

Terracotta statue of the sungod Shamash, from Ur, c.1900 B.C.

native tongue with their own Semitic dialect, thus making Sumerian a classical language. Their consolidation of the kingdoms of Akkad and Sumer united the whole of the territory lying between the Two Rivers, making possible the rise of a widespread Akkadian culture that had as its basis the rich inheritance of the classic Sumerian period.

The Akkadians applied their new cultural acquisitions to all departments of social life with considerable enthusiasm, so that business and culture alike flourished in the Old Akkadian period. Excavations at the site of ancient Gasur have testified to the prosperity of this age, and tablets that have been recovered include business accounts and records of commercial transactions. Under Naram-Sin, "the Mighty, God of Agade, King of the Four Quarters," there was a significant development of earlier artistic trends, which resulted in a high level of workmanship, and which in part has been preserved in the Victory Monument of Naram-Sin.[31]

What is particularly important in the development of Akkadian culture, however, is the manner in which they adopted the Sumerian religious concepts and used them as the basis of their own religious beliefs and practices. It is difficult to overestimate the importance that was attached in ancient Mesopotamia to the place the gods held in the universe. Sumerian tradition had conceded supremacy to them as early as the middle of the fourth millennium, and in the third millennium the gods had been organized into a pantheon under Ami the sky god and En-lil the storm deity. This celestial conclave had complete control over the cosmos, and regarded man as a particularly insignificant creature, amounting almost to an afterthought of divine creativity. Hence he was a servant, from whom was required unvarying and unquestioning obedience as he waited upon the will of the celestial beings.[32]

An extensive mythology was already in existence early in the third millennium in cities such as Nippur, the cult center of En-lil, and Shuruppak. This corpus of religious tradition spread quickly across ancient Babylonia, and the comparatively small number of city-states that were flourishing in that compact land in the third millennium made the communication of religious ideologies a matter of little difficulty. The Mesopotamian mind appeared to be satisfied with the early Sumerian accounts of the deities and their activities, though the numerical strength of the gods was sometimes enlarged and their worship modified according to local traditions.

The religious conservatism of these peoples is reflected in the fact that the deities cataloged in the second-millennium tablets recovered from Lagash and Shuruppak were regarded as canonical to the end of Babylonian history.[33] Indeed, one of the most significant features of religion in Semitic Babylonia is its almost complete dependence upon earlier Sumerian tradition and its perpetuation of that tradition through successive centuries. Thus the literary compositions of the Akkadians followed very closely the liturgical myths of Sumeria, although the native genius of the Akkadian scribes was such that the finished epics proved to be vastly superior in their content and dramatic form.

Revival at Ur

The Semitic empire Naram-Sin had established was overrun in the days of his son by a race known as the Gutians, who came from the Caucasus region. They were the dominant power in Akkad and Sumer for about a century (c. 2180–2070 B.C.), and their decline coincided with the rule of Gudea at Lagash. This man

Artist's impression of a ziggurat.

was a pious and kindly *ensi*, or governor, who in a vision was commanded to restore the temple of Eninnu, founded during the late Jemdet Nasr period. It was this sort of activity on his part that prepared the way for a dramatic revival of Sumerian culture during the splendid Third Dynasty of Ur (c. 2070–1960 B.C.). Ur-Nammu, "King of Sumer and Akkad," was the first ruler of this dynasty, and he followed the trend which Gudea had established by erecting the massive *ziggurat* at Ur.

Woolley excavated this site in 1923,[34] and found a great many bricks bearing the stamp and name of Ur-Nammu. The design of the *ziggurat* employed curves to convey the idea of delicacy combined with strength, while the slope of the triple staircase in relation to the angle of the walls helped to focus attention on the uppermost stage, where the shrine of the patron moon deity Nanna provided a fitting crown for the entire edifice. The immediate environs of the temple were regarded as sacred ground, and it was here that much of the business in the city was transacted. Goods and produce were stored in the temple magazines, which also contained workshops for the manufacture of woolen goods and the smelting of metal.

A limestone *stele*, five feet wide and about ten feet high, commemorating the happenings in the reign of Ur-Nammu, was found in the ruins of Ur. Although only fragments of it survived, it is clear that the *stele* depicted the progress achieved during this dynasty in matters of irrigation and agricultural pursuits. Several panels of the tablet depicted various stages in the construction of the *ziggurat* from the time when Ur-Nammu was commanded to erect the temple. The king himself was shown as a workman, carrying compasses, a trowel, and a pick.[35]

It is probable that the finishing touches were put to the *ziggurat* by Shulgi, the son and successor of Ur-Nammu, who reigned for fifty-eight years. He consolidated the empire he inherited, and encouraged the cultural and nationalistic renaissance of the Third Dynasty. He founded and restored many temples in Sumer and Akkad, bestowing particular attention upon the ancient Sumerian city of Eridu. Tablets that have been recovered from Lagash have demonstrated his capacity for careful political organization. All administration was centralized in Ur, and the local governors or *ensis* of provinces received their appointments from the king. It was part of their function to send regular intelligence reports to the capital, either by means of couriers or in person, a procedure that reduced the possibility of independent military activity by the *ensis*. Each governor was responsible for raising taxes and dispatching tribute to the central authority, one result of which was the establishing of a uniform system of weights and measures throughout the empire. The Third Dynasty of Ur was a time of great prosperity, as contemporary tablets have shown, and it is doubtful if the levels of business, commerce, agriculture, and general domestic activity were ever exceeded in subsequent days.

The Decline of Sumeria

The later years of the reign of Shulgi saw the first hint of a revived Semitic Babylonia, making it necessary for him to spend a considerable amount of time and effort in order to crush the revolts that erupted periodically in the warlike states lying to the east of the Tigris.

Under Amar-Sin, successor of Shulgi, the Sumerian empire began to feel the threat of Amorite invasion from the north and east. The Amorites lived in Palestine and Syria during the third millennium, but for some time they had been moving eastward to the Fertile Crescent along with other western Semites. During the reign of Shulgi they consolidated their hold on the land to the north of the Babylonian empire, and occupied certain ancient cities there, of which Mari, the subsequent capital of the Amorites, was one. Shu-Sin, who came to power after Amar-Sin had reigned for nine years, was unable to restore military control over the outlying provinces, and in the days of his successor Ibbi-Sin, the threat to Sumerian power became a reality with the Elamite invasions (c. 1960 B.C.) from the hills to the east. At the same time as the Elamites sacked Sumer, the Amorite chieftain of Mari, Ishbi-Irra, rebelled against Ibbi-Sin, occu-

pied Akkad, and carried him captive in chains to Anshan. A tablet from Nippur
has preserved as account of the wanton destruction that took place:

> The sacred dynasty from the temple they exiled,
> They demolished the city, they demolished the temple,
> They seized the rulership of the land. . . . [36]

So thorough was the devastation that the political and cultural dominance
of Sumeria suffered a mortal blow, leaving the formerly united empire of Akkad
and Sumer to the designs of military opportunists. This resulted in a reversion
to the idea of the old independent city-state living in precarious coexistence
with its neighbors. Thus the period that followed the Amorite and Elamite
invasions was one of continuous warfare among the more powerful communities
such as Kish, Erech, Babylon, Larsa, Isin, and Lagash. Of these, Isin, Larsa,
and Babylon became the dominant states, and the conquest of Isin by the
Elamite Rim-Sin of Larsa resulted in there being only two contenders for
leadership in southern Mesopotamia.

The kings of Larsa began to consolidate their position in Sumeria, and some
of the older cities were heavily fortified against attack. The Larsa dynasty also
revived Sumerian religion in an attempt to enlist the moral support of the conquered peoples, and it is a curious fact that there emerged during this period
the greatest literary and historical works the Sumerians ever produced. The
official pantheon was firmly established, and the various legends that dealt with
the activities of the gods were set down in writing and assumed their final form.
King lists were compiled, liturgical texts edited and collated, and magico-
medical procedures tabulated for subsequent generations. This great surge of
literary and religious activity that preserved the accumulated wealth of Sumerian
culture was providential, for no sooner had it run its course than disaster overtook the kingdom of Sumer once more.

The Period of Hammurabi

While the resources of the south had been progressively depleted by internal
warfare, the fortunes of Babylon were in the ascendancy. The First Dynasty of
Babylon, founded by Sumu-abum, produced a succession of rulers who extended
the territorial jurisdiction of their capital Bab-ilu (Gate of God), as it was originally called, and allied with neighboring city-states against the threat of Elamite
domination. The influence of Babylon suffered a temporary reverse when its
ally Isin was conquered by Rim-Sin, but a dramatic change took place when
the last great king of the First Dynasty, the outstanding soldier and administrator Hammurabi, came to the throne.

He marshalled his forces against the Larsa dynasty, and six years after the fall of Isin he defeated Rim-Sin and his allies, thus winning back Isin and Erech. The next twenty years were spent in reorganizing and strengthening his possessions, and after this he delivered a devastating blow to the aged Rim-Sin, which resulted in the overthrow of Elamite power in Sumeria. Hammurabi made Larsa his administrative headquarters in the south, and began the unification of his empire, despite the danger of attack from the powerful Amorite stronghold of Mari in the north. After thirty-one years on the throne Hammurabi finally removed this threat to Babylonian imperial security, and established the full glory of the Old Babylonian period, which lasted to the middle of the sixteenth century B.C.

Comparatively little of the city of Babylon as it existed in the days of Hammurabi (c. 1792–1750 B.C.) has survived, owing to the fact that sixth-century-B.C. reconstruction obliterated most of the buildings that were contemporary with Hammurabi. The few that have survived, however, show a genuine attempt at town planning during his reign, with property arranged in sections, and streets intersecting at right angles. This represented a considerable advance upon earlier conditions, for the site went back to earliest pre-Semitic times, and the city had developed around a religious shrine in the same haphazard way as that which characterized most other ancient sites in the plain of Shinar.

A number of diplomatic texts discovered at Mari by André Parrot, who excavated the site from 1933, proved to be correspondence between Hammurabi and the ambassadors of Zimri-Lim, the last king of Mari. These rulers had been allies for a number of years and were on friendly terms, as the following extract from a letter written by Ibal-pi-El, ambassador of Zimri-Lim to Hammurabi, indicates:

> When Hammurabi is occupied with any affair, he writes to me, and I go to him wherever he may be. Whatever the affair, he tells it to me.

However, Hammurabi had also been on good terms with another ruler, whose power he was subsequently to destroy. What is probably an intelligence report to Zimri-Lim contained an account of a letter sent by Hammurabi to Rim-Sin of Larsa in which Hammurabi said, "Do you not know that you are the person whom I love?" Evidently it was the custom of Hammurabi to remain on intimate terms with neighboring kings until he was in a position to destroy them quickly. But by whatever means he attained power, it cannot be denied that he was vastly superior to his contemporaries both in political acumen and military strategy. In these respects his only serious rival was Shamshi-Adad I (c. 1813–1781 B.C.), the Amorite ruler of Assyria.

Stele of Hammurabi , inscribed with three hundred sections from the code of Hammurabi. From Susa, c. 1750 B.C. The king is depicted standing in front of a seated deity on the black diorite stele.

The Code of Hammurabi

Almost immediately his empire began to feel the benefit of his clear thinking and farsighted administration. Hammurabi took a keen interest in the welfare of his people, and one of his first tasks was to establish a written code of laws that would be uniform for his realm. The movement towards a legal corpus had become apparent in the days of Ur-Nammu and Shulgi, but at that time civil law had been oral in nature, and comprised the decisions handed down in particular cases that had come before the courts. Hammurabi collected, classified, and modified these earlier Sumerian decisions, and extended their scope to cover almost all aspects of business, civil, social, and moral life. Though he doubtless incorporated other codes of law from the Old Babylonian period (c. 1830–1550 B.C.), such as those of Eshnunna and Lipit-Ishtar, his legislation stands as a monument of jurisprudence in antiquity.

A copy of this code was found in 1901 by J. de Morgan at Susa, where it had apparently been carried as a trophy of battle by Elamite warriors. It was an imposing *stele* of black diorite, and stood some six feet in height.[37] A bas-relief of Hammurabi standing before the sun deity Shamash, patron of justice, surmounted the fifty-one columns of cuneiform text written in Semitic Babylonian. A prologue stated that the gods had commissioned Hammurabi to "make righteousness shine forth in the land, to destroy the wrongdoer and the wicked man ... and to illumine the land," while a lengthy epilogue reaffirmed his desire to be known as "a lord who is a father to his subjects."

The legislation of the code was grouped into nearly three hundred sections,[38] of which many reflected a highly complex social background. Certain types of crime, such as kidnapping, were designated as capital offenses, while violations of morality were dealt with very severely also. A marriage had to be registered in order to be legal, but both contracting parties had equal rights in the matter of divorce. Certain sections of the code laid down the duties of taxation officers, soldiers, and civil servants, while others stipulated the required standards for a wide variety of business occupations and professions. The code recognized a threefold division of society in terms of the upper class, the artisan, and the slave, although no social stigma was attached to the latter. Legal satisfaction of wrong or injury was generally met by retaliation in kind and was modified to accommodate the various levels of society.

A number of close parallels exist between the Code of Hammurabi and the Hebrew laws of the Pentateuch, which is hardly surprising in view of the similarity of cultural heritage and racial antecedence. For example, where a man committed adultery with the wife of another man, the Code of Hammurabi (section 129) and the Mosaic law (Lev. 20:10 and Deut. 22:22) agreed that both should be put to death. The law of retaliation or *lex talionis* in the Code of Hammurabi was precisely the same as that in the Pentateuch (Ex. 21:23ff. and Deut. 19:21). On the other hand there are significant divergences. Hebrew law allowed a man to divorce his wife (Deut. 24:1), but did not agree with the Babylonian code (section 142) in permitting the wife to have the same privilege. The Code of Hammurabi is clearly deficient in spiritual thought, and in general it placed a lesser value upon human life than did the Mosaic legislation.

Legal codes were not the only product of this flourishing period of Semitic Babylonian culture. The stability and prosperity that had come to Akkad and Sumer with the consolidation of the empire under Hammurabi provided encouragement for the priestly classes to indulge in literary and educational pursuits. The Sumerian language had been replaced at an earlier time by Akkadian, but many Sumerian terms had survived, making it necessary for glossaries, word lists, and dictionaries to be compiled. The two centuries that followed the time of Hammurabi saw remarkable advances in the field of science. Mathematical texts that have been recovered from this period show that the Babylonians were

Babylonian boundary stone depicting the deity Marduk.

acquainted with a wide range of mathematical problems, and some of their techniques anticipated much later procedures. The so-called Venus Tablets of Ammizaduga brought to light their interest in the positions and movements of the stars. Following Sumerian custom they gave names to the various constellations and planets, and the lists they compiled remained standard throughout Babylonian history.

Babylonian Religious Epics

Hammurabi was anxious to promote the worship of the patron deity of Babylon throughout the empire, and accordingly he introduced modifications into the earlier religious traditions of Akkad in order to give prominence to Marduk, who was made the hero of a great epic of creation. This composition, sometimes called *Enuma elish*, from its opening words, was first found in the form of seven tablets at Nineveh, in the ruined library of Ashurbanipal (669–627 B.C.). Other fragments of the piece were unearthed subsequently at Uruk, Kish, and Ashur. Although the extant tablets are obviously late copies, the present form of the epic goes back to the time of Hammurabi and, as might be expected, depends upon even earlier Sumerian originals.

The story of creation began with two mythical personalities, Apsu, the subterranean sweet-water reservoirs, and Tiamat, the salt-water ocean:

> When above the heavens had not yet been named
> (And) below the earth had not (yet) been called by a name
> (When) Apsu primeval, their begetter
> Mummu, (and) Tiamat, she gave birth to them all,
> (still) mingled their waters together
> And no pasture had been formed (and) not (even) a reed marsh
> was to be seen . . .
> (At that time) were the gods created within them. . . . [39]

Tiamat, who was spoken of as a woman, and Apsu became parents of the deities, but when their boisterous offspring threatened to get out of control, Apsu determined to destroy them. Ea, the water deity, put Apsu to death, after which he begat the hero Marduk, the patron deity of the city of Babylon. Tiamat created powerful demonic forces to combat the threat posed by the appearance of Marduk, who was championing the cause of the remaining deities. In the battle that followed,

> When Tiamat opened her mouth to devour him
> He drove in the evil wind, in order that (she should) not
> (be able) to close her lips. . . .
> He shot off an arrow and it tore her interior;
> It cut through her inward parts, it split (her) heart. . . .
> He cast down her carcass (and) stood upon it. . . . [40]

After imprisoning the allies of Tiamat, Marduk fashioned the earth as a canopy to cover Apsu, and allotted to Anu, En-lil, and Ea their places in the cosmos. The fifth tablet of the Epic, which has survived in fragmentary form only, related how Marduk organized the celestial bodies to mark the days and months:

The moon he caused to shine forth; the night he intrusted (to her).
He appointed her . . . to make known the days.
Monthly without ceasing to go forth with a tiara. . . .[41]

Since the ancient Babylonians calculated their years in terms of lunar phases, the place of the moon as the regulator of times and seasons was obviously one of importance.

The sixth tablet narrated the creation of humanity, which arose, according to the Epic, from the spilled blood of a son and ally of Tiamat. Man was considered to be inferior to deity from the start, though claiming something in common with the nature of the celestial beings. The Epic concluded with an account of the way in which Marduk became head of the divine pantheon and claimed fifty titles representative of divine attributes.

This Epic, in the different forms in which it circulated in antiquity, presents obvious points of contact with the creation narrative of Genesis. In both accounts, the chaos gave place to an organized heaven and earth, and the order of events in creation followed a similar pattern. But as is so often the case when comparing Biblical and non-Biblical accounts of the same event, the differences between the two are even more important than the similarities,[42] leaving the Biblical account vastly superior to the Semitic Babylonian version. An even more celebrated literary product of the First Babylonian Dynasty was the Epic of Gilgamesh,[43] preserved in tablets that were also recovered from the library of Ashurbanipal. Like *Enuma elish*, the Epic of Gilgamesh depends on earlier Sumerian mythological cycles and traditions, but as a literary composition it is far superior to its antecedents in the liturgical collections of Sumeria. Gilgamesh was the legendary king of Uruk towards the end of the fourth millennium, and the Epic cycle, divided into twelve books, described his adventures in company with his friend Enkidu. When the latter died, Gilgamesh crossed the waters of death in an attempt to find Utnapishtim, who possessed a plant of life that would heal Enkidu. In the eleventh book, which preserves the Babylonian account of the Deluge, Utnapishtim told Gilgamesh how he was warned by Ea, the powerful Sumerian water deity, of a plot the gods were hatching to send a devastating flood upon Shuruppak. Utnapishtim was ordered to build an ark, and shortly after he had finished the task a terrible storm arose, which by its intensity frightened even the gods who had planned it:

Six days and (six) nights
The wind blew, the downpour, the tempest (and) the flood
    overwhelmed the land.
When the seventh day arrived . . .
The sea grew quiet, the storm abated, the flood ceased.
I opened a window and light fell upon my face. . . .
On Mount Nisir the ship landed . . . .[44]

A dove and a swallow that were sent out returned for want of a suitable resting place, but a raven did not reappear. After Utnapishtim had offered sacrifice to En-lil, he received the gift of immortality.

This account of the Flood, which has numerous features in common with the Genesis narrative of the Deluge, is a more fully developed form of the tradition that had existed in Sumeria at an earlier period. The name Utnapishtim or "Day of Life" is the Babylonian equivalent of the Sumerian form Ziusudra, and there are many other indications of dependence upon earlier Sumerian liturgical sources.

Other Babylonian Literature

The period of Hammurabi saw a great increase in the compiling and editing of magico-religious texts. Since the ancient Mesopotamians believed themselves to be so completely dependent upon the whim of the gods, it was obviously a matter of some importance for them to know how the deities might be influenced for good, or propitiated when they had been offended. The interpretation of omens called for considerable skill on the part of the priests, resulting in the use of divinatory methods such as astrology and hepatoscopy (the examination of postmortem livers) in an attempt to anticipate the trend of future events. Medical practice was controlled by the priesthood, and suitably qualified practitioners were empowered to undertake a surprisingly large number of medical and surgical procedures.

Because the incidence of disease was associated in the main with evil spirits, two classes of priests were designated for the important task of protecting individuals from sickness by means of spells, charms, and incantations. As many of the medical tablets that have been recovered from ancient Mesopotamia indicate, formulae for exorcism constituted an important part of the priestly equipment for righting the disease demons. What is especially interesting in the light of modern medical theory is the fact that the physicians of the second millennium B.C. were the first to practice psychotherapy. Not all medical activity was of a magical nature, however, for some medical texts comprise lists of herbs and therapeutic substances whose value is still such as to afford them a place in modern pharmacopoeias. But empirical therapy was generally allied with magical rites and incantations to produce the desired restoration to health. While Mesopotamian medicine was inferior as a whole to its Egyptian counterpart, there can be no doubt that it met the needs of the populace to a very considerable extent.

Babylonian thought during this period tended to be centered upon this present world, since theological speculation did not encourage men to hope for life in a world beyond the grave. Although the royal graves at Ur might be taken as an indication of some belief in a future existence, this need not necessarily be the correct explanation of the ceremonial burials. Indeed, some of the Akkadian myths were decidedly pessimistic about the question of immortality for the human race. It was left for the Mesopotamians to observe the order and harmony of the universe, and to believe that the omniscient deities would dispose of the ultimate value of life for the benefit of humanity.

The Horites

The beginning of the second millennium witnessed the rise of another very important ethnic group in the Fertile Crescent. These were the Hurrians, or Horites, as they are called in Genesis, and they appear to have originated in the mountainous regions to the northeast of Mesopotamia. Within five centuries they had spread throughout western Asia, and were found alongside Amorite settlements in Syria and Palestine. Until recent times, the Hurrians were known only through the Biblical references, but archaeological discoveries have proved that they were a powerful people who became most prominent in the Mitanni kingdom (c. 1470–1350 B.C.). In the second millennium they built up the city of Nuzu into a provincial center, and the culture they established there, as revealed in a wealth of clay tablets, had important links with the Patriarchal period as described in Genesis.

Excavations at Nuzu were first undertaken in 1925, under Edward Chiera, and the tablets that were recovered were found to be written in Babylonian, with the inclusion of certain native Hurrian loanwords. Most of the texts have been assigned to the fifteenth century B.C., which is some time after the Old Babylonian period ended. The customs and laws contained in the tablets exhibit striking parallels to those of Hebrew Patriarchal society, and will be considered more fully in the next chapter. As a result of these discoveries, it is possible to place Abraham and his immediate successors against the social background of the second millennium B.C. with complete accuracy.

The Habiru

About 2000 B.C., there arose an element of Mesopotamian society known as the Habiru. They were not primarily a race, for they included both Semitic and non-Semitic stock, and were probably nomads originally. According to the Nuzu tablets, they often gained economic security by hiring themselves out as slaves, either to wealthy households or to government authorities. On other occasions the Habiru appeared as aggressive, migratory groups, preying on unsuspecting communities and ambushing small caravans traveling along lonely trading routes. Some of them were craftsmen and musicians while others gradually abandoned their nomadic life and settled in urban centers.

Cuneiform texts also referred to these people as Hapiru, which is probably the Babylonian equivalent of the terms Apiru or Aperu of Egyptian writings. Because the name Habiru is almost equivalent phonetically to "Hebrew," many scholars have either identified the Habiru with the Biblical Hebrews, or else have regarded them as the precursors of the later Israelites. While there are still a number of unsolved problems connected with the Habiru, it would seem to be well in accord with the traditional history of the Hebrew people to associate their origins with one or more of the various groups in the Near East that were known by the name of Habiru in the second millennium.[45]

According to the narratives in Genesis, the ancestors of the Israelites originated in Mesopotamia. Noah, the son of Lamech, was tenth in descent from Adam (Gen. 5:3ff.), and the father of Shem, Ham, and Japheth. The latter were the eponymous ancestors of the Semitic, African, and Indo-European peoples respectively. From the line of Shem came Terah, the father of Abraham, who lived at first near the early Sumerian city of Ur. It is at this point that Hebrew origins really commence. Abraham is the first Biblical personage to be designated by the title "Hebrew," and his family may have had some connection with the group of Habiru that existed about 2000 B.C. in Larsa, nearly thirty miles away.

Probably some little time after this date, Terah and his family migrated from Ur to Haran, a town situated on the arch of the Fertile Crescent, in the region that was called Padan-Aram by later Biblical writers. Cuneiform references to Haran ("Harran" in the texts) indicate that at this time it was a prosperous city, being the junction of caravan trade between Carchemish and Nineveh, Mesopotamia and the Hittite empire in Asia Minor, and the communities along the eastern Mediterranean seaboard.

To this area of the Balikh valley, in the northwestern part of Mesopotamia, the Israelite writers of later days traced their progenitors, and set them against the background of culture and life that saw the last days of the magnificent Third Dynasty of Ur, and the rise of a distinctively Semitic tradition in the Near East. With what accuracy this was done will become evident in the following chapter.

NOTES

1. W. F. Albright, *The Archaeology of Palestine* (1949), pp. 55f.

2. W. F. Albright, *From the Stone Age to Christianity* (1940), pp. 93f.

3. W. F. Albright, *The Archaeology of Palestine*, p. 47.

4. W. F. Albright, *From the Stone Age to Christianity*, p. 92.

5. J. Finegan, *Light From the Ancient Past* (1949), p. 15 and pl. 1; W. F. Albright, *From the Stone Age to Christianity*, p. 90.

6. V. G. Childe, *New Light From the Most Ancient East* (1953), pp. 113ff.

7. J. Finegan, *op. cit.*, p. 17.

8. S. Piggott, *Prehistoric India* (1952), pp. 55ff.

9. *Ziggurats* are discussed in A. Parrot, *The Tower of Babel* (1955), pp. 26ff.

10. J. Finegan, *op. cit.*, pp. 20ff. and pl. 4–7.

11. H. Frankfort, *The Birth of Civilization in the Near East* (1951), pp. 55f.

12. S. Piggott, *Prehistoric India*, p. 20.

13. H. Frankfort, *op. cit.*, p. 67.

14. H. Frankfort, *Kingship and the Gods* (1948), pp. 237f.

15. Cf. J. B. Pritchard (Ed.), *Ancient Near Eastern Texts Relating to the Old Testament* (1950), pp. 263f.

16. C. L. Woolley, *The Sumerians* (1928), p. 21.

17. G. A. Barton, *Archaeology and the Bible* (1946), p. 320.

18. A. Heidel, *The Gilgamesh Epic and Old Testament Parallels* (1949), pp. 103f.

19. S. N. Kramer, *Sumerian Mythology* (1947), pp. 97f.

20. Cf. J. Finegan, *op. cit.*, pl. 8.

21. C. L. Woolley, *Ur of the Chaldees*, pp. 20ff.

22. A. Parrot, *The Flood and Noah's Ark* (1955), pp. 46ff. Stratigraphical sections of Ur and Kish are figured on pp. 46 and 48.

23. Cf. M. Burrows, *What Mean These Stones?* (1941), pp. 26f., 70f.

24. S. H. Langdon, *Semitic Mythology* (1922), p. 166.

25. C. L. Woolley, *Ur of the Chaldees*, pp. 72f.

26. *Ibid.*, pp. 74ff. and pl. 8(a).

27. J. Finegan, *op. cit.*, pl. 12; C. L. Woolley, *Ur of the Chaldees*, pp. 42f.

28. C. L. Woolley, *Ur of the Chaldees*, pp. 39ff.

29. C. L. Woolley, *The Sumerians*, pl. 9; *Ur of the Chaldees*, pp. 59f.

30. C. L. Woolley, *The Sumerians*, pl. 14 and pp. 50ff.

31. J. Finegan, *op. cit.*, pl. 17.

32. H. Frankfort (Ed.), *The Intellectual Adventure of Ancient Man* (1948), pp. 136ff.

33. W. F. Albright, *From the Stone Age to Christianity*, p. 143.

34. C. L. Woolley, *Ur of the Chaldees*, p. 89, pl. 9(a), (b); *The Sumerians*, pp. 141ff., pp. 23 and 24.

35. J. Finegan, *op. cit.*, pl. 20.

36. C. L. Woolley, *The Sumerians*, p. 169.

37. J. Finegan, *op. cit.*, pp. 48ff. and pl. 22.

38. J. B. Pritchard (Ed.), *op. cit.*, pp. 164ff.

39. A. Heidel, *The Babylonian Genesis* (1951), p. 8.

40. *Ibid.*, pp. 40f.

41. *Ibid.*, p. 44.

42. J. Finegan, *op. cit.*, p. 53.

43. A. Heidel, *The Gilgamesh Epic and Old Testament Parallels*, pp. 16ff.

44. *Ibid.*, pp. 85f.

45. W. F. Albright, *From the Stone Age to Christianity*, pp. 182f. On the origin and nature of the Habiru see M. Greenberg, *The Hab/piru* (1955), pp. 3ff.

3. The Patriarchal Period

CHRONOLOGY OF THIS CHAPTER

Middle Bronze Age	1959–1550 B.C.
Late Bronze Age	1500–1200 B.C.

The Mari Age

FROM THE TIME OF SARGON OF AGADE, A CONTINUAL STREAM of Semitic peoples had been pouring into Mesopotamia from the western desert. They were predominantly Amorites, and during the period that followed the collapse of the Third Dynasty of Ur, they settled in the northern portion of the Fertile Crescent. This area became known subsequently as Assyria, and though it remained independent from Akkad and Sumer politically, it nevertheless shared the same cultural traditions. While Babylon and Larsa were striving for dominance in Mesopotamia, the Amorites established control over the northern reaches of the Fertile Crescent, and their capital Mari became one of the most brilliant cities in the Near East. Under Shamshi-Adad I (c. 1813–1781 B.C.), a senior contemporary of Hammurabi, the power of the Amorites was dominant in Assyria, and it was only curbed after some years of adroit political activity, when Hammurabi defeated Zimri-Lim and destroyed Mari.

The Mari age was one of considerable political and cultural importance for Assyria. From the twentieth century B.C., the Amorites managed to displace the Akkadians from the higher political offices throughout Mesopotamia. So effectively was this accomplished that some three hundred years later the Amorites monopolized almost every position of political importance in the Near East.[1] Archaeological excavations at Mari have made it clear that their cultural attainments kept pace with their military and political ambitions. Parrot discovered a highly developed civilization there, which was flourishing before the time of Sargon of Agade. An early Dynastic temple of Ishtar was unearthed at the northwest edge of the site of Mari, and one of the statues that was recovered bore the inscription:

Lamgi-Mari, king of Mari, high-priest of Enlil, dedicated his statue to Ishtar.[2]

The columns of this building and the courts that surrounded it followed the traditional Sumerian architectural pattern. Another temple at Mari was surrounded by huge guardian lions, fashioned in bronze, a forerunner of the *shedu* or huge winged creatures that were prominent in Assyrian buildings of a much later period. The royal palace, when excavated, covered more than six acres and contained over two hundred and fifty rooms and courts. The pottery drains that went deep down beneath the foundations were found to be in good working order after three thousand five hundred years, and a bathroom that was excavated contained two terra-cotta bathtubs, beside which were simple toilets.[3]

But even more important was the discovery of over twenty thousand clay tablets in various rooms of the palace. They included correspondence between Hammurabi and Zimri-Lim, the last king of Mari,[4] as well as a huge collection of business documents, carefully filed in the royal archives. Other tablets were written in the Old Babylonian Human language, while a few contained rituals connected with the worship of Ishtar. The place magic and divination occupied in the daily lives of the Amorites was graphically illustrated by the recovery of tablets from Mari dealing with techniques for divination. One favorite method was that of hepatoscopy or liver examination, and actual clay models were supplied as a guide to the prognosticators. Some thirty-two of these models were excavated, and they carried inscriptions on them relating to the sort of events that had taken place subsequent to the inspection of a liver of that particular shape and appearance.

Divination was obviously important in time of battle, and the armies had a number of astrologers as part of their general staff. If the omens were unfavorable, only the most foolhardy would disregard them, as the following tablet would seem to indicate:

I and Ibbi-Amurru have been preparing for the campaign of Warad-Ilishu at Agdamatum, but our omens are not favorable. These omens I have sent my lord. May my lord pay very close attention to these omens.[5]

Some tablets contained references to the Habiru, though they were of a rather indeterminate nature. A letter to the king of Mari informed him that an Amorite named Yapakh-Adad "has built the city of Zallul on this side of the Euphrates, and is dwelling in that city with two thousand troops of the Habiru of the land." Such references merely indicate that the Habiru were living in certain localities in some numbers, and afford no additional information as to their nature and status in the kingdom.

This period of Amorite history is of great importance because it embraces the Patriarchal age, and throws considerable light on the narratives of Genesis that describe the lives and times of Abraham, Isaac, and Jacob, the progenitors of the Israelites. The Patriarchal period corresponds roughly to the Middle Bronze Age (c. 1950–1550 B.C.), a time which was marked by the movement of various groups of nomadic peoples in the Near East, and which was characterized by the cultural and social patterns depicted in the Patriarchal narratives.

Terah, the father of Abraham, migrated with his family from Ur to Haran about the third quarter of the twentieth century B.C., during which time the region was probably under Amorite control. Some of the place names that survived in the area of the Balikh River appear to have originated with the ancestors of Abraham. The cities of Serug, Terah, and Nahor were all located in the vicinity of Haran, and the Mari letters mention the city of Nahor, the home of Rebekah, quite often, speaking of it as Nakhur, a flourishing locality where some of the Habiru lived.[6] The names Abraham, Isaac, Laban, Jacob, and Joseph seem to have been in fairly common use during this period, for in the second millennium, Abraham appeared as *A-ba-am-ra-ma*, *A-ba-am-ra-am*, and *A-ba-ra-ma*, while Jacob (*Ya-'equb'-el*) was in use as a place name in Palestine as early as 1740 B.C. In tablets from Chagar Bazar in northern Mesopotamia that have been dated at about 1725 B.C., a variant form of Jacob (*Ya-ah-qu-ub-il*) was used as a personal name. To the present, however, no actual traces of the Biblical Patriarchs themselves have been discovered, and in the nature of the case it is unreasonable to expect otherwise.

The Mari tablets contained an interesting reference to a warlike nomadic Amorite tribe known as the Banu-Yamina, or "Sons of the Right." They probably originated in the desert areas to the south of the River Euphrates, but, like other Semites of that period, they had migrated to the fertile areas lying to the north. These turbulent tribesmen were a source of embarrassment to the Mari rulers, and one of the tablets recorded the year in which Zimri-Lim "slew the chieftain of the Banu-Yamina at Sagaratum, and captured their princes." Another tablet from the royal archives spoke of the predatory nature of the Banu-Yamina:

> Once they made a raid, and took away sheep . . . a second time they made a raid, and took sheep, and I sent auxiliary troops who caught them and slew their chieftain, and brought back the sheep they had taken. . . .[7]

Some scholars have been attracted by the possibility of a connection between these Bedouin nomads and the Benjaminites of the Biblical narrative. The activities of the Banu-Yamina as depicted in the Mari tablets are in remarkable agreement with the tenor of the blessing of Jacob respecting the offspring of Benjamin: "Benjamin is a marauding wolf; in the morning he devours the prey, and at evening he apportions the spoil" (Gen. 49:27; cf. Judg. 20:17; I Chron. 12:2).

The Mari archives also spoke of the geographical counterparts of the Banu-Yamina in terms of the Banu-Sim'al or "Sons of the Left," whose original home lay to the north of the River Euphrates. These tribes were part of a larger number of Amorite nomads who were roaming about the Near East from Babylonia to Canaan, preying on civilized communities and occasionally coming into conflict with each other. Whether the ancestors of the later Israelites had any connection with these marauding tribes is at present uncertain.

When the Mari texts were first published it was observed that several of them referred to the various leaders of the plundering Banu-Yamina as *dawidum*. On the assumption that this term meant "chieftain," several scholars maintained that new light had been shed on the origin of the personal name "David." It is now thought on the basis of subsequent studies, however, that the word *dawidum*, which occurs more than twenty times in texts published to date, has actually nothing to do with the name "David," as formerly thought. The precise meaning of the term has not been established beyond question at the time of writing, although it may describe someone "beloved" or perhaps be a derivation from a word for "uncle," as some earlier scholars maintained.

In common with other Oriental peoples, the Amorites of the Mari age regarded the slaughter of an ass, or *khayaram qatalum*, as it was phrased in the tablets, as an essential feature in the establishing of a treaty between individuals or peoples. Thus, a government official wrote to Zimri-Lim:

> I sent that message to Bina-Ishtar, (and) Bina-Ishtar replied as follows: "I have killed the ass with Qarni-Lim and thus I spoke to Qarni-Lim under the oath of the gods: 'If you despise (?) Zimri-Lim and his armies, I will turn to the side of your adversary.'"[8]

This letter indicates that the oath of treaty or alliance was accompanied by the sacrifice of an ass, which ratified the treaty. The phrase in the tablets "to kill an ass" is thoroughly Semitic, and the fact that these words occur in this connection in Hebrew throws an interesting sidelight upon customs that existed among the ass-nomads of Patriarchal and later times. The tradition of concluding a covenant by means of sacrificing an ass appears to have survived among the Canaanite descendants of Shechem, whose eponymous ancestor had conceived a passion for Dinah, the daughter of Jacob (Gen. 34:2ff.). The Shechemites were known as "Bene Hamor," or "Sons of the Ass" (Josh. 24:32), and claimed allegiance to the deity Baal-Berith, or "Lord of the Covenant." During the conquest of Canaan, the Bene Hamor were incorporated into the Israelites, probably by means of a treaty.

The eleventh tablet of the Gilgamesh Epic in damaged condition. This is part of the seventh-century B.C. Assyrian version and contains an account of a great deluge.

Excavations at Nuzu

Archaeological discoveries at the Horite city of Nuzu in northeastern Mesopotamia also have an important bearing on the conditions that existed in the Patriarchal age. While a great many of the tablets that were unearthed there have yet to be published and studied, those which have been interpreted have shown the substantial historical value of the Patriarchal sagas by indicating in an indirect manner the way in which those narratives conformed to the background of the period as represented in cuneiform tablets and inscriptions. The Hurrians were the dominant ethnic group in the Near East during the second millennium, and as such they were close to the Biblical Patriarchs in time and locale. Clay tablets recovered by Chiera and others from archives in the ruins of Nuzu have preserved an excellent record of the social and cultural background of the period, revolutionizing earlier knowledge of the Patriarchal age, and clarifying some of the problems connected with the lives of Abraham and his successors.

Although some of the texts are of a legal nature, the majority are private documents bearing largely on personal affairs. For this reason, many of them were concerned in some way or another with adoption, which was one of the social institutions in Nuzu. Because the law prohibited the direct sale of land, it had become customary for such transactions to be made under the guise of adoption. Slaves were frequently adopted for this very purpose, and it appears that an individual could be adopted by more than one couple.[9] However, genuine adoptions were also common in Nuzu, especially in the case of childless couples, who frequently resorted to this procedure in order to obtain a son. In return for the inheritance thus bestowed, the adopted son was expected to discharge normal filial duties. But if the adopting parents had a son of their own subsequent to the adoption, the adopted son was required by law to surrender to the natural son the right of inheritance. These circumstances underlie the adoption by Abraham of his slave Eliezer as his heir presumptive (Gen. 15:2f.), a procedure that presumably was carried out in accordance with the custom prevailing in the locality. That such was not to be a permanent state of affairs, however, was revealed by God when He promised Abraham that his slave would not be his heir after all, since a son would be born to inherit the property of Abraham and continue his name.

The Nuzu tablets indicate that the institution of marriage was regarded as a means of procreation rather than a device for human companionship. The marriage contract provided that if the wife remained childless for any reason, she was obliged to give a handmaid to her husband, so that children might be born into the family circle. Thus, one marriage document read as follows:

If Gilimninu (*the bride*) will not bear children, Gilimninu shall take a woman of N/Lullu-land (*whence the choicest slaves were obtained*) as a wife for Shennima (*the bridegroom*).[10]

In conformity with this custom, Sarah gave Hagar, an Egyptian slave, to Abraham (Gen. 16:2), and two generations later, Rachel gave Bilhah to Jacob (Gen. 30:3). Under Nuzu law, any children that resulted from such a union were to remain in the family, and their expulsion was strictly prohibited. This factor accounts for the apprehension Abraham experienced (Gen. 21:11) when Sarah determined to expel Hagar and Ishmael after the latter had mocked Isaac, the puny son of Abraham and Sarah, on the day of his weaning feast. Despite the Divine dispensation that justified the acquiescence of Abraham in the matter (Gen. 21:1ff.), it would have been legally possible to vindicate the action of Sarah by an appeal to section twenty-five of the Sumerian code of Lipit-Ishtar (c. 1850–1840 B.C.), which laid down the principle that the act of expulsion was compensated for by the resultant freedom the dispossessed thereby obtained.

According to Nuzu customs, the "birthright" or title to the position of first-born was negotiable among members of the family, and in one instance the

The traditional burial place of Rachel, about a mile north of Bethlehem, was originally marked by means of a pillar erected by her husband. In the Christian era a monument in the form of a miniature pyramid was erected in the vicinity (c. A.D. 350). The building shown here was constructed by Crusaders in the twelfth century, and consists of a domed room with an adjacent vestibule.

privileges were transferred to a person who was adopted as a brother. Another tablet told of a man named Tupkitilla disposing by agreement of his birthright:

> On the day they divide the grove . . . Tupkitilla shall give it to Kurpazah as his inheritance share. And Kurpazah had taken three sheep to Tupkitilla in exchange for his inheritance share.[11]

Since these transactions were fairly common in Nuzu, there would be nothing particularly unusual in Jacob taking advantage of his famished brother to obtain his rights of primogeniture (Gen. 25:31ff.).

The relationship that existed between Jacob and Laban has been paralleled to some extent by a text from Nuzu, which tells of a man adopting a son, giving him his daughter as a wife, and establishing him and his offspring as heirs. The usual proviso regarding the birth of a natural son to the adopting parents was added, but in this instance the adopted son was to be allowed an equal share of the inheritance with the natural son. The terms of adoption also laid down that the adopted son was forbidden to enter into any additional marriage contracts on pain of forfeiting his right to the property. Furthermore, if the adopting parents had offspring subsequent to the adoption, the children born to the adopted son would not have any claim upon the estate.

The Genesis narrative (29:6ff.) gives no indication that Laban had any sons when Jacob joined his household, showing that Jacob was accepted as an adopted son rather than as a son-in-law. This fact is further borne out by the way in which Laban proclaimed his patriarchal rights (Gen. 31:43). Whereas under normal circumstances married women were the property of their husbands, Rachel and Leah were not free to leave the parental household because they still belonged to Laban, a situation that can best be explained by regarding their husband as an adopted son. Thus it was well within the power of Laban to punish all three conspirators for their guilt in fleeing from his authority. Instead, he contented himself with an agreement with Jacob, wherein he admonished him, in accordance with the prevailing customs, not to enter into further marital contracts (Gen. 31:50).

Where it was necessary for the inheritance to be shared, Nuzu law recognized as the leader of the family the one who had possession of the household idols. These were evidently the images or "teraphim" Rachel stole (Gen. 31:19), and a number of similar figurines were recovered from Nuzu. Since they were apparently associated with certain rights of leadership or inheritance, their theft was a serious matter, because sons had been born to Laban (Gen. 31:1) after his apparent adoption of Jacob, so that to them belonged rights of primogeniture by law.

The elaborate blessings that have been preserved in the Patriarchal narratives were a common feature of Nuzu society. In effect they were the last will and testament of the person who uttered them, and as such they were legally binding, whether they were committed to writing or not. One tablet from Nuzu recorded a court case where the plaintiff succeeded in upholding his right to marry a certain woman who had been willed to him in this manner. His account of the situation was as follows:

> My father, Huya, was sick and lying in bed and my father seized my hand and spoke thus to me: "My other older sons have taken wives, but thou hast not taken a wife, and I give Zululishtar to thee as wife."[12]

As is still the case in some Oriental countries, the two contracting parties to the marriage had not been consulted in advance about the arrangement in which they were to participate.

A rather curious custom mentioned in the Nuzu tablets was connected with the passing of shoes or boots between persons who were entering into some sort of contract. In certain of the texts the transaction seems to have bordered on illegality, as in one instance where an attempt was apparently made to sell land. Since all such property belonged to the gods, it was regarded as inalienable, and as such could not be bought or sold. However, by means of some special procedure that involved the passing of a pair of shoes and certain other items, the transfer of the property was given the semblance of legality. In later times in Israel, certain moral obligations were dispensed with in much the same manner. This occurred, for example, in connection with the occasion when Ruth was redeemed by Boaz (Ruth 4:7f.), and seems also to have been used by unscrupulous wealthy landowners in the eighth century B.C., who deprived the poor of certain legal rights in this manner (Amos 2:6; 8:6).

Although the texts from Mari and Nuzu are of undeniably great value in furnishing an authentic historical background for the narratives dealing with Abraham, Isaac, and Jacob, an even more important source of information for this same general period was discovered by Sir Leonard Woolley in Turkey. Excavating just before and just after World War II at Tell el-'Atshana (Alalakh) in what was originally northern Syria, he uncovered two levels containing royal palaces, one of which belonged to the period c. 1900–1780 B.C., and the other to the fifteenth century B.C. Rather more than four hundred and fifty texts were recovered from the ruins, and were found to be roughly contemporary with those from Mari and Nuzu. However, they are of considerably greater value for the Patriarchal period, since they are closer to that era in both chronology and geography.

These tablets furnish additional information about the preferential status that could be given to any son of a particular wife, as illustrated by the following marriage contract between a man named Irihalpa and his bride Naidu:

If Naidu does not give birth to a son . . . the daughter of his brother . . . shall be given (to Irihalpa) . . . if (*another wife*) Irihalpa gives birth to a son first, and afterwards Naidu gives birth to a son, the son of Naidu alone shall be the firstborn.

The position of firstborn son in the family normally implied that the person concerned could claim a double share of the inheritance on the death of the family patriarch. However, the traditions of Alalakh reinforce certain ones in existence at both Mari and Ugarit to show that the father was at liberty to disregard the natural sequences of primogeniture, and instead to choose his own firstborn from among his sons. This custom has obvious bearing upon the case of Manasseh and Ephraim (Gen. 48:13–20), the repudiation of Reuben (Gen. 49:3f.), and the elevation of Joseph (Gen. 48:22).

From the foregoing it will be evident that the social institutions recorded in the Patriarchal narratives are thoroughly representative of life in the second millennium B.C. The basic literary form of the accounts in Genesis strongly suggests that the activities of these ancient Hebrew personages were recorded on tablets,[13] in conformity with Near Eastern custom, and were not preserved by word-of-mouth transmission, as has been suggested by many scholars. Family trees, such as those occurring in Genesis were of great importance in the cultures of Mari and Nuzu, and there is no reason for thinking that the ancestors of the later Israelites were any less concerned about their genealogies than their Mesopotamian counterparts.

Until recently it was generally asserted by scholars that the mention of camels in the narratives of the Hebrew Patriarchs was an anachronism. While there is little doubt that the donkey was actually domesticated before the camel, it is equally certain that the latter was used in Oriental trading caravans at a very early period. When Parrot was excavating Mari he uncovered the remains of camel bones in the ruins of a house that belonged to the pre-Sargonid period (c. 2400 B.C.). Recently discovered cylinder seals from northern Mesopotamia that can be dated in the general period of the Hebrew Patriarchs depicted riders seated upon camels. A relief from Byblos in Phoenicia assigned by archaeologists to the eighteenth century B.C. actually showed a camel in a kneeling position, indicating its use as a beast of burden at that period.

Another eighteenth-century-B.C. witness to the domestication of the camel, this time from Alalakh in northern Syria, consisted of a cuneiform tablet containing a list of fodder for domesticated animals that specifically mentioned the camel under the designation GAM. MAL.[14] Archaeological excavations in northern India have also shown that the camel had been domesticated early in the second millennium B.C., and judging by its comparative scarcity it must have been an extremely valuable beast of burden. A somewhat later piece of corroborative evidence came from Tell Halaf, some sixty miles east of Haran.

It consisted of a sculptured slab from about the eleventh century B.C., and portrayed a dromedary to which a palanquin resembling a wooden box had been attached by means of crosswise girths, on top of which the rider was seated.[15]

These and other archaeological discoveries support the correctness of Hebrew tradition, which traced the origins of the Patriarchs back to the valley of the Balikh River. The documents from Nuzu and Mari show that the Patriarchal narratives reflect the laws and social customs that were current in the nineteenth and later centuries of Mesopotamian history. The parallels in language and proper names between the Mari records and the traditions of Genesis indicate the existence of a common cultural background,[16] and place Israelite tradition on a historic basis relative to the homogeneous culture of the Near East.

Middle Bronze Age Palestine

The essential topography of the Patriarchal sagas is also in harmony with the archaeology of the Middle Bronze Age. Excavations at Shechem, Bethel, Gerar, and elsewhere have proved that these towns were inhabited in the Patriarchal age. The work of Glueck in the Hashemite kingdom of Jordan revealed that Palestine was in the midst of a nomadic upheaval during the Third Dynasty of Ur, and the Middle Bronze Age sites that were excavated afforded evidence of large-scale destruction and abandonment of cities and towns. Before the end of the twentieth century B.C., the material culture deteriorated, and the sporadic raids by warlike nomads from the east and south brought about a quick decline in the density of human settlement. After this time the attacks of nomadic groups forced the virtual withdrawal of all sedentary occupation from the southern Transjordan area, a state of affairs that continued for some seven centuries.[17] According to Egyptian sources, Palestine and southern Syria relinquished tribal organization for a developing sedentary culture at the beginning of the nineteenth century B.C., and within a comparatively short time their civilization was organized in terms of city-states, while Transjordan continued to be depopulated, and ultimately reverted to a tribal system.[18]

A little prior to 1900 B.C., Terah died at an advanced age, and Abraham his son migrated westward to Canaan shortly afterwards. Contact was still maintained with Haran, however, for Abraham sent to Nahor for a wife for his son Isaac, and it was from the same region that Jacob also acquired his wives. The Mari texts recorded that Amorite tribes were active in the area of Haran in the early second millennium B.C., and it may well be that their movements coincided with the migrations of Abraham and his dependents. The life Abraham and his descendants lived was characteristic of the contemporary nomadism, except that their wanderings were confined to the thinly populated hill country and the arid locality to the southwest of the Dead Sea.

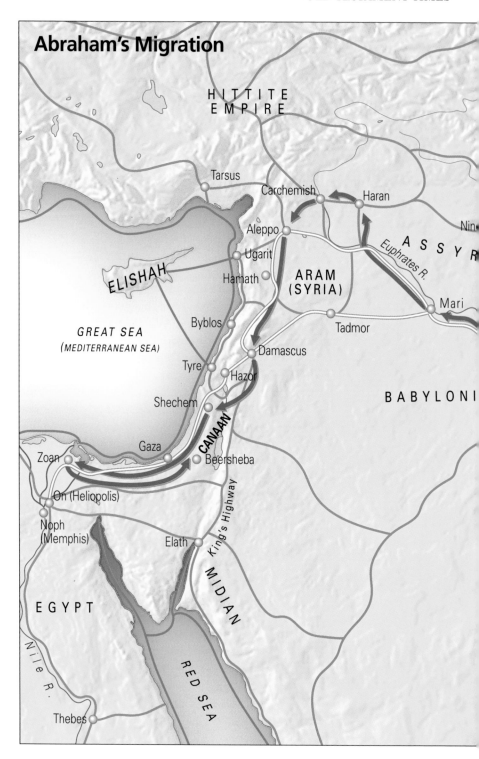

Abraham's Migration

HITTITE
EMPIRE

Tarsus

Carchemish

Haran

Nin•

ASSYR

Aleppo

Euphrates R.

Ugarit

ELISHAH

Hamath

ARAM
(SYRIA)

Mari

GREAT SEA
(MEDITERRANEAN SEA)

Byblos

Tadmor

Damascus

Tyre

BABYLONI

Hazor

Shechem

CANAAN

Gaza

Zoan

Beersheba

On (Heliopolis)

King's Highway

Noph
(Memphis)

Elath

EGYPT

MIDIAN

Nile R.

RED SEA

Thebes

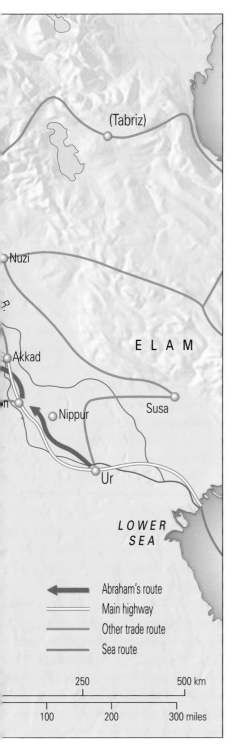

(Tabriz)

Nuzi

R.

Akkad

E L A M

Nippur

Susa

n

Ur

LOWER
SEA

→ Abraham's route
══ Main highway
── Other trade route
── Sea route

| 250 | | 500 km |
| 100 | 200 | 300 miles |

During and after the Middle Bronze Age this southerly region was known as the Negeb, which is rather inaccurately translated "the South" in some English versions. In point of fact the Hebrew term *negeb* means "dry" or "arid," and referred originally to climatic conditions rather than to a specific geographical region. The strategic and economic importance of the Negeb was evident as early as the beginning of the second millennium B.C., and the general route followed by the nomadic groups was governed to a large extent by the locations of wells and springs. Southern Syria, Palestine, and the Negeb proved to be convenient areas for the resettlement of those population elements which had been forced out of the Fertile Crescent from the nineteenth century B.C. by political and other pressures. The presence of copper ores in the eastern Negeb made the trading route from central Sinai northeastward to Judea of great importance, and recent excavations at Megiddo, Gezer, Ugarit, and other cities have shown that the control the Egyptians exercised over ancient Canaan enabled trading caravans to pass freely to and from Egypt.[19]

In the Middle Bronze Age the hilly regions of central Palestine were heavily forested, and because there was little arable land, the whole area was unsuitable for agricultural purposes. These conditions were ideal for nomadic tribes, however, and it was in this locality and farther to the south that Abraham and his descendants roamed for some years. The topography reflected in the Genesis narratives is quite credible, since the places visited by Abraham are known to lie in a zone whose annual rainfall is between ten and twenty inches, which is well suited to the requirements of sheep. The site of Mamre was associated with the Patriarchal wanderings, and after the days of Abraham the city of Hebron was founded there (c. 1700 B.C.). Two explanatory notes in Genesis (13:18; 23:19) indicated the original location of Mamre. The five cities of the Jordan plain south of the Dead Sea were also flourishing communities in the days of Abraham, but about the close of the twentieth century B.C., the Vale of Siddim, in which the cities of Sodom, Gomorrah, Admah, Zoar, and Zeboiim were situated, was overtaken by an earthquake and a calamitous conflagration, probably of volcanic origin. The depopulation of this region is described in Genesis 19, and the facts of the situation are fully borne out by archaeological excavations.[20]

An earlier rather than a later date for the presence of Abraham in Palestine seems indicated by the evidence relating to the destruction of Sodom (Gen. 19:24ff.). This city was probably located near the southern end of the Valley of Siddim, a tract of land that now lies submerged to the south of the Dead Sea peninsula, known as el-Lisan ("the Tongue"). From the description in Genesis 19:24, which mentions a heavy pall of black smoke, it would seem as though the catastrophe occurred in part through the igniting of gases from the asphalt and petroleum deposits around Jebel Usdum ("Mount of Sodom"), a large crystalline salt mountain over seven hundred feet high and five miles long, which is located along the south end of the west side of the Dead Sea.

The approximate date of this catastrophe can be estimated from the evidence furnished by the pottery excavated from Bab edh-Dhra'. This site was apparently used at the end of the third millennium B.C. by the people who lived in the "cities of the valley" as a festival center, being in demand for this purpose between about 2300 and 1900 B.C. Since visits by pilgrims and others to this locality ceased about 1900 B.C., it may be that the termination of interest in the site for religious and other purposes coincided with the destruction of Sodom and the other "cities of the valley." If this date for the destruction of Sodom and Gomorrah is correct, it would indicate that Abraham was living at the end of the twentieth century B.C., and was in Palestine by about 1900 B.C.

Probably the most intriguing document in the entire Patriarchal corpus is the fourteenth chapter of Genesis, which narrates the invasion of Palestine by an alliance of kings from Mesopotamia, and their defeat by Abraham. Until recently this material was regarded by critical scholars as legendary and unhistorical, but as a result of the work of Albright, Jirku, and Glueck, it has become increasingly clear that this chapter is a very ancient document that, when incorporated into the Genesis story, already needed to be explained by means of scribal glosses (as in 14:2, 3, 7, 17). While the identities of the four royal invaders have not been established as yet by archaeology, the circumstances of the narrative have been shown to correspond with the evidence presented by excavations in the Jordan valley. The Rephaim are known to have lived prior to the

Egyptian wooden model depicting oxen plowing.

fifteenth century B.C. in Syria and the regions to the east and south of the Dead Sea, because they are mentioned in administrative texts of that date which have been recovered from ancient Ugarit (Ras Shamra).[21] Together with the Zuzim and Emim they formed part of the pre-Israelite population of Palestine, and were renowned for their imposing stature. The Rephaim were known by different local names (cf. Deut. 2:11, 20f.), and seem to have been among the earliest people to settle in Moab and Ammon.

The sites of Ashtaroth and Karnaim were occupied in the Patriarchal period, while a small Bronze Age mound in eastern Gilead was identified with Ham. The invaders came through Bashan, a region south of the River Pharpar and east of the Sea of Galilee, where some of the Rephaim lived, and marched southward through eastern Gilead and Moab. Albright and Glueck have shown that these places were still thickly populated in the twentieth century B.C., and the discovery of a series of Early and Middle Bronze Age sites running down the eastern edge of Gilead and Moab indicated that the invading Mesopotamians were following a well-established trading route. This road actually extended as far south as Ezion-geber, which lay at the head of the Gulf of Aqabah, and it was subsequently known as the King's Highway (Num. 20:17).

It may be presumed that the reason for their aggressive intent was to be found in the rich prize of copper, asphalt, manganese, and other mineral deposits south of the Dead Sea. "Amraphel King of Shinar" used to be identified by scholars with Hammurabi of Babylon, but this is no longer acceptable.[22] The chronology of the Patriarchal period would be stabilized if a reliable identification of the four invading Mesopotamian kings could be made. This may emerge as the result of future excavations in the area, but in the meantime the chronology of the period under consideration must be placed between the twentieth and late seventeenth centuries B.C.

A final touch to the reality and nature of Patriarchal life has been provided from two Egyptian sources. The first is a scene painted on the tomb wall of Khnumhotep II, a powerful noble of the Twelfth Egyptian Dynasty, who was buried at Beni-Hasan in Middle Egypt. The tableau depicted thirty-seven Palestinian seminomads of the Patriarchal period visiting Egypt to bring the popular black eye-paint stibium. The nomads were typical bearded Semites, wearing long, gaily-striped clothing and sandals on their feet. They carried throw-sticks, javelins, and bows and arrows as weapons, and one of their number was shown to be playing on a lyre as he trudged behind his donkey. The fact that the mural portrayed portable bellows in the equipment of the Semites suggests that the company included at last one traveling tinsmith, and provides an authentic background for Genesis 4:20ff.

The second source that conveys the social atmosphere of the Patriarchal period is an Egyptian account of the adventures of Sinuhe, a nobleman who lived in the twentieth century B.C. This man was highly placed under Amenhemet I, founder of the Twelfth Egyptian Dynasty, and when the aged pharaoh died, Sinuhe fled to Palestine for political asylum. The "Tale of Sinuhe"[23] recounted his difficulties in crossing the Egyptian border, and the way in which he was rescued from death in the desert by a kindly Bedouin chieftain. When Sinuhe arrived in Syria, an important Amorite ruler befriended him, and gave him his eldest daughter in marriage. Sinuhe was made the ruler of a large Amorite tribe, which he led in marauding campaigns. His description of the Palestinian highlands is reminiscent of Deuteronomy 8:8:

> There were figs in it and vines,
> More plentiful than water was its wine,
> Copious was its honey, plenteous its oil;
> All fruits were upon its trees.
> Barley was there, and spelt,
> Without end all cattle.[24]

After the death of Terah, Abraham received a summons from God to leave his homeland, and in compliance he migrated with Sarah his wife and Lot his nephew to the land of Canaan. A famine compelled them to move farther southwest into more fertile Egyptian territory, and while they were there the beauty of Sarah attracted the attention of the pharaoh. He took her into his household with a view to marriage, having understood that Sarah was the sister of Abraham.

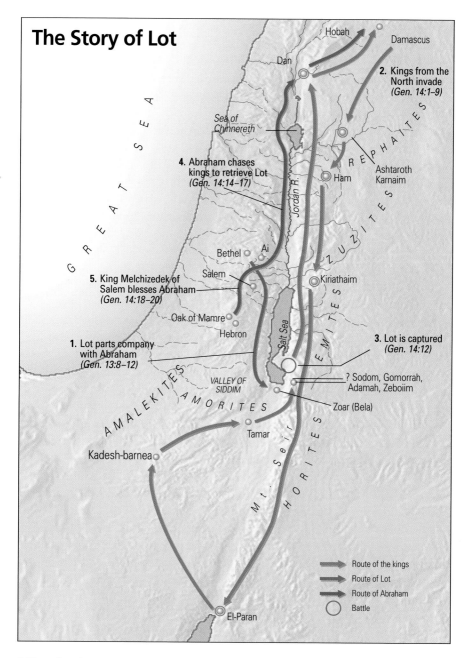

The Story of Lot

2. Kings from the North invade (Gen. 14:1–9)

4. Abraham chases kings to retrieve Lot (Gen. 14:14–17)

5. King Melchizedek of Salem blesses Abraham (Gen. 14:18–20)

1. Lot parts company with Abraham (Gen. 13:8–12)

3. Lot is captured (Gen. 14:12)

? Sodom, Gomorrah, Adamah, Zeboiim

Zoar (Bela)

Route of the kings
Route of Lot
Route of Abraham
Battle

When he discovered that she was actually his wife, however, he restored her to Abraham without delay, and permitted them to leave Egypt.

A repetition of this incident was to take place subsequently, when Abraham again conveyed the impression that Sarah was his sister, on this occasion to Abimelech, king of the city-state of Gerar (Gen. 20:2ff.). It is evident from these

83

two incidents that Patriarchal marriage customs differed considerably from those of later days. Sarah was in fact the half-sister of Abraham, being the daughter of his father but not of his mother (Gen. 20:12), which indicates that at this period it was quite permissible for nonuterine half-brothers and sisters to marry. If, however, such close relatives were not born of different mothers, they were not allowed to marry one another.

After Abraham had returned to Canaan, he entered into an agreement or covenant with God (Gen. 17:2ff.), which provided that God would make of him a great nation and be the protective Deity of his descendants in Canaan. Circumcision was instituted to commemorate the occasion, and the earlier names of Abram and Sarai were changed to Abraham and Sarah to indicate their new responsibilities in the covenant. Up to this time Sarah had been childless, and in conformity with custom had given her handmaid Hagar to Abraham so that children might be born into the household.

The first step in the fulfillment of the covenant with Abraham was completed with the birth of Isaac, despite the fact that Sarah was at an advanced age. She thus became the first of the four Hebrew matriarchs, and she asserted her authority by banishing Hagar and her adolescent son Ishmael to the desert. Although Sarah may have been justified to some extent in being angry when Ishmael mocked the infant Isaac during his weaning feast, her action in expelling Hagar and her son was not countenanced by contemporary Babylonian law. In due time, Ishmael became the eponymous ancestor of twelve tribes, who spread out through Transjordan and the territory bordering on the Gulf of Aqabah.

When Sarah died in Hebron, Abraham negotiated with Ephron the Hittite for the cave of Machpelah, in which Sarah was buried. The transaction followed typical Mesopotamian procedure as exemplified in numerous Babylonian and Assyrian contract texts, and the purchase price was weighed out, in accordance with the prevailing custom. Many centuries were to elapse before coinage put in an appearance on the historical scene.

The discovery of the Hittite legal code at Boghazköy has made possible a fuller understanding of the purchase by Abraham of the cave of Machpelah. It now appears that under Hittite law the one who purchased the entire property was under some sort of obligation to perform certain unspecified feudal services for the original owner once title to the land had been transferred. These services were no longer mandatory, however, if only a portion of the available property was purchased from the vendor. The narrative makes it clear that Abraham was just as anxious to avoid these legal obligations as Ephron was to impose them, although the normal procedures of courtesy were observed throughout the transaction. The mention of trees in the narrative is in conformity with contemporary Hittite practices, which required that the exact number of trees growing on each piece of property sold should be duly listed.

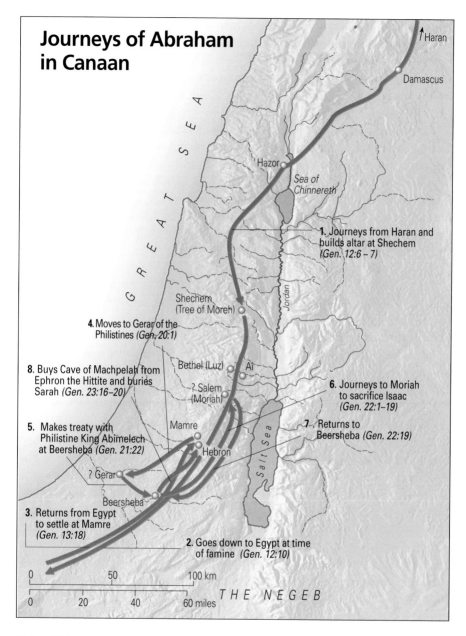

Journeys of Abraham in Canaan

Haran

Damascus

GREAT SEA

Hazor

Sea of Chinnereth

1. Journeys from Haran and builds altar at Shechem *(Gen. 12:6 – 7)*

Jordan

Shechem (Tree of Moreh)

4. Moves to Gerar of the Philistines *(Gen. 20:1)*

8. Buys Cave of Machpelah from Ephron the Hittite and buries Sarah *(Gen. 23:16–20)*

Bethel (Luz) Ai

? Salem (Moriah)

6. Journeys to Moriah to sacrifice Isaac *(Gen. 22:1–19)*

5. Makes treaty with Philistine King Abimelech at Beersheba *(Gen. 21:22)*

Mamre

7. Returns to Beersheba *(Gen. 22:19)*

Hebron

Salt Sea

? Gerar

Beersheba

3. Returns from Egypt to settle at Mamre *(Gen. 13:18)*

2. Goes down to Egypt at time of famine *(Gen. 12:10)*

| 0 | 50 | 100 km |

| 0 | 20 | 40 | 60 miles |

THE NEGEB

The Hittites

The mention of the Sons of Heth or Hittites in this narrative is by no means the first Biblical recognition of the Hittites. In Genesis 10, the offspring of the eponymous progenitor Heth were included in the group of nations of which the population of Canaan was composed. Precisely what connection these people had with the powerful non-Semitic Indo-European group that lived in central Asia Minor in the third millennium is difficult to establish. Speiser and others have suggested that since the ancient Hittite empire never extended into Canaan, the Biblical writers spoke loosely of non-Semitic inhabitants of Canaan as Hittites, when they should have been designated more accurately by the term "Hurrian."

Part of the confusion arises from the fact that the movement of the Indo-European Hittites into Asia Minor coincided roughly with the entrance of the Hurrians into Upper Mesopotamia from an Indo-Iranian source. The non-Semitic Hurrians, or Horites, as they are called in the Biblical narratives, spread farther westward, however, and penetrated into ancient Canaan. By the second millennium B.C. they were scattered all over the Near East, and were well established in Canaan in the days of Abraham. The Hurrians were conquered by the powerful Hittites about 1370 B.C., at the height of the New Empire period, and absorbed into the Hittite kingdom.[25]

But in any event, the Hurrian migration into Canaan was part of a wider movement of peoples, which included Hittites and perhaps Hivites, as well as Habiru and Semitic Hyksos. Although this may be contemporaneous with the Middle Bronze Age occupation of Asia Minor by the Hittites, it is quite distinct in its results. The Hittites of Asia Minor were the first Indo-Europeans to penetrate into Armenia and Cappadocia from the Caucasus region. They intermingled with the Anatolian Khatti whose territory they took over, and established a number of city-states. Some of these were in existence considerably prior to the period when Assyrian trading colonies were founded in Cappadocia to the east of the Khatti territory during the century when the Assyrians exercised temporary military control in Upper Mesopotamia (c. 1850–1750 B.C.). The Old Empire was established about 1800 B.C. by Pitkhanas, king of Kussar, and after two hundred years the Hittite kingdom extended from the Black Sea to Syria.

But under Mursilis I (c. 1600 B.C.), the Hittite empire was weakened by internal strife, and this paved the way for an increase in the influence of the Hurrians, who enlarged the Mitanni kingdom in northern Mesopotamia. The Mitanni probably came from the same region as the Hurrians, and there are reasons for believing that they occupied Upper Mesopotamia a little before the time of Hammurabi. The Mitanni dominated the region between Media and the Mediterranean during the Patriarchal period, maintaining a balance of power between the Hittites, Assyria, and Egypt. But a revival of Hittite power under Suppiluliuma (c. 1395–1350 B.C.) reduced the Mitanni kingdom to the position of a buffer state between Asia Minor and Assyria about 1370 B.C., and as a result Hittite influence was brought as far south as the Lebanon region.

Some ten thousand tablets recovered by Winckler in 1906 from Boghazköy in east central Asia Minor included the royal archives of the Hittite empire.

Wooden tomb-model of an Egyptian woman carrying a basket on her head. Wooden models of human and animal activities were frequently placed along with the deceased in Egyptian tombs.

The site was that of Khattusas, which for four centuries (c. 1600–1200 B.C.) had been the capital city of the Hittite kingdom. The extent of Hittite culture has been effectively portrayed by these tablets,[26] and it is now known that these ancient peoples were renowned horsemen, who claimed the distinction of having introduced the horse and horse-drawn chariot to the Near East.[27] They were also important in the development of the Iron Age (c. twelfth century B.C.) in Palestine, for cuneiform Hittite texts have shown that they monopolized the smelting and manufacture of iron for all trading purposes up to the time when Hittite power was broken about 1200 B.C.

Hittite religion was of a highly syncretistic nature, and borrowed deities from Sumer, Akkad, Nineveh, and Egypt. One tablet spoke of Marduk, god of Babylon, leaving Mesopotamia and living in Asia Minor for twenty-four years. This may perhaps be a reference to the campaign of Mursilis I against Babylon, which resulted in the city being devastated and the great image of Marduk being carried away among the booty.

Hittite legal codes have been found to contain enactments that are parallel to secular laws in the codes of Hammurabi and Moses. The general indications are that the same concepts of justice, law, and order prevailed throughout the whole of the Near East in the second millennium B.C. Hittite law recognized the inviolable nature of oaths, covenants, and treaties, and a refreshing feature of their legal system as compared with that of other Eastern countries was a marked respect for the status of womanhood. Whereas the principle of retaliation or *lex talionis* was common to the legislation of Hammurabi and Moses, a more humanitarian spirit prevailed in Hittite law.[28] In particular it was forbidden for severe physical mutilations to be imposed as punishment for those who offended against the law, with the possible exception of slaves, a marked contrast to some of the penalties that were prescribed as maximum sentences in the code of Hammurabi.

The Patriarchs in Palestine

While the Old Hittite kingdom was gaining in strength and influence, the Hebrew Patriarchs were pursuing their nomadic existence in Canaan. Abraham was unwilling to allow his son Isaac to marry a Hittite, i.e., native Canaanite, woman, so he sent his servant Eliezer to Haran to obtain a wife from his Aramean kinsfolk. A marriage was contracted on behalf of Rebekah, the prospective bride, by her brother Laban, acting on behalf of their aged father Bethuel, and Rebekah subsequently arrived in Canaan.

Shortly after this, Abraham died and was buried with Sarah in the cave of Machpelah. The union of Isaac and Rebekah, which at first had produced no offspring, was enriched by the birth of twins, Esau and Jacob, the former claiming the right of primogeniture. Esau was the favorite son of Isaac, and showed

A wooden tomb-model of an Egyptian granary. Grain was fed through holes in the roof and emptied through sliding hatches in the wall.

an interest in agricultural pursuits. This may perhaps be taken as an indication that Isaac marks the transition from nomadic to seminomadic living among the Patriarchs.[29] The Genesis narratives portray the relations between the various members of the family with great insight and delicacy of touch. With typical Oriental cunning, Jacob managed to purchase the birthright of Esau, and then deceived his blind father into a wrongful disposition of his final blessing. Because the latter was considered binding in accordance with contemporary custom, the trickery aroused the anger of Esau, and Jacob was sent for refuge to Haran, where he lived with his uncle Laban.

During his journey, Jacob experienced a Divine manifestation (Gen. 28:11ff.), which confirmed the covenant made with Abraham, and assured him of continued Divine blessing. When he arrived in Padan-Aram, he was apparently adopted by Laban, and contracted to serve him seven years for the hand of Rachel, Laban's daughter. At the end of this period, Jacob was tricked into accepting marriage with Leah, the elder sister of Rachel, and he was forced to work for another seven years without pay before gaining Rachel as his wife. In the meantime sons were born to Laban, which changed the entire situation for Jacob, if he had actually been adopted by Laban, as seems most probable, by depriving him of inheritance rights. Since their position in the family had now deteriorated, Rachel and Leah conspired with Jacob to flee from home, and prior to their departure Rachel stole the household idols, which under Nuzu law were the property of the natural rather than the adopted son. They were overtaken in flight by Laban, who remonstrated with them and demanded the return of the household gods or teraphim, which, after a search, he was unable to recover.

In the light of the customs that obtained at the time, Jacob, his wives, and all his property still belonged legally to Laban if Jacob was in the position of an adopted son who owed filial duties to the adoptive parents. This impasse was solved by a magnanimous gesture on the part of Laban, who allowed his daughters to depart with Jacob after having solemnized an agreement by which Jacob undertook to refrain from further marriages, and promised to respect the territorial boundaries of Laban.

On his way to Canaan, Jacob met his brother Esau near the rugged Jabbok canyon in eastern Palestine. Both men conducted themselves with dignity, and Esau graciously forgave Jacob, who bowed to the earth seven times as the custom of those days required on such occasions. Esau went to live in Edom, where he acquired considerable local authority as a Patriarch, while Jacob journeyed to Shechem and Hebron. On his arrival in Shechem, Jacob purchased land from the Bene Hamor, settled in the locality, and proceeded to devote himself to agricultural pursuits. When Dinah, one of his daughters, was the object of an amorous interlude at the hands of a Shechemite prince, two sons of Jacob, Simeon and Levi, carried out an act of deceit against the Bene Hamor. The resultant slaughter of the Shechemites annoyed Jacob, because he was without allies at the time and in a vulnerable economic position owing to his recent arrival in the locality. The incident passed without reprisal, however, and it may have added indirectly to the prestige of Jacob.

On receiving a Divine command to reside at Bethel, he moved his household, after insuring that all their domestic idols had been buried (Gen. 35:4). This is evidence of the fact that the Patriarchs still clung in some manner to their traditional Mesopotamian household gods. It would also indicate that such idolatrous affiliations were considered quite compatible with observance of the covenant of Jehovah, an attitude that was to persist among the Israelites for many centuries.

At Bethel God renewed His covenant with Jacob and in commemoration bestowed upon him the new name of "Israel." The family then moved again from Bethel to the neighborhood of Jerusalem, and it was here that Rachel died while giving birth to her second child, Benjamin. Shortly after this, another bereavement occurred in the family with the death of Isaac at an advanced age, and he was buried next to Esau and Jacob in the cave of Machpelah (Gen. 35:29).

The Joseph Narratives

At this point the Patriarchal narratives introduce the stories of Joseph, the elder son of Rachel, and favorite child of Jacob. The resentment with which his half-

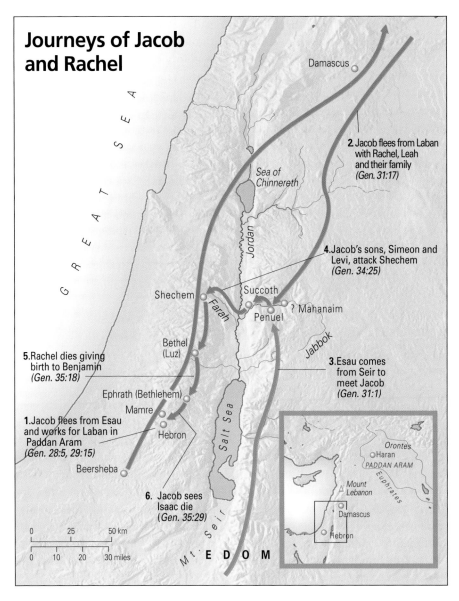

Journeys of Jacob and Rachel

Damascus

G R E A T   S E A

Sea of Chinnereth

Jordan

2. Jacob flees from Laban with Rachel, Leah and their family (Gen. 31:17)

4. Jacob's sons, Simeon and Levi, attack Shechem (Gen. 34:25)

Shechem   Succoth   ? Mahanaim

Farah

Penuel

Jabbok

Bethel (Luz)

3. Esau comes from Seir to meet Jacob (Gen. 31:1)

5. Rachel dies giving birth to Benjamin (Gen. 35:18)

Ephrath (Bethlehem)

Mamre

1. Jacob flees from Esau and works for Laban in Paddan Aram (Gen. 28:5, 29:15)

Hebron

Salt Sea

Beersheba

6. Jacob sees Isaac die (Gen. 35:29)

Orontes

Haran

PADDAN ARAM

Euphrates

Mount Lebanon

Damascus

Hebron

| 0 | 25 | 50 km |
| 0 | 10 | 20 | 30 miles |

Mt Seir

E D O M

brothers greeted his popularity with his father was increased when Joseph had two dreams that indicated that he would ultimately be vastly superior to them in position and authority. Out of spite they sold him as a slave to a trading caravan of Midianites who were traveling to Egypt, but gave the aged Jacob the impression that he had been devoured by wild beasts. The delicacy with which the reaction of Jacob is portrayed is characteristic of the exquisite beauty and drama of these narratives, which are among the most magnificent in the entire Bible.

When Joseph arrived in Egypt he became slave to Potiphar, an Egyptian military official, and soon was in charge of the entire household. When the wife of Potiphar conceived a passionate attachment for Joseph, he resisted her blandishments until in revenge the frustrated woman maligned Joseph to her husband, who had him imprisoned forthwith. This unfortunate incident has its counterpart in a thirteenth-century-B.C. tale of Egyptian life, entitled the "Tale of the Two Brothers." This romantic composition tells of the attempted seduction of a virtuous man named Bata by the wife of his older brother Anubis.

After admiring the physique of Bata, the amorous wife

> . . . stood up and took hold of him . . . then the lad (became) like a leopard with (great) rage at the wicked suggestion which she had made to him, and she was very, very much frightened. Then he argued with her, saying: "See here —you are like a mother to me, and your husband is like a father to me. . . . What is this great crime which you have said to me? Don't say it to me again!" [30]

Like Joseph, Bata was maligned for his virtue, but he was forced to endure a far greater degree of physical humiliation than was the case with Joseph. The latter enjoyed Divine favor even in prison, and his ability to interpret dreams not merely secured his release from captivity, but brought him to a position of great prominence in Egyptian political life.

When Pharaoh was unable to interpret a dream that portended famine, Joseph was brought before him for a royal audience, dressed in clean clothes and shaven in the Egyptian manner. When Joseph advised Pharaoh to store up the grain that would result from the period of plenty in anticipation of the famine that would follow, he was given the task of supervising the project. With this responsibility went the high office of vizier, which made him in effect the chief administrator of the country, and supervisor of the national economy. True to Egyptian tradition, he received from Pharaoh a signet ring, robes of honor, and a golden necklace. When he traveled about in the country he was second only in dignity and authority to the king of Egypt, and had attendants preceding his chariot crying "Pay heed." [31] Joseph then married the daughter of a priest of Heliopolis, and later had two sons, Manasseh and Ephraim.

The famine Joseph had predicted, and for which he had provided so amply, extended to the Semitic seminomads in Palestine and elsewhere, and they came periodically to Egypt to purchase grain. The elder brothers of Joseph were sent by the aged Jacob for this purpose also, and were recognized by Joseph, although they were unaware of his identity. The narratives that describe his dealings with

Wall-painting of Amenhotep I (c.1546–1525), from Thebes.

his brothers are masterful examples of drama and suspense, which culminated in the happy reunion of the entire family in Egypt. The pharaoh treated them hospitably, and settled them in Goshen, an area of the Nile delta well suited for grazing and for certain types of agriculture. The Beni-Hasan tableau, to which reference has already been made, depicted the arrival in Egypt of a party of west Semitic nomads of the Patriarchal period, which provides authentic background for the migration of Israel and his sons to Egypt. An Egyptian inscription of the fourteenth century B.C. confirms this by showing that frontier officials were accustomed to allowing the inhabitants of territory under Egyptian control to cross into the region of Goshen during times of famine.[32]

As the famine in Egypt grew progressively worse, Joseph gradually converted the land, its inhabitants, and their belongings into royal property. The people were required to till the land and contribute one-fifth of the produce to Pharaoh, but the priests were exempt from this provision since Pharaoh had already assigned crown lands for their use.

Many scholars have associated the Israelite settlement in Egypt with the conquests of the Hyksos (c. 1720–1570 B.C.) in that land. The Hyksos were probably part of the great nomadic movement from Mesopotamia that became pronounced about 1900 B.C. These "rulers of foreign lands," as the Egyptians described them, were a mixed group of Asiatic peoples, with a predominant Semitic element that probably included some nomadic Habiru.[33] In the eighteenth century, the Hyksos established a powerful kingdom in Syria and Canaan, which had previously been under Egyptian control. They fortified the land at strategic points, one of which was Jericho, by means of forts enclosed by ramparts of beaten earth (*terre pisée*), which were known by the Hebrews as "*khaserim*" (Deut. 2:23). By about 1720 B.C. they swarmed into Egypt itself, and for nearly two centuries they controlled most of the country from their capital at Avaris, the later Tanis, in the Nile delta. The Hyksos were a warlike people of considerable material prosperity, and were the first to introduce the horse and horse-drawn chariot into Egypt as a military weapon.

If there was some connection between the Hyksos and the nomadic Hebrews, the entry of the latter into Egypt would have been less difficult under Hyksos rulers than under an Egyptian dynasty,[34] since native Egyptians were not particularly tolerant of foreigners, especially if political opportunists were numbered among them. But before the implications of this situation can be examined further, it will be necessary to place this entire period against the larger background of early Egyptian history.

NOTES

1. L. Finkelstein (Ed.), *The Jews, Their History, Culture and Religion* (1949), I, 4.

2. G. E. Mendenhall, *The Biblical Archaeologist*, XI (1948), No. 1, p. 5.

3. *Ibid.*, p. 8 and pl. 5.

4. *Ibid.*, pp. 12ff.

5. *Ibid.*, p. 18.

6. *Ibid.*, p. 16.

7. *Ibid.*, p. 17.

8. *Ibid.*, p. 18, from G. Dossin, *Syria* (1938), p. 108.

9. C. H. Gordon, *Introduction to Old Testament Times* (1953), p. 101.

10. C. H. Gordon, *The Biblical Archaeologist*, III (1940), No. 1, p. 3.

11. *Ibid.*, p. 5.

12. *Ibid.*, p. 8.

13. D. J. Wiseman, *New Discoveries in Babylonia About Genesis* (1958) pp. 45ff.

14. R. K. Harrison, *Archaeology of the Old Testament* (1962), p. 29.

15. J. Finegan, *Light From the Ancient Past*, p. 55 and pl. 25. Cf. W. F. Albright, *From the Stone Age to Christianity*, p. 120.

16. W. F. Albright, *From the Stone Age to Christianity*, pp. 179ff.

17. N. Glueck, *The Other Side of the Jordan* (1940), pp. 114ff.

18. L. Finkelstein, *op. cit.*, I, 5.

19. M. Burrows, *What Mean These Stones?*, p. 174.

20. W. F. Albright, *The Archaeology of Palestine and the Bible* (1935), pp. 133ff.

21. C. H. Gordon, *Introduction to Old Testament Times*, p. 86.

22. M. Burrows, *op. cit.*, pp. 70f.

23. J. B. Pritchard (Ed.), *Ancient Near Eastern Texts Relating to the Old Testament*, pp. 18ff.

24. J. Finegan, *op. cit.*, p. 82.

25. Cf. F. F. Bruce, *The Hittites and the Old Testament* (1948), pp. 17f.

26. O. R. Gurney, *The Hittites* (1952), pp. 63ff.

27. C. H. Gordon, *Introduction to Old Testament Times*, p. 74.

28. O. R. Gurney, *op. cit.*, p. 95.

29. C. H. Gordon, *Introduction to Old Testament Times*, p. 113.

30. J. B. Pritchard (Ed.), *op. cit.*, p. 24.

31. This is the correct meaning of the phrase translated in Genesis 41:43 as "Bow the knee." Cf. C. H. Gordon, *Introduction to Old Testament Times*, p. 125.

32. G. E. Wright and F. V. Filson (Eds.), *The Westminster Historical Atlas to the Bible* (1945), p. 29.

33. Cf. E. A. Speiser, *Ethnic Movements in the Near East* (1933), pp. 34, 48, 51.

34. H. M. Orlinsky, *Ancient Israel* (1954), p. 34.

4. Ancient Egypt to the Amarna Age

CHRONOLOGY OF THIS CHAPTER

New Stone Age (Neolithic)	6000–4500 B.C.
Chalcolithic Age	4500–3000 B.C.
Early Bronze Age	3000–1950 B.C.
Middle Bronze Age	1950–1550 B.C.
Late Bronze Age	1500–1200 B.C.

The Neolithic Period

ON THE SOUTHWEST BORDER OF THE ARABIAN DESERT LAY the land bridge of the Sinai peninsula, which linked the Near East with the historic land of Egypt. The antiquity of the terrain that lay on either side of the River Nile may be judged from the fact that communal life had its beginnings there about the time that the Neolithic settlers were pioneering the Sumerian mud flats and marshes. The richness of the alluvial soil made it possible for these early communities to exist along the entire length of the Nile, while the favorable climatic conditions encouraged their growth and development. Unfortunately, heavy deposits of mud in the lower reaches of the Nile valley have prevented archaeologists from recovering more than the merest traces of these predynastic times. But in Upper Egypt, three sites identified with the modern villages of Badari, Deir Tasa, and Nagada have preserved Neolithic artifacts that date as far back as 5000 B.C.

The pottery excavated from Deir Tasa was very rough in nature, showing uneven patches of coloring on the outside that apparently were the result of poor temperature control when the pottery was being fired. The shape of the articles varied from shallow rectangular containers to beakers with a rounded base and a projecting rim at the top. A great many of the ceramic objects were

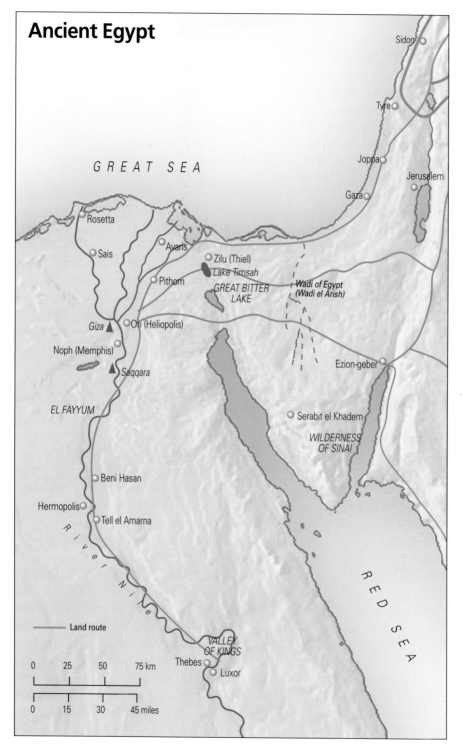

Ancient Egypt

SIDON

TYRE

Joppa

Jerusalem

GREAT SEA

Gaza

Rosetta

Sais

Avaris

Zilu (Thiel)

Lake Timsah

Pithom

GREAT BITTER LAKE

Wadi of Egypt (Wadi el Arish)

Giza

On (Heliopolis)

Noph (Memphis)

Ezion-geber

Saqqara

EL FAYYUM

Serabit el Khadem

WILDERNESS OF SINAI

Beni Hasan

Hermopolis

Tell el Amarna

River Nile

RED SEA

Land route

0   25   50   75 km

0   15   30   45 miles

VALLEY OF KINGS

Thebes

Luxor

distinguished by patterns of various sorts, but in the main the pottery designers confined their artistic efforts to modifications of simple geometric patterns. Grains of barley and emmer wheat were recovered from Tasian settlements, along with the saddle querns that were used to grind the cereals to flour. Despite these evidences of an approach to a sedentary economy, a scattering of flint arrowheads and fishhooks made from shell or horn indicates that the staple foods were gained by hunting and fishing.[1] Excavations at the six-acre site of Merimdeh, a few miles north of Cairo, uncovered artifacts from the same period as those of Deir Tasa, and in addition furnished evidence of the domestication of pigs, cattle, sheep, and goats.

About 4000 B.C. Tasian culture took on a more elaborate form, which first appeared near Badari, in Middle Egypt, during Chalcolithic times. Though seminomadic, the Badarians made serious attempts to cultivate grain and develop the domestication of animals. There is some evidence that their economy was influenced by trade, for they used an eye paint made from powdered green malachite that was probably imported from the Sinai peninsula. Badarian pottery was of exquisite texture and design, with bowls and beakers forming the main types of surviving vessels. Some vases were made from basalt, while ivory was used for small bowls, ladles, and female figurines. The Badarians are thought to have possessed a degree of familiarity with the malleability of copper, although they apparently did not understand the fusion of metals.

In the middle of the fifth millennium B.C., the Badarians were succeeded in Upper Egypt (i.e., the south) by the Amrateans, who mark the real commencement of the predynastic period (c. 4500–2900 B.C.). They were more sedentary in nature than their predecessors, and they are thought to have been the first to attempt systematic cultivation of the Nile valley. In the Nagada I stage of Upper Egyptian culture they became quite prominent, and expanded along the entire course of the Nile. Excavation of Amratean sites has shown that they cultivated and wove flax as well as manufactured a wide assortment of small copper tools and implements. Their basalt and alabaster vases were generally inferior to those of the Badarians, however, and in metallurgy they gave no indication of technical advances upon their predecessors.[2]

In the Nagada II phase, the Gerzean influence spread from Lower Egypt (i.e., the north), and paved the way for an urban and economic revolution in the upper reaches of the Nile. They were probably the first of the predynastic peoples to institute trade with Mesopotamia and India, and they were responsible for a wide expansion of agriculture. Whereas Amratean culture had depended on hunting to supplement the food derived from the cultivation of crops, the Gerzean economy was based wholly on agriculture, in which artificial irrigation probably played an important part. Cast-metal implements and weapons unearthed at Gerzean sites show that they had mastered the art of casting metal, and the use of copper in this period is indicative of extended trade with localities outside the Nile valley itself. From Asian sources came silver, lapis lazuli, lead, and other commodities, while cylinder seals that have been recovered from Gerzean graves are probably contemporary Mesopotamian products. Cosmetic techniques as practiced by the Badarians and Amrateans were developed in Gerzean culture, and palettes made in the shape of various animals were widely used for the pulverizing of green kohl or malachite for toilet purposes.

The advent of foreign influences has been seen in the presence of innovations in dress, ornaments, and implements. Flint knives and daggers were altered in shape and design, while radical changes took place in the manufacture of pottery. Decorated vases of light-colored clay, on which various patterns in shades of red and brown were painted, replaced the red pottery ornamented with white paint which had been the typical ceramic ware of the Amratean period. There were also significant changes in the matter of burials. Whereas cemeteries that dated from an earlier period showed that the corpse was generally wrapped in some sort of covering and buried in a contracted position facing the west, those which were located in Gerzean deposits indicated a lack of regular orientation, a more elaborate form of grave, and evidences of ritual procedure at the time of burial in the form of deliberately shattered pottery.

Predynastic Egypt

One of the most important contributions to the development of pre-dynastic Egypt was the expansion of community life that took place in Gerzean times. This was the basis of the territorial divisions or "nomes," as the classical writers called them, which were often tantamount to small kingdoms. Each nome or district had a special object of cult worship consisting of a sacred animal or plant, which became the emblem or fetish of the territory. The depicting of these nome emblems on pottery, and the inclusion of animal figures in the hieroglyphic nome designation of various gods led scholars to the conclusion that a totemistic form of religion existed during the early and predynastic period of Egyptian history. Certainly the predynastic inhabitants of Upper Egypt worshiped a composite animal as the cult object of the god Set, and the reverencing of the ram or goat, which was common in all periods of Egyptian religion, had its origin at this time.[3] But the most that can be said with certainty is that a modified form of fetishism and totemism characterized predynastic Egyptian religion.

The regional divisions ultimately accumulated to the point where there were twenty nomes in Lower Egypt (i.e., the Delta region) and twenty-two in Upper Egypt. The discovery of an elaborate tomb at Hierakonpolis, the seat of the Horus cult in Upper Egypt, gave rise to speculation that kingship came into being at this period. Decorated palettes recovered from the same site were found to portray a kingly personage in association with clan totems, lending further support to this conclusion. During the Gerzean period the nomes of Egypt combined, with the result that two powerful states, Upper and Lower Egypt, came into being. Gerzean culture dominated Upper Egypt for a time, and may even have effected a temporary union of the Two Lands. But the first single rule over a unified kingdom was that of Menes of Thinis, which marked the beginning of the Protodynastic period (c. 2900–2700 B.C.).

Because Thinis was far to the south, Menes built the fortified city of Menfe, or Memphis as the Greeks called it, near the apex of the Nile delta. The cemetery of the Thinite pharaohs was located in the desert near Abydos, and the excavation of the tombs revealed that a wealth of stone and copper vessels, jewelry, and other articles had been interred with the mummies. The site also yielded a number of royal names including Aha, Zer, and Narmer, although these may be cult titles rather than personal designations. Sir Flinders Petrie ultimately identified the "Horus Narmer" with Menes, the founder of the First Dynasty. One side of a large votive palette recovered from Hierakonpolis[4] portrayed a scene in which Narmer, wearing the crown of Upper Egypt, was beating an enemy chieftain into submission. On the other side of the palette he was shown walking in procession, wearing the crown of Lower Egypt. The union of the Two Lands was the underlying theme of the hieroglyphic record known as the Palermo Stone, which recorded the succession of pharaohs from the time of the First Dynasty.

Protodynastic Egypt

The beginning of the Protodynastic period was marked by an increase of trade with the peoples of the Near East and a significant development of the civilized arts. The older and more stable culture of Mesopotamia was represented in Egypt in a variety of ways. A mural decoration from a painted tomb at Hierakonpolis depicted a Mesopotamian type of boat rather than the variety commonly found in Egypt. Cylindrical seals recovered from early Protodynastic sites were found to be those of the Jemdet Nasr period, while building techniques that began to be employed at this time clearly reflected the architectural practices of Mesopotamia.[5]

In the predynastic age there appeared two cults that were more distinctive and less localized than their contemporaries. One, which was popular in Lower Egypt prior to the First Dynasty, was the cult of Re at Heliopolis, a city not far from Memphis. Re was the sun god, who was held to have originated from the waters of the Underworld, and was self-created. From him came other cosmic deities, who in turn gave birth to such notable gods of the Egyptian pantheon as Isis, Set, Osiris, and Nephthys. By the end of the Protodynastic period the cult of Re had gained considerably in influence, and in a very short time its doctrines proclaimed that the pharaoh was a son of Re, or even the sun deity

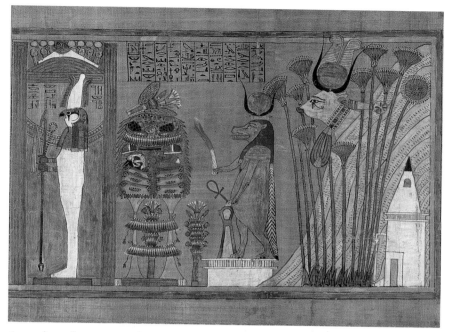

A meadow of papyrus reeds, painted on an ancient Egyptian papyrus.

himself. Complicated liturgies were gradually devised, which involved the pharaoh in a daily representation of the purification rites the Sun was believed to undergo. This procedure proved to be a considerable ritual burden in later days, as may well be imagined.

The other ancient cult was that of the god Thoth, son of the falcon deity Horus, which was associated with Hermopolis in the Nile delta. The cult emblem of Thoth was an ibis on a raised standard, and this deity was credited mythologically with the creation of the world, the control of nature, and the bestowal of culture upon humanity. As the god of wisdom, Thoth was honored by a number of epithets that reflected his primordial genius. He was also supposed to accompany Re the sun deity into the Underworld, where he acted as the scribe who recorded divine judgments in the "weighing of the hearts."

In the Thinite period a third religious cult arose in Memphis, and took Ptah as its supreme god. He was associated with ancient fetishes, but was always depicted in human statuesque form. According to his cult, he claimed priority over all other deities and was considered contemporary with the Underworld waters themselves. The doctrinal tenets of Memphite theology were of an intellectual nature, which contrasted noticeably with the crudities of other cults. Ptah was the great cosmic Mind, the First Cause, who by the projection of his thought had produced the world and its contents. Even the deities were but manifestations of his creative thought, and in his words resided almighty power.[6]

Old Kingdom Period

Probably the most majestic of any of the periods in ancient Egyptian history began with Djoser, first king of the Third Dynasty. This was the Old Kingdom period (c. 2700–2200 B.C.), which lasted until the Sixth Dynasty. The reign of Djoser was renowned for the work of Imhotep, a talented individual who was at once a magician, priest, architect, physician, and sage. For his royal master he designed a terraced mausoleum of unprecedented proportions, and erected it on a *mastaba* or platform to a height of nearly two hundred feet. This was the renowned "Step Pyramid" at Saqqara, which was the prototype of the great pyramids erected during the Old Kingdom period. The largest of these edifices was built in the Fourth Dynasty by Khufu (Cheops), its founder, at Giza. Covering thirteen acres of land, its construction took thirty years, and the cost in terms of men and material was prohibitive.

Just east of Giza across the Nile workmen toiled all the year round in the great limestone quarries to excavate the huge blocks of stone needed for the building of the pyramid. Five hundred miles up the Nile near Aswan other workmen were busy quarrying red and gray granite, while from other locations in the Sinai peninsula came black and green diorite, and white, peach, and rose alabaster. Each summer these huge blocks of masonry were floated down the Nile to the specially-constructed wharf near the site of the pyramid. The blocks were then placed on rollers or sleds and hauled up the great ramp leading to the pyramid by more laborers, some of whom were slaves. At the site the masonry blocks were given their final surface finish and then lifted into place by means of cradles, beams, and levers with fine precision.

When complete (c. 2680 B.C.), the pyramid was more than twice the height of the Imhotep structure, and was veneered with a magnificent casing of white limestone, which gave it a most impressive appearance. Prodigious feats of craftsmanship and engineering were involved in its construction,[7] and it is as much a monument to the skill and abilities of its designers as it is to the memory of Khufu. In all it took 100,000 men twenty years just to erect the structure itself, each side of which faced one of the cardinal points of the compass, and measured 767 feet at the base. The pyramid when complete contained approximately 2,300,000 stone blocks weighing an average of two and a half tons, making for a total weight of 5,750,000 tons. Some of the massive stone blocks were actually as much as sixty tons each in weight, and were placed with great accuracy on a layer of cement no thicker than a sheet of writing paper.

While the Great Pyramid gives the impression of being intact when viewed from a distance, its exterior surface has actually been marred by pillagers who have removed several courses of blocks for the construction of other buildings. The highly polished granite capstone with which the pyramid was completed has been taken away in this manner, along with almost all the smooth outer

Pharaoh Khafre departed from tradition by having his features embodied in the sphinx that stands to the east of the Second Pyramid of Giza, which he erected.

facing of Tura limestone, and the effect has been to lower the height of the pyramid from an original 480 feet to about 450 feet.

Succeeding pharaohs continued the fashion of pyramid erection, but Khafre, who followed Khufu, departed somewhat from tradition by having his features embodied in the sphinx that stands to the east of the Second Pyramid of Giza, which he erected. This edifice was in some respects an even more spectacular achievement than the Great Pyramid of Khufu, having slightly steeper sides, which were covered with granite and limestone slabs. It covered an area of more than eleven acres, measured 706 feet on each side at the base, and was 457 feet in height. The cubic area of this second largest pyramid has been estimated at sixty million cubic feet of rock. The total weight is thought to be about 5,309,000 tons, which is about half a million tons less than the Great Pyramid. As with this latter, unscrupulous builders removed a great deal of the limestone facing in order to use it in other types of construction, and this pillaging has resulted in a ten-foot reduction in its vertical height. The workmanship that went into the pyramid of Khafre was inferior to that expended on the Great Pyramid, and as a consequence its errors of linear measurement are double, and its errors of angles are almost four times as great by comparison.

In the Fifth Dynasty it became customary for inscriptions to be carved on inner walls of the pyramids. These texts dealt with the themes of judgment and eternal felicity and are known as the "Pyramid Texts." A special group of five pyramids containing texts was located near the Step Pyramid of Djoser, and the individual structures have been dated between 2450 and 2250 B.C. Although they are inferior in construction to the Step Pyramid, they are extremely important because of the writing they contain on the walls of the vestibules and interior chambers. In some of the latter even the ceilings were covered with texts that were carved carefully into the surface, or else painted in vertical columns of hieroglyphics. For the most part these inscriptions contained an assortment of magical spells, incantations, hymns, and prayers, all of which were provided for the use of the deceased king as he stood before the judgment seat of Osiris. A number of the Pyramid Texts are so archaic in their literary style that Egyptologists are of the opinion that they may have been composed at the beginning of the Old Kingdom period, and some even in the Protodynastic era.

First Intermediate Period

With the end of the Sixth Dynasty the splendor of the Old Kingdom waned, and the next dynasty introduced the period of social upheaval that has been designated the First Intermediate period (c. 2250–2000 B.C.). Probably the greatest single contributory cause to the instability that marked this phase of Egyptian history was the lack of a strong centralized government.

The Seventh and Eighth Dynasties exercised a weak rule from Memphis, whereas the two succeeding dynasties arose in the locality of modern Cairo. Thus it is not surprising that the First Intermediate period was one in which culture was eclipsed, and political intrigue was made to serve the ambitions of men whose only goal was the attainment of their material desires. It may have been the needs of the age that aroused an interest in the cult of the god Amon-Re of Thebes, the only other national deity to present a serious challenge to the claims of the mighty Ptah. Amon-Re was worshiped at Thebes, and in later centuries he became an object of popular veneration. He was held to be a unity of spirit and matter, and like some of his counterparts in Egyptian cultic worship was allegedly self-created. He was less of a religious figure than some of

Amon-Re was worshiped at Thebes, and later became an object of popular veneration.

the other members of the pantheon, and in later times he was honored as a political deity, particularly in Thebes.

Social revolution and Asiatic infiltration were features of life in the Delta region during the First Intermediate period. For a time the Eighth Dynasty pharaohs at Memphis tried to exercise some sort of authority over the local princes of Upper Egypt, but their efforts met with increasing resistance. In the Ninth and Tenth Dynasties certain kings in Middle Egypt tried to restore order in the Delta region, but in the process they quarreled with the princes of Thebes to the south of Upper Egypt. These latter gained the upper hand and finally conquered the Middle Egyptian rulers, thus making it possible for Egypt to be united once again under a strong central rule. With the Eleventh Dynasty the First Intermediate period came to an end.

Middle Kingdom Period

The Twelfth Dynasty, which was founded by Amenhemet I, began the second great age of Egyptian history, known as the Middle Kingdom period (2000–1780 B.C.). It saw a revival of society along feudalistic lines, as well as the commencement of a program of territorial expansion into Nubia. The mineral wealth of the Sinai peninsula was developed so that a prosperous mining industry resulted, and its products played an important part in the social life of the Middle Kingdom period. Incidental evidence of the wide communication Egypt had with the Near East during this time is furnished by the Tale of Sinuhe, to which reference has already been made, and by the Beni-Hasan tableau, which was concerned primarily with trade relations between Egypt and the Semitic nomads of Canaan and Arabia.

Although Amenhemet I had come from Thebes in Upper Egypt, he saw that the most effective control would be gained over the entire land only when his capital was more centrally located. Accordingly he established the seat of his kingdom near Memphis in Middle Egypt, where he organized a central treasury to which all the nomes in Upper and Lower Egypt contributed. This device served the twofold purpose of financing the kingdom and keeping the pharaoh in touch with all parts of his realm, so that the possibility of a military *coup* was greatly minimized. Apart from the campaign in Nubia, the influence of the Twelfth Dynasty was felt in Canaan with the invasion of Sesostris III, who penetrated as far as central Palestine. The extent of Egyptian influence in Canaan and Phoenicia generally in the Twelfth Dynasty is indicated by the nineteenth-century-B.C. Execration Texts, which recorded the names of the enemies of Egypt on bowls and figurines that were then cursed magically and smashed. The names that have been recovered from the fragments include certain Nubians and Egyptians, as well as some potentially hostile Semitic princes and the districts from which they came.

The Twelfth Dynasty appears to have carried on a consistent program of agricultural development, first initiated by Amenhemet I, and once the concept of kingship had won the confidence of those nobles who were jealous of their local autonomy certain changes were made in the administration of the country as a whole. Under Sesostris III, who subdued Nubia and extended the influence of Egypt into Palestine as far as Shechem (called "Sekmem" in the Egyptian texts), the restoration of royal power and prestige resulted in the

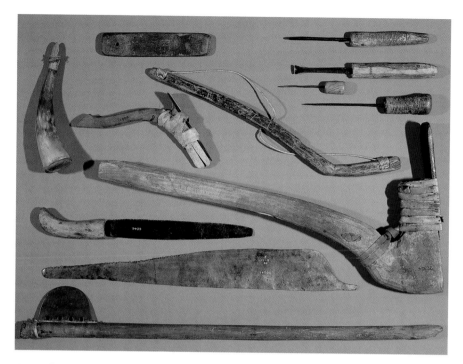

A set of ancient Egyptian carpenter's tools discovered at Thebes.

disappearance of the powerful landed princes. In their place were installed civil servants from the central administrative authority whose only loyalty was to the pharaoh, and this move brought a degree of political stability to the country as a whole.

The Middle Kingdom period proved to be the golden age of classical literature in Egypt, of which short stories and works of propaganda were the most outstanding. Of the former, the best and most familiar is the Tale of Sinuhe, a graphic narrative of a distinguished Egyptian official who was forced to seek political asylum in Palestine and spent a number of years there as a tribal chief before his honorable recall to his homeland.[8] Representative of propaganda writing was the Prophecy of Neferty, a work that assumed the style of prophetic utterance in order to proclaim Amenhemet I as the savior of Egypt and outline his program of administrative and social reform. Middle Kingdom Egypt, well organized and sensitive to the vulnerability of its Asiatic frontier, was in all probability the Egypt Abraham knew. This is illustrated by the fact that the instructions Pharaoh gave to his followers with regard to Abraham (Gen. 12:20) when he left Egypt for Canaan are exactly paralleled in reverse by those given to the returning exile Sinuhe. Pictorially the Beni-Hasan tableau, depicting a group of thirty-seven Asiatics visiting Egypt, shows the ease with which Semites could cross the heavily protected northeastern frontier into Egypt.

The Middle Kingdom period was also one of religious consolidation and the subordination of local deities to the all-powerful Re. The myths concerning the suffering, death, and resurrection of Osiris were developed into the form of a ritual, which became increasingly popular as time went on. The Twelfth Dynasty saw the principle of the Pyramid Texts applied to society as a whole, and from this time on religious texts for the guidance and protection of the deceased in the Underworld were written on the inside of the coffin. Combined with the Osirian rituals, these Coffin Texts assured mortal men that virtue was its own reward, and that final felicity was contingent upon the morality of the life lived on earth.

Second Intermediate Period

But the Middle Kingdom period suffered from political upheaval, and it was this which finally brought about its end in 1780 B.C. The two successive dynasties were unable to regain control of the situation because they were confronted by the threat of foreign invasion. Finally, about 1720 B.C., the initiative was snatched away from the Egyptians by the inroads of the Hyksos, who poured into the Two Lands in horse-drawn chariots. In order to exercise control over their territory in western Asia, they established their capital at Avaris (Tanis) in the Delta region. This was a strategic move, designed to afford them surveillance over all but the most distant reaches of Upper Egypt, and it achieved its purpose admirably for a century and a half. The Hyksos were of mixed Semitic-Asiatic stock, and probably included a proportion of Habiru. Manetho summarized the events that made every Asiatic shepherd "an abomination to the Egyptians" when he described the situation that led to the subjugation of Egypt:

> There came unexpectedly men of lowly birth from the eastern regions, who marched in, confident of victory against our country. By sheer weight of numbers they subdued it, without striking a blow. Having overpowered our rulers, they burned our cities savagely, demolished the temples of the gods, and treated the inhabitants in a hostile manner. They slew some of them, while the wives and children of others were made slaves. . . .[9]

The Hyksos, whose name in Egyptian meant "chiefs of foreign lands," seem to have capitalized on the fact that at the time of their invasion Semitic slaves were to be found in Egypt as far south as Thebes. Besides establishing their capital at Avaris, they took over the kingship of Egypt at Ithet-Tawy, near Memphis, a center Amenhemet I had built specifically for the purpose of administering his regime. The Hyksos at first made few changes in the general pattern of the regular Egyptian civil service, preferring for the sake of stability and continuity to employ the officials of the preceding regime. As time went on, however,

The pyramids of Giza.

they appointed naturalized Semitic officials to high administrative office in the country, one of the best known from this period being the chancellor Hur.

Significant points of contact between the Hyksos and the Habiru have been suggested by archaeological evidence. During this dark period of Egyptian history, the fortunes of Canaan prospered and considerable development in the arts and crafts took place. The Hyksos organized a system of feudal city-states in Canaan, and built fortifications in which huge earthwork enclosures were erected to accommodate their chariotry. Hyksos cemeteries were invariably situated outside city boundaries, and their excavation has provided considerable information as to their social and religious outlook. The discovery of jar burials of babies under foundation stones or floors may be an indication that they sacrificed their firstborn. Their worship appears to have followed the pattern of the Baal fertility cults, and artifacts recovered from Hyksos levels in Palestine have included cultic objects in a crude human form with grossly exaggerated sexual features.

Archaeological excavations at Tanis (Avaris) have revealed the presence of huge defensive fortifications that conform readily to the pattern of known Hyksos defense works in Palestine. From this same site a stele was recovered, which was dated about 1320 B.C. Apparently it had been erected by order of Ramses II (c. 1290–1224 B.C.) to commemorate the four-hundredth anniversary of the founding of Avaris, and as such it furnished a date of about 1720 B.C. for the beginning of Hyksos rule in the Nile delta.

The scribal explanation in Numbers 13:22 that associated Hebron (known to the Patriarchs as Mamre) with Zoan (Avaris) implies that some Hebrews were involved in Hyksos enterprises, and were in Egypt when Avaris was founded. A further connection between the Hebrews and Egypt can be seen in the prediction of Genesis 15:13, which said that the offspring of Abraham would be afflicted for four hundred years, a period of time that was lengthened by thirty years in Exodus 12:40. When the reference in Genesis is connected with that in Numbers, it is a cogent argument for associating the Patriarchal movements with the Avaris era.

More direct contact with contemporary Semitic peoples may be seen in the fact that two Hyksos leaders bore the names "Jacob-el" (May El protect) and "Jacob-baal" (May Baal protect), both of which have elements in common with the name of the third great Hebrew Patriarch. The local color of the narratives that recount the career of Joseph seems well suited to this period of Asiatic domination, for the Egyptians, who were never particularly tolerant to politically ambitious foreigners, would be powerless to prevent the rise of a talented Semite such as Joseph, especially if he had the support of the Hyksos conquerors.[10] In addition, it can scarcely be considered a coincidence that the Hebrews were most firmly established in Goshen, in the eastern part of the Nile delta, where the Hyksos had their capital. Finally, the third-century-B.C. Egyptian historian Manetho, to whose work reference has already been made, preserved the tradition that a large number of Hyksos moved from Avaris to Palestine, where they built the city of Jerusalem.

The narrative dealing with the life of Joseph indicates that the land of Goshen was near the Egyptian capital and that the Hebrews had ready access to the royal court. Since Thebes in Upper Egypt was the capital of the Two Lands both before and after the Hyksos period, the location of Avaris as the seat of government would be in complete accord with the conditions described in Exodus. The position Joseph enjoyed in Egypt was similar to that accorded to other notable non-Egyptians such as the chancellor Hur. Like so many others, Joseph was a Semitic servant in the household of an important Egyptian official. Although the royal court was characteristically Egyptian, the Semite Joseph was readily appointed to high office, evidently that of vizier, which made him second only to Pharaoh in rank.

Further evidence of a connection between the Avaris era and the Patriarchal migration to Egypt may be seen in the statement that Joseph bought up all the land for Pharaoh during the years of famine (Gen. 47:13). This procedure resulted in the displacement of the older landed nobility and the creation of a new class of serfs, a situation that reflects closely the conditions of social upheaval in Palestine when the Hyksos were in power there. In the light of this and other evidence, there would seem to be reasonable ground for supposing that Jacob and his family entered Egypt about 1700 B.C., when the country was under the control of Asiatic foreigners.

Apart from these inferences, the period of Hyksos rule in Egypt is one of considerable obscurity, due chiefly to the lack of Egyptian historical inscriptions during this embarrassing time of conquest by foreign invaders. It seems reasonably certain, however, that the Israelites were in Egypt when the Hyksos were in power in the Two Lands, and that they remained behind in the Delta region after the Middle Kingdom period had come to an end about 1780 B.C. It is possible that some aspects of the work of Joseph survived from the latter end of the Second Intermediate period (1780–1570 B.C.), which included the rule of the Hyksos in Egypt. When the invaders were finally expelled, the land, with the exception of temple property, belonged to Pharaoh, as it had previously when Joseph organized the country to meet the threat of famine.

Probably during the early part of the Hyksos regime, the aged Jacob fell ill, and called his sons together for his final blessing, in the traditional manner. The younger son of Joseph was preferred above the elder, and the twelve sons of Jacob, from whom the tribes of Israel subsequently traced their descent, were blessed by their father in a penetrating review of their several characters and abilities. Jacob expressed a final wish to be interred in the ancestral burial ground in Hebron, and this was duly fulfilled. After the death of Jacob, Joseph and his brothers continued to live in Egypt, and the Hebrews became increasingly prosperous. Joseph himself died as a very old man, and on his deathbed he prophesied that God would take the Israelites back to the land of their ancestors. His final request was that his bones might accompany the Israelites in their migration, and when he died, he was embalmed in the usual Egyptian manner.

New Kingdom Period

Meanwhile, national resentment was smoldering against the hated Asiatics, and shortly after 1600 B.C. the native rulers of Thebes rebelled against Hyksos domination. Sekenenre, a ruler of the Eighteenth Dynasty, was apparently killed in a preliminary battle for liberation, and the fight for freedom was carried on by his sons Khamosis and Ahmosis I. The Egyptians rallied to the cause, and Ahmosis launched a campaign against Avaris, which soon fell to his forces. This was the signal for a concerted effort to expel the Hyksos, and about 1570 B.C. the hated invaders were finally driven from the Nile delta. They retreated to their Canaanite strongholds and made a determined stand at Sharuhen in southern Canaan, but after a siege of three years they were forced to surrender. Egyptian forces then occupied the old Hyksos empire in Syria and Palestine and, freed from the threat of foreign domination, Ahmosis I of Thebes, founder of the Eighteenth Dynasty, established the New Kingdom (c. 1570–1150 B.C.).

This period has been described as probably the most brilliant in the whole of Egyptian history. Almost from the beginning of Egyptian liberation there was a dramatic resurgence of activity in the fields of architecture, literature, and artistic effort. Profiting from their unpleasant and humiliating experiences under the Hyksos, the Egyptians reorganized their armies, and attained a high degree of proficiency in the military use of the compound Asiatic bow and the horse-drawn chariot. This new weapon became the most important source of Egyptian power in the New Kingdom period, and was the monopoly of the upper military classes. The old feudalism of the Twelfth Dynasty was replaced by a dictatorship, with the result that the beginning of the New Kingdom period found the common people in the position of serfs, who tilled the land for its royal owner under conditions similar to those Joseph had instituted in time of famine, and which may well be a relic of earlier Hyksos administration.

When Ahmosis I died, about 1546 B.C., he was succeeded by his son Amenhotep I, who reigned for twenty years. About 1525 B.C., Thotmes I, son-in-law of Ahmosis I, came to the throne and established firm control over the Egyptian provinces of Syria and Canaan. His daughter was the remarkable Queen Hatshepsut, and through her the kingship descended in conformity with the ancient Egyptian social system known as the matriarchate, by which inheritance passed through the female, rather than the male, of the family.

In compliance with the matriarchate, the son and successor of Thotmes I, who was the half brother of Hatshepsut, married the queen, thus becoming the pharaoh Thotmes II. He died a few years after one of his concubines had borne him a son, Thotmes III, and while this boy shared nominal rule with Hatshepsut, it was clearly the latter who exercised regal domination in Egypt. She adopted the title of "king," somewhat to the surprise of her subjects, and wore the double crown of Upper and Lower Egypt.

She was a woman of compelling personality, who expanded Egyptian influence abroad and erected a number of imposing buildings at home, the most ambitious of which was her mortuary temple near Thebes. Her death allowed Thotmes III to express his long resentment of her influence by defacing and mutilating her monuments and inscriptions. He himself, however, was a very able ruler, and he led successful campaigns in Syria and Palestine, one of which defeated a coalition of Canaanite and Hyksos forces at Megiddo,[11] about 1480 B.C. Over the next eighteen years Thotmes III built up a large empire in the Near East, extending as far as the Euphrates. In addition, he gave careful attention to domestic problems, with the result that Egypt attained to great heights of imperial stature. In keeping with royal convention, Thotmes III erected a number of obelisks to commemorate his exploits. One of these monuments, from Heliopolis, is the so-called Cleopatra's Needle, on the Thames embankment in London, while a similar obelisk is in New York City.

When Thotmes III died, about 1436 B.C., he was succeeded by his son Amenhotep II, a powerful and valiant warrior who was renowned for his skill

Egyptian sculpture of priest with an offering-table, Dynasty 18, c 1450 B.C.

as an archer. The successor of Amenhotep II was Thotmes IV (c. 1422–1413 B.C.), who renewed diplomatic contacts with Asia by marrying a Mitanni princess. A mural from this period, found in a tomb at Thebes, depicts the arrival of a group of Syrians bringing tribute to the royal court. Their bearded faces and costumes mark them clearly as Semites.[12]

Amenhotep III succeeded to the throne about 1413 B.C., and reigned until c. 1377 B.C. Under his rule the magnificent Eighteenth Dynasty reached its height in a blaze of cultural splendor. Amenhotep continued the tradition of friendly relations with the Asiatic powers by marrying a number of native princesses. This was primarily a political device, for the beginnings of disquiet and revolt in the northern parts of the Egyptian empire were making themselves felt. Indeed, while the reign of Amenhotep III fell in one of the most fascinating and colorful periods of Egyptian history, it also marked the political decline of the New Kingdom.

Amenhotep IV became pharaoh about 1377 B.C., after being coregent with his father for some years. He was of a sensitive intellectual disposition, and was influenced by his mother to a considerable extent. He established his capital city Akhetaton at the modern site of Tell el-Amarna, some two hundred miles south of Cairo. The locale has given its name to the Amarna Age, as a convenient designation of the fifteenth and fourteenth centuries B.C., when Amenhotep III and IV ruled Egypt. What is probably the earliest international diplomatic correspondence was unearthed from the royal archives at Tell el-Amarna. Included among other texts were nearly four hundred clay tablets, written in Akkadian cuneiform by the rulers of foreign states and Egyptian dependencies. Babylonian cuneiform was the official language for international correspondence of all sorts, and facilities for learning the language existed at Akhetaton. These documents throw considerable light on the way in which the Egyptians administered their holdings in Canaan.

At the beginning of the Amarna period, the Mitanni kingdom was still holding the balance of power between the Hittites and the Egyptians. Syria was garrisoned by the Mitanni, but Canaan claimed both Egyptian and Hittite spheres of influence, while the petty kingdoms of Palestine affected allegiance to one or the other of these two great powers. To insure the loyalty of their provincial chieftains, the Egyptians set up administrative centers in Gaza and Joppa, from which commissioners exercised government. Local autonomy was respected as long as it did not interfere with the flow of tribute and forced labor to Egypt, but if petty kings formed alliances against their suzerain, reserve forces of slaves and mercenaries were employed to suppress whatever revolts arose. When it became evident at the beginning of the Amarna Age that Egyptian power was in decline, fortresses were erected in Canaan so that armies might be on hand to quell any rebellion in its initial stages.

This system of provincial government appears to have worked quite well when powerful pharaohs were in charge of government affairs. When this was not the case, however, corruption was rife, and the periodic deterioration of discipline among the Egyptian soldiers, combined with the rivalry that not infrequently arose between the vassal states, presented serious administrative problems to government officials. Such a state of chaos and disorder prevailed at the time of Amenhotep IV, and some of the Amarna tablets consisted of letters written to Egypt by Canaanite chieftains, complaining of internecine warfare

Head of Ramses II (c. 1290-1224 B.C.).

and aggression. One letter from the deputy governor of Jerusalem speaks of the predatory Habiru who were invading various cities in Canaan with considerable success, while other tablets give evidence of political intrigue and military maneuvering. These texts afford valuable information as to the conditions that existed in Palestine somewhat prior to the Hebrew occupation, and show that the Amarna Age was one of political deterioration in the Egyptian empire.

Amenhotep IV, husband of the beautiful Nefertiti, forsook political and administrative interests for religious pursuits, and in the sixth year of his reign he instituted a thoroughgoing reform of Egyptian polytheism. He dispensed with the complex system of deities, and revived the Old Kingdom concept of solar monotheism by making the sun deity Re supreme. This was in accord with the teachings of the priests at Heliopolis, the seat of sun worship. Amun, the ram-headed deity of Thebes, had for some time been associated with Re in cultic rites, so that the sun god had become known as Amun-Re, "the father of the gods, the creator of men, the lord of all being." As a final step towards the liberation of sun worship from its mythological origins, Amenhotep revived the ancient solar title of Aton, suppressed the cult of Amun, and founded his new city Akhetaton ("Horizon of Aton") on a site free from any associations with earlier cultic deities. To complete the transformation he changed his name from Amenhotep (or Amenophis) to Ikhnaton, because the former was partly composed of the divine name Amen (Amun). Inscriptions and monuments that contained the names of suppressed deities were mutilated so as to remove all traces of the earlier polytheism, and the new religion was rigidly enforced in the Two Lands.

In one of the tombs at Tell el-Amarna there was found the magnificent Hymn to the Sun, which enshrined the spiritual concepts of the new faith in words of singular beauty, reminiscent of Psalm 104:

> When thou didst rise in the eastern horizon,
> Thou didst fill every land with thy beauty. . . .
> Though thou art far away, thy rays are upon earth;
> Though thou art in the face of men, thy footsteps are unseen. . . .
> When thou shinest as Aton by day
> Thou drivest away the darkness. . . .
> How manifold are thy works!
> They are hidden before men,
> O sole god, beside whom there is no other. . . .
> Thou settest every man into his place,
> Thou suppliest their necessities. . . .
> How benevolent are thy designs, O lord of eternity!
> Thou makest the seasons . . .
> Winter to bring them coolness,
> And heat that they may taste thee.[13]

With this religious reformation came a change in the traditional forms of Egyptian art, and new aesthetic concepts were introduced. This resulted in a less formal portrayal of the human figure than had previously been the case, and the statues of Ikhnaton generally depicted a serenity of character that could not have been effected under the older canons of artistic representation. Probably the finest *objet d'art* to emerge from ancient Egypt was the superb bust of the beautiful Nefertiti, which not merely communicated the likeness of the fair queen in a striking manner, but spoke eloquently of the cultural and artistic refinement of this period.

The revolution Ikhnaton instituted caused a good deal of resentment, especially among the suppressed priesthoods, to whose prestige the reformation had dealt a serious blow. When Ikhnaton died at an early age, the pent-up forces of the suppressed Amun cult broke out in a fanatical attempt to restore the ancient religious situation. The reforms of Ikhnaton were swept aside, the capital city of Akhetaton was abandoned, and the cult of Amun was restored to its former position of authority.

The period that followed the death of Ikhnaton was marked by a further deterioration in Egyptian power and the rise of Hittite influence in Palestine and Syria. Political motives probably inspired the beautiful Nefertiti to contract a marriage with a son of Suppiluliuma, the powerful Hittite monarch. This was a most unusual departure, for hitherto the Egyptians had neither allowed their women to marry foreigners, nor had princes from other countries been permitted to ascend the Egyptian throne. Although the arrangements were confirmed by Nefertiti, Egyptian traditionalism gained the upper hand, and a serious international crisis was caused by the murder of the son of Suppiluliuma as he journeyed to Egypt for the marriage.

At this point, Tutankhaton, husband of the third daughter of Ikhnaton, came to the throne, and regained some measure of control over the situation. Obeying the dictates of popular feeling, he removed his capital to Thebes, and changed his name to Tutankhamun ("Beautiful in life is Amun") so as to eradicate from it all traces of the hated Aton religion. He did not reign for long, however, and when he died at the age of eighteen, he was given a sumptuous burial in the Valley of the Kings in gratitude for the restoration of the Amun priesthood. The opulence and splendor of that occasion were hidden from human eyes until the tomb of Tutankhamun was discovered by Howard Carter in 1922, and the world learned once again of the magnificence of the Amarna period.

Although Tutankhamun was a comparatively minor pharaoh, the artifacts that have been recovered from his tomb are among the most splendid of their kind in the world. The archaeologists who discovered the location of the tomb itself were delighted to find that it had not suffered from the activities of robbers, as had other larger tombs in the Valley of the Kings. As early as 1910 the location of the last resting place of Tutankhamun was established in a general way, but it was not until 1920 that the actual stairway that led to the sealed tomb was discovered by Lord Carnarvon and Howard Carter. In 1922 the excavators opened several anterooms containing an astonishing array of furniture, ornaments, clothing, weapons, and food for the departed king, and in the following year before a distinguished audience the door leading to the sepulchral chamber proper was broken down and the burial shrine was revealed.

Beyond this chamber lay a second shrine, whose doors were bolted and sealed, and close by was a treasure chamber in which a large chest, guarded by beautifully executed statues of four Egyptian deities, contained the mummified viscera of the king. When the burial chamber itself was finally explored later that year, it was found to comprise an enormous yellow quartzite sarcophagus covered with religious inscriptions and topped with a magnificent rose granite lid. When this was removed, a superbly executed golden effigy of the young king was revealed, and beside the religious symbols worked into the forehead was a tiny wreath of flowers, the last fond gift of a sorrowing queen to her deceased husband. This magnificent outermost coffin enclosed a second of equal splendor, and within this was the third and last, made of solid gold adorned with jewels. When the mummy was finally exposed, it was seen to have been decorated with a great many objects of gold and precious stones, the value of which cannot properly be determined. The fantastic profusion of valuable articles of all kinds is an eloquent testimony to the esteem in which the young king was held by the Amun priesthood for the way in which he had rehabilitated their cult, and at the same time it furnishes some small indication of the enormous wealth possessed by the royal families of ancient Egypt.

The Nineteenth Dynasty

An Egyptian general, Haremhab (c. 1345–1318 B.C.), the founder of the Nineteenth Dynasty, restored imperial glory to some extent by staving off disaster at the hands of the Hittites, and instituting a program of domestic reorganization that included certain measures of social reform. Under Seti I (c. 1317–1290 B.C.), military campaigns were pursued in Palestine against the Canaanites and Hittites, while Ramses II (c. 1290–1224 B.C.) continued an aggressive policy towards the Hittites. A series of battles took place, and hostilities concluded ultimately with a treaty of nonaggression in which northern Syria was ceded to the Hittites, whereas southern Syria and Palestine remained under Egyptian control. For the first time in Egyptian history, a Hittite princess exercised the functions of queen of Egypt by marrying Ramses II, the son of Seti I, about 1267 B.C. When previous marriages had been contracted between pharaohs and Asiatic nobility, the women had been received into the Egyptian royal household but had not been accorded public recognition as queen. Thus the Hittites gained a resounding diplomatic triumph at the expense of an enfeebled Egypt.

Early in the Nineteenth Dynasty, Ramses II moved his capital from Thebes to the old Hyksos city of Avaris (Tanis), which had been reconstructed by Seti I and which was subsequently enlarged considerably by Ramses II. Excavations at Tell el-Retabah uncovered what is believed to be the ancient city of Pithom, which was built, or perhaps rebuilt, by Hebrew slave labor for an Egyptian pharaoh. Some of the massive brickwork is still in evidence, and shows that the walls of Pithom were made of "bricks without straw" such as were employed in the Israelite *corvee* (Ex. 1:14; 5:7f.). The Egyptian store-city known to the Hebrews as Raamses (Ex. 1:11) was in fact Tanis,[14] the capital of the Nineteenth Dynasty, which Ramses II enlarged. Since the Biblical account used the name by which the city was known for a period of two centuries only (c. 1300–1100 B.C.), it is probable that the Hebrew tradition dated from this time.[15]

Israel in Egypt

Despite the fact that many scholars have attempted to disprove the historicity of a prolonged Israelite sojourn in Egypt, the historical conditions that existed from the nineteenth century B.C. in the Near East and Egypt are in full accord with the Biblical tradition in this respect. The rise of Semitic influence in Lower Egypt had culminated before the end of the eighteenth century B.C. in the Hyksos domination of the Two Lands. It is probable that the migration of Jacob into Egypt was connected with the increase of Hyksos power, and if this is the case, the rise of Joseph to political prominence would have been a matter of comparatively little difficulty. But Semitic fortunes in Egypt were reversed with the expulsion of the Hyksos by Ahmosis I, and according to contemporary sources, the Semites who remained in the Delta area were enslaved, or made to work as peasants in the region of the old Hyksos capital.

This situation appears to correspond with that described in the first chapter of Exodus, though the identity of the "pharaoh who knew not Joseph" is by no means clear. Certainly the enslavement of the Hebrews could commence with Ahmosis, but their actual affliction by Egyptian overseers is most probably to be associated with the work of construction at Pithom and Raamses under Seti I and Ramses II. The beatings the Hebrews endured add an unfortunately authentic touch to the situation, for this was standard procedure in ancient Egyptian life for encouraging progress in any kind of work.[16] Despite the conditions under which they existed, the Hebrews increased in numbers, and to counter this trend, the Egyptians promulgated a law providing for the destruction of all male children born to Semitic women.

From this situation there emerged the infant Moses, who shortly after birth was hidden by his mother in a boat of papyrus reeds at a place on the river that was used by the daughter of Pharaoh for bathing. When she discovered the baby, she adopted him into her household, gave him an Egyptian name, and brought him up as an Egyptian. This event antedated by several centuries the cuneiform legend (c. 800 B.C.) of Sargon I of Akkad:

My *changeling* mother conceived me; in secret she bore me.
She set me in a basket of rushes, with bitumen she sealed my lid.
She cast me into the river which rose not (over) me.
The river bore me up and carried me to Akki, the drawer of water. . . .
Akki, the drawer of water, (took me) as his son (and) reared me.[17]

The narratives dealing with the earlier part of the life of Moses are well known. His education was probably gained in the priestly circle of Heliopolis, where the complex motifs of the cult of Re would form the background of his instruction. There can be little doubt that he would become familiar with the religious beliefs and practices of ancient Canaan, which were already exerting considerable influence over worship in the Near East. He would also be in touch with the dialects of Canaan, as well as with Babylonian cuneiform, which was the normal vehicle for diplomatic communication. Moses was probably familiar with the maxims of such renowned Egyptian sages as Ptah Hotep,[18] the institution of solar monotheism by Ikhnaton and its overthrow under Tutankhamun, and the wide range of priestcraft that would be included in the education of one who came from the royal household.

There is nothing particularly unusual about the idea of a west Semite being brought up in court circles in ancient Egypt. During the New Kingdom period the pharaohs had several residences in the Delta region, and the children of concubines were educated in the royal *harims* for leadership in the state. There is clear evidence that at least from the time of Ramses II onwards, Asiatics were brought up in the *harims* of the pharaoh with a view to holding various offices. Indeed, western Semitic influence had so far penetrated the court of Ramses II that his eldest daughter was called by the thoroughly Semitic name of Bint-Anath.

Such contacts as Moses had with the Semites who lived east of the modern Suez Canal led to his marriage with the daughter of a Midianite priest, and while he was living in this region south of the Dead Sea he received a theophany, in which God appeared to him under the name of Jehovah. Moses was ordered to return to Egypt with his brother Aaron, and was commissioned to lead the enslaved Israelites out to an ultimate destination in Palestine.

The arrival of Moses in Egypt as leader of the captive Israelites coincided with the period of their greatest oppression. Moses was somewhat reluctant to undertake the responsibilities of his vocation, but after meeting with his brother Aaron and the elders of Israel (Ex. 4:27–31), he went before Pharaoh to request permission for the Israelites to go into the wilderness to celebrate a feast of their God. This request was refused by Pharaoh on the ground that it would encourage idleness among the Hebrews, not because there was anything unusual about such a proposal. Egyptian ostraca that recorded the day-to-day activities of workmen frequently included notations concerning absenteeism, and one such journal spoke of workmen "offering to their god."

In consequence of this rebuff to Moses, a succession of closely related natural calamities befell the Egyptians, culminating in the death of their firstborn. At this juncture, the Israelites prepared to leave the land, and the Passover festival was instituted (Ex. 13) to commemorate the Divine deliverance from Egypt. The Israelites began their Exodus by moving southeastwards from Raamses to Succoth, but were prevented from taking the northern route along the Mediterranean because of the danger presented by the Philistines, a wild maritime people who had migrated from the Aegean to Canaan somewhat before the twelfth century B.C. Having been diverted into the Wilderness of Etham, the Israelites were ordered to encamp near Pihahiroth, between Migdol and the sea (Ex. 14:1).

It was at this encampment that the Egyptian charioteers overtook the fleeing Israelites, thereby precipitating the events that resulted in the Exodus proper and the destruction of Egyptian forces. Prior to the discovery of Raamses, the Biblical account of the Exodus was viewed with considerable scepticism by many scholars, some of whom claimed that the actual route followed was the military road from Raamses to Gaza, known as the "Way of the Land of the Philistines." Others argued that it was improbable that the Israelites had actually crossed the main body of the Red Sea, and suggested that they had in fact followed the old trading route linking Memphis with Ezion-geber at the head of the Gulf of Aqabah. Part of the misunderstanding rested upon the translation of the Hebrew name *Yam Suph* by "Red Sea," for the correct rendering is "Marsh Sea" or "Reed Sea." Thus the names "Red Sea" (Ex. 13:18) and "the sea" (Ex. 14) are probably meant to indicate the Lake of Reeds, situated in the marshlands between the Bitter Lakes and the town of Zilu (Thiel). It is hardly probable that the oceanic gulf extending from the Indian Ocean to the Gulf of Suez can be meant, for reeds do not occur in this area. While the name *Yam Suph* was used in antiquity in a loose fashion to designate the Red Sea proper as well as the Gulfs of Suez and Aqabah, it again appears unlikely that either of the latter was the *Yam Suph* of the Exodus narrative. The principal reason is that the Israelites were depicted as crossing a body of water that presented a natural obstacle to travel in the Sinai wilderness, and neither the Gulf of Suez nor the Gulf of Aqabah fulfills this requirement. The Red Sea is at the southern end of a geological fault that extends from Syria along the Jordan valley and the Gulf of Aqabah into Africa. In antiquity the area north of the Gulf of Suez consisted of a succession of small lakes and marshy ground where papyrus reeds grew in abundance. Egyptian documents of the thirteenth century B.C. spoke of a great Papyrus Marsh, which existed in the locality of Tanis in the

Nile delta.[19] Probably the crossing was made in the area of Lake Timsah, a body of water that lay somewhat north of the Bitter Lakes. Shallow stretches of water such as existed in this region would be more easily parted by a wind in the manner described in Exodus 14:21, which is an accurate record of a natural phenomenon occurring periodically in different parts of the world.

The Date of the Exodus

The chronology of the Exodus has presented problems that are undoubtedly among the most perplexing in the whole of Hebrew history. It has been the subject of heated debate for a number of years, and the difficulties are by no means resolved at present. The two main conflicting views have a difference of over one and a half centuries between them, and both can be supported to some extent by the Biblical narratives. The earlier dating places the Exodus in the reign of Amenhotep III of the Eighteenth Dynasty, while the later one regards it as occurring in the Nineteenth Dynasty, when Ramses II ruled Egypt.

The fifteenth-century date depends partly upon a chronological note in I Kings 6:1, which states that Solomon began to build the Temple in the four hundred and eightieth year after the Exodus, and partly upon the date of the conquest of Canaan, including the fall of Jericho, as well as other archaeological material. Assuming that the reference to Solomon is to a date about 961 B.C., the Exodus would have taken place about 1441 B.C. The excavations of Garstang at Jericho provided further support for this date when it was announced that Jericho had fallen to the invading Israelites prior to 1400 B.C.[20] It was also stated that diplomatic contact between Jericho and Egypt ceased under Amenhotep III (c. 1413–1377 B.C.), making Amenhotep II (c. 1436–1422 B.C.) the pharaoh of the Exodus. The fall of Jericho had been preceded by the Israelite occupation of Moab, which according to Jephthah in Judges 11:26 extended over a period of three hundred years. If a date of c. 1100 B.C. is given for Jephthah, the occupation of Moabite territory would have taken place about 1400 B.C., which again gives a fifteenth-century-B.C. date for the Exodus.

Circumstances of Egyptian history have also been adduced in favor of a date at this time, thereby making Thotmes III, the great Egyptian empire-builder, the pharaoh of the Israelite oppression. A mural in the tomb of Rekhmire, the vizier of Thotmes III, depicts a brick-making scene, where slaves are moistening lumps of Nile mud, adding sand and chopped straw, and placing the mixture into molds for baking in the sun. The mural carries an inscription reminiscent of advice given by the taskmasters to the enslaved Hebrews, "The rod is in my hand; be not idle."

The mention of the invading Habiru in the Tell el-Amarna tablets (c. 1400–1360 B.C.) was taken as particularly significant for an early date of the Exodus. The Habiru were equated with the conquering Hebrews, and the dis-

Sunset over Jebel Musa, Mount Sinai, in the Sinai peninsula, Egypt.

turbed political conditions as reflected in the tablets were held to be those which existed in Canaan before the Israelite invasion. Thus the plea of Abdi-Hiba, governor of Jerusalem, in a letter to the pharaoh Ikhnaton in which he requested aid against the marauding Habiru:

> Let the king . . . send archers against the men who transgress against the king, my lord. If there are archers (here) in this year, then the lands . . . will (still) belong to the king, my lord. If there are no archers, the lands . . . will (no longer) belong to the king . . .[21]

was regarded as a native Canaanite version of the conquests of Joshua.

The arguments for placing the date of the Exodus in the thirteenth century B.C. were based in part on the reference in Exodus 1:11, which implies that the Israelites were in bondage when the cities of Raamses and Pithom were being built or enlarged, making Seti I or Ramses II the pharaoh of the Israelite oppression. Contemporary inscriptions referred to people known as Apiru who were laboring for Ramses, and these were identified by many scholars with the Habiru. A *stele* found at Raamses recorded that the city was founded four hundred years before the erection of the monument, and since the date of the latter was about 1320 B.C., the capital city of the Hyksos was founded c. 1720 B.C. As noted earlier, the connection between the Hyksos invasion of Egypt and

123

the Hebrew occupation of the land of Goshen was thought to be implied by the tradition in Exodus 12:40, which gives a four-hundred-and-thirty-year Egyptian sojourn for Israel, and which is probably based on the Avaris era. This usage was further alleged from the reference in Numbers 13:22, which states that Hebron was built seven years before Zoan (Avaris), using the Avaris period as a medium for dating. On this basis, the Exodus would have occurred some four hundred and thirty years after Avaris-Tanis was founded, furnishing a date about 1300 B.C.

Additional evidence for a thirteenth-century date for the Exodus emerged from the work of Glueck in Transjordan. He discovered that after the time of Abraham, the territories of Edom and Moab became denuded in population until about the middle of the thirteenth century B.C.[22] From this it became evident that the conditions of population that necessitated the circuit of Edom and the difficult campaigns against the Ammonites in Heshbon (Num. 20–21) could scarcely have existed until the thirteenth century, after which time Edom was densely populated.

An even later date for the fall of Jericho, c. 1250 B.C., was suggested by Vincent, an eminent Palestinian archaeologist, who rested his conclusions to some extent upon the discovery of imitation Mycenaean vases at Jericho. These had probably been imported from Greek sources when the Minoan civilization of Crete (c. 2000–1000 B.C.) had exercised an important cultural influence over the Mediterranean lands, and belonged properly to the Late Bronze II period (c. 1375–1200 B.C.), after which they were no longer imported. However, other archaeological considerations weigh heavily against so late a date for the Exodus, including the fact that a whole series of Canaanite cities such as Lachish and Bethel fell in the thirteenth century B.C.

It will be apparent from this brief survey of the situation that no sequence of dating is without its difficulties. The fifteenth-century date presents problems for the chronology of the Patriarchal period also, for taking the Genesis narratives as they stand, it would appear that a period of two hundred and fifteen years elapsed between the arrival of Abraham in Canaan and the migration of Jacob to Egypt. If the statement that Israel was in Egypt for four hundred and thirty years (Ex. 12:40) is considered independently of the Hyksos movement, it would presumably mean that Abraham entered Canaan some six hundred and forty-five years before the Exodus, about 2086 B.C. Since he was seventy-five years of age at that time (Gen. 12:4), his birth would have taken place about 2161 B.C., somewhat prior to the Third Dynasty of Ur (c. 2070-1960 B.C.). This date seems a little early, judged by the trend of the migrations in Mesopotamia subsequent to the twentieth century B.C. If, however, Abraham entered Canaan about 1900 B.C., as the archaeological evidence relating to the destruction of Sodom and Gomorrah seems to indicate, a prolonged Israelite sojourn in Egypt would point to a thirteenth-century date for the Exodus.

The Cave of Machpelah, Hebron, by tradition the resting-place of the patriarchs Abraham, Isaac, and Jacob.

According to Genesis 15:13, the descendants of Abraham were to be afflicted in a strange land for four hundred years, while the tradition of Exodus 12:40 extends the sojourn to four hundred and thirty years. The Septuagint Greek version of the latter text, however, reduced it to two hundred and fifteen years. Probably two traditions are involved here; the first, indicating a prolonged stay, appears to have computed the length of the sojourn from the time when the Hyksos entered Egypt (c. 1720 B.C.), while the Septuagint reckoned the actual "bondage" from the time when the Hyksos were expelled. In any case, both traditions would indicate a date towards the beginning of the thirteenth century B.C., if the Patriarchal migrations were connected with the Avaris era.

Part of the difficulty in interpreting the reference in I Kings 6:1 correctly lies in the fact that the Oriental peoples often used numbers to signify more than purely mathematical considerations. Indeed, the attitude of the earlier Biblical writers towards general computation has much in common with that of the modern Bedouin Arab. Where a fair degree of chronological exactness is required, genealogies are far more important to the Oriental mind than the Occidental method of reckoning in terms of days, months, and years. This is one of the reasons for the prominence of genealogies in Biblical narratives generally, and it also accounts in part for the usage of "round numbers" to express approximate duration of time.

Thus, the phrase "forty years" was synonymous with the concept of a "generation," while in Genesis 50:26 the period of one hundred and ten years, which marked the life span of Joseph, was the traditional Egyptian figure for a full life or advanced old age. It is not always easy on occasions to determine whether the Biblical numbers are being used literally or symbolically. Where there appears to be a motif or cycle involving sevens, forties, and the like, it is probable that other than purely literal considerations are involved. When the reference in I Kings 6:1 is examined from this standpoint, it is found to comprise a matter of twelve generations of forty years each. This appears to involve a double cycle, and may be related in some manner to the idea of successive generations as applied to the twelve tribes. If the number is taken literally, however, it argues strongly for a fifteenth-century date of the Exodus.[23]

The evidence that the excavations of Garstang at Jericho presented for an early dating has suffered seriously from subsequent work at the site, carried on under the supervision of Dame Kathleen Kenyon since 1951. Sellin, Watzinger, and Garstang had shown that Jericho was occupied in Neolithic times, and that several cities were erected on the site during the Chalcolithic era (4500–3000 B.C.). Later cities, which Garstang identified alphabetically, dated from 3000 B.C., and the fourth of these, City D, built about 1500 B.C., was held to be the one overthrown by Joshua about 1400 B.C. But excavations undertaken since 1951 have shown that practically nothing is known about the site as it existed in the time of Joshua, owing to natural erosion and human destruction. Since no traces of Late Bronze Age walls were unearthed, and no remains of contemporary ceramics were discovered, it has become almost impossible to say when its overthrow at the hands of the Israelites took place. Recent discoveries at Jericho have demonstrated beyond question the immense antiquity of the site, and have thrown further light on the nature of the pre-pottery Neolithic communities there.[24] No new information has been forthcoming to date on the chronology of the Exodus, however, and it may be some years before a new appraisal of the problem of the date is possible.

Objections to the thirteenth-century date generally envisage the conditions of the Eighteenth Dynasty as being ideal for the enslavement of the Hebrews. Some scholars have argued that the reference to the treasure city of Raamses in Exodus 1:11 is to the building of the original Hyksos capital of Avaris-Tanis about 1720 B.C., by Israelite labor, and not to its enlargement under Ramses II (c. 1290–1224 B.C.). This view assumes that the Israelites entered Egypt about 1870 B.C., during the strong Middle Kingdom period, and that they were enslaved when the Hyksos conquered Egypt about 1720 B.C. The name "House of Ramses" (Per-Re'emasese), by which Tanis was known for two centuries (c. 1300–1100 B.C.), is held to be a modernized form of the archaic Zoan-Avaris in the same way that Laish (Gen. 14:14) was subsequently modified to Dan, with the reference being, as far as Tanis was concerned, to the original Hyksos capital.

The possible relationship between the Habiru of the Amarna tablets, the Hebrews, and the Aperu (Apiru) has also been urged as an argument against the thirteenth-century date of the Exodus. On this view, the Hebrew conquest of Palestine was actually the Habiru invasion of which the princes of the Canaanite states complained in correspondence sent to Amenhotep III and IV. Unfortunately it is by no means clear that there was any relationship between the Habiru, the Hebrews, and the Aperu, and the problem is very complex, to say the least.[25] Some scholars who identify the Habiru and the Hebrews have disclaimed any connection between the Habiru and the Aperu, but no clear evidence on this matter has been forthcoming to date.

The earliest references to the presence of Aperu in Egypt date from the time of Amenhotep II, who is the pharaoh of the Exodus, according to the fifteenth-century sequence of dating. The Aperu may have been employed in part as mercenary troops, and they are definitely depicted in inscriptions from the time of Ramses II as laborers performing heavy manual work in quarries and at the sites of buildings. But even if some relationship existed between the Hebrews and the Aperu, the fact that the latter were in Egypt from the fifteenth to the middle of the twelfth century B.C. would indicate that at least some of them did not leave the country with the Hebrews, whatever the date of the Exodus actually was.

Some scholars have also questioned the validity of the surface explorations in Transjordan made by Glueck; and even Albright, who supported his general conclusions, has admitted that some modifications may be necessary.[26] Accordingly it has been argued that the gap in the sedentary population of the Arabah and the Transjordan regions between 1900 and 1300 B.C. was not so pronounced as Glueck has maintained. Thus there may well have been sufficient organized resistance among the Edomites and Ammonites to justify the situation described in Numbers 20–21. In any event, the conquests of the roving Israelites may have been matched by the military prowess of other warlike nomads, or of tribes whose economy was of a simple agricultural variety, such as may have been true of the Edomites and Ammonites in the fifteenth century B.C.

It will appear from the above considerations that a good deal of care has to be exercised in the interpretation of archaeological data, and its correlation with the Biblical narratives. While archaeological excavations often serve a useful purpose in illuminating ancient history and social life, they can also present a variety of special problems, and the subjective nature of some of the conclusions that may be drawn frequently makes for considerable difference of opinion among experts. The date of the Exodus is one of the most problematical issues facing the Biblical archaeologist, but it is not too much to hope that it will be resolved in the future by further discoveries in Egypt or Canaan.

NOTES

1. V. G. Childe, *New Light From the Most Ancient East*, pp. 33f.

2. *Ibid.*, pp. 57f.

3. E. A. W. Budge, *From Fetish to God in Ancient Egypt* (1934), pp. 75ff.

4. J. Finegan, *Light From the Ancient Past*, p. 73 and pl. 28.

5. H. Frankfort, *The Birth of Civilization in the Near East*, pp. 82f.

6. E. A. W. Budge, *op. cit.*, p. 16.

7. I. E. S. Edwards, *The Pyramids of Egypt* (1947), pp. 86ff; B. Mertz, *Temples, Tombs and Hieroglyphs* (1964), pp. 85ff.

8. J. B. Pritchard (Ed.), *Ancient Near Eastern Texts Relating to the Old Testament*, pp. 18ff.

9. In Josephus, *Contra Apion.*, I, 14.

10. H. M. Orlinsky, *Ancient Israel*, p. 33.

11. C. H. Gordon, *Introduction to Old Testament Times*, pp. 58f.

12. J. Finegan, *op. cit.*, p. 40.

13. *Ibid.*, p. 97

14. G. E. Wright and F. V. Filson (Eds.), *The Westminster Historical Atlas to the Bible, p. 37.*

15. W. F. Albright, *From the Stone Age to Christianity*, p. 194.

16. C. H. Gordon, *op. cit.*, pp. 130f.

17. J. B. Pritchard (Ed.), *op. cit.*, p. 119.

18. *Ibid.*, pp. 412ff.

19. W. F. Albright in *Old Testament Commentary (*1948), p. 142.

20. J. Garstang, *Joshua-Judges* (1931), p. 146.

21. J. B. Pritchard (Ed.), *op. cit.*, p. 488.

22. N. Glueck, *The Other Side of the Jordan*, pp. 125ff.

23. J. W. Jack, *The Date of the Exodus* (1925), pp. 200ff.

24. Kathleen M. Kenyon, *Digging Up Jericho* (1957), pp. 51ff.; *Archaeology in the Holy Land* (1960), pp. 43ff.

25. H. H. Rowley, *From Joseph to Joshua* (1950), pp. 45ff.

26. Cf. H. H. Rowley (Ed.), *The Old Testament and Modern Study* (1951), p. 4.

5. The Wilderness and Canaan

UNDER DIVINE DIRECTION, MOSES HAD BEEN ENABLED TO deliver the descendants of the Patriarchs from the shame of forced labor in Egypt. This in itself was a disaster of considerable magnitude for the former captors, who had employed a heavy proportion of slaves for work on building projects since the time of Amenhotep II. The conquests of this enterprising warrior in Syria and Canaan had resulted in large numbers of Semitic and non-Semitic groups being carried captive: Among these were 3,600 Aperu who, to judge from contemporary inscriptions, were particularly valuable for heavy laboring tasks. The ambitious building schemes of Ramses II were also implemented by means of slave labor, and the brutality of the Egyptian *corvée* served to inspire a deep hatred of the captors and an earnest desire to escape from bondage when a suitable opportunity presented itself.

That such a large group of captive people should have been able to escape from a powerful nation was neither impossible nor entirely unknown in the ancient Near East. A Hittite document described a similar occurrence in the late fifteenth century B.C. in which the inhabitants of some mountain settlements and townships in the Hittite kingdom suddenly decided that they no longer wished to live under Hittite control. Accordingly they collected all their belongings and went as a group to live in the land of Isuwa, and although the Hittites were understandably disturbed by this sudden blow to their national pride, they were unable to bring the group back by force until the time of the powerful Hittite monarch Suppiluliuma.

The Egyptians, however, were less fortunate in their attempts to retain, and then to pursue and recapture the fleeing Hebrews, since God had arrayed against them the forces of nature in the shape of nine powerful plagues, a supernatural calamity that comprised the tenth plague, and the catastrophe that overtook the Egyptian chariotry at the *Yam Suph.* What was unique about the situation that involved the Hebrews was that they had been called out of bondage as a nation to render service to a specific Deity along the lines of a covenant obligation. While those inhabitants of ancient Anatolia who fled to the land of Isuwa may well have considered themselves economically and politically oppressed, they had no definite commission or calling to some exalted spiritual destiny, and seem only to have been trying to improve their social and political fortunes.

The narratives of Exodus 12:38 and Numbers 11:4 make it clear that many of these slaves took advantage of the Israelite departure from Egypt to make good their own escape. These non-Israelite elements formed a considerable proportion of the liberated slaves and serfs whom Moses led out into the desert regions beyond the borders of Egypt. This movement was the beginning of a journey that lasted for a whole generation, during which time an unruly mob was forged into a worshiping community in preparation for the occupation of the Promised Land of Canaan.

The Route of the Exodus

Reec
Shihor Lak
? Baal Zephon
Rameses
Pithom
Bitt
On (Heliopolis)
Noph (Memphis)
E G Y P T
Nile

Traditional route of th
Alternative routes
Border fortress
Track
0   50   100
0   20   40   60 mile

Route of the Exodus

The precise route that was followed after the crossing of the *Yam Suph* has been a matter for some debate, particularly since the precise location of Mount Sinai (Horeb) is still uncertain. The Sinai peninsula, bounded on the southwest by the Gulf of Suez and on the southeast by the Gulf of Aqabah, consisted of sev-

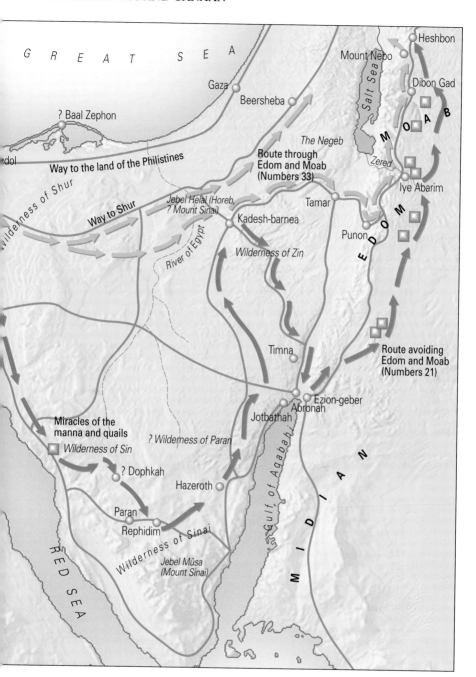

eral distinct desert areas, separated by mountains and the River of Egypt, the modern Wadi el-Arish, which drained the surplus rainfall from the Wilderness of Paran into the Mediterranean Sea. In antiquity it formed the boundary between Sinai and Palestine (Num. 34:5). The first part of the journey took the

Israelites southeast along the Gulf of Suez into the Wilderness of Sin, a desert area at the foot of the Sinai plateau, well inland from the Red Sea. This locality is usually identified with Debbet er-Ramleh, a sandy tract extending below Jebel et-Tih in the southwest of the Sinai peninsula, although another suggested location is on the coastal plain of el-Markhah. Et-Tih is part of a large limestone formation that as it projects into the peninsula of Sinai becomes fringed with sandstone outcrops. South of the plateau of et-Tih the peninsula contains a triangular area of granite and other hard crystalline rocks that form several mountain ranges, including the traditional Mount Sinai. At the northwest and northeast corners this area is separated from the limestone plateau by the outcroppings of sandstone that in antiquity contained substantial deposits of turquoise and copper ores.

Despite the rugged and barren grandeur that is typical of the scenery of Sinai, it must not be imagined that the peninsula is either an impassable desert or a tract of land entirely devoid of vegetation. Wells and springs are to be found within a day's journey of each other all down the west coast from the Suez area to el-Markhah, and the water table is generally close to the surface of the gravelly ground. Some sort of vegetation can be found in the *wadis*, and where there is permanent water, such as at an oasis, the vegetation flourishes accordingly. Some of the mountains in the limestone range have small plateaus at their bases, and these provide modest grazing areas for herds and flocks. A great many of the tamarisk and acacia trees that grew in the Sinai peninsula in antiquity have been cut down, and although this may have affected the amount of rainfall slightly, there seems to have been no significant change in the nature of the winter rainy season over the centuries.

The traditional route of the Exodus is by no means as impossible as some scholars have imagined in the past, although there are obvious difficulties connected with the identification and nomenclature of specific sites. Many of the places at which the Hebrews stopped were named in connection with events that occurred during the wanderings (e.g., Num. 11:34), and since no sedentary population remained to continue the tradition, the names did not receive any particular topographical fixity. The Wilderness of Shur can be identified with a tract of land in the northwestern part of the Sinai isthmus, between the present line of the Suez canal on the west and the Wadi el-Arish on the east. From this area the Hebrews passed south through the Wilderness of Sin along the western coastal strip of the Sinai peninsula, and it was at this period that they experienced their first murmurings of unrest.

These were satisfied by the appearance of quails, a small pheasant-like bird, which probably flew in with the winds from the sea (cf. Num. 11:31). This incident also confirms indirectly the tradition that the Hebrews followed a southerly (Sinaitic) rather than a northerly (Mediterranean) escape route from Egypt, the latter having been forbidden to them in any event (Ex. 13:17f.). Quails only

Mount Sinai lies within a triangular area of granite and other hard crystalline rocks that form several mountain ranges.

land on the Mediterranean coast of the Sinai peninsula from Europe in the autumn and at dawn. By contrast, the hungry Israelites encountered them in the spring, in the evening, and during the month of March. These considerations exclude the Mediterranean coast from the escape route followed by the Israelites, and directly favor the southerly route by the Gulfs of Suez and Aqabah.

It was in the Wilderness of Sin that the Israelites also came into contact with the mysterious substance they called manna, and which was to form a prominent part of their diet during the wilderness wanderings (Ex. 16:35). It appeared on the ground each morning after the dew had fallen, and in appearance was small, whitish in color, and sweet to the taste. It did not keep overnight, and in order to be available for use on the sabbath it had to be cooked or baked in advance. Some partial parallels have been seen in the honeydew excretions on tamarisk twigs produced by certain insects in the month of June. These drops fall to the ground at night and are eaten by ants the following morning. The substance is supposed to be rich in carbohydrates and to have considerable pectin and sugar content also.[1] The interpretation of manna in terms of insect excretions is not acceptable to those scholars who regard manna as some kind of fungous growth, however, and the nature and provision of this food must be assigned to the realm of the miraculous.

The next stage of the journey took the Israelites to Rephidim, perhaps to be identified with the Wadi Refayid, where an acute shortage of water was miraculously remedied. At this time Joshua, the son of Nun, rose to prominence as the leader selected by Moses to ward off an attack by Amalekite tribesmen, which he did with great success. Here, too, Jethro (Reuel), the shepherd-priest of the Midianite tribe of Kenites, and father-in-law of Moses, visited the Israelite leader and assisted him in organizing courts of law to hear the disputes that were arising among the Israelites continually. There are good reasons for regarding as accurate the tradition that locates the Kenites in the area to the south and east of the Gulf of Aqabah, opposite the Sinai peninsula. The name "Kenites" means "belonging to the copper-smiths," and it is probable that they were attracted to the Sinai peninsula by the renowned copper mines at Serabit el-Khadem, a site some fifty miles from the traditional location of Mount Sinai.

Copper and iron had been mined from an early period in the Jordan valley and the Wadi Arabah to the south, and the Kenites doubtless made use of the deposits of copper and turquoise near the Wadi Serabit also. The presence of nomadic metalworkers such as the Kenites implies at least a semisedentary form of occupation in the regions of Midian and Sinai, and this would certainly be influenced by the presence of the ancient trading routes between Egypt and the Near East. The Kenites belonged to the Midianite peoples, who were among the first of the nomadic Bedouins to domesticate the camel. This period, then, marks the transition from the use of the ass to that of the camel in nomadic travel. Since the Israelites were restricted to ass-nomadism, the traditional route of the wilderness wanderings (Num. 33) kept them within easy reach of oases in the desert, and the grazing lands to the southwest of the Dead Sea.[2]

The Revelation at Sinai

With the departure of Jethro, the Israelites moved to a new encampment in the desert of Sinai, where they stayed for almost a year. This period was one of great importance for the unifying of the wandering multitude, for it was in the Sinai desert that Moses met with God to receive the Decalogue and other legislation that were basic to the faith and life of the later Israelite nation. The mountain from which God revealed the Law was named Horeb in the book of Deuteronomy, though the other books of the Pentateuch referred to it as Sinai. The identification of the site is by no means certain, but the great weight of tradition indicates Jebel Musa, the "Mountain of Moses," a prominent peak in a rugged range of granite hills, as the original Mount Sinai.[3] The precise distinction between Horeb and Sinai is also uncertain. Some scholars have identified Horeb with a separate mountain, Jebel Serbal, which formed part of the Sinai range, and which had a well-watered oasis on its northern side, but this conclusion is doubtful. Probably the name Horeb was a local description of the

A bronze statue of the sacred bull of Apis, Memphis. Bull worship, associated with fecundity, was prominent in the pre-exilic cultic rites of the Hebrews.

whole district, whereas Sinai was the designation of the particular mountain in the range where the Law was given.

The revelation Moses received culminated in an event that was of supreme significance for the Israelites. A solemn agreement or covenant was contracted between God and Moses, which in effect constituted the nomadic Israelites as the Chosen People of God. Henceforward they were to be a united group with an awareness of national status, implemented by Divine protection. God covenanted to bring His people into the Promised Land of Canaan if they would undertake to recognize Him consistently as the one true God, and to offer worship and allegiance to Him alone.

As observed previously, covenants were widely used in the Near East during the second millennium B.C., both at the international and at the more personal level. Mendenhall has pointed out striking similarities between the covenant in Exodus 20 and the international suzerainty treaties of the fourteenth and thirteenth centuries B.C. that were recovered principally from Hittite sources at Boghazköy.[4] These legal undertakings between a great king and a vassal began with a title or preamble in which the instigator of the covenant was identified (cf. Ex. 20:1). This was followed, in second-millennium-B.C. covenants only, by a historical prologue, in which the previous relations existing between the two contracting parties were mentioned (cf. Ex. 20:2), along with the assurance that the past generosity of the overlord was the basis for gratitude and future obedience on the part of the vassal.

Then came the obligations the suzerain wished to impose on the vassal, consisting of general (cf. Ex. 20:3–17, 22–26) and detailed (cf. Ex. 21–23; 25–31) stipulations, along with a prohibition against the vassal engaging in foreign alliances (cf. Ex. 34:14). A further clause in the treaty stated that the document itself should be kept carefully by the vassal (cf. Ex. 25:16; 34:1, 28–29) and read in public at intervals, generally at least once in each generation (cf. Deut. 31:10–13). A concluding section listed those gods who witnessed the pagan secular treaties (replaced in the Old Testament by memorial cairns [Ex. 24:4], the law-book itself [Deut 31:26], or the people as participants [Josh. 24:22]), and enumerated the blessings or curses that would occur according to whether the covenant was honored or not (cf. Lev. 26:14–33; Deut. 28:1–14).

Since the Sinai covenant corresponds so closely in form to the international treaties of the second millennium B.C., it appears that the covenant actually originated in the thirteenth century B.C. at the latest, that is to say, within the lifetime of Moses, as the Biblical tradition claims. This covenant was renewed just before the entrance into Canaan, as preserved in the book of Deuteronomy, which is in fact a covenant-renewal document, and again in the time of Joshua at Shechem. While the use of this form by the Hebrews involved a structure that was familiar throughout the ancient Near East, it was given a unique character by being made the expression of a spiritual relationship between a people and its sovereign God. Once this covenant had been ratified in a formal manner by the sprinkling of blood (Ex. 24:3ff.), it became binding on both the Great King and the vassal Israelites.

The Tabernacle

Subsequent to this momentous event Moses again communicated with God, during which time he received directions for the construction of a portable place of worship known as the Tabernacle. The specifications of this sanctuary as contained in Exodus 26–27, 35–38 indicate that it was an elaborate and colorful structure. It consisted of a rectangular enclosure that covered an area of about twelve hundred square yards. This court was surrounded by a series of linen curtains suspended by hooks from silver rods attached to columns of acacia wood. Entrance to the court was gained through tapestries draped over an opening in the east wall, beyond which was the altar of burnt offering and the laver. At the far end of the court was the Tabernacle proper, a rectangular structure about fifty-five feet long and fifteen feet wide, made of acacia wood and richly ornamented with silver. The eastern end of the Tabernacle was closed by means of a curtain suspended from silver rods, which were attached to five pillars overlaid with gold.

The Tabernacle contained two compartments, of which the outer one was known as the Holy Place, and measured thirty feet by fifteen feet. In this antechamber were placed the seven-branched candlestick, the table of shewbread, and the golden altar of incense. The small inner chamber was called the Holy of Holies, or Most Holy Place, in which rested the Ark of the Covenant, an oblong chest of acacia wood overlaid with gold. The lid of the Ark supported two golden cherubim with outstretched wings, and when the Divine presence rested upon the Ark in the form of a luminous cloud known as the *Shechinah*, the lid was spoken of as the Mercy Seat.

The Ark occupied the most sacred place of the sanctuary, and it was seen only by the high priest on special occasions. The Levites of the house of Kohath were delegated to carry the Ark and the sacred vessels of the Tabernacle whenever the Israelites moved their encampment and journeyed through the wilderness. All public religious services took place in the Tabernacle court, which was open to the sky, and the sanctuary became both the focal point of communal worship and a symbol of religious unity.

Such tent shrines were by no means unknown in the ancient world. An early Canaanite writer (c. 700 B.C.) described a primitive Phoenician structure that was apparently placed on a cart and pulled by oxen. In pre-Islamic times the *qubbah*, a miniature red-leather tent, was used for carrying the idols and cultic objects revered by the particular Arab tribe. These tents were valued for the guidance they were thought to give to the tribe in its wanderings, and in time of war were venerated for the protection they conferred. The *qubbah* was used as a rallying point, a locale for the giving of oracles from the deity, and also as a place of worship. A similar portable shrine portrayed on a bas-relief from a much earlier period, that of Ramses II (c. 1290–1224 B.C.), showed the tent of the divine king placed in the center of the Egyptian military camp.

From the preceding millennium in Egypt has come the splendid portable tent canopy of Queen Hetepheres I, mother of Cheops, the pharaoh who built the Great Pyramid about 2700 B.C. The bed canopy comprised a framework of long beams at the top and bottom, separated by vertical rods and corner posts and fitted with horizontal beams across the top. The structure was made of wood overlaid with gold leaf, and had hooks on all sides to which curtains could be attached. The beams and rods were fitted into sockets in such a way that the structure could be dismantled and rebuilt rapidly in the same manner as the Hebrew Tabernacle some fourteen centuries later.

The significance of the covenant relationship that existed between God and

A replica of the Hebrew Tabernacle set up in southern Israel.

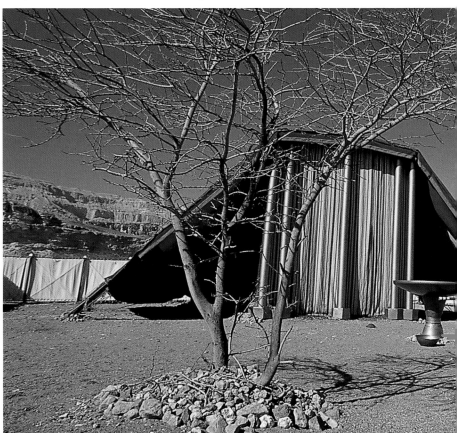

the Israelites was not immediately appreciated by the latter, and the prolonged absence of Moses on Mount Sinai encouraged an outburst of idolatry. Aaron, the elder brother of Moses, was persuaded to make a golden calf from the trinkets and ornaments of the Israelite women, after which the whole multitude indulged in an orgy of idolatrous veneration reminiscent of the cultic rites found in the worship of the bull Apis at Memphis in the New Kingdom period. This apostasy was sternly rebuked by Moses, who reduced the calf to powder and compelled the Israelites to drink the water of a desert stream into which he had thrown the remains of the image.

After this episode the covenant was renewed when atonement had been made, and the construction of the Tabernacle proceeded in accordance with the instructions Moses had received from God. Aaron, the descendant of Levi, the third son of Jacob, was consecrated as the first high priest of Israel, with the privilege of retaining the office in his family on an hereditary basis. The priestly robes Aaron wore when pursuing his duties matched the splendor and color

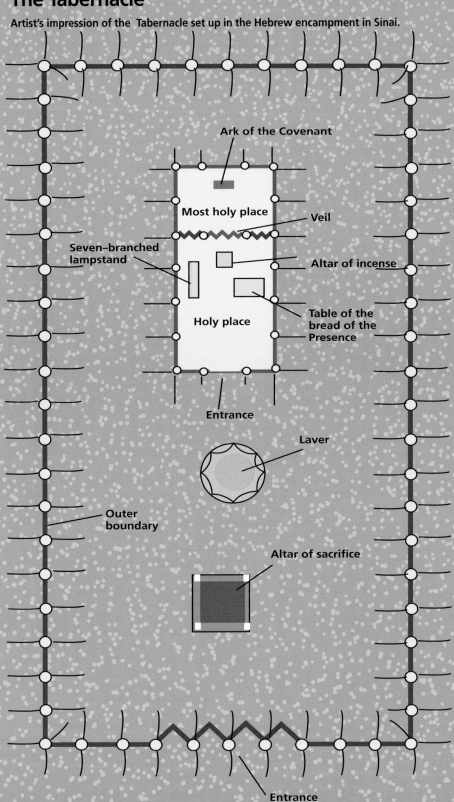

The Tabernacle

Artist's impression of the Tabernacle set up in the Hebrew encampment in Sinai.

Ark of the Covenant

Most holy place

Veil

Seven–branched lampstand

Altar of incense

Table of the bread of the Presence

Holy place

Entrance

Laver

Outer boundary

Altar of sacrifice

Entrance

of the Tabernacle furnishings, and were made, like the Tabernacle itself, from materials that were readily accessible. Even the semi-precious stones that decorated the ephod were available locally.

The second Passover was celebrated two years after the departure from Egypt, while the Israelites were still in the Sinai wilderness. About this time the solemn responsibility of the priestly office was emphasized dramatically when Nadab and Abihu, sons of Aaron who had been consecrated as priests, were struck down by God after they had offered incense in an improper manner (Lev. 10:1ff.). From the solemn injunction given to Aaron immediately afterwards (v. 9), it would appear that Nadab and Abihu were intoxicated while performing their priestly functions.

The Departure from Sinai

The sojourn at Sinai finally drew to a close, and the Israelites moved forward under the guidance of the cloud and the nocturnal fiery glow. Several of the points at which they paused have yet to be identified, but it is probable that they journeyed to the northeast, roughly parallel to the Gulf of Aqabah. The supplies of food were plainly deficient at this time (Num. 11:1ff.), and serious discontent was only averted by the arrival of a flock of quails. Food poisoning appears to have been contracted by the Israelites and resulted in heavy mortality, which was interpreted as an indication of Divine retribution. The incident was commemorated by naming the locality Kibroth-hattaavah, or "graves of lust."

The Sinai wilderness near St Catherine's Monastery.

From Kibroth the company went to an oasis named Hazeroth, probably to be identified with 'Ain Khadra. Here Aaron and Miriam indulged in a fit of pique against the leadership of Moses, and Miriam was punished by being temporarily afflicted with a skin disease of a leprous nature (Num. 12). The next few stages of the journey northward were pursued in the Wilderness of Paran to the northwest of the Gulf of Aqabah, and after many short encampments the Israelites arrived at Ezion-geber, a site which at that time was probably little more than a group of wells and palm groves near present-day Aqabah, the Elath of the Old Testament. This place was one of the important stations along the caravan route from Egypt to the east, and in later times it became a flourishing seaport city.

After a short stay at Ezion-geber, the Israelites proceeded to Kadesh-barnea in the Wilderness of Sin. The exact locality of Kadesh is indeterminate, and Woolley, who explored the Wilderness of Sin, thought that the usual identification of Kadesh with 'Ain Qudeis was improbable. He favored the Kossaima plain, northwest of 'Ain Qudeis, which he held would be sufficiently fertile to have supported the nomads for some time. This site, 'Ain Qudeirat, has in fact considerably more vegetation and water than 'Ain Qudeis, and as such is a better location for Kadesh-barnea. Most probably all the springs in the area were used by the Israelites at one time or another during their lengthy stay there, with 'Ain Qudeirat doubtless being the principal one. Certainly the general location of 'Ain Qudeirat and 'Ain Qudeis suits the topographical requirements of the Exodus narratives very well indeed.

Kadesh-barnea was also the junction of a number of trading routes, and it was probably along one of these that spies were sent to Hebron in order to examine the borders of Canaan, with a view to invasion from the south. Although the luscious grapes from the Valley of Eshcol were proof of the bounty the land offered, the formidable appearance of the inhabitants deterred attempts at invasion, and the Israelite defeat at Hormah, added to the sentence of a forty-year stay in the wilderness, lowered the morale of the people considerably.

Contacts with Transjordan

After leaving Kadesh they went northward to Mount Hor on the borders of Edom, where Aaron died. Passing down the Wadi Arabah, they returned to Ezion-geber, and asked permission from the Edomites to travel along the "King's Highway" (Num. 20:17). The road in question was well known in the Early Bronze Age (c. 3000–2000 B.C.), for it ran north and south through central Transjordan, linking the territories that from the thirteenth century B.C. were known as the kingdoms of Edom, Moab, and Ammon. Between the twenty-third and the twentieth centuries B.C., a series of settlements sprang up along this route, particularly in the fertile uplands of central Transjordan, which supported a thriving agricultural economy. Reference has already been made to the fact that this was probably the route that was followed by the Mesopotamian kings whose exploits are recorded in Genesis 14. If Glueck is correct in supposing that sedentary occupation in Transjordan lapsed from the nineteenth to the thirteenth centuries B.C., it would appear that the resistance that was offered to the Israelite advance by the people of Edom (Num. 20:14ff.) is best understood in the light of a thirteenth-century date for the Exodus.

Because it was not possible for the Israelites to travel through Edomite territory along the "King's Highway," they were compelled to make a laborious circuit of the kingdom of Edom through difficult terrain. This provoked a good deal of resentment against Moses, and the people were punished by means of poisonous serpents (Num. 21:5ff.). When the journey was resumed, the Israelites kept within a short distance of the borders of Edom, and seem to have obtained provisions from the Edomites (Deut. 2:3ff.) without being molested. They passed the mining area of Punon in the east central Arabah, paused for a time at the oasis of Oboth, and then crossed the northern border of Edom at the brook Zered, the modern Wadi el-Hesa, which formed the boundary between Edom and Moab.

Conquests in Transjordan

The border appears to have been strongly fortified on the Moabite side to the north, and the Israelites avoided the danger of attack by a circuit to the east. They crossed the River Arnon, the modern Wadi Mojib, which formed the northern boundary of Moab, and came into the land of Gilead, which was Amorite territory. When Moses requested permission from Sihon, the king of the Amorites, to pass through the country, he was refused and the result was a battle in which Sihon was decisively defeated. A like fate overtook Og, king of Bashan, and his people, the powerful and aggressive Rephaim, who had terrorized the Israelites in the Patriarchal period. Balak, the Moabite king, wished to avoid conflict with the victorious Hebrew nomads, and to this end he engaged Balaam, a pagan soothsayer who lived at Pethor in northern Mesopotamia, to invoke a curse upon them (Num. 22–24) as they advanced into the Jordan valley. This was fully in accord with the Babylonian practice of employing diviners and astrologists as staff advisers to military forces, and the Mesopotamian soothsayers were consequently in considerable demand for this purpose.

Balaam was a highly proficient soothsayer who had been trained as a *baru* or master diviner, and his activities have been amply illustrated by cuneiform texts from various parts of Mesopotamia. In the third millennium B.C. diviners had become so proficient in their methods that their fame spread everywhere in the Near East, and in consequence they were in great demand. Visits to Syria,

Palestine, and even Egypt were not uncommon, and it is interesting to note in this connection that when Beth-shan was being excavated, the personal seal of one of the Babylonian diviners was uncovered in the ruins.

When the story of the activities of Balaam is read in the light of the techniques employed by the Babylonian *baru,* it becomes quite intelligible. According to the rules of the profession the divination had to be carried out very early in the morning, since the best results were believed to be obtained before the sun had actually risen. Three attempts were made, which again conforms to the general principles of professional divination, since the number three played an important role in Babylonian magic. The attempt to rob the Israelites of their strength by placing curses upon them drew on the same principles of sympathetic magic as those found in the Execration Texts of the nineteenth century B.C. in Egypt. Quite probably the reason why Balaam suddenly abandoned his efforts at divination (Num. 24:1) was his realization that he was being thwarted by a higher power, and that as a result he might well lose his professional reputation as a diviner. Understandably enough, when this occurred, Balak refused to pay Balaam the fee he had promised in return for his services.

The territory that had been conquered was suitable for grazing and so it was allotted to the tribes of Reuben, Gad, and the half-tribe of Manasseh, who owned a considerable number of flocks and herds. From this region the Israelites moved to the north of the River Arnon, and crossed the mountainous ridge extending north and east from the shore of the Dead Sea. They encamped in the land of Moab within easy reach of the ancient Hyksos fortress of Jericho, and shortly after this, the death of the aged Hebrew leader Moses occurred.

The Work of Moses

The figure of Moses towers over other Israelite personalities of the second millennium B.C. Although he may have lacked the persuasive rhetoric of the demagogue, he was a man of singularly deep spiritual insight, who knew as if by instinct how to communicate the revelation of the Divine will to his fellow men. The range of his vision was seldom obscured by the exigencies of the moment, and he possessed the rare faculty of being able to relate his spirituality to practical considerations without diminishing the vitality of his communion with God. Even though he was a man of remarkable fortitude and resource, he must often have been deeply discouraged by the failure of the unruly multitude of liberated slaves to catch a glimpse of their future glory as the people who stood in covenant relationship with the God of heaven and earth. Indeed, his marshalling of personal spiritual reserves in the frequent emergencies and crises that overtook the nomadic Israelites is the one quality that marks him out as the greatest leader in the history of the Hebrew people.

To Moses was assigned the forbidding task of exerting a stern religious discipline over a wayward and discontented assembly that not infrequently repudiated its newly gained freedom in a bid to renew the idolatrous associations of former days. The rigors of the long journey that intervened between the Exodus and the victorious entrance into Canaan would have defeated the highest aspirations of a lesser man. Although his moral standards were never lowered for one moment, the cumulative effect of dissension and apostasy over this period of time was such that it left a mark upon the character of this redoubtable leader. Without the genius of Moses it is doubtful if the Israelite tribes would ever have attained to such a consciousness of national and religious unity as that which resulted from the experience of the wilderness wanderings. Even though they might have made good their escape from Egypt under different leadership, they would have been virtually compelled to adopt a seminomadic existence in the inhospitable Sinai peninsula, or in the southern reaches of Transjordan, and to have remained weak and disunited, a ready prey to the marauding Bedouins from the powerful thirteenth-century kingdoms situated to the east and south of the Dead Sea.

Instead of this, they emerged from the hardships of their sojourn in the wilderness as a people united in their loyalty to God and convinced that they had an important role in the revelation of His will to mankind. Their morale was high because they believed that victory would attend their entrance into the Promised Land, a conclusion amply vindicated by the defeat of such formidable opponents as Sihon and Og.

This level of religious aspiration was by no means an incidental product of the Mosaic leadership and discipline. Indeed, it was one of the objectives towards which Moses labored most diligently, and it displays the renowned Israelite leader in his capacities as prophet and priest. It is impossible to understand the later history of the Hebrew people without an appreciation of the fact that the new revelation of the Divine nature and purpose that was given to Moses formed the basis of the monotheistic doctrines characteristic of subsequent Israelite religious thought. With true prophetic insight Moses revealed the character of God and the implications of Divine morality for the Chosen People. The events of the Exodus were divorced from any connection with the realm of accident or coincidence, and were invested with a spiritual significance that demonstrated beyond doubt the overruling providence of a compassionate Deity who had elected to associate Himself with the fortunes of an unpredictable and rebellious people.

For Moses, the central theme of the covenant relationship was an unquestioning loyalty and devotion to the God who had manifested His superiority over heathen deities, and had delivered His people from harsh captivity into an adoptive relationship of mutual trust and respect. This God was sovereign over the whole earth, unlike the majority of Egyptian deities that claimed territorial jurisdiction only, and beside Him other gods were as nothing. His nature was one of compassion and forgiveness, which manifested itself in gracious acts of sustaining love, but which revolted in stark hatred when deeds of injustice, immorality, and oppression were in evidence. The Decalogue laid down the concept of the moral law for all subsequent generations, and by making it the link between God and men, it demonstrated that religion and morality were inseparably connected. The ethical monotheism Moses proclaimed was basic to the religious ideals of the Hebrew people and provided the major themes that were developed in later prophecy.

In his capacity as a priest, Moses marked the point of transition from the Patriarchal custom of family priesthood to the Israelite tradition of a priestly tribe descended from Aaron the Levite. While Moses received assistance in the performance of his priestly duties, he remained the chief intercessor for the people, and acted as a mediator between them and God. He was responsible for implementing the legislation regarding the worship and sacrificial ritual of the Tabernacle,[5] though his fidelity to the concept of ethical monotheism consistently subordinated ritual performance to considerations of morality.

But the abiding genius of Moses is to be seen in his traditional role of lawgiver. He was the divinely appointed agent for the revelation of a legislative system that was to be the basis of Israelite life and polity in subsequent ages. At the head of this corpus of law stood the Decalogue and the terms of the covenant relationship, and they were followed by a wide variety of laws, some of which were suited to the life of nomadic people while others anticipated the sedentary occupation of Canaan. A few generations ago it was held that Moses could not possibly have committed his legislation to writing, but archaeological discoveries in the Sinai peninsula and Transjordan have necessitated a modification of this extreme view.

Inscriptions found in the turquoise mines of Serabit el-Khadem in the Sinai peninsula, which in antiquity were controlled by the Egyptians, have shown that for some time prior to the Mosaic period there existed an alphabetic script of an early variety scholars have named "proto-Sinaitic." These inscriptions, which numbered about twenty-five in all, were discovered by Sir Flinders Petrie in 1904, and dated by him about 1500 B.C.[6] Albright deciphered the inscriptions in 1947, and traced their origin to the use of an alphabetic script by Semitic slaves from Canaan, who were being forced to work the turquoise mines in the days of Thotmes III. Other scholars, however, date them considerably earlier, assigning them to the Middle Kingdom period of Egyptian history.

In any event, several means of linguistic expression were available in the Mosaic period for transmitting written communications. The Tell el-Amarna tablets show that Babylonian cuneiform was the *lingua franca* of that time, while Egyptian hieroglyphic writing had been in existence for many centuries. The Canaanites of the Late Bronze Age (c. 1550–1200 B.C.) employed a linear alphabetic variety of writing, a native cuneiform language (Ugaritic), and a syllabic script in use at Byblos in Phoenicia, as well as Akkadian cuneiform and Egyptian hieroglyphics in their communications. The nature of commercial enterprise between Egypt and the Near East in the second millennium B.C. was such that it was virtually impossible for the major centers of commerce in Egypt to be unfamiliar with languages other than their own. One of the earliest Biblical references to writing was concerned with the defeat of an Amalekite raid on the Israelite encampment in the Sinai peninsula (Ex. 17:14), in the vicinity of Serabit el-Khadem. In the light of archaeological discoveries at that site there seems no valid reason to doubt the antiquity of the Hebrew tradition that ascribed literary activity to Moses.

Early Near Eastern Law Codes

Until the discovery of other ancient legal collections in the Near East, the Mosaic code was thought to be the only representative of its kind. The finding of the Code of Hammurabi at Susa in 1901 made it clear that the Israelite legal enactments were anticipated by a number of other law codes in ancient Babylonia. At the same time it served to demonstrate the unique spirit of the Mosaic legislation, and dealt a mortal blow to older critical views that had maintained that legal material such as existed in the Pentateuch was anachronistic.

One of the earliest legal sources upon which the Code of Hammurabi drew was the group of enactments promulgated by Urukagina, king of Lagash about 2380 B.C. This Sumerian *ensi* pledged to Ningirsu, patron deity of Lagash, that he would not allow the orphans and widows of his city to be exploited by ruthless individuals. In an attempt to modify the power of the *ensi* and restore theocratic rule in Sumeria, Urukagina initiated legislation that largely removed the privileges acquired by palace dignitaries, civic officials, and other administrative personnel, and restored them to the temple as the vital administrative center of the community. Urukagina also ended certain abuses that had arisen under his predecessors, such as lowering the fees for burials and prayer services, and vindicating the right of the ordinary man to his property. This legislation, as with most other "codes" in Mesopotamia, arose out of the promulgation of legal decisions as a means of guiding judges in court, and should not be taken as representing precise stipulations for the regulation of all legal matters. The laws are essentially collections of precedents that were intended as a general standard of justice for the guidance of legal authorities, and were doubtless amenable to a certain freedom of interpretation.

Another early collection of laws to emerge from Babylonia antedated the Code of Hammurabi by nearly two centuries. Known as the Code of Eshnunna, it was recovered from tablets found at Tell Abu Harmal near Baghdad.[7] The code was written in Semitic Old Babylonian, and incorporated the legislation of the king of Eshnunna (c. 1885 B.C.). Some of the laws dealt with the establishing of prices for cereals and other products, while one section (53) of the code was significant in that it constituted the earliest parallel to Hebrew law. This provision laid down the procedure to be followed when determining the value of oxen that had been fighting and had sustained fatal injuries, paralleling the legislation in Exodus 21:35.

The Code of Eshnunna was followed about a decade later by the enactments of Lipit-Ishtar, king of Isin (c. 1875 B.C.), a district of central Babylonia. The Code employed what appears to have become a standard literary form, for the legislation of Hammurabi followed exactly the same pattern. A prologue that stated that Lipit-Ishtar established justice under the protection of En-lil introduced the main body of the legal enactments, which were concluded by means of an epilogue. The tablets, which were written in Sumerian, are fragmentary, and contain thirty-five enactments that legislated for life in a feudal society. They dealt with such diverse matters as the hiring of boats, the procedure to be followed for those who defaulted in the payment of taxes, and laws governing property, inheritance, and marriage.[8]

The wealth of legal material that was unearthed at the site of ancient Nuzu, near Kirkuk in modern Iraq, greatly augmented existing knowledge of jurisprudence in the ancient Near East. These laws dated from the fifteenth century B.C. and, as has already been observed, have provided a basis for a fresh appraisal of the customs and laws that formulated the pattern of social life in the Patriarchal period. But the most striking precursor of Hebrew law was the celebrated Code of Hammurabi, which was seen to be based upon earlier legal material from Babylonia. Because of a common Semitic background and a degree of similarity in cultural heritage, the Mosaic legislation clearly resembles that of Hammurabi in many areas, and this superficial consonance led many scholars to believe that the legal codes of the Hebrews were nothing more than modifications or adaptations of the earlier Babylonian material.

While there are many close parallels in the enactments of Hammurabi and Moses, there are differences of sufficient importance to discount any theory of Hebrew dependence upon Babylonian jurisprudence. The Code of Hammurabi was a body of civil law adapted to the needs of an urban Mesopotamian society, whereas the Mosaic legislation was primarily ritualistic and religious in nature, and suited to the needs of a pastoral economy. Even where topics of a similar nature received the attention of the two codes, there are striking differences in matters of detail, as for example in the laws concerning divorce. Although the priestly legislation in the Mosaic code contains many elements in common with other priestly rituals in the Near East, the points of divergence are even more significant in dissociating Hebrew law from its precursors in the field of jurisprudence.

Two important types of law are apparent in the Code of Hammurabi, and these have been styled "apodictic" or "categorical," and "casuistic" or "case-

Misty view of the Mountains of Moab from the western side of the Dead Sea.

law." The first of these two classes comprises brief categorical law that normally occurs in the form of a prohibition. The second variety, which is the dominant form present in the collections of legal precedents so far recovered from the ancient Near East, lays down precise specifications as to how particular legal issues are to be dealt with procedurally. Both classes are reflected in the Pentateuchal legislation, and occasionally elements of the apodictic type of law occur in the middle of case-law procedures. Thus in Exodus 21:7–11, in which certain specific legal situations emerging from a general statement on the theme of female slavery are discussed, the expression "since he has dealt faithlessly with her" (v. 8) introduces a categorical aspect into the question of the slave's rights.

Despite the fact that the Mosaic code shows some degree of affinity with other great bodies of law that emerged from the cultures of the Near East and Egypt, it has a distinct character that attests to its superiority over the legal codes of neighboring peoples. Its resolute monotheism could command devotion towards God and man in a way that does not occur in other contemporary legislation. The enactments of the Mosaic code were not merely laws that required obedience, but were the embodiment of a spirituality that enriched the character of the individual whose life was governed by them. The Hebrew legislation assigned a greater value to human life, demanded higher respect for the honor of womanhood, and allotted more dignity to the position of the slave than is to be found in any of the legal codes of other nations in the Near East.

Part of the excavated site at Arad, a ninth-century B.C. town in the Negeb. The site went back to the Bronze Age and was mentioned by name in Egyptian texts of the Amarna period.

In attempting to assess the historical background of early Israelite legislation, it must never be forgotten that the precursors of the Israelites proper, who had lived in the Goshen region of the Nile delta for well over two centuries, had their own laws and customs, based upon a settled agricultural economy and presupposing close relations with foreign peoples. It may well be that some of the legal traditions from this period, which antedated that of Moses, were adapted to the needs of a rather different mode of life and then incorporated into the growing body of customary law in the wilderness period.

Joshua as Leader

When the legal basis for later Israelite life had been established and the wandering Hebrews had pitched their camp across the Jordan from Jericho, the task of the great Hebrew lawgiver was over. After seeing a panorama of the Promised Land from Mount Nebo, identified with the modern Khirbet ei-Mekhaiyet, Moses died and was buried in Moab. A short time before his decease, Moses had consecrated Joshua as his successor, and the latter now took over full leadership of the Israelites. The conquest of Canaan was his ultimate goal, and accordingly he made immediate plans for the crossing of the Jordan and the assault on Jericho. The capture of this stronghold was a prerequisite to military success in Canaan, for it stood among the crags of the Judean wilderness on a site that dominated the entrance not merely to the Jerusalem plateau, but also to the whole of Canaan.

The strategic importance of Jericho was established in remote antiquity by the way in which it stood sentinel over one of the chief permanent fords of the Jordan River.

The site of ancient Jericho (Tell es-Sultan) was the scene of considerable archaeological activity during the twentieth century. In 1907, the German Oriental Society sent out Sellin and Watzinger to conduct excavations there, and the result was a well-documented account of the Middle Bronze period at Jericho, which included a detailed account of the ceramic ware that had been recovered. The work was discontinued after two years, and was only resumed in 1929 by Professor Garstang of Liverpool University. In the next seven years he excavated the various levels of the site, and assigned alphabetical designations to the successive layers that were unearthed. The excavation of Jericho was resumed in 1952 by a group of British and American archaeologists under the direction of Dame Kathleen Kenyon, the director of the British School of Archaeology in Jerusalem.

These excavations have penetrated to levels of habitation reaching back to at least the fifth millennium B.C., indicating that the site was one of the oldest in the whole of the Near East. While other peoples were only at the beginning of life in unprotected village communities, the Neolithic inhabitants of Jericho were enjoying life in a walled city of about eight acres in area. Evidences of pre-pottery Neolithic communal activity were augmented by the discovery in 1956 of a huge defensive ditch, some thirty feet in width, which had been cut eight feet down into bed rock. Surmounting this ditch was an eighteen-foot wall, above which was a circular stone bastion. The culture of this period was of the "irrigation" type, capable of supplying grains such as millet, barley, emmer wheat, and subtropical fruits, including figs, dates, and grapes.

It is probable that the location of Jericho contributed to its prosperity in antiquity, for it stood at the junction of several of the routes that were traversed by the Oriental spice caravans. Its strategic importance was established in remote antiquity by the way in which it stood sentinel over one of the chief permanent fords of the Jordan River. To the east Jericho was sheltered by the plateau that formed the Moab uplands, while to the south stretched the barren ranges bordering the Dead Sea. The site itself was in the long rift valley through which the River Jordan flowed, and although it stood some five hundred feet above the level of the Dead Sea, it was still some eight hundred feet below the level of the Mediterranean.

In summer the temperature at the bottom of the rift valley reached tropical proportions, while in winter the warmth of the air trapped in the gorge contrasted pleasantly with the cold and snow of Jerusalem, which was situated seventeen miles to the southwest. These climatic conditions were enriched by the presence of a sweet spring, known today as 'Ain es-Sultan, which was a perennial source of water for those who frequented the locality. Traditionally this spring was the one purified by Elisha, and it supplies the only water in the neighborhood that is not brackish to the taste.

When the Hyksos dominated Canaan, they fortified Jericho strongly with huge defense glacis and used it as a base for attacks upon the Egyptian empire. But after they were expelled from Egypt (c. 1550 B.C.), Jericho became one of the large city-states in Canaan, and was ruled by its own king, who was subject to Egyptian administrative control during the Amarna period. The unhealthy nature of feudal organization in Canaan combined with the internecine strife of the various city-states to produce a distinct decline in the level of Canaanite civilization by the time that Joshua and his forces were preparing to invade the land. Although the massive fortifications erected by the Hyksos were still in evidence in many parts of the country, the moral fiber of the Canaanites was seriously weakened by centuries of internal warfare and by the debilitating effects of indulgence in a debased form of religious activity. To this extent the ground was prepared for the victorious campaigns of Joshua and the Israelites. Jericho was the first and probably the most formidable obstacle to victory, and its fate was destined to serve as an indication of what was in store for the land as a whole when Israelite fervor was pitted against the feeble resistance of the demoralized inhabitants of Canaan.

NOTES

1. Cf. F. S. Bodenheimer, *The Biblical Archaeologist,* X (1947), No. 1, pp. 2ff.; W. Keller, *The Bible as History* (1956), p. 112.

2. W. F. Albright, *From the Stone Age to Christianity,* pp. 196f.

3. J. Finegan, *Light From the Ancient Past,* p. 129.

4. G. E. Mendenhall, *The Biblical Archaeologist,* XVII (1954), No. 3, pp. 26ff.

5. R. K. Harrison, *The Zondervan Pictorial Bible Dictionary* (1963), pp. 821ff.

6. W. F. M. Petrie, *Researches in Sinai* (1906), pp. 129ff.; W. F. Albright, *The Archaeology of Palestine,* pp. 188f.

7. J. B. Pritchard (Ed.), *Ancient Near Eastern Texts Relating to the Old Testament,* pp. 161ff.

8. *Ibid.,* pp. 159ff.

6. The Promised Land and the Nation

CHRONOLOGY OF THIS CHAPTER

Early Iron Age (Iron I)	1200–970 B.C.
David	1011/10–971/70 B.C.

THE TERRITORY THE VICTORIOUS ISRAELITES WERE TO occupy had been settled for many centuries as a result of periodic incursions of Semitic peoples from northern Mesopotamia. Even before the beginning of the third millennium B.C., the sites of Jebus (the later Jerusalem), Gebal, Gezer, and Beth-shan had been established, and in the second millennium the country was occupied by Amorites, Hittites, Horites, and some smaller Semitic groups. The inhabitants referred to their country as Canaan, or Kinakhna as it was called in the Amarna tablets, and this was the older native designation of Palestine, a name by which the land became known subsequent to the Philistine occupation of the twelfth century B.C. The form "Canaan" that occurred in Biblical and Egyptian texts was probably Hurrian in origin, and may have meant "land of the purple," an allusion to the use of the murex mollusks in the dye industry of Phoenicia. The boundaries of Canaan suggested in Genesis 10:19 included all the territory that lay to the west of the Jordan between Gaza and Sidon, although the Amarna letters thought of Canaan primarily in terms of the Phoenician coast.

Geographical Features

The physical features of the land fell into a rough pattern of four parallel strips, bordered by the Mediterranean Sea and the Arabian Desert. This division was caused by the presence of two mountainous ranges, one of which ran from

154

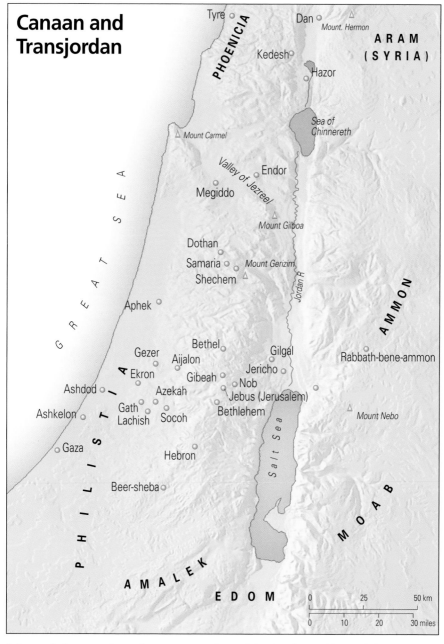

Canaan and Transjordan

Mount Lebanon along the western edge of the Jordan valley, while the other extended southward from Mount Hermon to the east of the Dead Sea and continued to Mount Hor in Edom. The parallel sections thus formed consisted of the coastal strip called the Maritime Plain, the central mountainous range extending southward from Mount Lebanon, the valley of the Jordan, and the plateau

Assyrian relief depicting a Phoenician ship.

of eastern Palestine stretching eastward from Mount Hermon to Mount Hor. North of Mount Carmel the coastal plain narrowed considerably, but to the south it gradually widened until at Gaza it extended about sixteen miles inland. Farther south lay the arid district of the Negeb, an area of about 360 square miles in extent. Prior to the Israelite conquest there were several important cities located on the coastal trading route, but the majority of the inhabited cities were to be found in the central mountainous district.

This was a rugged area intersected throughout by valleys or *wadis*. It was thickly wooded, so that it was of limited value for agricultural purposes other than the grazing of flocks and herds. The uplands to the east of the Jordan were apparently well populated by the thirteenth century B.C., for it was there that the powerful kingdoms of Bashan, Ammon, Moab, and Edom were to be found. At this time the land west of the Jordan was settled from Beer-sheba to Laish (Dan), a distance of one hundred and fifty miles. The Canaanites showed a marked preference for the lowlands, and avoided the already sparsely populated mountainous districts whenever possible.

Canaanite City-States

Because Palestine occupied the position of a land bridge between Asia, Africa, and Europe, it was subjected to a continual movement of peoples in ancient times. Its meager natural resources contrasted unfavorably with the fertility of

GREAT SEA
(MEDITERRANEAN SEA)

Plain of Phoenicia

UPPER GALILEE

LOWER GALILEE

PLAIN OF ESDRAELON

MOUNT CARMEL

Plain of Sharon

C O A S T A L   P L A I N

C E N T R A L   R A N G E

JORDAN VALLEY

MOUNT EPHRAIM

Plain of Philistia

SHEPHELAH

Mountains of Judah

WILDERNESS OF JUDEA

E A S T E R N   R A N G E

D E S E R T

N E G E B

metres	feet
1,000	3,281
500	1,640
200	656
0	0
below sea level	

0   25   50 km

0   10   20   30 miles

the Nile valley or the Babylonian plain, but it had a tactical importance that no other land in the Near East possessed. For many centuries the great empires used the land of Canaan either as a buffer state to protect themselves against the military ambitions of aggressors, or as a coveted advance base from which to launch a program of imperial expansion. Thus Palestine had a part of major importance to play in preserving the balance of power in the Near East, and it is difficult to overestimate the strategic value that accrued to the possession of that rugged and often inhospitable territory.

The admixture of Amorites, Hittites, Jebusites, and others who had entered the land of Canaan during the early part of the second millennium appears to have become most pronounced about 1600 B.C. By this time the majority of the immigrants had consolidated their settlements in the country, and were beginning to take advantage of the way in which the Mitanni kingdom controlled the balance of Near Eastern power about 1550 B.C. to assert themselves as independent peoples. This was encouraged to some extent by the Egyptian administration of Palestine after the Hyksos had been expelled from Egypt, for the native Canaanite rulers were permitted to organize the economy of their city-states along feudal lines. The incessant bickering that took place among these petty kingdoms was tolerated by the Egyptians as long as it precluded the rise of powerful Canaanite coalitions and allowed a steady stream of taxes to flow into the Egyptian treasury.[1]

The culture of the Canaanite city-states reached back to the third millennium, and because of the strategic position of Palestine it was able to exercise considerable influence over life in other nations of the Near East in successive centuries. Semitic influence was felt increasingly from the fourteenth century B.C. in the religious life of Egypt, with the result that the worship of the Canaanite deities Baal, Anath, and Ashtaroth became very popular. These gods were identified with the Egyptian deities Set, Nephthys, and Isis, and were worshiped in the capital city of Avaris-Tanis during the Nineteenth Dynasty. Egyptian officials frequently bore names of a distinctly Semitic character, and one of the Egyptian commissioners in Palestine during the Amarna period was a man called Yanhamu, who may even have been of Semitic stock.

The cosmopolitan nature of Canaan is indicated by the fact that during the Amarna period four distinct scripts were employed in Canaanite writings in addition to Akkadian and Egyptian, as has already been observed.[2] The influence of Semitic terminology during this period was considerable, and Egyptian documents of the thirteenth century B.C. have been shown to contain a great many Semitic words. While it is still true that the Amarna tablets furnished important information about the language of Canaan, which varied only slightly from the Semitic dialect of the Hebrews, the discovery of clay tablets and other artifacts at Ras Shamra has placed the Amarna Age of Canaan in an entirely new perspective.

Bronze figurine of Baal, Canaanite god of war.

Ras Shamra (Ugarit)

In the second millennium B.C. , Ras Shamra was known as Ugarit, and being situated on the north coast of Syria, it was a flourishing commercial and cultural center. After its destruction by the Philistines about 1200 B.C., it disappeared from the pages of history until the discovery of the Amarna letters in 1887, but it was only when Schaeffer unearthed some tablets at Ras Shamra in 1929 that the importance of the site became apparent. The tablets that were found were inscribed in several types of cuneiform, and following the custom of Mesopotamian Akkadian the script was written from left to right. Hundreds of these tablets were excavated after 1929, and those which contained the then unknown language of Ugaritic were painstakingly deciphered. Ugaritic was

159

found to belong, with Hebrew, Aramaic, and other Canaanite dialects, to the north-west branch of the Semitic language group. The tablets were dated about the first third of the fourteenth century B.C., although it was recognized that the script that was employed antedated that period somewhat.

The cuneiform writing of the Ugarit tablets is of importance as being alphabetic, rather than syllabic, in nature. The ancient Egyptians have been credited generally with the introduction of alphabetic writing, but they combined it in practice with a system of syllabic (where each sign represents a syllable) and logographic (where each sign stands for a word) writing to produce the complicated hieroglyphic script familiar from antiquity. The Canaanites appear to have been the first to use the principle of alphabetism in cuneiform, and it was then transmitted through the Hebrews and Phoenicians to the Greeks, who modified it and gave the alphabet its characteristic classical form. Perhaps the necessity for keeping pace with the demands of international commerce led to the adoption of the new variety of cuneiform at Ugarit, since it was certainly more convenient for use in business than the cumbersome script of Mesopotamia.

When the site of Ugarit was being excavated, part of a royal scribal library came to light, containing several hundred clay tablets, some of which were written in an ancient Canaanite dialect ante-dating the Mosaic era. It is not overstating the case to say that these tablets, written in a previously unknown Semitic language reduced to an unfamiliar cuneiform script, represented the most important discovery in the field of ancient literature during the present century. The texts included poetry and prose, the former group consisting of mythological cycles and legends dealing with gods and men, while the prose compositions treated of such widely divergent topics as land ownership, taxation, conscription, statistics, and veterinary practice.[3]

Ugaritic and Hebrew Poetry

Most of the literary compositions exhibited a characteristic poetic form of particular importance because it contains a great many parallels in grammar, style, and verbal usage to Hebrew poetry. This is especially the case where the earlier poems of the Old Testament are concerned, and the consonance in style and vocabulary between their verse forms and those of Ugaritic literature is most striking. As a result, it is now evident that the apparent textual anomalies that were regarded by critical scholars as being present in the Psalms and other Hebrew poetic compositions are not true corruptions of the Hebrew text. Instead, the vast majority of them are seen to be accurate reflections of peculiarities in Canaanite grammar and forms of speech, whose significance had lapsed with the passing of time. Thus, the textual emendations of Kittel and others will require drastic revision in the light of the evidence presented by the Ras Shamra texts.

One familiar feature of Hebrew poetry consists of a pattern of repetitive parallelism, as illustrated by Psalm 92:9:

> For behold thine enemies, O Lord,
> For behold thine enemies shall perish.
> All the workers of iniquity shall be scattered.

which is paralleled by a verse in the Epic of Baal and Anat (68:5ff.) as follows:

> Lo thine enemies, O Baal,
> Lo thine enemies wilt thou smite.
> Lo thou wilt vanquish thy foes.[4]

This is a characteristic pattern, which is repeated frequently, with some variations, in Hebrew and Ugaritic poetry.

A comparison of these two literary traditions indicates that from a linguistic, grammatical, and syntactical standpoint the Canaanite dialect of Ugarit is closely related to the Hebrew of the psalter. Archaic forms in the Psalms have their counterpart in the pagan myths of Ras Shamra, while similar combinations of words, organized in terms of the same poetic stresses, are to be found alike in the Hebrew and Canaanite compositions. On the whole, however, there is a more noticeable spontaneity attaching to Hebrew poetry and less emphasis upon purely stylistic considerations than is to be found in the myths of Ugarit.

From the abundance of parallels that have been shown to exist between Ugaritic and Hebrew poetry, and from the remarkable consonance in language and thought forms, it is evident that the Canaanites and Hebrews drew somewhat differently upon the same variety of linguistic and idiomatic expression. While the theology of the Hebrew writings is totally divergent in that it is avowedly monotheistic, there is often a notable degree of similarity between the descriptions of Jehovah and those of the Ugaritic gods. Thus Baal is spoken of as the "Rider of the Clouds" (cf. Ps. 68:4; 104:3), who sits on a throne in the heavens (cf. Ps. 2:4; 103:19), and hurls down lightning and thunderbolts (cf. Ps. 18:13; 77:18; 144:6).

Social institutions recorded by the Hebrews are also paralleled in the mythological texts of Ugarit, as in the case of the blindness Nahash the Ammonite determined to inflict upon the inhabitants of Jabesh-gilead (I Sam. 11:1ff.). This has its equivalent in the Legend of Aqht (1:165ff.), where King Daniel invoked blindness upon the town where his son was murdered:

> Woe unto thee, City of Mourners
> Near which Aqht the Hero was smitten!
> May Baal make thee one-eyed
> From now and unto eternity. . . .[5]

Such a community of literary interest has provided a new and independent criterion for the dating of early poetic material in the Hebrew Bible. An illustration of this is furnished by the song of Miriam (Ex. 15), which until recently was dated by critical scholars in the period subsequent to the building of the first Temple because of the reference to "the mountain of thine inheritance" (v. 17), which was interpreted as Mount Zion. But the discovery in the Canaanite Baal Epic of the phrase "the mountain of mine inheritance" ('nt III.25ff.), used with reference to the remote northerly home of Baal,[6] shows that the description was poetic rather than topographical, and thus removes the obstacle to a date within the Mosaic period where it properly belongs. An early dating must now be assigned also to other poetic utterances such as the Balaam oracles (Num. 22–24), the blessing of Jacob (Gen. 49), and the final oration of Moses (Deut. 33).

The thought patterns and vocabulary that occur in the ancient mythological texts of Ras Shamra have illuminated to a considerable extent some of the obscure figures of speech found in the Hebrew psalter. The mention of "dragons" and "leviathan" in Psalm 74:13f. recalls the Ugaritic legend of Baal and Anat (62:50), where the sea serpent Tannin was invoked for magical purposes. The Hebrew divergence from the pagan myth is significant, however, for the psalmist roundly asserts the superiority of the God of Israel, and rejoices in the destruction of the monsters and their alleged magical powers.

Such allusions to pagan legends are few, however, and constitute nothing more than the exercise of poetic imagery in order to heighten the general literary effect. This device has obvious stylistic value, and it was appreciated, among others, by Milton, who incorporated many allusions to pagan mythology in his literary compositions. It should be noted, however, that the references to pagan myths and cult objects in Hebrew poetic literature are generally of the most disparaging kind, in consonance with the ethical monotheism of the writers.

Canaanite Religion

As the myths of ancient Ugarit indicate, the religion of the Canaanite peoples was a crude and debased form of ritual polytheism. It was associated with sensuous fertility-cult worship of a particularly lewd and orgiastic kind, which proved to be more influential than any other nature religion in the Near East. The principal deity acknowledged by the Canaanites was known as El, who was credited with leadership of the pantheon. He was a rather shadowy figure who was worshiped as the "father of man" and the "father of years." A *stele* unearthed at Ras Shamra showed him seated upon a throne with a hand upraised in blessing, while the ruler of Ugarit presented a gift to him.[7] His consort was Asherat, the counselor of the gods, and known to the Israelites as Asherah.

Their offspring was the fertility deity Baal, sometimes known as Haddu (Hadad), the god of rain and storm. He succeeded El as the reigning king of the Canaanite pantheon, and lived in the lofty mountainous regions of the remote northern heavens. A *stele* from ancient Ugarit portrayed him in his role of storm deity, standing with a mace in his upraised right hand and a thunderbolt at his left side. His titles included the epithets Zabul (Lord of the earth) and Aliyn (the One who prevails), the latter being prominent in Ugaritic poetic literature. The theme of the Baal and Anat cycle was that of his struggle with Mot, the deity of misfortune, who had challenged the kingship of Baal (Text 51:VII). The latter descended to the Underworld realm of Mot, and there was slain. When his death was followed by a seven-year cycle of famine, Anat, the consort of Baal, revenged herself by killing Mot, after which she planted his body in the ground. Aliyn Baal then recovered, and a seven-year period of prosperity ensued, followed once more by the resurgence of Mot.[8] The ritual is strongly reminiscent of the Isis and Osiris mystery cult of Egypt, though the nature of Baal was interpreted somewhat differently by the Canaanites. For them he was essentially a fertility deity, though he was not indispensable in fertility rituals, and he does not appear to have been a seasonal deity, as was first thought.[9]

It is important to realize that the critical views of the Wellhausen school regarding the evolutionary nature of Canaanite religion have undergone drastic change as a result of careful study of the Baal epic and other Ugaritic literature. Baal is no longer to be thought of as a spirit that becomes associated with a particular locality and develops the functions of a vegetation deity. Nor must the title Baal be regarded as a generic name for a host of local deities, each of which had jurisdiction over a limited extent of territory. Instead, Baal must now be granted the status of a "high god," a cosmic deity who was the acknowledged head of a pantheon, and who was worshiped in various communities under his own name or as Hadad, the storm deity.

The depraved nature of Canaanite religion is indicated by the character of Anat, the sister-spouse of Baal, who was variously identified with Astarte, Asherah, and Ashtoreth in cultic worship. An Egyptian text of the New Kingdom period described Anat and Astarte as "the great goddesses who conceive but do not bear." The Canaanites evidently regarded their fertility goddesses as combinations of virgins and begetters of life, and they spoke of Anat in her role of sacred prostitute as "*qudshu*," "the holy one." This term is somewhat related to the Biblical term for "holy," but it is important to realize that among Semitic peoples generally the idea of "holiness" was applied to anything that had been dedicated to the service of a deity. Because the moral connotation of the Hebrew term was completely lacking in contemporary Semitic usage, it is hardly correct to speak of *qudshu* as being applied "in the perverted moral sense," as Unger does.[10]

Cult objects such as lilies (representing sex appeal) and serpents (symbolic of fertility) were associated with the sensuous worship of Anat, and plaques recovered from Ras Shamra depicted her nakedness and fecundity.

A center dedicated to Anat worship was excavated at Gebal (Byblos), a very important site in ancient Phoenicia, which was notorious for its fertility rites and ceremonial prostitution. Terracotta figurines of Astarte have been unearthed at a great many sites throughout Palestine, and they invariably represented a naked woman with exaggerated sexual features. This contrasted strikingly with the appearance of Egyptian goddesses in the New Kingdom period, who were always decorously clothed.

Another equally vicious characteristic of Anat worship was the fiendish savagery of the composite goddess. A fragment of the Baal Epic (II:7ff.) shows her indulging in a massacre of young and old alike:

> She smites the people of the *seashore*
> Destroys mankind of the sunrise. . . .
> She *piles* up heads on her back
> She ties up hands in her bundle. . . .
> Anat *gluts* her liver with laughter
> Her heart is filled with joy.[11]

Egyptian texts represented Astarte and Anat as goddesses of violence and war, showing them naked astride a galloping horse, waving weapons of battle.[12]

With the worship of Asherah were associated a number of cult objects or symbols, in which she was thought to reside. The most prominent of these appears to have been some object of wood such as the image of the goddess herself, which was erected beside the altars of incense and the cone pillars of the Canaanite shrines. Whatever the nature of the emblem, it was held in abhorrence by the faithful Israelites, and was capable of being cut down and burned. The Hebrew name "Asherah" is generally rendered "grove" in the King James Version, following the tradition of the Greek and Latin versions, which related the cult object to the place where it was worshiped.

It will be evident from this brief survey of Canaanite religion that its sordid and debased nature stood in marked contrast to the high ethical ideals of Israel. The absolute lack of moral character in the Canaanite deities made such corrupt practices as ritual prostitution, child sacrifice, and licentious worship the normal expressions of religious devotion and fervor. In consequence there could be no compromise between the morality of the God of Israel and the debased sensuality of Canaanite religion.

The prose documents from ancient Ugarit have enabled scholars to obtain a clear picture of social life in Phoenicia and Canaan in general during the fourteenth century B.C. The king was the head of the community state, which was organized along theocratic lines. The priesthood played an important part in the control of social life and, following Mesopotamian custom, extended its

Occupation mound of the Canaanite settlement at Beth-shan. Part of the site was occupied by a fourteenth-century B.C. Canaanite temple. The fortress, an important strategic location, finally fell to Israel in the tenth century B.C.

influence to the military sphere also. The chiefs of the army were drawn from the upper classes of society in Ugarit, and like the Egyptian aristocracy of the New Kingdom period they placed great emphasis upon the chariot as a military weapon.

While tribal organization was found to a considerable extent in Ugarit, it was being replaced increasingly by the concept of urban or provincial membership. People were ceasing to be regarded as belonging to tribes and were being recognized as citizens of a particular town or province. Professional guilds had arisen, embracing the various arts and crafts in Ugarit, and marking an advanced stage of social organization.[13]

The patriarchal concepts of Mari and Nuzu characterized the life of the ancient Canaanite families. A man might possess one or more wives, and his offspring received the rights of inheritance in return for the satisfactory performance of domestic duties. Slavery was common in Ugarit as elsewhere, and wealthy households employed a number of male and female servants, who appear to have had rather less freedom than their Mesopotamian counterparts. In a country where several languages were current, education was restricted to the upper classes, and the complexities of reading and writing were generally left to scribes who had been specially trained for the task.

As a seaport city, Ugarit carried on a flourishing copper trade with Cyprus, while the discovery of an iron battle-axe dated c. 1400 B.C. showed that commercial relations with the Hittite empire, which at that time monopolized the manufacture and export of iron, were well established. The Phoenician traders were well known to the pharaohs of the Nile valley also, and they played an important part in the spread of the Minoan culture in the lands bordered by the Mediterranean Sea.

Ugarit and the Aegean

Quite aside from other considerations, the discoveries at Ras Shamra are of great importance because they have added a new dimension to knowledge about the origins of Near Eastern culture and its dissemination during the second millennium B.C. An increasing amount of archaeological evidence from Minoan sites indicates that, until some time after 1500 B.C., Greece, Ugarit, and Israel all belonged to the same cultural sphere, in which the most significant element in the complex makeup of all these peoples was Phoenician. The texts from Ras Shamra make it clear that ancient Ugarit was the heir of all the preceding great cultures from Sumer to Egypt, and had the closest relations with peoples such as the Hittites and Hurrians, who were of prime importance for Mycenaean times but who disappeared from history in a welter of international upheaval.

On this basis it is clearly a mistake to assume that Israel and Greece represented two entirely distinct cultural entities, since the Ras Shamra epics supply unmistakable organic parallels that link the preprophetic Hebrews with the prephilosophical Greeks.[14] The trend of cultural development in antiquity now makes it evident that in the second millennium B.C. the Greeks and Hebrews were members of the same international order in the Near East. From the first millennium B.C. down to the fourth century B.C. the Greeks and Hebrews each produced their distinctive classical contributions, but with the conquests of Alexander both were drawn together once more into the Hellenic variety of culture.

Recent excavations in Crete have thrown interesting light upon the origins of Minoan culture, and have tended to associate its beginnings increasingly with the Nile delta region. It now seems probable that, whereas the pre-Minoans of Crete came from the mainland and from Anatolia, the Minoans themselves must have come from a southern climate, since they made little attempt to provide central heating in their homes and palaces. Most probably the Minoans came from the Nile delta region, since Cretan archaeology has yielded a great many artifacts that were imported from, or else imitated the workmanship of, Egypt. Their Lower Egyptian origins seem further indicated by the fact that

Minoan chronology is linked to Near Eastern history principally through Egyptian scarabs and other pharaonic inscriptions found in the Cretan excavations. This is certainly in harmony with the traditions of Genesis 10:13–14, which correctly derived the Cretans (called the "Philistines" and "Caphtorim") from Egypt. C. H. Gordon has pointed out that the significant differences between Egypt and Minoan Cretan culture subsist in the fact that classical Egyptian culture was produced primarily in Upper Egypt, whereas Lower Egypt was much more a part of the Mediterranean world, with many of its inhabitants being Semitic and non-Egyptian in character.[15] If this assessment of the origins of Minoan culture is correct, it shows that the Delta area was in a real sense the cradle of Western civilization. From it came the Minoans who founded the first advanced culture of Europe, and later on emerged the Hebrews of the Exodus period who migrated to their Promised Land. Thus the precursors of classical Greek and Hebrew culture were kindred Delta peoples.

Although ancient Ugarit was prosperous in the economic field and advanced in social organization, its fabric was seriously weakened by the demoralizing sensuality of Canaanite Baal worship. It was this same degenerating influence that presented the invading Israelites with problems of a more serious nature than the overthrowing of heavily fortified towns or the occupation of rugged mountain terrain. In the last resort, the success of the Israelite conquest of Canaan would be determined by the way in which the invaders dealt with the threat to morality posed by the insidious crudities of Canaanite cult worship.

Not all of the dangers that lurked in the Promised Land may have been apparent to the Israelites as they camped across the Jordan from Jericho. To them, the main difficulty lay in gaining an immediate foothold in Canaan, and the first step in this direction was taken when the Jordan was dried up for a time to enable the Israelites to cross. This phenomenon was probably the result of a landslide upstream that blocked the flow of the river, similar to those which have occurred twice within living memory, in 1906 and 1927. Having erected a cairn to commemorate this providential circumstance, the Israelites dedicated themselves to their task by renewing the ordinance of circumcision, after which they commenced psychological warfare against the already apprehensive inhabitants of Jericho.

The City of Jericho

The Middle Bronze Age had seen the development of this extremely ancient site by the Hyksos, who fortified it by means of a huge defensive embankment When the Hyksos retreated to Canaan after their expulsion from Egypt, they offered some resistance from Jericho, but they were soon overcome and suffered the loss of their fortress by fire. Garstang unearthed parts of the palace storerooms and a number of houses dating from the close of the Middle Bronze period, all of which showed unquestionable indications of destruction by fire. Jericho was rebuilt at the beginning of the Late Bronze Age (c. 1550 B.C.), though on a considerably smaller scale than previously. The city was fortified by means of a double wall of mud brick, the inner one following the general direction of the foundations upon which the Early Bronze Age wall had been erected. Sun-dried mud bricks were employed for the work, and this, combined with the uneven coursing of the walls resulting from the irregular nature of the foundations, made for an inferior standard of construction.

This was "City D," which Garstang believed to be the one conquered by Joshua and his followers. The outer wall, originally about thirty feet high and six feet thick, had been almost completely destroyed, and the inner wall, of about the same height but from twelve to fifteen feet thick, had suffered a like fate, which Garstang attributed to seismic disturbances.[16] The house in which Rahab lived was probably near the main city gate, and may have straddled the two defensive walls. The rubble Garstang examined contained fragments of blackened brick, ashes, smoke-stained pottery, charred timbers, and other evidences of destruction by fire, an event that Garstang dated in the fourteenth century B.C.

Excavations that began in 1951 under the leadership of Dame Kathleen Kenyon have necessitated some revision of the picture Garstang presented.[17] Very few traces of the Joshua period have been discovered in the mound, and no traces of Late Bronze Age walls have been unearthed, a situation that conflicts curiously with the careful description of what Garstang took to be Late Bronze Age fortifications. Although recent investigation has established the antiquity of the site beyond any doubt, it is almost impossible to make any pronouncement at present on the nature of the fortified city that was overthrown by Joshua, or the date when this event took place. From what is known, however, it appears quite feasible for the Israelite forces to have marched around the city seven times in one day (Josh. 6:4).

The overthrowing of Jericho was followed by the slaughter of the inhabitants and the destruction of their property. Although this resulted from the direct command of Jehovah, it is not quite so inconsistent with Divine morality as some scholars have suggested.[18] In the first instance, the sparing of Rahab and her family is characteristically humanitarian, and constituted an appropriate reward for assisting the spies whom Joshua had sent to survey the defenses of the city. Secondly, the real issue at stake was that of the morality of Jehovah as against the depraved rituals of Canaanite religion. There could be no form of compromise between the two, and if the strict ethical code of Israel was to be established permanently, the suppression of Canaanite orgiastic worship was inevitable. Nor could there be diminution of effort in the resolute stand against the nature rituals and debased fertility cults of Canaan without the integrity of Hebrew religion being affected immediately. From a cultural standpoint, Near

Ruins of Jericho. It was around this six-acre site that Joshua led the marching Israelites. "... the wall fell down flat. ... And they utterly destroyed all that was in the city. ... And they burnt the city with fire."

Eastern society sustained little loss when the decadent civilization of Canaan fell under the hammer blows of the invading Israelites. Had they only exterminated it completely, the whole trend of their subsequent history might well have been vastly different.

The Conquest of Canaan

The accounts of the military campaigns in Canaan contained in the book of Joshua are evidently of a selective nature. The sequences appear to be condensed somewhat, so that the conquest seems to have been completed in a comparatively short time. It is quite within the bounds of possibility that some of the campaigns that took place were not included in the book of Joshua, since the purpose of the author was to show that the Israelites had finally occupied the land promised to their forbears.

The conquest was pursued in three distinct stages, the first of which involved the occupation of eastern Palestine prior to the fall of Jericho. The second phase consisted of the capture of Jericho and Ai, the league with the royal city of Gibeon, the defeat of the five kings who had allied to fight against Gibeon, and the capture of a group of cities that included Lachish and Hebron.

The final stage of the occupation took the Israelite forces into Galilee and northern Palestine, where Joshua fought against a Canaanite coalition headed by Jabin, king of Hazor. Although the Israelites were victorious, none of the fortified cities was destroyed except Hazor, which appears to indicate that they were anxious to retain the cities intact while at the same time insuring that their military power was broken. By the time the campaign had been brought to a conclusion, no less than thirty-one petty kings had been subdued. Nevertheless there were still some formidable cities that remained to be reduced, such as Jerusalem and Megiddo. Despite the apparently speedy conclusion of the military campaign and the occupation of Canaanite territory, the book of Joshua makes it clear (13:1ff.) that the gains that had been made were far from being consolidated even in the lifetime of Joshua.

Archaeological excavations along the route of the occupation have afforded clear indications of violence and destruction during the second half of the thirteenth century B.C. , which affected the stability of life in Canaan for the next two centuries. The site of Ai, lying one and a half miles to the east of Bethel, was excavated in 1933 by Madame Marquet-Krause, at which time the ruins of an Early Bronze Age city were uncovered. The remains of the temples, palaces, and city walls indicated that the city was completely destroyed about 2200 B.C., and was not occupied again for about eleven hundred years, when a much smaller village settlement was established. Thus, the description of the assault and capture of a city whose population numbered twelve thousand (Josh. 8:25) probably refers to the destruction of neighboring Bethel rather than Ai.

The narrative does not distinguish very clearly between the warriors of the two cities (Josh. 8:17), and it may have been, as Vincent suggested, that Ai was a fortified outpost on the edge of Bethel. In any event, Ai was quite small in comparison with other sites (Josh. 7:3), and if its destruction involved the simultaneous overthrow of a neighboring site, there is no reason why the account should not have been subsumed under the narrative of the victory at Ai. Ancient Bethel was excavated in 1934 under the direction of Professor Albright and was found to have been established in the twenty-first century B.C. , shortly after the destruction of the Early Bronze Age community of Ai. In the thirteenth century B.C., the well-built Middle Bronze Age city was sacked and burned, as indicated by the great quantities of charred debris, burnt brick, and ashes that were unearthed at lower Late Bronze Age levels. This destruction probably resulted from the Israelite conquest of Canaan, though some scholars who assign an early date to the Exodus would associate it with the fall of Bethel to the tribe of Joseph (Judg. 1:22ff.), which occurred after the death of Joshua.

Excavations at Lachish, the modern Tell ed-Duweir, were begun in 1933 under the direction of J. L. Starkey, who showed that the site had been settled by cave dwellers in the Early Bronze Age. Subsequent communities built the site up into an important stronghold, and in the time of Joshua it was a former royal Canaanite city, controlled by an Amorite governor. The Hyksos period was represented by a huge defensive fosse of the sort that provided an enclo-

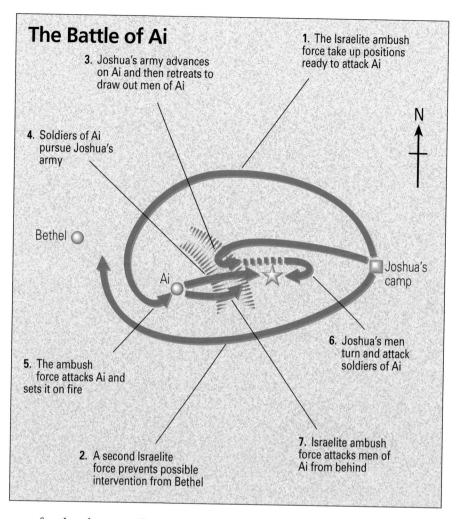

The Battle of Ai

1. The Israelite ambush force take up positions ready to attack Ai

3. Joshua's army advances on Ai and then retreats to draw out men of Ai

4. Soldiers of Ai pursue Joshua's army

Bethel

N

Ai

Joshua's camp

6. Joshua's men turn and attack soldiers of Ai

5. The ambush force attacks Ai and sets it on fire

2. A second Israelite force prevents possible intervention from Bethel

7. Israelite ambush force attacks men of Ai from behind

sure for the chariotry. Between the fifteenth and thirteenth centuries three Canaanite shrines were erected in the enclosure, and artifacts from the site have suggested the existence of a form of worship having much in common with Hebrew sacrificial ritual. A potsherd that contained an Egyptian inscription recording a business transaction was recovered from Late Bronze Age levels, in the midst of debris that spoke of the violent destruction of the city. The ostracon or potsherd was dated about 1230 B.C., which would imply that the city fell in the thirteenth century, probably to invading Israelites.

The characteristic occupational levels of Canaanites, Egyptians, Hyksos, and Hebrews were in evidence when Debir was excavated from 1926. The older name of this site was Kiriath-sepher, and it is now identified with Tell Beit Mirsim, thirteen miles southwest of Hebron. Here again a layer of charred debris separated subsequent Hebrew deposits from the Late Bronze Age remains

171

beneath, dating the destruction of the city at about 1200 B.C. Scholars who maintain a fifteenth-century date for the Exodus regard the attack of Joshua on Debir (cf. Josh. 10:38f.) in terms of the destruction of its inhabitants only, and the fall of the city proper as the result of Israelite destruction under Othniel, the nephew of Caleb (Judg. 1:11ff.).

Apart from a few soundings made by Garstang at Hazor, the modern Tell el-Qedah, in 1926, nothing was known about the Galilean campaign of Joshua. In 1954, an expedition from the Hebrew University of Jerusalem led by Dr. Yadin began to excavate the mound. To the northwest they unearthed a large enclosure surrounded by an embankment of beaten earth. Ancient Hazor, the strongest of the pre-Israelite city kingdoms, was also one of the most populous towns in Canaan, and the camp enclosure served not only to accommodate the famous chariotry of Hazor, but also a number of dwellings.[19]

Of the seventeen occupational levels at Hazor, the earliest is thought to be dated around 4000 B.C., which is eloquent testimony to the antiquity of the site. The rampart around the enclosure was found to date from the Middle Bronze Age II period, contemporary with the Hyksos deposits. Nearby were found some potsherds, one of which had Proto-Sinaitic script upon it. A cemetery dating from the Middle and Late Bronze Age was excavated in the center of the camp enclosure, which indicates that the last period of settlement there was apparently terminated by the Israelite conquests under Joshua. As far as is known at present, this destruction is to be dated in the thirteenth century B.C., and may well be associated with the Galilee campaign (Josh. 10:36f.). But as with Debir, if an early date is assigned to the Exodus, the final destruction of Canaanite civilization in Hebron may have taken place in the Judges period (cf. Judg. 1:10).

The Meneptah Stele

Independent evidence of the fact that the Israelites were well established in western Palestine about the time that Lachish and Debir fell was provided by an Egyptian source. This is the celebrated Stele of Meneptah,[20] which recorded the success of his early campaigns in Palestine. A large black granite monument erected by Amenhotep III was inscribed by Meneptah in the fifth year of his reign (c. 1220 B.C.) in the exaggerated language that commemorated military engagements of any degree of success whatsoever in ancient Near Eastern life. The list of defeated foreigners included the inhabitants of Libya (Tehennu) and the Israelites:

> Devastated is Tehennu;
> The Hittite Land is pacified;
> Plundered is Canaan with every evil;

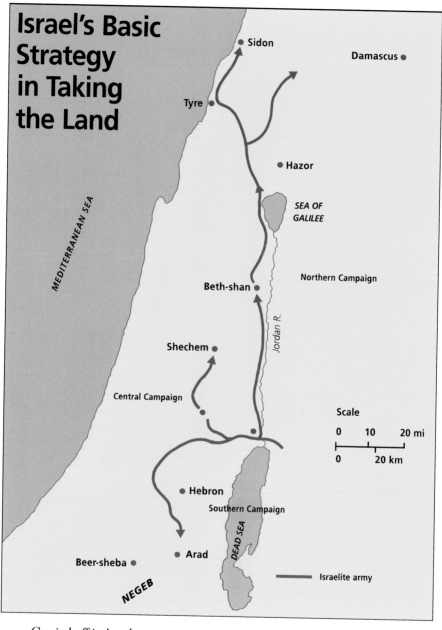

Israel's Basic Strategy in Taking the Land

Carried off is Ascalon.
Seized upon is Gezer;
Yenoam is made a thing of naught;
Israel is desolated, her seed is not.
Palestine has become a defenseless widow for Egypt;
Everyone that is turbulent is bound by king Meneptah. . . .[21]

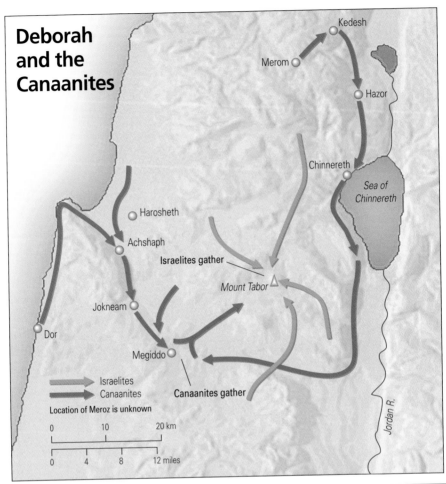

Deborah and the Canaanites

Kedesh

Merom

Hazor

Chinnereth

Sea of Chinnereth

Harosheth

Achshaph

Israelites gather

Mount Tabor

Jokneam

Dor

Megiddo

Israelites
Canaanites
Canaanites gather

Location of Meroz is unknown

Jordan R.

0   10   20 km

0   4   8   12 miles

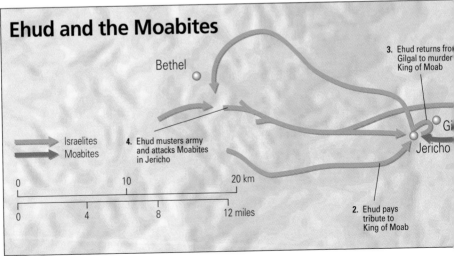

Ehud and the Moabites

3. Ehud returns fro
Gilgal to murder
King of Moab

Bethel

Israelites
Moabites

4. Ehud musters army
and attacks Moabites
in Jericho

Gi

Jericho

2. Ehud pays
tribute to
King of Moab

0   10   20 km

0   4   8   12 miles

In this list of names, Israel is the only one to be written with the determinative symbol indicating "people" rather than "land." This would imply that the Israelites were in western Palestine in some strength, but that they were not as yet fully sedentary. On the other hand, the inscription may contain a scribal error at this point, resulting from carelessness, since the *stele* contains other errors of writing also.

Under the leadership of Joshua, the Israelites occupied much of Canaan and overcame military resistance to the degree that the tribes could begin sedentary life in comparative peace. It must not be imagined, however, that the subjugation of the land was completed in the time of Joshua, for although the Israelites continued to absorb the inhabitants of Canaan into their own cultural patterns, there were notable centers of resistance to Israelite military power, including the fortresses of Megiddo, Beth-shemesh, Gezer, and Jerusalem.

The Rise of the Judges

When the death of Joshua robbed the Hebrews of resolute leadership, a period of transition ensued that saw the degeneration of national unity and the rise of more individual tribal activity. Local resistance to the Israelite invaders was a feature of this period, and it became necessary in the end to reconquer and consolidate some of the territory that had been acquired under Joshua. One reason for the success of Canaanite opposition was the inferior state of Hebrew technology, especially in the matter of horse-drawn chariots and other weapons of warfare, such as the strong compound Asiatic bow. When an emergency situation arose, a judge was raised up by God to lead the people to victory, and in consequence this phase of Hebrew history is known as the Judges period.

This era was marked by the increasing idolatry of the Israelites and the rise

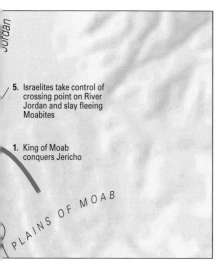

of powerful Canaanite resistance in many parts of Palestine. Eglon, king of Moab, enslaved some of the Israelites for eighteen years, and they were finally delivered by Ehud. Jabin, king of Hazor, presented a formidable threat to Israelite security by the might and mobility of his armed forces. His general, Sisera, who commanded a group of nine hundred iron-fitted chariots, roamed at will among the northern tribes. Deborah, the judge and prophetess, appointed Barak as the commander of the Hebrew forces mobilized to defeat the men of Hazor, and in the ensuing battle Sisera was defeated. He fled to an ally, Heber, the Kenite, whose wife Jael sheltered him, and then put him to death when he slept from exhaustion. The magnificent song of Deborah (Judg. 5) commemorated the ultimate defeat of Jabin and his forces in language that has seldom been surpassed in epic poetry for beauty and vigor of expression.

Midianites and Ammonites

A serious blow to the economy of the Hebrew tribes was dealt by the incursions of the Midianites. These people were camel-riding nomads,[22] who followed the custom of raiding Israelite crops at harvest time and terrorizing the populace generally. They allied with the Amalekites and brought such oppression to bear upon the Israelites that the latter were forced to flee to strongholds in the hills. The situation was finally remedied by Gideon, who began his campaign against the Midianites with a dramatic assault upon the idolatrous practices of Israel (Judg. 6:25ff.). He then assembled the northern tribes of Zebulun, Asher, and Naphtali together with his own tribe of Manasseh. With a selected company of men armed with lamps, trumpets, and pitchers, he caused complete confusion among the Midianites and Amalekites in a surprise attack at night. The resulting victory offended the Ephraimites, who felt slighted at not being asked to fight with the forces of Gideon. But when they were complimented on their capture of the Midianite princes Oreb and Zeeb, the breach was healed. Gideon succeeded in reestablishing the worship of Jehovah, although idolatry was evidently never very far from the thoughts of the Israelites (Judg. 8:27). He refused to accept the idea of hereditary rule in his desire to maintain the theocratic concepts of the law, and this was one of the causes of dissension among his sons after his death.

A four-horned stone altar from Megiddo, c. tenth century B.C.

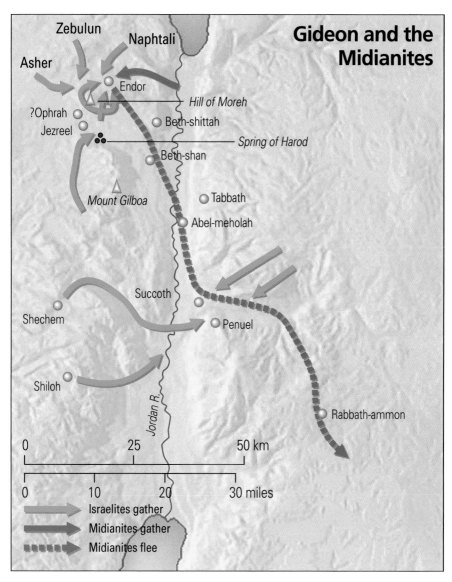

Gideon and the Midianites

A subsequent lapse into idolatry brought upon the Israelites further calamities in the form of Ammonite oppression. A champion of the cause of God appeared in the person of Jephthah the Gileadite, a man of considerable ability and initiative. The kingdoms of Transjordan offered staunch resistance to his plan of conquest (Judg. 11:17ff.), but he finally won a decisive victory over the Ammonites. Ephraimite jealousy was once again aroused, and the sad spectacle of intertribal warfare followed, resulting in the defeat of the Ephraimites.

The Philistines

After the death of Jephthah, a succession of judges ruled Israel, during which time the threat of Philistine oppression became more acute. The Philistines were a maritime people of non-Semitic stock who migrated from the Aegean, and particularly from ancient Caphtor (Crete) to Canaan about 1175 B.C., settling in the coastal plain. Small groups of Philistines had lived on the southern border of Palestine in Patriarchal times (Gen. 26:1, 14), but the twelfth-century migration was of a different order. The Philistines had been driven out of Crete and Asia Minor by invaders from the north, and before settling in Canaan they attacked Egypt. Ramses III repelled them with heavy losses in a naval battle, and forced them to turn their attention to the coastal areas of southwestern Palestine.[23] Here they established a confederation of five cities, Gaza, Gath, Ashkelon, Ashdod, and Ekron, upon which their military strength very largely depended.

Apart from their closely-knit political organization, their power was felt in the economic area of Israelite life also. The Philistines had learned the uses of iron from the Hittites, who had controlled the manufacture and export of that metal. When Hittite power waned about 1200 B.C., the Philistines acquired a monopoly of the supply of iron, and used it to fashion agricultural implements of various sorts, including sickles, axes, and plows. To insure the stability and permanence of their military power, they equipped their forces with weapons

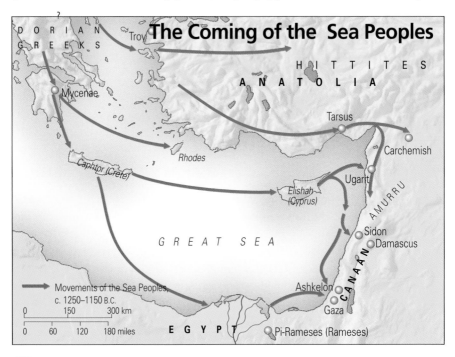

manufactured from iron, and made them mobile by furnishing them with iron-fitted chariots from which to attack the enemy. This technological advance combined with Israelite conservatism to give the Philistines a distinct advantage in economic and military spheres in Canaan, providing a situation they were quick to exploit.

The Israelites came into sporadic conflict with the Philistines during the Judges period, and one of the champions of Israel during this time of Philistine ascendancy was Samson, a man of superior physical strength but of indifferent moral character. It is probable that the modern Wadi el-Seirar was the site of some of his exploits, which, though dramatic in nature, failed to deliver Israel from Philistine oppression.

The Rise of Centralized Rule

The general state of unrest among the tribes at this time may be gathered from the narratives that deal with Micah of Ephraim (Judg. 17). He was a wealthy man who, at the instigation of his mother, made cultic images and established his own shrine in which his son acted as priest. An itinerant Levite joined the household, but when the Danites were migrating northward he was captured by them, and his cultic equipment was confiscated despite the objections of the true owner. The Danites invaded the peaceful city of Laish in northern Palestine, and established it as their tribal center. This town (Dan) ultimately marked the northernmost limits of the Israelite kingdom.

The closing chapters of the book of Judges reveal the social chaos that prevailed among the tribes, and indicate that there was an urgent need for some centralized temporal authority in the form of a king. The most important religious center at this time was Shiloh, a place to which Joshua had brought the tribes after the main phase of the occupation had ended. Here the Ark of the Covenant had been deposited, and the worship of the sanctuary was conducted by Eli the priest, along with his corrupt sons Hophni and Phinehas. The disorder, weakness, and immorality to which the nation had fallen victim were epitomized by the conduct of affairs at Shiloh (I Sam. 22:22ff.), and it fell to Samuel, the last of the judges and the first of the prophets, to institute social and religious reforms in an attempt to remedy the chaos of contemporary tribal life.

The narratives of the early life and call of Samuel are set against this background of religious depravity and social disorder. The weakness of Israelite morale was clearly demonstrated by the loss of the sacred Ark to the valiant Philistines and the debacle that followed. It is probable that the shrine at Shiloh was destroyed at this time (cf. Jer. 7:12, 14), and if this took place, it robbed the Israelite tribes of their central sanctuary, thus contributing further to the weakness of the nation.

The situation was saved to some extent for the Israelites by an unexpected calamity which overtook Dagon, the grain deity of Ashdod, and which assumed the more serious proportions of a virulent epidemic outbreak among the local populace. The symptom of inguinal buboes (I Sam. 5:9), the presence of rodents (I Sam. 6:5), and the fact that the disease spread quickly along lines of communication indicate that the epidemic was that of bubonic plague. The Philistines were quick to relieve themselves of the sacred Ark of Israel, which they rightly connected with the outbreak of the plague, and it was returned with a sin offering. A subsequent Philistine foray was met by a chastened, penitent, and revived Israel, and Philistine losses in battle were such that further raids were discouraged.

The disunity of Hebrew society was so great, however, that some modification of the theocratic ideal Samuel cherished was inevitable if the nation was to survive the growing weight of Philistine economic and military pressure. The people needed a tangible, unifying factor in the form of a leader, and were demanding the services of a king. Although Samuel was quick to point out the disadvantages implicit in a monarchical system, the will of the people prevailed. Thus God was no longer the sole ruler of the nation as He had been under the theocracy, and the modifications of this concept, which the monarchy introduced, were to have an important bearing upon the subsequent relations between prophet and king.

Rule of Saul

By Divine command Samuel anointed Saul, a man from the insignificant tribe of Benjamin, as ruler of the tribes. He was of a commanding appearance physically, and the Israelites gave him unreserved support in his task of unifying the nation. The early home and capital of Saul was at Gibeah, some four miles north of Jerusalem on the main road to Samaria. It claimed considerable importance as a military outpost for Israelite forces, since Jerusalem was still in Jebusite hands in the eleventh century B.C. Archaeological excavations at the site, identified with the modern Tell el-Ful, showed that there had been a total of twelve occupational levels there. Of four fortresses that were erected on the site, the second appears to have been that established by Saul (I Sam. 14:2)[24]. The two-storied structure was roughly square in shape, measuring fifty-five feet by fifty-one feet in area, with walls varying from eight to ten feet in thickness. In the cellars were found storage jars that still contained oil and grain, while household pottery and equipment lay nearby in profusion. Though the original site was only about two acres in extent, it was the first important political center of Israel, and continued to be a military outpost long after the capture of Jerusalem.

Shortly after Saul had assumed the office of ruler, the Ammonites made an attempt to subdue Jabesh-gilead in Transjordan, and messengers were sent to

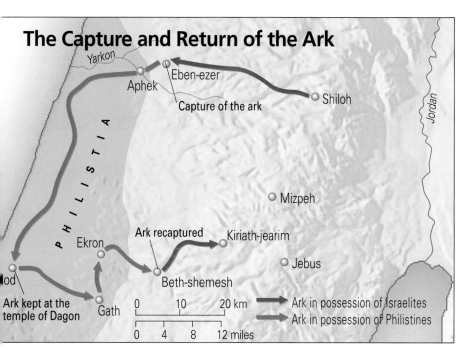

The Capture and Return of the Ark

Yarkon

Aphek

Eben-ezer

Capture of the ark

Shiloh

Jordan

P H I L I S T I A

Mizpeh

Ekron

Ark recaptured

Kiriath-jearim

Jebus

od

Beth-shemesh

Ark kept at the
temple of Dagon

Gath

0   10   20 km

0   4   8   12 miles

➡ Ark in possession of Israelites

➡ Ark in possession of Philistines

Saul to inform him of the emergency. His dramatic display of leadership resulted in an Israelite victory over the Ammonites and the rescue of Jabesh-gilead (I Sam. 11), which did much to heighten his prestige. Although Saul was little more than a rustic chieftain, he was a man of considerable pride and self-will, and as time progressed these characteristics asserted themselves increasingly in his rule of the people. A clash of authority between prophet and king appeared inevitable, and repeated disobedience of the Divine will on the part of Saul resulted in a deterioration of relations between himself and Samuel. The theocratic ideal was still stronger than that of the newly established monarchy, and Samuel was ordered by God to anoint David, son of Jesse, as successor to Saul in a move to preserve the unity of the nation. By this time it was evident that Saul was the victim of mental disturbance (I Sam. 16:14), and David was appointed to play the harp to him when he became depressed.

The Rise of David

Philistine military power had now reached such proportions that it threatened to disrupt the economic life of the Israelites, and a decisive victory in battle was an urgent necessity if Israel was to survive as a national entity. At this juncture David appeared as the champion of his people, and slew a formidable Philistine warrior under very unfavorable circumstances, turning the tide somewhat in favor of Israel. The adulation that was heaped upon him aroused a storm of jealousy in the mind of King Saul, which was not quelled by the devotion Jonathan and Michal, children of Saul, showed to him. Although Saul suspected David of treason, he promised David that he could marry Merab, his elder daughter. When the time for the solemnizing of the marriage arrived, however, she was given instead to Adriel the Meholathite, and David was persuaded to marry Michal, the younger sister of Merab. While this change still served the plans of the suspicious king admirably, it is probable that other considerations were also in view, the significance of which will be examined shortly.

The jealousy of Saul reached such proportions that David was advised by Michal and Jonathan of plots against his life, upon which he fled to Nob and obtained help from Ahimelech the priest. His presence there was betrayed by Doeg the Edomite, and he was forced to withdraw to the southwest of Jerusalem, where he hid in the cave of Adullam. Friends and malcontents joined him there, and he became captain of a group of warriors who were shortly confronted with the twofold task of staving off the attacks of Saul and at the same time ridding southern Canaan of Philistine domination.

When Saul heard the tidings that the priest of Nob had assisted the fugitive David, he raided the shrine and killed Ahimelech along with eighty-five other priests of Jehovah (I Sam. 22). Abiathar, one of the sons of Ahimelech, escaped and joined the forces of David, bringing with him the ephod, a sacred cultic object of linen (Ex. 28) from the shrine. Saul pursued David with frantic eagerness, and was only deterred in his quest by occasional Philistine raids (I Sam. 23:27). David experienced considerable difficulty in obtaining supplies, and he resorted to a polite form of brigandage in order to meet the needs of his forces. Thus Nabal (I Sam. 25:2ff.) was requested to supply food for David and his men in return for the "protection" they were conferring upon him by refraining from damaging his interests.

Nabal, an alcoholic, refused to consider this transaction, and the retribution David and his followers had planned to exact was only halted by the blandishments of Abigail, the beautiful wife of Nabal. When she subsequently communicated to her husband the method by which David had been appeased, Nabal had an apoplectic seizure and died within a few days. After this, David married Abigail after Michal had been taken from him and given to Phalti, the son of Laish. About that time he also took Ahinoam of Jezreel as his wife, and the two women shared his exile.

On two occasions David had an opportunity to kill Saul, but he refrained from harming the anointed ruler of Israel. In order to escape from the insensate jealousy of Saul, David went with his wives and followers and allied himself with Achish, king of Gath, who gave him control of the town of Ziklag (I Sam. 27). For the next year he made periodic raids upon the Amalekites and other enemies of the Israelites without, however, waging war against his kinsfolk. In the meantime, Achish prepared for a battle against Saul, and when he saw the nature of the forces arrayed against him, the Israelite king took the final step towards his own downfall by having recourse to occultism. At an earlier period Saul had outlawed occult practices in accordance with the strict injunctions of the Mosaic law (Deut. 18:10f.), but his state of dementia had reached such proportions that he was prepared to clutch at any means of assistance, however flimsy it might prove to be. The spiritualistic medium to whom Saul paid a visit conjured up the shade of the departed Samuel, who prophesied his death and the destruction of the Israelite forces.

When the Philistines were ready to attack Saul, they marched to Aphek in company with David and his warriors. Achish was suspicious of the loyalty of David under these circumstances, and excused him from taking part in the battle. David returned to Ziklag to find it destroyed by Amalekite raiders and its inhabitants captured. After consulting the sacred ephod, David received assurance of success if he pursued the raiders. Scarcely had he set out when he had the good fortune to come upon a straggler from the Amalekite raiding party, who guided him to the main encampment. In the battle that followed, David decimated the nomadic marauders and recovered all that had been stolen. Those who had participated in any way in the victory received a share of the spoils, as well as having their wives, children, and property restored to them, a procedure that set a precedent for later times (I Sam. 30:25).

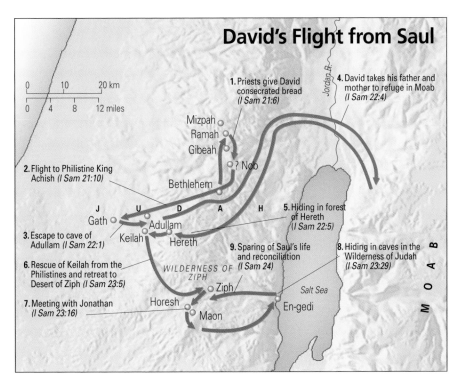

David's Flight from Saul

1. Priests give David consecrated bread (I Sam 21:6)
2. Flight to Philistine King Achish (I Sam 21:10)
3. Escape to cave of Adullam (I Sam 22:1)
4. David takes his father and mother to refuge in Moab (I Sam 22:4)
5. Hiding in forest of Hereth (I Sam 22:5)
6. Rescue of Keilah from the Philistines and retreat to Desert of Ziph (I Sam 23:5)
7. Meeting with Jonathan (I Sam 23:16)
8. Hiding in caves in the Wilderness of Judah (I Sam 23:29)
9. Sparing of Saul's life and reconciliation (I Sam 24)

Mizpah
Ramah
Gibeah
? Nob
Bethlehem
Gath
Keilah
Adullam
Hereth
WILDERNESS OF ZIPH
Horesh
Ziph
Maon
En-gedi
Salt Sea
Jordan R.
MOAB

183

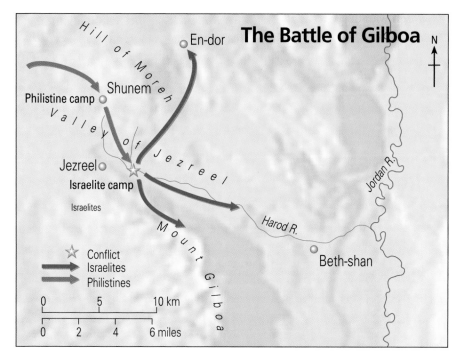

A crushing blow to the Israelite army was administered by the Philistine onslaught at Gilboa, in which Saul and his sons were slain, as Samuel had foretold. The body of Saul was mutilated and set up in Beth-shan, but it was recovered in a raid by warriors from Jabesh-gilead, an act that returned the bravery shown towards them at an earlier time by Saul. The lament David composed for the occasion was a poignant and beautiful tribute to those for whom he felt sincere affection, despite the change that had overtaken their relationships. The tragic circumstances of Gilboa were invested with a range of personal values that elevated the defeat above the level of its counterparts in current Near Eastern annals, and invested it with the true character of historiography.

The Matriarchate

It is perhaps in the realm of personal values and their application in the light of social custom that the explanation of the fury that characterized the attitude of King Saul towards David is to be found. The particular point at issue may well lie in the influence of the Egyptian matriarchate during the earliest stages of the Hebrew monarchy. This system of inheritance through the female line only was of immense antiquity, and exercised a profound influence over all levels of Egyptian society. Furthermore, there is some reason for believing that it affected the course of the Hebrew monarchy as it developed into an hereditary patriarchate.

A view of the River Jordan as it moves south along the course of a rift valley that is the lowest depression on earth.

Maachah, the great-grandmother of Saul, was the wife of Jehiel, who in I Chronicles 8:29 is described as the "father" of Gibeon. If she was named after the small city-state that lay at the foot of Mount Hermon, it may well have been in conformity with the ancient custom of bestowing upon the ruler the same name as that of the country being ruled, and making Maachah a royal personage in her own right. If the matriarchal system was valid to some extent, the concern David experienced when Merab was given in marriage to Adriel instead of to himself would be justified, since the husband of Merab would then be in the direct line of succession to the throne. Again, when David married Maachah, daughter of Talmai, king of Geshur (II Sam. 3:3), he would become heir to that small kingdom also, and it is interesting to note that it was to this place that Absalom fled after killing his brother Amnon (II Sam. 13:37f.).

If it is possible to identify Ahinoam, wife of David (I Sam. 25:43), with Ahinoam, daughter of Ahimaaz and wife of Saul, it would appear that David had managed to contract a marriage with the wife of the reigning king. If the matriarchate was at all valid in Palestine at the time, David would by this means have gained a clear title to the throne of Israel. Under such circumstances Saul would have urgent reasons for the destruction of David, since as long as the latter possessed the heiress to the kingdom, the throne would be his by right of marriage. In this connection the obvious attachment of Phaltiel to Michal (II Sam. 3:16), the former wife of David, is understandable if she was an heiress to the throne, for as her husband he would be in the direct line of succession.

It must be realized that this theory involving the influence of the Egyptian matriarchate is by no means free from difficulties, one of which concerns the true identity of Ahinoam and Maachah. Given some degree of validity, however, it might well assist in the understanding of the motives that prompted the political intrigue of the early Hebrew monarchy, and the actions that, judged by the standards of Western culture, might appear to be unnecessarily immoral, coarse, or brutal.

NOTES

1. L. Finkelstein (Ed.), *The Jews, Their History, Culture and Religion*, I, 14.

2. W. F. Albright, *The Archaeology of Palestine*, pp. 185f.

3. Cf. C. H. Gordon, *Ugaritic Handbook* (1947); *Ugaritic Literature* (1949).

4. C. H. Gordon, *Ugaritic Literature*, p. 15.

5. *Ibid.*, p. 99.

6. *Ibid.*, p. 19.

7. J. Finegan, *Light From the Ancient Past*, pl. 60.

8. C. H. Gordon, *Ugaritic Literature*, pp. 9ff.

9. *Ibid.*, pp. 3f.

10. M. F. Unger, *Archaeology and the Old Testament* (1954), p. 173.

11. C. H. Gordon, *Ugaritic Literature*, pp. 17f.

12. W. F. Albright, *Archaeology and the Religion of Israel* (1953), p. 77.

13. C. H. Gordon, *Introduction to Old Testament Times*, p. 83.

14. C. H. Gordon, *Ugarit and Minoan Crete* (1967), pp. 18ff., 151.

15. *Ibid.*, p. 30.

16. J. and J. B. E. Garstang, *The Story of Jericho* (1948), pp. 135ff.

17. Kathleen M. Kenyon, *Digging Up Jericho*, pp. 33, 51ff.; *Archaeology in the Holy Land*, pp. 177ff.

18. E.g., H. H. Rowley, *The Rediscovery of the Old Testament* (1946), p. 16.

19. Y. Yadin *et al.*, *Hazor* I (1958); *Hazor II* (1960).

20. J. Finegan, *op. cit.*, pl. 51.

21. S. L. Caiger, *Bible and Spade* (1936), pp. 111f.; cf. J. B. Pritchard (Ed.), *Ancient Near Eastern Texts Relating to the Old Testament*, p. 378.

22. L. Finkelstein (Ed.), *op. cit.*, I, 21.

23. J. Finegan, *op. cit.*, pp. 108f.

24. M. Burrows, *What Mean These Stones?*, pp. 141ff.

Near Eastern Chronology from the Hebrew Monarchy to 722 B.C.

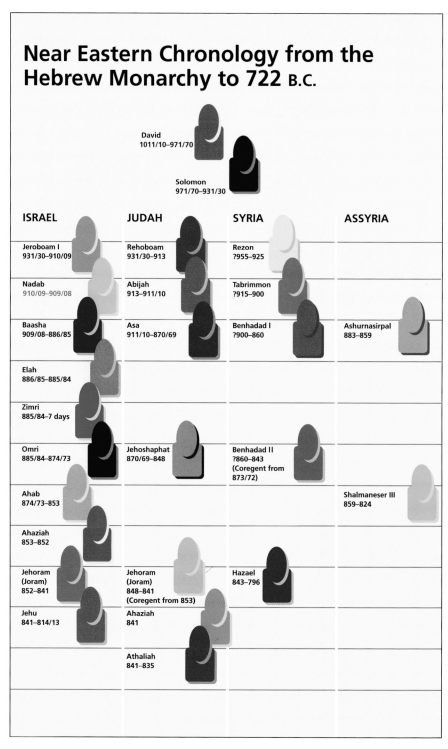

David
1011/10–971/70

Solomon
971/70–931/30

ISRAEL	JUDAH	SYRIA	ASSYRIA
Jeroboam I 931/30–910/09	Rehoboam 931/30–913	Rezon ?955–925	
Nadab 910/09–909/08	Abijah 913–911/10	Tabrimmon ?915–900	
Baasha 909/08–886/85	Asa 911/10–870/69	Benhadad I ?900–860	Ashurnasirpal 883–859
Elah 886/85–885/84			
Zimri 885/84–7 days			
Omri 885/84–874/73	Jehoshaphat 870/69–848	Benhadad II ?860–843 (Coregent from 873/72)	
Ahab 874/73–853			Shalmaneser III 859–824
Ahaziah 853–852			
Jehoram (Joram) 852–841	Jehoram (Joram) 848–841 (Coregent from 853)	Hazael 843–796	
Jehu 841–814/13	Ahaziah 841		
	Athaliah 841–835		

Near Eastern Chronology from the Hebrew Monarchy to 722 B.C.

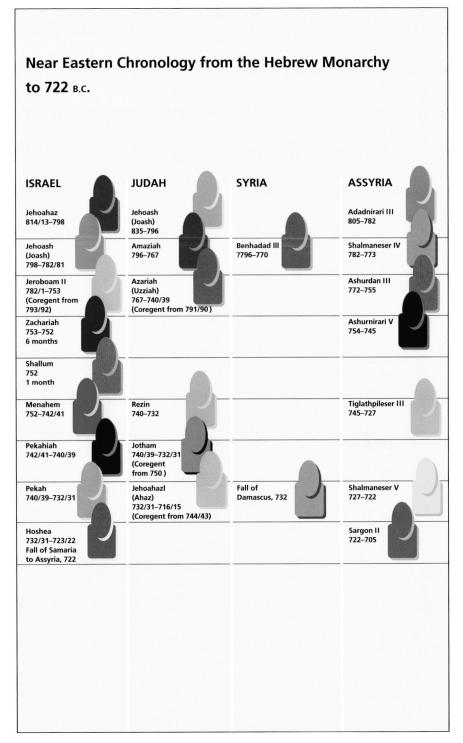

ISRAEL	JUDAH	SYRIA	ASSYRIA
Jehoahaz 814/13–798	Jehoash (Joash) 835–796		Adadnirari III 805–782
Jehoash (Joash) 798–782/81	Amaziah 796–767	Benhadad III ?796–770	Shalmaneser IV 782–773
Jeroboam II 782/1–753 (Coregent from 793/92)	Azariah (Uzziah) 767–740/39 (Coregent from 791/90)		Ashurdan III 772–755
Zachariah 753–752 6 months			Ashurnirari V 754–745
Shallum 752 1 month			
Menahem 752–742/41	Rezin 740–732		Tiglathpileser III 745–727
Pekahiah 742/41–740/39	Jotham 740/39–732/31 (Coregent from 750)		
Pekah 740/39–732/31	Jehoahazl (Ahaz) 732/31–716/15 (Coregent from 744/43)	Fall of Damascus, 732	Shalmaneser V 727–722
Hoshea 732/31–723/22 Fall of Samaria to Assyria, 722			Sargon II 722–705

7. The Kingdom United and Divided

CHRONOLOGY OF THIS CHAPTER

David	1011/10–971/70 B.C.
Solomon	971/70–931/30 B.C.
Fall of Samaria	722 B.C.

ALTHOUGH THE IMMEDIATE THREAT TO THE WELFARE OF DAVID had been removed by the death of Saul, the Philistine victory at Gilboa brought about a state of crisis in the political history of the Israelites. Not merely had they been robbed of leadership but they had also lost control of the fertile valley of Jezreel, which extended southeast from Mount Carmel to the River Jordan. The main highway from Syria to Egypt crossed the northern part of this valley, while to the south lay the principal trading route between Damascus and Jerusalem. The valley had long been coveted by invaders of Palestine because of its strategic importance, and with the Philistines in control, the breakdown of Hebrew society was virtually assured.

Anointing of David

Even more serious was the internal strife that arose over the matter of a successor to Saul. The northern tribes remained loyal to the house of the dead king, and accepted the rule of Ishbosheth, the fourth son of Saul. With the assistance of his general, Abner, he established his capital at Mahanaim in Transjordan, while David returned to the tribe of Judah and settled in the ancient city of Hebron. Here David was anointed ruler over the house of Judah, and governed for seven years. Under the circumstances, warfare between himself and the suc-

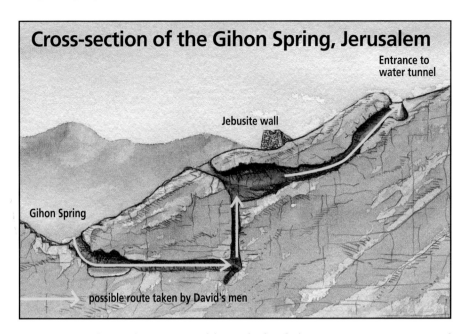

Cross-section of the Gihon Spring, Jerusalem

Entrance to water tunnel

Jebusite wall

Gihon Spring

possible route taken by David's men

cessors of Saul was almost inevitable, and a battle between opposing teams of warriors (II Sam. 2:15) began the process of deterioration that ended in the extinction of the house of Saul. Abner quarreled with Ishbosheth over one of the royal concubines, and immediately transferred his allegiance to David in the hope that this gesture would permit David to become ruler of the northern Israelite tribes as well as of Judah. But Abner discovered that as a prerequisite to the acceptance of his loyalty, David required the return of his former wife Michal, married at that time to Phaltiel (Phalti).

If the idea of the matriarchate was in force to any degree, this step would constitute a necessary preliminary to the recognition of David as king over Israel in addition to being ruler of Judah. When this matter had been settled to the satisfaction of David, Abner proceeded to influence the northern tribes in favor of accepting David as king, and he might well have become commander of the forces of Judah had it not been for the jealousy of Joab, whose brother Abner had killed previously. Joab had allied his forces with those of David, and had assumed command at Hebron, so that the appearance of Abner presented a threat to his position as general. In consequence Joab murdered him in cold blood, an act that evoked an angry rebuke from his master. Despite the delicacy of the situation, however, David used it to political advantage by giving Abner an honorable burial, and impressing the northern tribes with his own magnanimity and sincerity.

The turbulent career of Ishbosheth ended in his murder by two of his followers, who took his head to David at Hebron. Far from being rewarded, however, they were put to death as common murderers, an act that increased the prestige

An artist's reconstruction of Jerusalem in the time of David and Solomon

Irrigation channels

City gate

Citadel

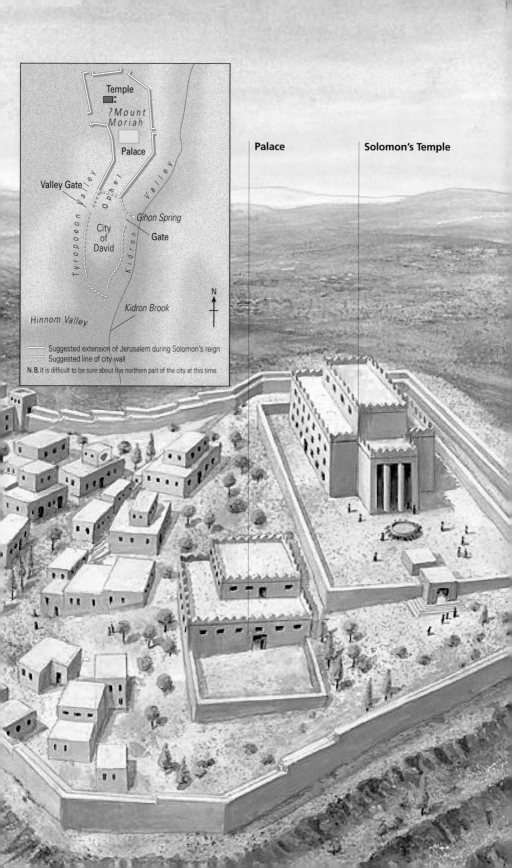

Temple

?Mount
Moriah

Palace

Valley Gate

Tyropoeon Valley

Ophel

Kidron Valley

Gihon Spring

Gate

City
of
David

N

Kidron Brook

Hinnom Valley

Suggested extension of Jerusalem during Solomon's reign
Suggested line of city wall
N.B. It is difficult to be sure about the northern part of the city at this time.

Palace

Solomon's Temple

of David in the north even more. The time was then considered ripe for the northern peoples to transfer their allegiance to him, and they entered into a covenant relationship with David by which he would become their ruler. Having accepted this responsibility, his immediate task was to implement the political unity of the tribes by means of an established kingdom.

The Establishing of a Capital

The question of a capital city was of some importance, and David displayed considerable political acumen by choosing a site that was outside the strict territorial range of the Israelite tribes, while at the same time being near the center of his newly united country. The proposed capital was Jerusalem, which at the time was a Jebusite stronghold, firmly established on a rocky plateau over three thousand feet above the level of the Jordan plain at Jericho. So impregnable did the native defenders consider the city that they taunted David and his men in a manner they shortly regretted. Precisely how the "Stronghold of Zion" was taken is uncertain, and until recently the passage relating to its capture (II Sam. 5:8) appeared to indicate access by means of a "gutter" (K.J.V.) or "watershaft" (R.S.V.). When Sir Charles Warren was conducting early excavations at Jerusalem, this theory seemed to be substantiated by the discovery of an underground water system instituted by the Canaanite inhabitants of the site around 2000 B.C.

Because of its location, Jerusalem was deficient in water supplies and depended largely upon underground cisterns and reservoirs. The nearest spring was in the Kidron valley to the southeast of the mount known as Ophel, and was called the Spring of Gihon. Still farther south, below the junction of the valleys of Kidron and Hinnom, was another source of water, the well Enrogel. Warren discovered that the Jebusites had dug a tunnel through the rock, after the manner of those at Gezer and Megiddo, which drew water from the cavern into which the Spring of Gihon emptied, bringing it under the mound Ophel into a deep recess some forty feet below the surface. This reservoir was approached by means of a vertical shaft, and it was comparatively easy for the inhabitants to lower vessels into the recess and obtain whatever water was needed.[1]

While it would not have been impossible to gain access to the fortress by this route, it would have presented formidable obstacles to a raiding party. It is not necessary to argue for such a procedure, however, for Ugaritic studies have shown that the word translated "gutter" or "watershaft" is a Canaanite word meaning "hook." Thus access to the city was gained by means of grappling-irons, scaling-hooks, and other devices of a similar nature. Excavations at Zion, the lower eastern hill of Jerusalem, unearthed a stout stone wall in which a large breach had been made, probably dating back to the time of David.

Jerusalem was formally established as the capital of the Hebrew nation, and

Part of a Jebusite wall in Jerusalem, excavated in the twentieth century.

became known as the "City of David." Being outside tribal jurisdiction, it owed loyalty to the king alone, and in its early stages it was a comparatively small city of about eight acres, populated by the personal followers of David. The new ruler applied his acumen to religious considerations as well as to national and social matters, taking an important step towards centralizing Hebrew religion in Jerusalem by transferring the survivors of the Nob massacre to his stronghold, and erecting a tabernacle to house the Ark. This sacred cult object was brought to its new resting place in procession, and David performed an ecstatic dance before the company, much to the disgust of his refined wife Michal.

Decline of Philistine Power

The growth of the young kingdom was regarded with some misgivings by the Philistines, who invaded the territory on two occasions with the intention of reducing the stronghold of Jerusalem. But David outmaneuvered them, and followed up his victories by the invasion of Philistia, in which Gath fell to his forces (I Chron. 18:1). Having nullified the military threat of Philistine power, he turned his attention to the other inveterate enemies of Israel, the nations of Transjordan. By combining military conquest with skillful diplomacy, David was able to extend the boundaries of his kingdom northward to central Syria and to the Euphrates valley in the northeast (II Sam. 8). The Philistines were reduced to the status of tributaries, and the accumulation of booty from his conquests made David a rich and powerful ruler. He next applied his energies to the organization of his kingdom and, following Egyptian patterns to some extent, built up a system of administrative officials answerable to himself alone as a means of centralizing authority and restricting the autonomy of the tribes. His army increased in size and efficiency, and was augmented by mercenary troops from Caphtor and elsewhere, who were intensely loyal to him.

David combined gifts of personality with shrewdness of dealing to become the most popular ruler in the history of the Hebrew monarchy. In one respect he epitomized the aspirations of every humble person by his rise to power. Once he was in control, his abilities were such that he managed to placate most of his opponents and establish political alliances of far-reaching importance. His basic kindness of heart was illustrated by the way in which he dealt with Mephibosheth, the crippled son of Jonathan, in restoring to him the estate of Saul and furnishing him with supplies at government expense. Such a leader inspired loyalty and generosity in his followers, resulting in such gestures as that of Joab at Rabbah-Ammon, which gave to David the honor of capturing the city (II Sam. 12:27).

Unrest in David's Household

But while David displayed great ability in establishing the growing Hebrew kingdom, he proved to be less successful in the ordering of his own household. Although his sons followed the current pattern of fratriarchal organization whereby the eldest was chief of the brothers and the second son was his immediate inferior,[2] there was a good deal of strife and unrest in the family as a whole. Matters came to a head when Amnon, the firstborn son, conceived an amorous attachment for his half sister Tamar, and violated her without requesting permission to marry her. For this he was subsequently killed by Absalom, the full brother of Tamar, who was then forced to flee to the kingdom of Geshur, from which his mother had come.

These events assumed an even greater significance than might be apparent on the surface if the matriarchate exercised any degree of influence in Palestine during the early monarchy. If such were the case, the action of Amnon in dishonoring Tamar need not be interpreted as the outcome of lustful speculation, but rather as a carefully planned attempt to seize the throne. Furthermore, the fact that Tamar pleaded as she did (II Sam. 13:13) might indicate that the marriage of Amnon to Tamar would have been permitted by King David, in accordance with the ancient custom that allowed considerable latitude when marriage to paternal relatives was being undertaken. While David had succeeded in establishing and organizing the kingdom, he failed to stabilize the position of the royal family in Israel by neglecting to make adequate provision for regulated hereditary succession.

David's Campaigns

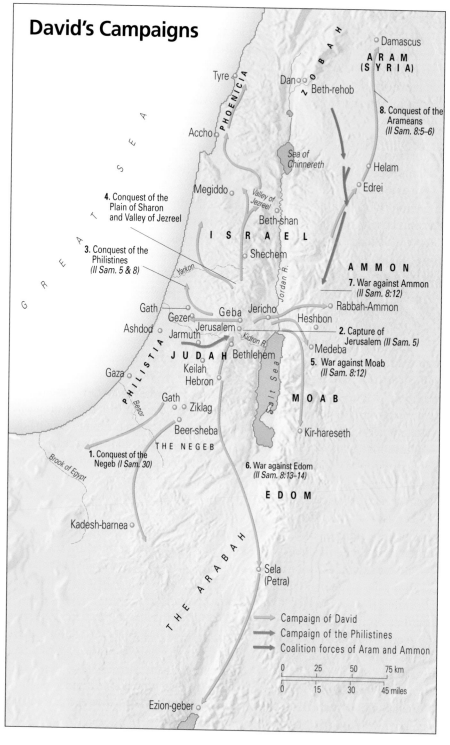

Damascus

A R A M
(S Y R I A)

Tyre

Dan
Beth-rehob

8. Conquest of the
Arameans
(II Sam. 8:5–6)

Accho

PHOENICIA

Sea of
Chinnereth

Helam

Megiddo
Valley of
Jezreel

Edrei

4. Conquest of the
Plain of Sharon
and Valley of Jezreel

Beth-shan

I S R A E L

3. Conquest of the
Philistines
(II Sam. 5 & 8)

Shechem

Yarkon

A M M O N

7. War against Ammon
(II Sam. 8:12)

Gath

Geba
Jericho

Rabbah-Ammon

Gezer

Ashdod

Jarmuth

Jerusalem

Kidron R.

Heshbon

2. Capture of
Jerusalem (II Sam. 5)

J U D A H Bethlehem

Medeba

Gaza

Keilah

Hebron

5. War against Moab
(II Sam. 8:12)

Gath

Ziklag

M O A B

Beer-sheba

THE NEGEB

Kir-hareseth

1. Conquest of the
Negeb (I Sam. 30)

6. War against Edom
(II Sam. 8:13–14)

Brook of Egypt

E D O M

Kadesh-barnea

Sela
(Petra)

THE ARABAH

Campaign of David
Campaign of the Philistines
Coalition forces of Aram and Ammon

0	25	50	75 km
0	15	30	45 miles

Ezion-geber

Joab, the crafty commander of the royal forces, realized the dangers inherent in the situation that arose from the death of Amnon at the hands of Absalom, and he enlisted a woman from Tekoa to help in effecting a reconciliation between David and the fugitive Absalom. With characteristic Oriental skill the woman applied a fictitious family situation to the crisis that confronted David, and by this means persuaded the king to pardon Absalom.

Intrigue in the Kingdom

The decision was to have unhappy consequences, for Absalom was as handsome and popular as his father had been in earlier days, and he was capitalizing upon this to build up a following among the people. Some time after his return, Absalom assembled the malcontents of Judah and then marched on Hebron, forcing David and his household to flee across the Jordan. Some of the foreign mercenary troops David had employed demonstrated their loyalty to him at this juncture. Under their commander Ittai of Gath they insisted upon serving his interests in the emergency, however precarious the situation might be, and would brook no argument to the contrary (II Sam. 15:19ff.), despite the pleas of David.

During his flight the exile king was met by Ziba, servant of Mephibosheth, who told him that his master was now disloyal to the house of David, and was preparing to seize the throne of Judah. For this crafty tale Ziba was rewarded by David with the landed property of his master, which was subsequently reapportioned when the truth was discovered (II Sam. 19:24ff.). Even more serious a situation for the unity of the nation arose from the reproach Shimei the Benjaminite hurled at the fleeing king. Shimei was of the same tribe as the defunct Saul, and he felt that David had usurped the royal prerogatives in assuming the kingship. It is a singular tribute to the magnanimity of David that he was later able to forgive Shimei when he met him on his return to Jerusalem (II Sam. 19:16ff.).

Ahitophel, the adviser to David who had espoused the cause of Absalom in the revolt, advised the latter to possess the harem his father had abandoned in his flight, so as to demonstrate his supremacy. He further requested permission to assemble a large fighting force and pursue David before he could rally support and crush the revolt. Other advice prevailed, however, and in despair Ahitophel committed suicide (II Sam. 17:23). During this time David was receiving regular intelligence reports from the priests of the sanctuary in Jerusalem, and when he felt that he had sufficient military backing, he organized his forces against an impending attack by Absalom. The armed strength of Judah was deployed by Joab near Mount Ephraim, while the aged David waited in Mahanaim for news of the battle. In the engagement that followed, the Israelites suffered heavy losses and Absalom was forced to flee. His luxuriant hair became

Excavations at Megiddo have revealed the remains of stables and hitching posts used by Israelite chariot forces.

entangled in a low tree, and when Joab arrived on the scene he slew Absalom, despite orders from David to the contrary.

The narratives that tell of the way in which the sad news was brought to David, and the profound emotional reaction that overtook the aged ruler, are among the most dramatic and expressive in the Hebrew Bible. When Joab could see that the feelings of David for his dead son threatened to turn triumph into defeat and lower the morale of the troops, he rebuked David sternly, and persuaded him to think in terms of victory. David then returned to Jerusalem, and absolved Mephibosheth, who disclaimed the slightest thought of disloyalty, and Shimei, who had previously stoned David and his men when they were in flight.

Unrest Among the Tribes

It soon became apparent that the tribes of Israel and the people of Judah were by no means at peace with one another. Rivalry broke out, and Sheba, a Benjaminite, revolted, backed by popular feeling among the northern tribes. David had nominated Amasa, the cousin of Joab, as commander of his forces in succession to Joab, despite the fact that he had supported Absalom in the earlier revolt. He failed to take immediate punitive action against Sheba, however, and Joab murdered him out of revenge (II Sam. 20) and disbanded his forces. A famine followed this abortive revolt, and it was blamed on the slaughter of the Gibeonites by Saul at an earlier period. To effect proper satisfaction, David surrendered seven descendants of the house of Saul and the Gibeonites put them to death, after which the famine ended. David recovered the bodies for burial, and also obtained the remains of Saul and Jonathan, which were interred in the family grave. When a revival of Philistine aggression took place, David assigned the conduct of affairs to some of his most valiant warriors, with gratifying success.

Perhaps with the thought of conscription, taxation, or a large-scale *corvée* in mind, the aged David ordered a census of the nation to be taken, much against the advice of Joab, to whom the execution of the task was committed. Apparently the motive was not of the highest order, as David himself subsequently discovered (II Sam. 24:10), and God offered him a choice of punishments. David wisely selected one that placed him solely within Divine mercy.

The Last Days of David

The final days of the once virile ruler were a pathetic picture of senility. A young woman named Abishag was chosen to nurse the enfeebled king, who was by now an invalid and unable to exercise rule. Adonijah, the fourth son of David, plotted to seize the throne and supplant the favored Solomon, son of Bath-sheba. Joab was persuaded to cast in his lot with Adonijah, who also received the support of Abiathar the priest. But a more powerful coalition that supported Solomon was headed by Zadok the priest and Nathan the prophet, who persuaded Bath-sheba to go to David and tell him of the way in which Adonijah was usurping the kingdom. This was done, and the testimony of Bath-sheba was confirmed independently by Nathan, much to the alarm of David, who ordered Solomon to be crowned king in Gihon. When news of this event came to Adonijah, he fled to the sanctuary in terror, but was allowed to go home unharmed.

Finally the life of the aged ruler drew to a close, and after giving a solemn charge to Solomon he died and was buried in his capital. The personality of David had exercised a profound influence over the young Hebrew nation, and he remained its ideal king ever after. During his lifetime he had laid the foundation of a realm that was to become increasingly prosperous under his son Solomon, and despite occasional lapses of character as in the Bath-sheba incident, his ideals for the development of the kingdom were those of the ancient covenant of Moses. What he lacked in consistency was remedied by a simplicity and earnestness of character that at once made him generous in victory and resolute in defeat. His poetic compositions, which set a pattern for subsequent psalmists, remain as a monument to the spirituality of this towering personality who guided the infant nation through the early stages of its growth.

Model reconstruction of the ancient Israelite stronghold of Megiddo, built to dominate the valley of Jezreel.

The Reign of Solomon

Following the death of David, Solomon immediately consolidated his hold on the throne, and again there is some evidence that the influence of the matriarchate was still being felt. In this connection the position of Abishag is of some interest since, although her relationship to David was primarily that of a nurse rather than a marital partner, she appears to have been recognized after the death of David as having, to some extent at least, a claim on the throne. This is evident from the indignant reply of Solomon to the request by Adonijah, presented through Bath-sheba, that he be given Abishag as his wife (I Kings 2:17), possession of whom would imply right of succession to the throne. To Solomon, this threat to his kingly position could only be removed at the expense of breaking an earlier oath to spare the life of Adonijah, with the result that the latter was put to death for his indiscretion. Joab, the faithful servant of David, was also killed for offering allegiance to Adonijah in his attempt to seize power, while the priest Abiathar was banished to Anathoth for his part in the intrigue. Shimei, who had been ordered to live in Jerusalem under the surveillance of the authorities, violated his parole after three years, and when he returned to the city he also was put to death.

As a young man Solomon was of a profoundly religious disposition, and like the Sumerian *ensi* Gudea of Lagash he received oracles from God in the form of dreams. He was a person of great intellectual ability who became legendary at a comparatively early age. He was credited with a great many poetic compositions, and was particularly adept at crystallizing the manifold aspects of life in the form of literary proverbs, a practice that was also popular in Egyptian court circles at that time. In a day when contemporary rulers were scarcely renowned for their intellectual abilities, his prowess excited the curiosity of people from far and near, and the visit of the queen of Sheba was typical of this.

Probably with political as well as other considerations in view, Solomon married an Egyptian princess, who came to live at his court. This in itself is an indication that Egypt was in a comparatively weak state, since several centuries earlier the women of Egypt had been flatly denied permission to leave their native land in order to marry foreigners. Under the rule of David, Israel had increased in influence, while Egypt was declining, and Solomon was beginning to reap the benefits of the policy his father had pursued. He continued the process of diminishing tribal authority by establishing twelve administrative districts, each of which was to be responsible for supporting the royal household for one month of each year. These districts replaced the traditional tribal pattern to a large extent, and were controlled by governors who stood high in the royal favor.

Remains of an Israelite Chalcolithic temple at Megiddo.

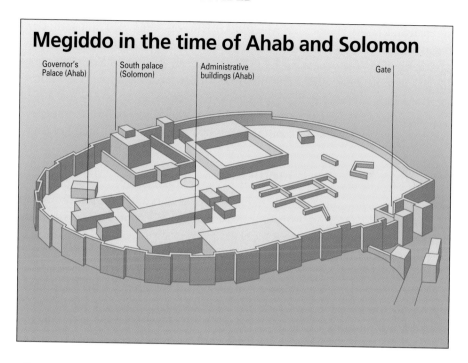

Megiddo in the time of Ahab and Solomon

| Governor's Palace (Ahab) | South palace (Solomon) | Administrative buildings (Ahab) | Gate |

Campaigns in Syria

In order to secure the borders of his kingdom, Solomon engaged in a series of military campaigns. One of these expeditions was launched against Hamath on the River Orontes in Syria, some one hundred and twenty miles north of Damascus. Hamath had been a flourishing city under the Hittites, and recent excavations there have uncovered a great many Hittite inscriptions. The region was well irrigated, and as such was suitable for the "store cities" of Solomon (II Chron. 8:4). An increasing source of trouble was the Aramean dynasty of Hadad the Edomite, who was attempting to free the Edomite people from the control of Israel.

Accordingly Rezon, the general of Hadad, seized control of Damascus, and in an attempt to check the threat posed by this move Solomon fortified the ancient Bronze Age city of Hazor. Excavations there have shown that in the reign of Solomon it was a center for chariotry, and some of the hitching posts going back to that period have been recovered. The Lebanon region was similarly fortified, and to guard against Edomite raiding parties Solomon protected the flow of copper and other goods from the port of Ezion-geber northward through the Arabah.

Whereas David had refused to employ chariots, Solomon saw their value as a military weapon, and he built up a number of divisions that were stationed in strategic positions throughout his kingdom. These fortified towns included

Jerusalem, Gezer, Hazor, and Megiddo (I Kings 9:15ff.), and archaeological excavations at these sites have uncovered the remains of chariot enclosures and stables. At Megiddo, the level IV B contained a group of stables that could have accommodated about five hundred horses. There is some doubt, however, as to whether this level belongs to the time of Solomon or Ahab of Israel. The structure of the masonry in Megiddo corresponds to the description in I Kings 7:12, and may have been the result of Tyrian architectural influence.

Solomon and the Phoenicians

Solomon took advantage of the decline in Egyptian and Assyrian power to expand the economic interests of his vast realm. One of his first political acts was to confirm the alliance that had existed between David and Hiram, king of Tyre. The Israelites had never shown any desire to attack the powerful fortresses of the Phoenician coast, and the ratification of a treaty of friendship with Hiram had the effect of placing the economic wealth of the maritime kingdom at the disposal of Solomon without the effort and risk of a military campaign. The domestication of the camel as a beast of burden had revolutionized the caravan trade throughout the Near East, making it possible to transport much heavier loads over longer distances. Since Solomon controlled the frontier districts of Transjordan, he had an actual monopoly of the entire caravan trade between Arabia and Syria.

From this commercial activity Solomon derived a great deal of revenue, partly by exacting tolls and partly by engaging in trade with other nations. He built a large navy, which was based at Ezion-geber, and was manned by Phoenician sailors. It carried the products of Palestine to the ports of the East and brought back gold, silver, and other luxury commodities (I Kings 10:22). His control of the sea routes enabled Solomon to import horses from Asia Minor and chariots from Egypt, which he then sold at a fixed price. He also exploited the rich mineral resources of the Arabah, and obtained Phoenician workmen to supervise the mining and smelting of copper around Ezion-geber and in parts of the Jordan valley.

The furnaces these technicians and artisans constructed were discovered by Glueck in 1938 at Ezion-geber, and proved to be excellent examples of tenth-century-B.C. copper refineries.[3] The Phoenicians had acquired considerable experience in the construction of furnaces, and they located the Solomonic ore refineries in the best possible position when they erected them at Ezion-geber (Tell el-Kheleifeh) so as to take the greatest advantage of natural contours. The place was situated between the hill country of Sinai and the rocky plateau of Edom, and as a result it received the full force of the howling windstorms that swept down the Wadi Arabah from the north.

When the site was excavated, an unusual building was found at the north-

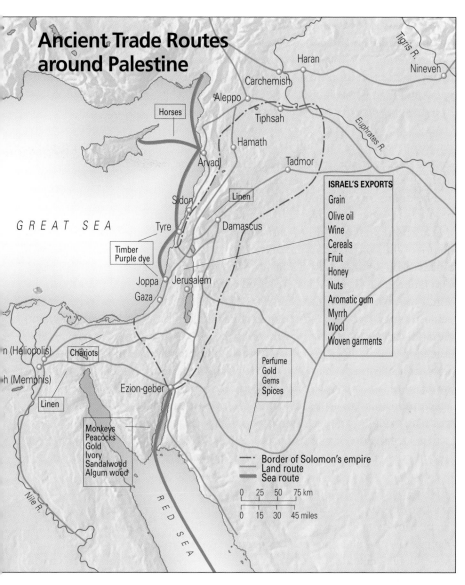

Ancient Trade Routes around Palestine

Haran
Nineveh
Carchemish
Aleppo
Horses
Tiphsah
Hamath
Arvad
Tadmor
Sidon
Linen
GREAT SEA
Tyre
Damascus
Timber
Purple dye
Joppa
Jerusalem
Gaza
n (Heliopolis)
Chariots
h (Memphis)
Ezion-geber
Linen
Monkeys
Peacocks
Gold
Ivory
Sandalwood
Algum wood
Nile R.
Tigris R.
Euphrates R.
RED SEA

ISRAEL'S EXPORTS
Grain
Olive oil
Wine
Cereals
Fruit
Honey
Nuts
Aromatic gum
Myrrh
Wool
Woven garments

Perfume
Gold
Gems
Spices

--- Border of Solomon's empire
=== Land route
▬▬ Sea route

0   25   50   75 km
0   15   30   45 miles

west corner of the mound, and on being completely exposed its north wall was found to be entirely blank except for two horizontal rows of holes. These were linked to a series of air ducts that ran through the center of the main walls and were connected to the upper row of holes so as to form flues. To smelt the ore, the laborers placed it in crucibles inside the smelter, and then lit a fire of brush or wood under the container of ore. The wind blowing down the rift valley was caught in the flues and directed to the fire, which became intensely hot even when using small amounts of fuel and smelted the ore into ingots that were shipped elsewhere for manufacture into various kinds of articles.

While it is probable that copper ore was brought from Sardinia or Spain to Ezion-geber for smelting, there were certainly sufficient deposits of copper and iron in the soft sandstone outcroppings to allow mining to be undertaken there in the days of Solomon. The excavators found the remains of several small furnaces at Tell el-Kheleifeh near the places where the ore had been mined, and from the presence of numerous slag heaps it would seem that considerable processing of ore had taken place at the time the refineries were built. Near the slag heaps were the ruins of the foundry rooms and the living quarters of the miners themselves. From the austere nature of the latter it appears that many of those who worked at Ezion-geber were slaves.[4]

The emphasis Solomon placed upon the mining industry of the Arabah resulted in copper becoming his principal export commodity, and the monopoly he exercised guaranteed him substantial profits. It was probably the serious nature of the competition for Near Eastern trade that prompted the queen of Sheba (Saba) to undertake a journey of about twelve hundred miles by camel. Oriental canons of politeness assigned cultural and intellectual reasons for the visit, but the success of the venture (I Kings 10:1, 2, 10) gives reason for supposing that practical issues involving commercial treaties and the demarcation of trading zones were also very much to the fore. There is every reason to give credence to the historicity of the Biblical narrative concerning the queen of Sheba, for although queens were not prominent in the history of southern Arabia after the sixth century B.C., cuneiform inscriptions have been found which indicate that, especially in northern Arabia, tribal confederacies were frequently ruled by queens from the ninth to the seventh centuries B.C.[5]

The expansion of economic life in Israel and the increased burden of central government administration made the imposition of direct taxation a necessity for the life of the nation. This took the form of the *corvée* or forced labor, special levies, tribute in weighed silver, the current medium of exchange, or gifts of the staple produce of the land. Originally the *corvée* had been intended for the non-Israelite inhabitants of the land, but the ambitious nature of the commercial and building projects Solomon was promoting demanded the energies of the Israelites in the *corvée* also. Forced labor was organized in such a way that ten thousand men were at work each month in the mines, forests, or cities, under conditions that were little removed from slavery. The discontent this produced among those who treasured the freedom of the nomadic life was augmented by the increasing control that was exercised over all levels of society by the officials of the central government. The standing army, lavishly equipped with costly horses and iron-fitted chariots, proved to be a substantial and continuing drain upon public funds, while the expansion of the royal household made for increasing burdens of taxation upon the nation as a whole, and particularly upon the peasants.

An important piece of written evidence from this period was unearthed at tenth-century-B.C. levels at Gezer. Known as the Gezer Calendar, it comprises a small limestone tablet inscribed in the old Phoenician script. It has been suggested that a schoolboy had written it as part of his writing exercises, but whether this is so or not the tablet gives valuable insights into the agricultural activities that were undertaken in the appropriate months of the year. A translation by W. F. Albright is as follows:

The shedu or winged bull, a popular theme in Assyrian mythology. This five-legged specimen stood over ten feet in height and guarded the gateway to the palace of Ashurnasirpal in Nimrud.

His two months are (olive) harvest; his two months are grain-planting; his two months are late planting; his month is hoeing up of flax; his month is barley-harvest; his month is harvest and festivity; his two months are vine-tending; his month is summer fruit.[6]

Quite aside from the way in which tenth-century-B.C. Israelite agricultural practices are illustrated, the tablet is also important because of the fact that certain linguistic affinities it has with the second book of Samuel enable that composition to be dated with confidence in the tenth century B.C.

Because Solomon failed to increase the agricultural productivity of the country to any great extent, the balance of trade was heavily offset by his ambitious building and economic projects. All available surpluses of Israelite grain and oil were shipped to Phoenicia in exchange for Phoenician men and materials. Since agricultural productivity in Israel was barely sufficient to meet domestic needs, Solomon quickly incurred a debit balance of trade with Tyre by following this policy, and encouraged the spread of inflation in his kingdom. Some attempt to remedy the situation was made when Solomon agreed to cede to Hiram twenty towns in Galilee as part payment for goods and services received (I Kings 9:11).

Solomonic Buildings in Jerusalem

The most spectacular of the public works Solomon undertook were to be found in Jerusalem. He repaired the damage done to the city walls when David had captured the fortress from the Jebusites, and he erected a defensive station, known as the Millo, at the northern end of the old city.[7] Solomon then drew heavily upon Phoenician skill in the designing and construction of a series of buildings, of which the Temple was one. The plan of this building was characteristically Phoenician, and similar sanctuaries built between 1200 and 900 B.C. have been unearthed in northern Syria, particularly at Tell Tainat (Hattina).

Within a short time the Temple eclipsed all other religious shrines among the Hebrew people. It formed part of a group of buildings, and took seven years to erect as against thirteen for the construction of the royal palace. This discrepancy would suggest that the Temple may have served originally as a royal chapel. The building itself was a narrow rectangular limestone structure, about thirty-five yards long and ten yards wide. It stood on a larger platform in a manner somewhat reminiscent of Babylonian shrines. There were two landings in the flight of steps that led to the entrance of the Temple, while in the portico to the right and left were the two free-standing pillars of burnished copper known as Jachin and Boaz. Columns of this sort were a common architectural feature of temples in Syria during the first millennium B.C., and in later centuries they were to be seen in Assyrian and western Mediterranean shrines also. The purpose of the columns in the Temple of Solomon is by no means clear, but they probably served as huge cressets or fire altars.

Sir Austen Layard oversees the excavation of Ashurnasirpal's palace at Nimrud in the mid-nineteenth century.

Beyond the portico lay the main chamber or Holy Place, extending into the Temple for a distance of about twenty yards. The floor was made of stone, on which a covering of cypress wood was laid, and the chamber itself was lined with cedar, decorated with inlaid gold leaf. Beyond the Holy Place lay the Holy of Holies, in which stood two cherubim, fashioned from olive wood and overlaid with gold. This latter was a characteristic Syro-Phoenician decoration, and may have been a representation of a winged sphinx where it occurred in pagan temples. The Ark rested in the Holy of Holies, and was overshadowed by the symbolic presence of the Lord. The furnishings of the Temple far exceeded the moderate fittings of the wilderness Tabernacle, and show a marked indebtedness to Phoenician religious theory and practice. The large metal basin ("molten sea") that replaced the laver of the Tabernacle and stood between the porch and the altar of the Temple appears in particular to have had mythological associations.[8]

When the Temple had been completed it was dedicated with appropriate ceremony, and the priests, Levites, and singers who had ministered before the Ark in the time of David saw the fulfillment of an inspiration that had been denied the famous father of Solomon. No expenditure of time, money, or skill had been lacking in the construction of the magnificent central shrine of the Israelite nation, and the oration Solomon delivered at the feast of the dedication was in every sense worthy of that splendid occasion.

Artist's reconstruction of Solomon's Temple

Molten Sea
(metal basin)

Jachin

Boaz

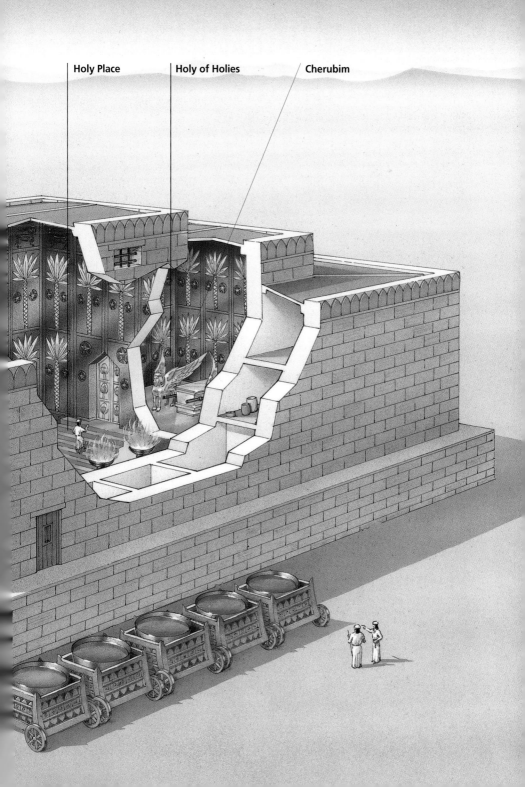

Holy Place   Holy of Holies   Cherubim

Last Days of Solomon

The later life of Solomon was marked by religious apostasy and indulgence in polygamy. The wives and consorts who were brought into the royal household continued the worship of their native deities, for whom shrines and priests were often made available in Jerusalem (I Kings 11:7). Prolonged expenditures on a lavish scale had sown seeds of dissension among the populace for a number of years, while outside the kingdom, Rezon, the vigorous founder of the Damascus dynasty, proved to be an increasing source of trouble in the later days of Solomon.

The death of the latter removed from the scene a colorful personality who in his lifetime had transformed the concept of kingship from the idea of charismatic or divinely inspired leadership current in the days of the early monarchy to that of typical Oriental despotism. The strain this process placed upon the internal economy of the nation was not alleviated by the fact that the sources of national income had been diminishing for some time prior to the death of Solomon, whereas government expenditures continued at a high level.

Division of the Kingdom

When Rehoboam, the son of Solomon, came to the throne, he was confronted with an economic crisis of a particularly grave nature. He presented himself at Shechem for acceptance by the ten northern tribes, who were keenly interested in whatever proposals he had to make for the future conduct of national life. They had as their spokesman the former chief of the *corvée* in the north, a man named Jeroboam, who had fled to Shishak, king of Egypt, when Solomon suspected him of fomenting revolt among the enslaved Israelites. The leaders of the ten tribes recalled Jeroboam when Solomon died, and on the accession of Rehoboam it was decided that Jeroboam should present the case on behalf of the northern tribes for a reduction in taxation and relief from the distasteful *corvée*.

But instead of following a policy of alleviating economic distress and reducing the menace of inflation, Rehoboam took the advice of the counselors who wished to see even sterner measures of dictatorship applied to the already heavily burdened nation. As a result, the northern tribes renounced their allegiance to the house of David and formed a separate northern kingdom known as Israel. Their resistance to the regime of Rehoboam was such that he fled for refuge to Jerusalem, whereupon the northern tribes entered into a covenant with Jeroboam, whom they appointed as their ruler.

He was a shrewd man, who was determined to maintain his kingdom independently of the southern tribe of Judah, and to this end he established his capital at Shechem, and subsequently at Tirzah. For political reasons he strengthened the religious influence of the shrines at Dan and Bethel, where he introduced golden calves into the cult worship. Albright and others have held that these were intended to portray an invisible deity mounted upon a young bull of gold,[9] but this view does not take sufficient account of the motives that prompted bull worship. Jeroboam was anxious to provide counter-attractions to the worship of the central shrine in the kingdom of Judah, and he felt that his interests would be served most effectively by the introduction of this form of religious expression into Israel. He was essentially an apostate who established a new, non-Levitical priesthood in his kingdom, and fostered a series of religious festivals that were thoroughly pagan in character. The institution of calf worship was an open abandonment of the Mosaic ideal, and was intended to appeal to people who were already familiar with the Canaanite worship of the bull as a symbol of reproduction. The ancient bull cult of Memphis, which had its roots in the Old Kingdom period of Egypt, exercised a powerful influence over Egyptian and Hebrew thought alike, and there is every probability that Jeroboam had had personal experience of it during his sojourn in Egypt.

Moreover, Jeroboam also maintained fertility-cult groves in Samaria, shrines where the licentious rituals of the Canaanite agricultural deities were observed, and sanctuaries for the worship of Canaanite gods such as the Moabite Chemosh, Milcom, and Ashtoreth. Although he ruled the people of Israel for only about twenty-two years (931/30–910/09 B.C.), he established a tradition of religious apostasy which became the hallmark of the northern kingdom, and which at the outset encountered severe prophetic denunciation (I Kings 14:7ff.).

Shishak in Judah

Despite the fact that the tribe of Judah and the remnants of the tribe of Benjamin remained faithful to Rehoboam, he was seriously handicapped by the lack of economic and military resources. In consequence he was unable to resist the invasion that came from the south in the fifth year of his reign. Taking advantage of the political crisis in Palestine, Sheshonk I of Egypt (945–924 B.C.), the powerful founder of the Twenty-Second Dynasty, invaded the southern kingdom, destroyed several fortresses, and carried off a great many of the golden treasures from the Temple. An account of this campaign was contained on a bas-relief found at Karnak (Thebes), where no less than one hundred and fifty-six Palestinian towns were alleged to have been captured, including Beth-horon, Gibeon, Megiddo and Ajalon.[10] Excavations at Megiddo showed evidences of looting and burning at a level roughly contemporary with the campaign of Sheshonk, and his inscribed mutilated *stele,* which was also recovered there, proved that he had occupied the site.

One of the panels of the Black Obelisk of Shalmaneser III, depicting Israelite captives bringing tribute. The kneeling figure may represent Jehu.

Scribal Methods of Reckoning

The way in which the chronologies of the kings of Israel and Judah were compiled in various Old Testament books has provoked a good deal of scholarly discussion in the past. On the basis of apparent internal contradictions, many writers felt that the various lists were almost worthless as historical sources, and it was only as a result of the work of E. R. Thiele that these chronologies have been shown to be thoroughly reliable in character. As was so often the case in Old Testament studies, the scholars looked at the writings of Oriental peoples from a strictly Occidental point of view, and were perplexed when their computations failed to agree with those of the Hebrew scribes.

Thiele showed that the chronological data in question must be examined consistently in terms of ancient scribal methods of reckoning. These involved such devices as accession years, non-accession years, coregencies, and synchronisms, which although comparatively unfamiliar to the Western mind were a regular part of the Near Eastern scene, and were used with consistency and precision by the ancient scribes.

As far as the regal chronologies in the Old Testament are concerned, it appears from the researches of Thiele that the normal principles of computation were employed in differing ways at various periods to produce an internal consistency that harmonizes with the chronological patterns of neighboring states.[11] Thus at the time of the division of the kingdom, Israel followed the non-accession-year system current in Egypt, and continued in this fashion until the

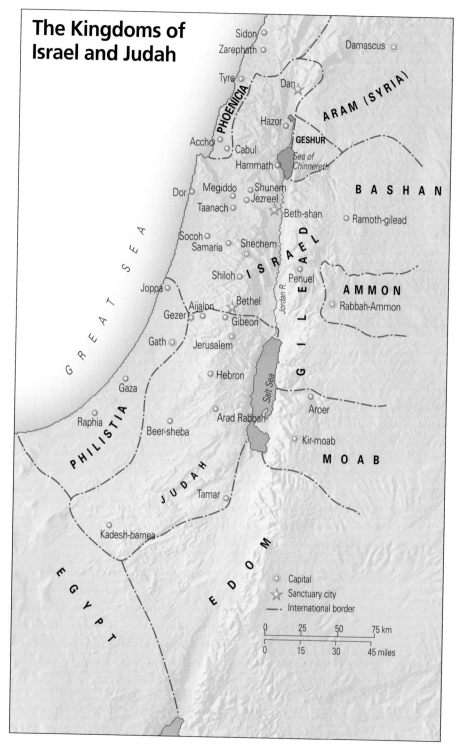

The Kingdoms of Israel and Judah

Sidon
Zarephath
Damascus

Tyre
Dan

PHOENICIA

ARAM (SYRIA)

Hazor

Accho
Cabul
Hammath
GESHUR
Sea of Chinnereth

Dor
Megiddo
Shunem
Jezreel
BASHAN

Taanach
Beth-shan
Ramoth-gilead

Socoh
Samaria
Shechem

ISRAEL

Shiloh
Penuel

Joppa
Gezer
Aijalon
Bethel
Gibeon

GILEAD

Jordan R.

AMMON
Rabbah-Ammon

Gath
Jerusalem

Hebron

Salt Sea

Gaza

Raphia
Beer-sheba
Arad Rabbah
Aroer

PHILISTIA
Kir-moab

JUDAH
MOAB

Tamar

Kadesh-barnea

EGYPT

EDOM

GREAT SEA

◎ Capital
☆ Sanctuary city
— International border

0   25   50   75 km
0   15   30   45 miles

end of the ninth century B.C., when under Jehoash a change was made to the accession-year system in use in Babylonia, and this was employed until the northern kingdom was taken into captivity.

In the time of Rehoboam, Judah used the accession-year method of calculating the length of reigns, and carried on in this fashion until the middle of the ninth century B.C. But from Jehoram to Joash the reigns were reckoned according to the non-accession-year system, while from Amaziah to the end of the history of Judah the accession-year method was employed once more.

Thus it will be evident that at the division of the kingdom Israel and Judah were using different systems of chronological reckoning, but that from the middle of the ninth century to the close of their respective histories both kingdoms utilized the same system of computation, namely, the non-accession method to the beginning of the eighth century B.C., and the accession-year system from that time forward. In the present book most of the dates for the Hebrew kings will be given in double form because the Hebrew year does not coincide with the normal pattern of our civil year.

Growth of Syrian Power

While Sheshonk was subjugating Judah, the Aramean dynasty of Damascus was increasing in strength and becoming the dominant power in Syria. The discovery in 1940 of the inscribed *stele* of Benhadad at a site in northern Syria has given general confirmation to the list of early Syrian rulers mentioned in I Kings 15:18, although the position of Rezon, the founder of the Damascene state, is still uncertain. The growth of Syrian power in the initial stages was encouraged by the hostility that existed between Israel and Judah, and the unrest that characterized the Israelite dynasty itself. When Jeroboam I died (910/09 B.C.), his son Nadab succeeded him for two years, but he was murdered by Baasha of Issachar in the Philistine town of Gibbethon. This took place in the third year of the reign of Asa, king of Judah (911/10–870/69 B.C.), who became king after the death of Abijah (913–911/10 B.C.), the son and successor of Rehoboam. Baasha fortified the town of Ramah, five miles from Jerusalem, as a military outpost threatening the border of Judah (I Kings 15:17), and in desperation Asa appealed to Benhadad of Syria for assistance, sending as a bribe some of the remaining Temple treasures. Benhadad responded to this entreaty by driving Baasha back to his capital city Tirzah, while Asa marched on Ramah and demolished it. He salvaged material from the ruins of Ramah and with it he constructed two other fortresses in the kingdom of Judah. This gesture of friendship by Benhadad was to his political advantage, for by his intervention he gained control of the prosperous caravan routes to the ports of Phoenicia, enabling him to increase the wealth and prosperity of his capital city Damascus, just as Solomon had done for Judah in an earlier generation.

Rise of Omri

When Baasha died (886/85 B.C.), his son Elah reigned for two years, and then was assassinated in Tirzah by Zimri (I Kings 16:9ff.), an ambitious chariotry commander, who then assumed the rule. Omri, the general of the army under Elah, was engaged in a campaign against the Philistines when Elah was slain, and on hearing the tidings he returned immediately to Tirzah. After a rule of only seven days, Zimri committed suicide, and the crisis that was precipitated led to a period of civil war. Four years later (880 B.C.), Omri gained control of the situation and established a new dynasty (I Kings 16:23), the *Bit-Humri* (House of Omri) of Assyrian cuneiform records.

He moved the capital of Israel to the hill of Samaria, which had been unoccupied until this time, and built strong fortifications around it.[12] He endeavored to offset the Syrian control of commerce by establishing trading alliances with Phoenicia, and arranged a marriage between Ahab, his son and successor, and Jezebel, daughter of the king of Tyre. To protect his borders, Omri attacked Moab and gained control of the northern part of the kingdom. The celebrated Moabite Stone, which was discovered in 1868, spoke of the part Omri played in the campaign against Moab:

> Omri, king of Israel . . . oppressed Moab many days because Chemosh was angry with his land. And his son succeeded him, and he also said, "I will oppress Moab."[13]

Although Omri developed Samaria as a commercial center, the economy of the nation prospered at the expense of the small landowners and the peasants, who were forced to give up their holdings of land and property to the wealthy upper classes. While commercial enterprises were flourishing, the artisans were becoming increasingly poor, and were living under conditions that were little removed from servility. The domestic and foreign policies of Omri were continued by his son Ahab (874/73–853 B.C.), who endeavored to strengthen his kingdom, against ultimate Syrian invasion. The fortifications and the splendid royal palace of Samaria were completed in his reign, and a number of fortresses, including Jericho, were reinforced also at this time. He entered into an alliance with Judah in order to protect his southern border, and the treaty resulted in the marriage of his daughter Athaliah to Jehoram (Joram), the crown prince of Judah (II Kings 8:18). His diplomatic links with Tyre brought the worship of Melkart, the Tyrian Baal, into vogue in Israel, and for this apostasy he was sternly rebuked by the prophet Elijah, who foretold a punitive drought and famine.

After nearly four years of this privation, Elijah demonstrated in a dramatic encounter with the priests of this orgiastic Baal cult the moral and spiritual superiority of the God of Israel (I Kings 18), and as a result of the slaughter of the Baal priests he brought upon himself the fury of Jezebel. The state of the national economy was reflected in the corruption that enabled Ahab to obtain the vineyard of Naboth (I Kings 21), an injustice that sealed the doom of Ahab and Jezebel. The prophet Elijah followed the example of Samuel in endeavoring to relate the will of God to the contemporary political and social situation. These two men were the early representatives of a prophetic tradition that was unique in the annals of ancient Near Eastern life. Reference has already been made to the astrologers of Babylonia and Ugarit, who purported to forecast the trend of events under particular circumstances, and who typified prophetism outside the Israelite nation. The Hebrew prophets differed from these soothsayers and diviners in that they scorned magic, denied the authority and existence of pagan deities, and sought consciously to mediate the Divine will to a nation that was thought of in theocratic terms.

Hebrew Prophetism

Of the Hebrew names applied to the prophets as representatives of a spiritual movement in Israel, the term *nabhi'* was undoubtedly the most widely used. Originally it was thought to have been derived from a root indicating a "speaker," but it is now known that its basic meaning is "to call." The *nabhi'* was thus an individual who had been called by God for some specific purpose, and who thus stood in a particular spiritual relationship with Him.[14] The prophet was essentially a charismatic figure who was authorized to speak to the Israelites on behalf of their God. Before the time of Samuel such individuals were generally designated as a "man of God," and in the time of Saul and David this expression was apparently synonymous with *nabhi'*. The utterances of the Hebrew prophets were the direct consequence of their spiritual relationship with God, and in essence they comprised variations on the theological and covenantal themes enshrined in the Law. In point of fact there is no single prophetic doctrine that was not already present, at least in embryonic form, in the Torah, thus making the prophets commentators rather than doctrinal pioneers.

Frequently the Hebrew prophets were commissioned by God from the ranks of the people, as with Elisha and Amos, to warn the nation of the punishments that would follow upon persistent wickedness. They were resolute in emphasizing the holiness of God, and their criticisms of contemporary morality were undertaken in an attempt to point the way towards a sound religious life for the nation. On occasions it fell to their lot to reveal the Divine counsels in connection with some particular situation, as may be illustrated by reference to Elijah (I Kings 18:17ff.), Amos (4:4ff.), Jeremiah (26:12ff.), and Ezekiel (27:2ff.). At all times they spoke with that sense of authority which was inseparable from their conviction of Divine inspiration. While the prophets often dealt with contemporary political, social, and religious issues in their utterances, they were also acutely conscious of the fact that the future is inherent in the present. In consequence they experienced little difficulty in surveying the more distant historical scene and predicting the outcome of current political and social patterns with remarkable accuracy. The modern antithesis between forthtelling and foretelling would therefore have been meaningless to the Hebrew prophets.

The earliest prophets, Samuel, Elijah, and Elisha, conveyed their messages by means of oral utterances, which were probably recorded fairly soon after the events themselves had occurred. But in the century following the death of Elisha, an important development in Hebrew prophetism took place with the rise of the literary prophets, represented by Amos, Hosea, Micah, Isaiah, and their successors. While these men exercised the characteristic functions of the oral prophets, they also reduced their inspired messages to written form, in which poetry often occurred as frequently as prose. These literary productions are among the most treasured legacies of the ancient Hebrews, and are an indispensable prerequisite to any study of Israelite history and religion.

The great writing prophets preserved the traditional monotheistic faith of the ancient Hebrews in times when the obligations of the covenant were either ignored or forgotten completely. They emphasized afresh the major themes of the Mosaic law and related them to the contemporary scene. Their intense patriotism never clouded their vision of the Divine purpose for the Chosen People, and although they could grieve for the doom that would inevitably overtake their land and nation, they were never in doubt as to the ultimate triumph of good over evil.

Religious communities such as the "sons of the prophets" were in existence during the days of the oral prophets, and may have consisted of schools or prophetic guilds. Such groups appear to have settled in different parts of Palestine, and were generally found in remote areas. Samuel maintained one of these schools at Ramah (I Sam. 19:20ff.), while others were located at Bethel, Gibeah, and Gilgal. Their members engaged in worship at local shrines (I Sam. 10:5), and accepted payment for their professional services (I Sam. 9:7f.). But the prophetism in which they engaged was of the ecstatic variety, and as such was markedly different from the rational, controlled utterances of the oral and literary prophets. None of the latter was a product of the prophetic guilds, and after the death of Elisha the "sons of the prophets" gradually disappeared from the recorded historical scene.

Assyria in Palestine

About the year 855 B.C., Benhadad and his allies finally swept down on Samaria (I Kings 20), but were repulsed with heavy losses. The following year, another Syrian attack at Aphek, east of the Sea of Galilee, resulted in a costly defeat for

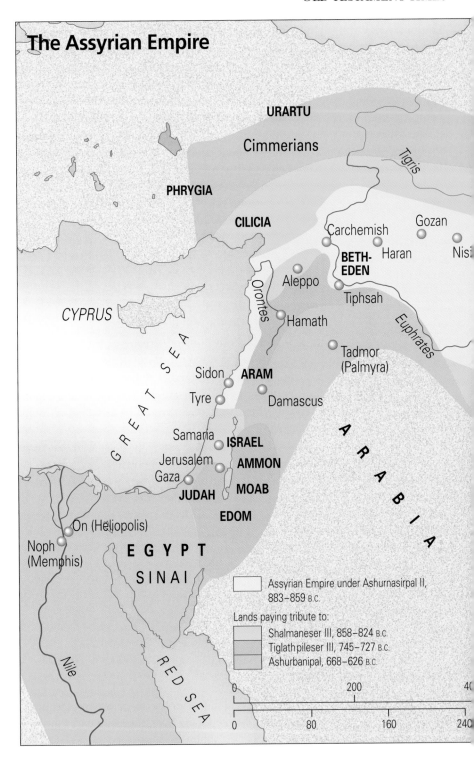

The Assyrian Empire

URARTU

Cimmerians

Tigris

PHRYGIA

CILICIA

Gozan

Carchemish

BETH-EDEN Haran Nisi

Aleppo

Tiphsah

Orontes

Hamath

Euphrates

CYPRUS

Tadmor
(Palmyra)

G R E A T   S E A

Sidon ARAM

Tyre Damascus

Samaria

Jerusalem ISRAEL

Gaza AMMON

JUDAH MOAB

EDOM

A R A B I A

On (Heliopolis)

Noph
(Memphis)

E G Y P T

S I N A I

Nile

R E D   S E A

Assyrian Empire under Ashurnasirpal II,
883–859 B.C.

Lands paying tribute to:

Shalmaneser III, 858–824 B.C.
Tiglath pileser III, 745–727 B.C.
Ashurbanipal, 668–626 B.C.

0		200	4(

0	80	160	240

Benhadad, and the power of Syria might have been broken completely had it not been for the appearance of a powerful Assyrian expedition against Palestine (c. 853 B.C.). Under Ashurnasirpal II (883–859 B.C.) the military power of Assyria reached new heights. The brutality with which the Assyrian campaigns were conducted is indicated in a contemporary inscription:

> I built a pillar over against the city gate, and I flayed all the chief men who had revolted, and I covered the pillar with their skins; some I walled up within the pillar, some I impaled upon the pillar on stakes, and others I bound to stakes round about the pillar. . . .[15]

Shalmaneser III (859–824 B.C.), the son and successor of Ashurnasirpal, brought the might of Assyria to bear on Syria and Palestine, and in the crisis that arose Ahab and Benhadad allied against the common enemy. A full-scale battle was waged at Kharkar on the Orontes River in Syria in 853 B.C., in which huge numbers of Israelite and Syrian infantry and chariots inflicted a decisive defeat upon the Assyrians. In conformity with normal procedure in such instances, Shalmaneser III claimed a great victory, and his Monolith Inscription recorded in exaggerated language a description of this battle, along with other significant events of his reign.[16] The annals stated that Hadadezer (Benhadad) and Ahab the Israelite led the opposing forces, and this fact provides independent confirmation of the ninth-century-B.C. date of Ahab.

The Assyrian defeat had been sufficient to check further military enterprises on their part for several years, and soon

Assyrian relief from Nimrud depicting Ashurnasirpal flanked by an eagle-headed protective spirit c 865 B.C.

the old hostility between Syria and Israel flared up. One important result of this resurgence of animosity was that Ahab was killed while trying to recover Ramoth-gilead from Syrian control. Jehoshaphat, king of Judah and father of Jehoram, husband of Athaliah, assisted Ahab in this campaign, but to no avail (I Kings 22). Ahab was succeeded by Ahaziah (853–852 B.C.), who was forced to send an expedition almost immediately against Mesha, the rebellious vassal king of Moab, who had been defaulting in payments of tribute that had been imposed in the days of David. Ahaziah was injured in an accident that happened shortly before he set out against Mesha, and Elijah foretold his death (II Kings 1:2ff.), which occurred about a year afterwards. Because he left no male successor, his brother Jehoram became ruler of Israel about the year 852 B.C., and reigned for a period of eleven years (852–841 B.C.).

Events in Judah

Jehoram continued the alliance his father Ahab had established with Judah, and he enlisted the aid of Jehoshaphat of Judah in quelling the revolt of the Moabites. Elisha prophesied a remarkable victory for Israel and Judah, and in the battle that followed, the Moabites were cut off and suffered heavy losses (II Kings 3). During the reign of Jehoram the prophet Elisha took an active part in political affairs, and his warnings enabled Jehoram to escape from the grasp of the marauding Syrians. But when the king lapsed into idolatry, he was advised by Elisha that God would punish him at the hands of the Syrians. Shortly after this, Samaria was heavily besieged, and the inhabitants were reduced to cannibalism (II Kings 6:28ff.), but the city was saved when the Syrians mysteriously withdrew in disorder.

Jehoshaphat, king of Judah, died in 848 B.C., after a prosperous reign in which he continued the reforms of his father Asa. He was succeeded by his eldest son Jehoram (Joram), the husband of Athaliah, daughter of Ahab, under whose influence Baal worship revived in Judah (II Kings 8:18). During his reign Jehoram was confronted with an Edomite revolt, and this encouraged a joint invasion of Judah by Arabian and Philistine forces (II Chron. 21:16f.), who sacked the palace and captured his wives and sons, with the exception of Ahaziah, who succeeded him (853 B.C.).

About the year 843 B.C. Benhadad fell sick and was murdered by Hazael, a court official who had been told by Elisha that he would become ruler of Syria (II Kings 8:7ff.). The accession of this usurper was mentioned in an inscription

Relief from Nimrud depicting Ashurnasirpal on military campaign.

of Shalmaneser III from Asshur, "Hazael, son of a nobody, seized the throne."[17] He had reigned only a few months when the throne of Israel was also seized by a usurper in the person of Jehu. This man had been anointed by Elisha (II Kings 9:6) and commissioned to overthrow the dynasty of Ahab and succeed to the throne. His rise to power was hastened when Ahaziah of Judah, the grandson of Ahab and nephew of Ahaziah, the eighth king of Israel, joined with Jehoram of Israel in attacking Hazael of Syria. Jehoram was wounded at Ramoth-gilead, and retreated to Jezreel in order to recuperate. Jehu followed him there and killed him on the very piece of land Ahab had taken by treachery from Naboth. This deed marked the beginning of a drastic purge in Israel, which continued with the slaying of Ahaziah of Judah, the evil queen Jezebel, and the rest of the house of Ahab. The pagan shrines that had been built by Ahab were also demolished, and the Baal priests who had been responsible for conducting the sensuous rituals were put to death.

When her son Ahaziah died, Athaliah seized control of the government and killed all the members of the royal house in Judah except the young prince Jehoash (Joash). He was rescued by his aunt and concealed in the Temple for the six-year period in which Athaliah reigned (841–835 B.C.). At the end of that time Jehoiada the high priest produced Jehoash in the Temple as the lawful king, and when a formal covenant had been ratified Jehoash was anointed king. Athaliah, who was an avid Baal worshiper, arrived at the Temple too late to prevent the anointing, and was slain by command of Jehoiada. The reign of Jehoash brought material prosperity to Judah, and the influence of Baal worship declined. But when Jehoiada died, Jehoash lapsed into idolatry, encouraged a revival of Canaanite worship, and erected a number of pagan religious shrines. Zechariah, the son of Jehoiada, protested at this reversion to idolatry, and was put to death in the Temple court (II Chron. 24:20ff.).

Further Assyrian Attacks: Hazael

In the eighteenth year of his reign (841 B.C.), Shalmaneser III attacked the Syrian coalition, which consisted mainly of Israel, Damascus, and the coastal city-states. Jehu chose to pay tribute to Shalmaneser rather than join in the fight against Assyria, and this internal weakness of the coalition left Hazael to face the full weight of the Assyrian attack. The famous Black Obelisk of Shalmaneser, found in the palace at Nineveh in 1846, depicted a captive kneeling humbly before his overlord and proffering gifts:

> Tribute of Jehu, son of Omri. Silver, gold, a golden bowl, a golden beaker, golden goblets, pitchers of gold, lead, staves for the hand of the king, javelins, I received from him.[18]

Shalmaneser III

Hazael withstood the attack of 841 B.C., and for four years resisted the threat of invasion, after which the Assyrians were compelled to withdraw from Syria to defend their northern borders. Hazael took advantage of the opportunity to extend his territory into Israel, whom he attacked relentlessly in return for their failure to support him in 841 B.C.

When Jehu died in 814/13 B.C., he was succeeded by his son Jehoahaz, who reigned for about fifteen years (814/13–798 B.C.). Throughout this period he was kept in subjugation by Hazael, who compelled him to reduce his armed forces and pay tribute. Israelite territory now comprised little more than the hill country of Ephraim, and Hazael, bent on the expansion of his kingdom, marched south and occupied the Philistine plain. He destroyed Gath and threatened to invade Jerusalem, but Jehoash (Joash), king of Judah, placated him by giving him Temple treasures (II Kings 12:17f.), and remained his vassal until he was murdered by his servants in the Millo, the citadel palace erected by David in Jerusalem.

With the death of Jehoash in 796 B.C., Amaziah his son came to the throne of Judah. He liquidated the murderers of his father, and in order to strengthen his kingdom he hired a large force of Israelite mercenary troops and marched against the Edomites. He won a decisive victory south of the Dead Sea, and occupied Sela, the Edomite capital. His misfortunes began when he honored the pagan gods of Edom in preference to the God of Israel, and continued when, as the result of a rash military challenge to Jehoash, king of Israel, he was defeated at the battle of Beth-shemesh. Jerusalem was plundered and Judah became virtually subject to Israel, thus robbing Amaziah of much of his desired security. As the result of an intrigue he was murdered at Lachish, and was succeeded by his young son Azariah (Uzziah), about 767 B.C., who had been coregent from 791/90 B.C.

The Eighth Century B.C.

The reign of Uzziah was one of great economic prosperity for Judah, and the religion of Jehovah gained the ascendancy over Baal worship. Uzziah developed the agricultural holdings of Judah, and insured the military security of the nation by raising a large army. New defense works were built in Jerusalem and military outposts in Judah were strengthened. Uzziah then engaged in war with the Philistines in the west, and recovered Elath, the important port of the Gulf of Aqabah, from Edomite control. This port had been lost to Edom by Jehoram some eighty years earlier, and on its recapture Uzziah refortified it and made it the headquarters of his foreign trade. The material prosperity of his reign gave Uzziah a sense of pride, and this culminated in an attempt to usurp the functions of the high priest (II Kings 15:5). For this he was punished with leprosy, and on his death (740/39 B.C.) he was buried in a special tomb. The

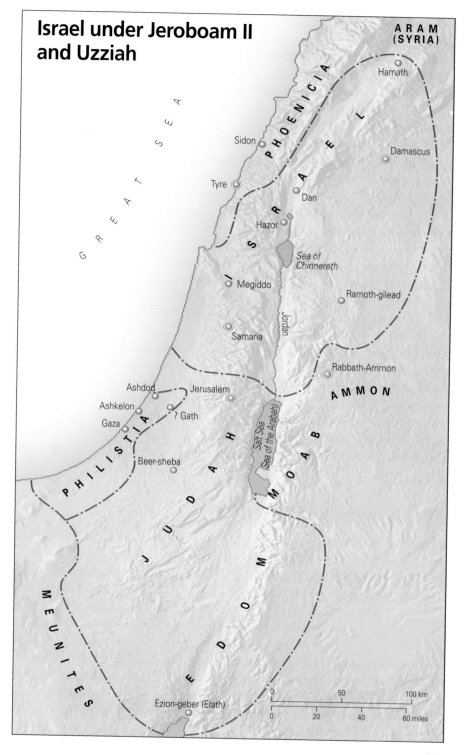

Israel under Jeroboam II and Uzziah

A R A M
(S Y R I A)

Hamath

GREAT SEA

PHOENICIA

Sidon

I S R A E L

Damascus

Tyre

Dan

Hazor

Sea of Chinnereth

Megiddo

Ramoth-gilead

Jordan

Samaria

Rabbath-Ammon

Ashdod

Jerusalem

A M M O N

Ashkelon

? Gath

Gaza

P H I L I S T I A

J U D A H

Salt Sea (Sea of the Arabah)

M O A B

Beer-sheba

M E U N I T E S

E D O M

Ezion-geber (Elath)

0		50		100 km
0	20	40		60 miles

religious ceremonies associated with the occasion probably contributed to the call of Isaiah (Isa. 6:1ff.).

The political ambitions of Hazael of Syria were checked by the rise of Assyrian power in the person of the formidable Adadnirari III (805–782 B.C.), and he was unable to stem the invasion from the east. Israel and Philistia revolted against Hazael and paid tribute to Assyria, while Hazael himself suffered heavy losses, and according to contemporary Assyrian annals also paid large sums of tribute.[19] The Assyrians took no immediate steps to consolidate their territorial gains, and this enabled Israel under Jehoash (Joash), successor of Jehoahaz and the third king of the Jehu dynasty, to regain some of the cities conquered earlier by Hazael. The latter died about the time that Jehoash came to the throne (798 B.C.), and was succeeded by his son Benhadad II. He was no match for the vigorous leadership Jehoash displayed, and Aramean prestige in southern Syria suffered accordingly (II Kings 13:25). By the time Jehoash died (782/81 B.C.), he had recovered much of the territory previously lost to the Aramean regime, and had reduced Judah to the position of a vassal state.

Jeroboam II succeeded Jehoash as king of Israel, and with his accession a period of splendor and prosperity, reminiscent of the days of David, began in the northern kingdom. Benhadad III was forced to defend himself against an attack by Zakir, king of Hamath, who was making a serious bid for power in Syria, and this fact, combined with the weakness of Assyria at this time, removed the threat of warfare in Israel.[20] Jeroboam followed the retreating Syrians and occupied their capital city of Damascus, while subsequent territorial gains restored the northern kingdom to the boundaries of the Davidic realm (II Kings 14:25). The belief that the golden age of the early monarchy had returned was fostered further by the economic prosperity of Judah under the rule of Uzziah, a contemporary of Jeroboam II.

The Corruption of Society

Phoenicia was still the dominant commercial power in the Near East, despite the rise of competition from Greece. Israel derived the benefit of trade relations with Phoenicia from tolls that were levied upon the caravan trade passing through the country. Increased territorial holdings poured wealth into the coffers of Samaria, and the economic evils that had been present in the time of Solomon appeared once more. The rich upper classes had no scruples about the way in which they acquired land and possessions, so that the peasants became increasingly poor and were often deprived of their small holdings in an illegal manner. A desire for luxury caused the simple dwellings of brick to be replaced with buildings of hewn stone, and the ivory decorations for which the palace of Ahab had been famous (I Kings 22:39) were widely copied in the mansions of the rich landowners.

A considerable number of these elaborate ivory pieces were unearthed during the excavations at Samaria, and while the artifacts were not particularly large in size, they demonstrated a high standard of technical proficiency in their manufacture. The influence of Egypt is reflected in the style and subject matter of the carvings, which depict familiar plants and animals of Egypt such as lilies, lotus, papyrus reeds, bulls, lions, and deer. A medallion of singular beauty and delicacy shows the infant Horus seated upon a lotus plant. His left hand is raised to his lips and in his right hand he holds a short flail. Above his head are three symbolic figures, and the whole scene is carved in relief.[21] In general the ivories took the form of small separate panels, which, because of their size, could be inlaid in furniture or used to decorate walls.

Other archaeological discoveries in eighth-century levels at Samaria have confirmed the splendor the Biblical narratives attribute to that period. The strong fortifications that had withstood the Syrian siege (II Kings 6:24ff.) were reinforced on the orders of Jeroboam, and other buildings were erected in the capital, including a magnificent limestone palace flanked by a strong rectangular tower. Excavations at the northern extremity of the palace courtyard revealed the existence of a cemented pool, and it is thought that this may have been the celebrated "Pool of Samaria" in which the armor and bloodstained chariot of Ahab were washed after the burial of the defunct monarch in Samaria (I Kings 22:38).

The well-known Samaritan (or Samarian) ostraca (potsherds) are generally held to date from the early eighth century B.C. (c. 778–770 B.C.), for they exhibit the same type of ancient Hebrew script as that current in the days of the prophet Hosea. The ostraca, recovered from one of the palace storehouses, consist of administrative documents that list royal revenues of wine and oil. One potsherd contains the name of the treasury official to whom the wine was dispatched, the district from which it had come, and the names of the peasants whose taxes had been paid in this manner. But even more significant is the light they throw on contemporary society in Israel. The great increase in wealth and material prosperity of the northern kingdom was due principally to the cessation of hostilities with Syria. These struggles had placed certain limits upon the normal development of agriculture, and had forced the northern peoples away from the poorly defended villages into the comparative security of walled cities. This brought about an urbanizing of what had been a predominantly pastoral community, and in the process the Israelites were introduced to the more unpleasant aspects of city living.

The nature of city life in Palestine during the preexilic period throws some light on this situation. At the time of the Hebrew conquest, the invading Israelites were overawed by the grandeur of the Canaanite cities (cf. Deut. 1:28), unaccustomed as they had been during the wilderness period to sedentary life. Excavations at Canaanite sites have shown that, because of their comparative inexperience in the techniques of building, the Israelites adopted the general architectural styles of the structures in the conquered cities.

At this time the large residences of wealthy Canaanite households were divided up into apartments, in which several Israelite families lived along with some domestic animals. When smaller houses began to be built in the cities, they were generally placed close beside the larger ones without any hint at town planning. Consequently streets as such were seldom laid out in Israelite towns, and in effect comprised the narrow alleys of about seven feet in width that separated the various houses and wound up and down without any particular direction in view.

Pedestrians picked their way carefully along these passages in single file, avoiding the filth underfoot and keeping a respectable distance from such animals as were being led from one part of the city to another. While bigger cities often had spaces reserved for shopkeepers' stalls, the effect was still that of a noisy, cluttered Oriental bazaar. Since few Israelite towns or cities had open spaces within their walls, the merchants generally gathered inside the city gate in order to sell their goods, and this added further to the general congestion.

Old Testament writers seem to have taken for granted the ever-present mud and filth of the city streets (cf. Isa. 5:25; 10:6), which was augmented by broken pottery, fragments of bricks, household garbage, and ashes. In the summer heat the stench became almost unbearable, and the generally unsanitary conditions of city living made epidemic disease a continuous threat.

In time of peace the city population usually exceeded the available accommodation, and during the summer those who were able moved outside the city proper to join the few permanent villagers who lived in small cottages in the nearby fields. They stayed there to sow seed and graze their cattle, and only returned to the city when the onset of winter compelled them to do so. This practice became particularly popular from the ninth century B.C. onwards, when for the first time in their history Israelite cities experienced acute overcrowding. In times of economic distress, when peasants from nearby agricultural regions flocked to the city to obtain some sort of livelihood, the physical, social, and moral problems of city life became particularly severe.

The Economic and Moral Crisis

The dramatic increase of trade and commerce encouraged the rise of a mercantile class, whose principal object seemed to be the rapid acquisition of money. Greed and dishonesty in business cast their shadow upon the prosperous northern kingdom, encouraging a widening of the gap between the rich and the poor. The upper classes lived in selfish luxury, for which only the finest of commercial and agricultural products would suffice. This attitude made heavy demands upon the already impoverished peasants and farmers, and the complete

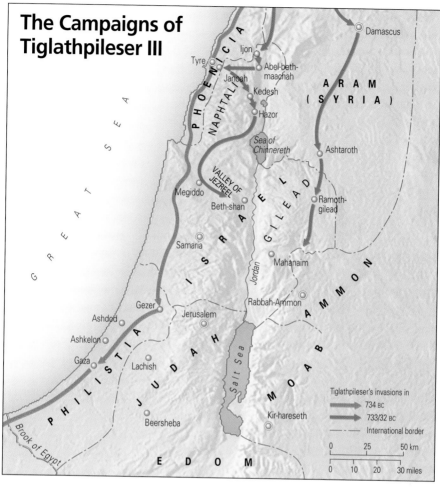

The Campaigns of Tiglathpileser III

Damascus

Ijon

Tyre

Abel-beth-maachah

Janoah

Kedesh

A R A M

(S Y R I A)

Hazor

P H O E N I C I A

N A P H T A L I

Sea of Chinnereth

Ashtaroth

VALLEY OF JEZREEL

Megiddo

Beth-shan

Ramoth-gilead

G I L E A D

S A R A B A H

Samaria

Mahanaim

Jordan

Gezer

Jerusalem

Rabbah-Ammon

A M M O N

Ashdod

Ashkelon

J U D A H

Gaza

Lachish

P H I L I S T I A

Beersheba

Salt Sea

Kir-hareseth

M O A B

Tiglathpileser's invasions in

734 BC

733/32 BC

International border

0   25   50 km

0   10   20   30 miles

Brook of Egypt

E   D   O   M

G R E A T   S E A

indifference the rich merchants and landowners adopted towards them was an ominous echo of an earlier age of material prosperity.

Despite the fact that the mineral resources of the Wadi el-Arabah had been developed by Solomon so that Ezion-geber became an important industrial center, the most significant feature of all Palestinian life was its agriculture. The quiet pastoral existence reflected in the Gezer Calendar (c. 925 B.C.), which outlined the agricultural work normally undertaken in the different months of each year,[22] was typical of the nation, and furnished the assurance of a stable Israelite economy. But when rich landowners began to oppress the peasants and to deprive them of their holdings, they undermined the foundations of their society as a whole. The Samaritan ostraca depicted the exaggerated demands of the wealthy, who used "pure clarified wine" and refined anointing oil, thereby providing independent corroboration of the circumstances that provoked the grim warning given by Amos (6:6) to those in Samaria who "drink wine in bowls, and anoint themselves with the finest oils, but do not grieve over the ruin of Joseph."

Because the lot of the small farmers was becoming increasingly intolerable, there was an inevitable drift from the land to the cities, thus bringing about a further weakening of the general economy. In consequence, the rise of an urban proletariat during the first half of the eighth century B.C. proved to be an important social phenomenon that was to have almost immediate consequences for the well-being of the nation. For men like Amos and Hosea, who were acutely aware of the pressing social problems in Israel, the deterioration of national life was a matter for deep concern and prophetic denunciation. The survival of the northern kingdom could only be assured if "judgment ran down like waters, and righteousness as a mighty stream" (Amos 5:24).

Amos taught that God was supremely righteous, hence any violations of justice or morality could only result in stern punishment. Ruin, not prosperity, was her certain fate if Israel continued apostate, even though she was God's covenant people (Amos 3:2). Hosea agreed with this view of the penalty for national sin (Hos. 5:1–14; 6:4–11), but in a powerful marriage analogy he pleaded tenderly with Israel to forsake her heathen lovers and return in repentance and faith to a loving and merciful God (Hos. 6:1–3; 14:1–3).

The Decline of Israel

The economic and moral inequities that were an integral part of the social pattern during the reign of Jeroboam II were the logical outcome of the pagan religious activities of the people of Israel. Justice and social morality were regarded as commodities of little value, and were swept aside in a wave of corruption that engulfed the nation as a whole. The prophets Amos and Hosea protested vigorously against the debased practices of Baal worship and its implications for the social life of the nation. Amos in particular exposed the extravagance that characterized the way of life in Samaria, and castigated the false values upon which such conduct was based. His denunciations irritated Amaziah, the idolatrous priest at the shrine of Bethel, to the point where he charged Amos with conspiracy against Jeroboam (Amos 7:10ff.). There is little evidence that the king himself was affected by the prophetic utterances of either Amos or Hosea, for the latter was no more successful in persuading Jeroboam and the Israelites to abandon their idolatrous ways than his contemporary had been.

Prophetic predictions that the house of Jeroboam would fall before the sword and the Israelites would be taken into captivity began to be fulfilled after Jeroboam died in 753 B.C. His son Zechariah, who succeeded him, reigned for six confused months, after which he was assassinated by Shallum, a claimant to the throne. With the death of Zechariah the dynasty of Jehu came to an end, and ushered in a period of civil unrest and strife similar to that which had

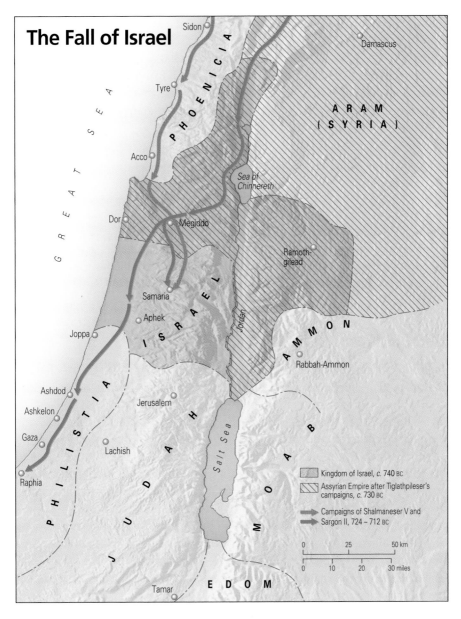

The Fall of Israel

marked the beginning of the house of Jehu. Shallum reigned for one month, and then was killed by Menahem, governor of Tirzah, the older capital of Israel, who seized the throne and crushed all opposition to his regime. But whatever military ambitions he might have entertained were thwarted by a resurgence of Assyrian power. After the death of Adadnirari III (782 B.C.), Assyria was ruled over by three weak kings, Shalmaneser IV (782–773 B.C.), Ashurdan III (772–755 B.C.), and Ashurnirari V (754–745 B.C.), who presented no threat to the western powers. But about the time that Jeroboam II died, a powerful warrior, Tiglathpileser III (745–727 B.C.), or Pul, as he was known in Babylonia, usurped the Assyrian throne and brought new vitality to the empire.

He appeared with an army on the northeastern frontier of Israel during the reign of Menahem (II Kings 15:9), who deemed it wise under the circumstances to become tributary to him. In the annals of Tiglathpileser the event was described as follows:

> As for Menahem, terror overwhelmed him . . . he fled and submitted to me . . . silver, colored woollen garments, linen garments . . . I received as his tribute.[23]

Menahem was succeeded by his son Pekahiah in 742/41, who was unable to appease the Assyrians as his father had done, and after two years was assassinated by a military group under Pekah, who then succeeded him. The new king sought to restore the political fortunes of Israel, and allied with Rezin, king of Damascus, the Philistine states, and some of the Transjordan kingdoms against Assyria.

The Last Days of Israel

In Judah, Jotham had succeeded his father Uzziah about 740 B.C., after having been regent for several years. He was anxious to maintain the material prosperity of previous years, and apart from enforcing the payment of tribute Uzziah had levied upon the Ammonites, he pursued a consistently peaceful policy. Towards the end of his reign, the alliance between Rezin and Pekah threatened the security of Judah, and when Ahaz, the son and successor of Jotham, came to the throne (732/31 B.C.), he was faced with the growing might of the Syrian coalition. Despite harassing attacks, he resisted all invitations to join the alliance, even when the confederates laid siege to Jerusalem. At heart, however, he was a reckless individual, and although Isaiah prophesied Divine deliverance (Isa. 7), Ahaz, alarmed by the capture of Elath on the Gulf of Aqabah and its occupation by Syrian peoples, appealed urgently to Assyria for help. Tiglathpileser, whose own security was menaced by the Syrian coalition, accepted the treasures from the Temple and the royal palace that Ahaz had sent by way of tribute (II Kings 16:7ff.) and marched against the coalition.[24]

He swept down into Syria, and when Damascus fell in 732 B.C., after a protracted siege, he killed Rezin and accomplished the destruction predicted in prophecy (Amos 1:4; Isa. 8:4; 17:1). He then turned against Israel and carried captive the tribes of Reuben, Gad, and the half-tribe of Manasseh, which were transported to Mesopotamia in the first captivity of Israel (II Kings 15:29).[25] With the death of Rezin the Aramean dynasty of Damascus terminated, leaving Assyria as the dominant power in the Near East.

Low relief of Tiglathpileser III.

Pekah was slain in 732/31 B.C. by Hoshea, whom Tiglathpileser made a vassal and from whom he exacted heavy tribute, as recorded in the Assyrian annals:

Paqaha (Pekah) their king they deposed and I placed Ausi' (Hoshea) over them as king . . . talents of silver as their tribute I received from them. . . .[26]

When Tiglathpileser died in 727 B.C., his son Shalmaneser V (727–722 B.C.) succeeded him, and Hoshea, who was an intensely patriotic individual, took this as an opportunity for discontinuing payment of tribute to Assyria and forming secret affiliations with Egypt. In reprisal, Shalmaneser imprisoned Hoshea and besieged Samaria for three years (II Kings 17:3ff.). Before it fell, Shalmaneser was succeeded by Sargon II (722–705 B.C.), who overthrew the Israelite monarchy and carried the remaining northern tribes captive to Assyria. In the Khorsabad annals he stated with characteristic exaggeration:

I besieged and captured Samaria, carrying off 27,290 of the people who dwelt therein. 50 chariots I gathered from among them. . . .[27]

Sargon followed the current practice of replacing deported peoples with others who would be loyal to the regime. Accordingly he brought groups of non-Semitic peoples from Babylonia, Elam, and elsewhere, and settled them among the artisans and peasants who had been left behind in the northern kingdom. As the result of intermarriage, a mixed population arose, which ultimately took the name of Samaritans, after the capital of the fallen kingdom. They gradually assumed the nature of a religious sect rather than a nation, and they came to occupy an important position in the history of later religious developments in Palestine.

The End of the Northern Kingdom

The second captivity of 722 B.C. marked the end of Israel as a separate kingdom, thus terminating its long history of turmoil and unrest. From a religious standpoint, its fall was the logical outcome of the idolatrous practices that had been in existence for so long, despite the repeated warnings of prophecy. The people were morally depraved, and had repudiated the covenant obligations to such an extent that they had virtually passed from memory. From a political point of view, the power of Syria had proved to be no match for the repeated onslaught of the Assyrian military machine, and after a time it became apparent that any nation that allied with Syria could only expect to share her ultimate fate. With the abandonment of the theocratic ideal, the northern kingdom had no choice but to engage in political affiliations, which, it was hoped, would assist her in becoming prosperous and powerful. But apart from the days of Jeroboam II, this policy produced little that was even of immediate political benefit, and forced the eighth-century-B.C. prophets to the conclusion that God would use human designs for the vindication of His righteous nature, and employ foreign nations as the rod of His anger to punish His wayward and idolatrous people.

NOTES

1. F. Kenyon, *The Bible and Archaeology* (1940), p. 176.

2. C. H. Gordon, *Introduction to Old Testament Times*, pp. 158f.

3. N. Glueck, *The Other Side of the Jordan*, pp. 50ff.

4. *Ibid.*, pp. 89ff.

5. Wendell Phillips, *Qataban and Sheba* (1955).

6. W. F. Albright, *Bulletin of the American Schools of Oriental Research* (1943), No. 92, pp. 16ff.

7. J. Finegan, *Light From the Ancient Past*, p. 150.

8. W. F. Albright, *Archaeology and the Religion of Israel*, p. 148.

9. W. F. Albright, *From the Stone Age to Christianity*, p. 229.

10. J. Finegan, *op. cit.*, p. 113.

11. E. R. Thiele, *The Mysterious Numbers of the Hebrew Kings* (1965 ed.), pp. 5ff.

12. C. C. McCown, *The Ladder of Progress in Palestine* (1943), pp. 192ff.

13. Cf. J. Finegan, *op. cit.*, p. 157.

14. W. F. Albright, *Samuel and the Beginnings of the Prophetic Movement* (1961), pp. 5ff.

15. Cf. J. Finegan, *op. cit.*, p. 170.

16. *Ibid.*, pp. 171f.

17. M. Burrows, *What Mean These Stones?*, p. 281.

18. J. Finegan, *op. cit.*, pp. 172f. and pl. 73.

19. D. D. Luckenbill, *Ancient Records of Assyria and Babylonia* (1926), I, Sects. 735, 740.

20. L. Finkelstein (Ed.), *The Jews, Their History, Culture and Religion*, I, 38.

21. J. Finegan, *op. cit.*, pl. 66.

22. Cf. *ibid.*, p. 153.

23. D. D. Luckenbill, *op. cit.*, I, Sect. 816.

24. *Ibid.*, I, Sect. 801.

25. *Ibid.*, I, Sect. 815f.

26. *Ibid.*, I, Sect. 816.

27. *Ibid.*, II, Sect. 55.

Near Eastern Chronology
715–581 B.C.

JUDAH	ASSYRIA	BABYLONIA
Hezekiah 716/15–687/86 (Coregent from 729)	Sennacherib 705–681	
Manasseh 687/86–642/41 (Coregent from 696/95)	Esarhaddon 681–669	
	Ashurbanipal 669–627	
Amon 642/41–640/39		
Josiah 640/39–609		Nabopolassar 626–605
Jehoahaz II 609– 3 months		
Jehoiakim 609–597		Nebuchadnezzar II 605–562
Jehoiachin 597–3 months First Captivity 15/16 March 597		
Zedekiah 597–587 Second Captivity 587		
Gedaliah 586–582 Third Captivity 581		

8. The Fall of Judah

THE COLLAPSE OF THE NORTHERN KINGDOM BEFORE THE onslaught of Assyria presented serious problems for Judah. Jehoahaz was still paying substantial tribute to the Assyrian empire, and although the economy of Judah was relatively stable, the position of the nation in other respects was extremely vulnerable. The Assyrians seemed bent on conquering Egypt, or at the least on reducing her power, and the southern kingdom formed an important advanced base for such an objective. For Judah to revolt against her Assyrian overlords and seek the protection of Egypt would merely serve to expedite Assyrian plans for the extension of imperial interest in the west. Since the military resources of Judah were totally inadequate to meet the threat of invasion, the greatest security for the southern kingdom appeared to lie in preoccupation with domestic affairs and the renunciation of alliances with foreign powers.

These were the difficulties that confronted Hezekiah (716/15-687/86 B.C.), the son and successor of Jehoahaz I, when he acceded to the throne. He was a deeply religious man who, at the beginning of his reign, was guided by the prophet Micah to undertake a program of religious reformation aimed at reversing the religious policies of his father and eradicating the noxious influence of Baal worship from the southern kingdom. He destroyed all the high places where pagan religious ceremonies had been held, and disposed of all cultic objects that might have any heathen significance, including the copper serpent which Moses had made and which had been preserved in the Temple (II Kings 18:4). The recent downfall of Israel added sanction to the reforms, and the consequent purification of religious life led to a revival of Jehovistic worship.

The reign of Hezekiah was one of considerable economic prosperity, resulting from careful organization and development of national resources. He regained control of the cities in the plain of Philistia, and built up the defenses of the kingdom as a whole. Taking advantage of the struggle of power between Egypt and Assyria, he expanded the commercial activity of Judah and brought husbandry to an advanced level (II Chron. 32:27f.). His military successes against the Philistines encouraged him to think of revolting against Assyria and allying with Egypt, but Hezekiah was not supported in this policy by the prophet Isaiah, who saw all too clearly its consequences (Isa. 18:1–7; 30:1–7).

Like his contemporary Micah, Isaiah devoted his attention principally to Judah and Jerusalem (Isa. 1:1), whereas Amos and Hosea had concentrated upon the sin of the northern kingdom. Isaiah appears to have been of noble birth, and as such had ready access to the royal court, where his advice was generally listened to with respect even if, in the end, it was disregarded. Already during the prosperous reigns of Uzziah (767–740/39 B.C.) and Jotham (740/39–732/31 B.C.) the prophet Isaiah was proclaiming the last days of the southern kingdom, no doubt to an incredulous audience.

When Ahaz of Judah (732/31–716/15 B.C.) declined the invitation extended by Damascus to join an anti-Assyrian coalition, he was threatened with subjugation by Pekah of Israel and Rezin of Syria. On this occasion Isaiah comforted Ahaz with the assurance that the plot against him would come to nothing, and that the kings who appeared to be so menacing would themselves be liquidated in a very short time (Isa. 7:3–9). Ahaz was apparently unconvinced, however, both by this assurance and by the promise of Immanuel, the son of a virgin, who would be born to the house of David (Isa. 7:10–15), and as a result he committed the foolish act of asking Tiglathpileser III of Assyria for help.

Isaiah seems to have withdrawn from political life for a time after the Assyrians made Judah tributary in 734 B.C. (cf. Isa. 8:11–22), but when he saw that there was a possibility of the nation participating in foreign alliances, he uttered a warning against such procedures. In particular Isaiah insisted that Judah should not rely upon aid from Egypt (Isa. 19:1–22), and he counseled consistently against alliances with that country (Isa. 30:1–7; 31:1–3).

Assyrian Threats to Jerusalem

In 705 B.C. Sargon of Assyria died and was succeeded by his son Sennacherib. Although he was not as forceful a leader as his father had been, he continued the westward expansion of the Assyrian empire. Sennacherib fortified Nineveh, his capital city, erected a series of magnificent buildings, and restored some of the older religious shrines, thus making the city one of the most splendid in the Near East. At the beginning of his reign, Sennacherib was confronted with the attempt of Merodach-Baladan, king of Babylon, to resist the growing power of Assyria. This man had sent ambassadors to Hezekiah shortly after the latter had fallen victim to a serious illness (II Kings 20), with the aim of drawing Judah into a confederacy of Near Eastern powers formed to resist Assyrian aggression.

Although Isaiah predicted that membership in the projected coalition would result in the destruction of the kingdom and the exile of the people in Babylon, Hezekiah decided to support the scheme Merodach-Baladan had advanced. At the same time he entered into an alliance with Egypt, in the belief that such a move would check the rise of Assyrian power. But as a precautionary measure he strengthened the defenses of Jerusalem, and even while this work was being carried out, the Assyrian forces swept to the Mediterranean coast in 701 B.C., isolated the city of Tyre, and reduced Ashkelon, Joppa, Timnath, and Ekron. An Egyptian

The celebrated prism of Sennacherib, dated c. 686 B.C. and recovered from Nineveh. It records events in the reign of the Assyrian monarch Sennacherib (705-681 B.C.).

expeditionary force that had been dispatched to the aid of the beleaguered towns suffered defeat, and was forced to withdraw.[1]

Hezekiah made hurried preparations to safeguard Jerusalem from attack, and ordered his engineers to construct a tunnel that would bring the water from the Spring of Gihon into the city proper. This tunnel was excavated through solid rock for a distance of nearly six hundred yards, and when it was completed it emerged just inside the southeastern corner of the old city, where what

241

Hezekiah's Tunnel emerged where the Pool of Siloam was later situated.

was later known as the Pool of Siloam was situated. The conduit referred to in II Kings 20:20 and II Chronicles 32:30 was a memorable engineering accomplishment, for the excavators worked with hand-tools from opposite ends, meeting in the center. The tunnel narrowed somewhat from the Siloam Pool end, but nevertheless it maintained an average height of six feet.

The presence of an inscription on the right-hand wall, some twenty feet from the Siloam entrance, was revealed in 1880, and on examination subsequently it was found to have been written in eighth-century-B.C. script (c. 701 B.C.). It consisted of six lines inscribed in classical Hebrew,[2] and gave the following account of the termination of the excavations:

View down Hezekiah's Tunnel. The conduit was an engineering accomplishment, for the excavators worked with hand-tools from opposite ends, meeting in the center.

The boring through is completed. And this is the story of the boring through: while they plied the drill, each toward his fellow, and while there were yet three cubits to be bored through, there was heard the voice of one calling to another, for there was a crevice in the rock on the right hand. And on the day of the boring through the stone-cutters struck, each to meet his fellow, drill upon drill; and the water flowed from the source to the pool for a thousand and two hundred cubits, and a hundred cubits was the height of the rock above the heads of the stone-cutters.[3]

In order to gain further respite, Hezekiah endeavored to placate Sennacherib by offering him tribute. The Assyrian annals interpreted the situation as follows:

As for Hezekiah the Jew, who did not submit to my yoke, 46 of his strong walled cities, as well as the smaller cities in their neighborhood . . . I besieged and took. . . . Himself, like a caged bird, I shut up in Jerusalem, his royal city. . . . As for Hezekiah, the terrifying splendor of my majesty overcame him . . . and his mercenary troops . . . deserted him.[4]

243

The Assyrian Withdrawal

With characteristic exaggeration the annals of Sennacherib described the tribute exacted from Hezekiah, which consisted of thirty talents of gold, eight hundred talents of silver, and a wide variety of valuable merchandise. The account in II Kings 18:14, however, indicates that Hezekiah paid only three hundred talents of silver and thirty talents of gold.

While Sennacherib was besieging Lachish, he sent one of his officials, whose title, Rabshakeh, alone has survived, to Jerusalem in order to persuade the citizens to surrender. Speaking in Hebrew, he addressed all who could hear, and stated that the campaign being waged by Sennacherib had the sanction of Jehovah, and that Hezekiah could not therefore save his people from disaster. But though he promised good treatment for all those who surrendered, the morale of the Judeans remained unshaken by this attempt at psychological warfare. Hezekiah was assured independently by Isaiah that God would deliver Jerusalem miraculously from the Assyrian forces, with the result that he ignored the Assyrian threats (Isa. 36:1–37:38).

It is significant that Sennacherib did not claim the capture of Jerusalem in view of the devastating plague, probably bubonic in nature, which routed the Assyrians (II Kings 19:35). Again it is characteristic of the times that no mention of this reverse occurs in the annals of Sennacherib, for defeats or failures

Assyrian relief depicting the capture of a town.

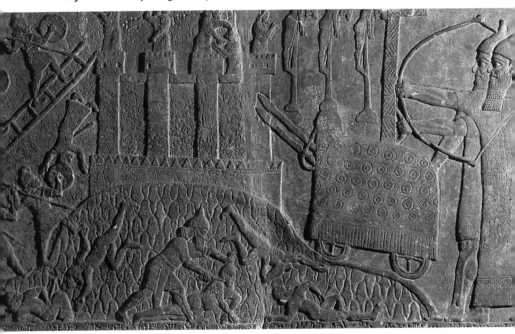

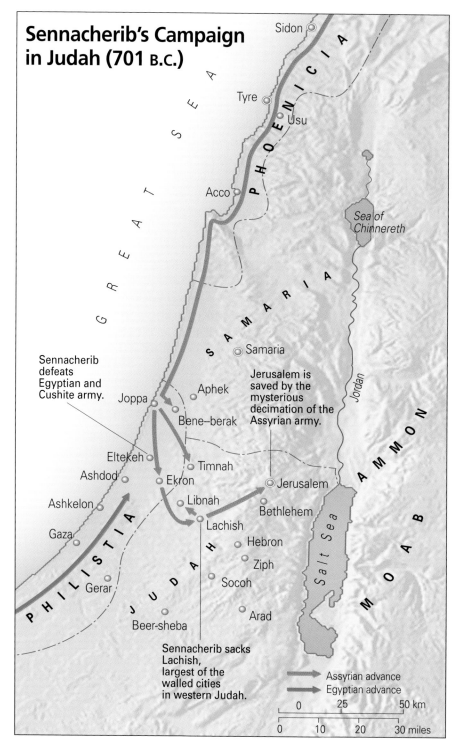

Sennacherib's Campaign in Judah (701 B.C.)

Sidon

Tyre

Usu

Acco

GREAT SEA

PHOENICIA

Sea of Chinnereth

SAMARIA

Samaria

Sennacherib defeats Egyptian and Cushite army.

Joppa

Aphek

Jerusalem is saved by the mysterious decimation of the Assyrian army.

Bene–berak

Jordan

Eltekeh

Timnah

Ashdod

Ekron

Jerusalem

AMMON

Ashkelon

Libnah

Bethlehem

Gaza

Lachish

Salt Sea

PHILISTIA

Hebron

Ziph

JUDAH

Socoh

Gerar

MOAB

Beer-sheba

Arad

Sennacherib sacks Lachish, largest of the walled cities in western Judah.

→ Assyrian advance
→ Egyptian advance

| 0 | 25 | 50 km |
| 0 | 10 | 20 | 30 miles |

were invariably ignored when chronicles were being compiled by Near Eastern nations. After this episode, Sennacherib returned to Nineveh from Judea, and in 681 B.C. was assassinated by his sons (II Kings 19:37), being succeeded by Esarhaddon (681–669 B.C.).

The withdrawal of the Assyrian army from Jerusalem was hailed as a national deliverance, and it encouraged Hezekiah to set about restoring the material prosperity of his kingdom. The remainder of his reign passed uneventfully, and about 686 B.C. he was succeeded by his son Manasseh.

The Reign of Manasseh

This man reacted violently against the religious policy of his father, and rebuilt the Canaanite shrines that had been destroyed previously. The Biblical writers unanimously condemned him for his reintroduction of pagan forms of worship, which included the veneration of the astral bodies, the adoration of Astarte, and the encouragement of immoral Baal cults throughout the kingdom. One of his more flagrant violations of morality was to establish the worship of Moloch, an Ammonite deity, to whom parents sacrificed their children by making them pass through fire, a practice strictly forbidden in the Mosaic law (Lev. 20:2ff.). During the long reign of Manasseh (687/86–642/41 B.C.), the people of Judah sank to new depths of depravity and moral degradation.

The chronicler of II Chronicles 33:11ff. preserved a tradition that stated that God punished Manasseh for his wickedness by deportation to Babylon, where, after a period of imprisonment, he apparently repented of his former way of life. To the present there is no archaeological evidence to substantiate this tradition, although one cuneiform text from the time of Esarhaddon contained a reference to a visit made by Manasseh to Nineveh at the command of the Assyrian ruler:

> I summoned the kings of Syria and those across the sea–Baalu, king of Tyre, Manasseh, king of Judah . . . Musurri, king of Moab . . . twenty kings in all. I gave them their orders.[5]

Since Babylonia was a vassal of Assyria, and Esarhaddon was in process of rebuilding Babylon,[6] which his father had destroyed, it is probable that the visiting rulers were shown the magnificence of the restored city before being allowed to return home. Some scholars see the captivity of Manasseh as a punishment for membership in the coalition of Phoenicia, Edom, and Egypt that revolted against Assyria c. 650 B.C.[7] But Judah did not join in this revolt, and

Assyrian relief depicting Sennnacherib watching a march-past.

Assyrian relief illustrating the deportation of prisoners, c. 630-612 B.C.

so was not the victim of Assyrian retribution when the revolt was finally crushed. A parallel to this tradition is afforded by the capture and subsequent release of the pharaoh Necho I by Ashurbanipal, as narrated on the Rassam Cylinder.[8]

On his return to Jerusalem, Manasseh instituted a religious reformation in Judah and restored the worship of Jehovah to the sanctuaries. His reign was comparatively uneventful from a political standpoint, although he took the precaution of installing garrisons in all the fortified towns throughout Judah and strengthened the defenses of Jerusalem still further against a possible attack by Assyria. His lengthy rule terminated in 642/41 B.C., when he was succeeded by his son Amon. Like his father, he worshiped pagan gods at the beginning of his reign, and after a two-year period on the throne he was murdered in a palace conspiracy in 640/39 B.C.

The Rule of Josiah

His eight-year-old son Josiah succeeded him, and reigned until the year 609 B.C. His piety was evident from an early age, and in the twelfth year of his reign he began a program of religious reformation in which the pagan Canaanite shrines were destroyed and the worship of Jehovah was restored. He gave this matter his personal supervision, and when it had been completed to his satisfaction, he turned his attention to the repairs that had to be made to the fabric of the Temple (II Kings 22:3ff.).

During the course of the renovations, a copy of the ancient law was discovered by Hilkiah the high priest, and it was brought to the king. On hearing its contents read aloud, Josiah was overcome with remorse because of the way in which the Divine precepts had been ignored in previous days. After receiving a favorable oracle from God, he instituted another religious reformation of a far-reaching character, supported by priests, prophets, and government officials, and based on the newly recovered Book of the Law.

The fact that the scroll was discovered at the time when the fabric of the Temple was being restored suggests that it may have been deposited in the foundations during the period when the building was being erected. Occasionally such documents were recovered by Near Eastern rulers who were possessed of antiquarian interests, as in the case of Nabonidus of Babylon (556–539 B.C.), who was a notable religious antiquary and archaeologist. During his reign he excavated the temple of Shamash at Sippar in lower Mesopotamia and recovered the foundation records of Naram-Sin, the son of Sargon. The custom of incorporating records and other material into the foundations of buildings is very ancient, and originally it had magical connotations.

The precise nature of the scroll itself is difficult to determine. Traditionally it comprised the whole Pentateuch, but the fact that it is spoken of as "the Book of the Covenant" (II Chron. 34:30), and that it could be read within a reason-

Assyrian relief of Tiglathpileser III setting out on an expedition. He is standing in a war chariot accompanied by his driver and an armed attendant.

ably short time, may indicate that it consisted of one part of the Pentateuch only. Scholars have claimed that the scroll either contained or perhaps even consisted of the book of Deuteronomy, but this is a matter that in the nature of the case cannot be proved. Most probably the law scroll consisted of the Decalogue, the covenant code, the regulations regarding the Tabernacle, and some portions of the ancient laws of holiness contained in the first seven chapters of Leviticus.

A theory that demands more serious consideration, however, is the one that claims the scroll to have been forged shortly before its discovery about 621 B.C. This view, as Gordon indicates, is based on an incorrect understanding of the nature and function of legal codes in the ancient Near East. Although such codes were based in part on public opinion, tradition, and earlier legal decisions, whether written or oral, they did not exercise any significant influence over the affairs of everyday life. Once written they were placed in archives for safekeeping, and were not used as works of reference except on infrequent occasions by scholars. The general public did not have access to them, and the documents constituted in effect little more than original sources for purposes of research. Decisions made in Mesopotamian law courts seldom if ever appealed to written constitutions, and while codified laws such as those of Hammurabi were in existence, they had virtually no influence at all upon legal practice or social behavior. Thus there would be no need for Josiah to possess a written

Assyrian bas relief of Ashurbanipal feasting with his queen at Nineveh.

Assyrian bas relief depicting the imperial guard.

law code as an authoritative pre-requisite for a religious reformation. Nor would he even need to appeal to such a code, since he had already initiated one such reformation at an early period in his reign without the benefit of reference to sacred or legal documents.

So far from a forgery being circulated, as a great many scholars have alleged, the significance of the discovery in the Temple is that a lost and forgotten sacred book had been recovered. Its contents were so pointed and embarrassing that because of its intrinsically holy nature it was adopted as the permanent religious legislation for the nation.

Josiah destroyed the high places of Canaanite religion, and centralized worship at Jerusalem. The astral worship of Manasseh and Amon was prohibited, and the Moloch fire rituals in the valley of Hinnom were terminated. The Passover had long fallen into disuse, and on the instructions of Josiah it was reintroduced with all the traditional ceremony. Although Josiah set an example of piety for the nation of Judah, there were many who did not follow his lead, and in consequence the calamities that had been predicted for the nation (II Kings 22:20) loomed on the horizon. The prophecies of Zephaniah, who was contemporary with Josiah, contained a general denunciation of idolatry in Judah and the threat of Divine retribution, while at the same time they asserted the superiority of Jehovah over all other deities and nations.

The Babylonian Empire

→ Routes of exiled Judeans

▓ Babylonian empire

0	250	500 km

0	100	200	300 miles

The Zenith of Assyrian Power

Under Esarhaddon the power of Assyria reached its height with the defeat of Taharka, the king of Egypt (c. 671 B.C.), who suffered heavy losses. The annals of Esarhaddon claimed a great victory:

> . . . daily without cessation I slew multitudes of his men, and him I smote five times with the point of my javelin. . . . Memphis, his royal city, in half a day, with mines, tunnels, assaults, I besieged, I captured . . . I burned with fire. . . .[9]

Taharka apparently survived both his wounds and his defeat, however, whereas Esarhaddon died (669 B.C.) on his next campaign against Egypt, and was succeeded by his son Ashurbanipal (669–627 B.C.). He brought the prestige of Assyria to its highest point, and although he waged war with vigor, he was also renowned for his cultural interests. He established a huge royal library in which was housed as much of the historical, scientific, legal, and religious literature of Babylonia and Assyria as his scribes could collect. This material was unearthed in 1853, and among the tablets were Assyrian copies of the Babylonian Creation and Flood narratives, subsequently deciphered by George Smith of the British Museum in 1872. Magnificent bas-reliefs depicting hunting and other scenes in the royal life were also recovered from the palace at Nineveh, which in style represent the climax of art in Assyria.

Ashurbanipal consolidated the gains Esarhaddon had made in Syria and Egypt, and inflicted a further defeat upon the nephew of Taharka, who had succeeded him in 664 B.C. Memphis and Thebes fell in 662 B.C., and the enormous amount of booty that was acquired from these cities was mentioned in the annals of Esarhaddon:

> Silver, gold, precious stones, the goods of the palace . . . great horses, the people men and women . . . booty, heavy and countless, I carried away from Thebes . . . with a full hand I returned safely to Nineveh, the city of my lordship.[10]

In general, however, Ashurbanipal followed a policy of appeasement towards Egypt, and established Necho, an Egyptian prince, as vassal pharaoh.

In 652 B.C., the power of Assyria was shaken by violent internal strife. The king of Babylon, who was the brother and vassal of Ashurbanipal, revolted, and was subdued only after four years of bitter strife. Taking advantage of the situation, the Egyptians, Phoenicians, and some of the Transjordan peoples rose in revolt against Assyria. Judah did not become a member of the coalition, however, which was crushed when Babylon was subdued in 648 B.C., and so was not affected politically by the insurrection.

The Rise of Babylon

Babylonian tablet recording the fall of Nineveh.

Ashurbanipal himself died in 627 B.C., and at once the Assyrian empire crumbled. Babylon asserted her independence in 626 B.C., while Assyria was threatened from the north by the invasions of a warlike people known as the Scythians. They inhabited the regions to the north and east of the Black Sea, and were a barbarous, nomadic group, who wandered over the vast area between the Caspian and the Black seas. About 626 B.C. they pushed southward through Palestine in the direction of Egypt, and to Zephaniah and Jeremiah their conquest of the northern defenses of Judah was the beginning of Divine retribution. The Scythians apparently followed the coastal route to Egypt, but they were turned back to Ashdod by the Egyptians. Herodotus claimed that Psamtik I (c. 633–609 B.C.), the father of Necho, bribed the Scythians to return to their native land, though to what extent this was true is difficult to say.

In 616 B.C. the Babylonians under Nabopolassar allied with the Medes, attacked Assyria, and began a systematic reduction of strong points throughout the empire. Ashur, the capital city, fell in 614 B.C., and after a further two years of bitter fighting Nineveh fell in 612 B.C. All resistance was crushed with the conquest of Haran, which had been occupied by a remnant of the Assyrian army in 610 B.C. The might of the Assyrian empire was at an end, and its fall signally vindicated the predictions of Zephaniah (2:13ff.) and Nahum (3:1ff.). The Tigris was used as a boundary for dividing up the empire, the Babylonians taking the territory to the west and south, while the Medes occupied the land to the north and east. The marriage of the daughter of the Medan king to

Nebuchadnezzar II, son of Nabopolassar, completed the proceedings, and the New Babylonian empire (612–539 B.C.) arose.

With the fall of Assyria, the pharaoh Necho asserted himself and marched into the coastal plain of Palestine. The R.S.V. interprets his motive as expressed in II Kings 23:29 quite correctly by saying that he went "to" the king of Assyria rather than "against" him, as in the K.J.V. and R.V. The Babylonian Chronicle, published by Gadd in 1923, makes it clear that Necho was marching to the aid of the Assyrian forces, who were in temporary possession of Haran. Josiah did not wish Necho to assist the hereditary enemies of Judah, and attempted to stop him at Megiddo, but he was assassinated there in 609 B.C. Jehoahaz II, son of Josiah, was made king by the people, but after three months he was deposed by Necho in favor of his elder brother Jehoiakim, whom Necho made his tributary, requiring him to pay one hundred talents of silver and one of gold (II Kings 23:33).

The Work of Jeremiah

While these events were taking place, the influence of the prophet Jeremiah was being felt increasingly in the political circles of Judah. He had been born into an old priestly family at Anathoth about 640 B.C., shortly after the death of Manasseh, and he was greatly influenced by the religious reformation of Josiah, as well as by the teachings of Hosea. His prophetic mission commenced with the death of Ashurbanipal, and from the outset he denounced Temple and cultic worship alike in favor of the ethical monotheism implicit in the traditional Mosaic religion. Although he was a man of mild disposition, he attacked with great vigor some of the respected institutions and personages of his day, including the Temple priests (Jer. 26:8ff.), false prophets (Jer. 23:9ff.), and government officials (Jer. 36:12ff.). For this he earned the enmity of vast segments of the populace, and his ministry was marked consistently by opposition, imprisonment, and direct persecution.

Jeremiah saw the dangers of the position Judah occupied in the international struggle for power. The Assyrian empire had disintegrated, and its place had been taken by a powerful Babylonian regime. Egypt was again asserting its claim to a voice in the affairs of the Near East after more than a century of decline, and appeared certain to challenge Babylonian military power sooner or later. If Judah allied with Egypt, she would suffer severe consequences if an Egyptian defeat took place, or if the Babylonians occupied the country and used it as an advanced base for attacking Egypt. Jeremiah foretold that Judah would be overwhelmed by the might of Babylon under Nebuchadnezzar (Jer. 25:9ff.), and he made dramatic attempts to influence the foreign policies of his country so that Judah would become a vassal of Babylon, and so be spared destruction (Jer. 27:6ff.).

The Westward Advance of Babylon

In 605 B.C. Necho marched to the Euphrates, and Nabopolassar sent his son Nebuchadnezzar with an army to fight against him. A decisive battle was fought at Carchemish that year, in which the Egyptians were routed and were pursued by the Babylonian forces as far as the Egyptian border. Judah now fell within the territory of the New Babylonian empire, and when Nebuchadnezzar succeeded to the throne in 605 B.C. on the death of his father, he consolidated his gains by compelling Judah to pay tribute to Babylon (II Kings 24:1).

The evidence presented by Daniel (1:3) would indicate that Nebuchadnezzar required the presence of Judean hostages in Babylon in 605 B.C. as evidence of good faith on the part of Jehoiakim. Daniel himself was among those deported to Babylon under this provision, along with members of the royal house and some of the intelligentsia of Judah. The allegation of an anachronism in the narrative (Dan. 1:1), in which the third year of Jehoiakim is equated with the fourth year of that king in Jeremiah 25:1, is now known to have been based on a misunderstanding of chronological sequences in antiquity. In Babylonia, the year of accession was reckoned separately, being followed by the first year of the reign. In Palestine, the year of accession was regarded as the first year of the reign. Thus Daniel computed his chronology according to the Babylonian system, while Jeremiah followed the one current in Palestine.

The First Captivity of Judah

After being tributary to Babylon for three years, Jehoiakim, who was a political opportunist, rebelled against his overlord in a desperate bid for independence, despite the consequences Jeremiah had predicted as an outcome of this policy (Jer. 22:18). Babylonian retribution was not long delayed, for in 597 B.C. the Chaldean armies invaded Judah and attacked Jerusalem. Jehoiakim died that year, perhaps as a result of a court uprising, and was succeeded by his son Jehoiachin, otherwise known as Jeconiah or Coniah. He capitulated to the invading forces after only three months' rule, and was taken as a prisoner to Babylon along with the royal family, the court, the upper classes, and the artisans. The Temple was looted and the treasures were taken to Babylon as booty. Tablets excavated from a vaulted building near the Ishtar Gate of ancient Babylon afford independent confirmation of this "first captivity" of Judah. The texts, which are dated between 595 and 570 B.C., were written in cuneiform, and contained memoranda of rations of barley and oil issued to the captive princes and artisans, including "Yaukin, king of the land of Yahud." This is a direct reference to Jehoiachin, and some of the tablets referred also to his five sons who accompanied him to Babylon.[11]

The discovery in 1956 by D. J. Wiseman of four additional tablets of the celebrated Babylonian Chronicle in the British Museum provided the first extra-Biblical account of the Babylonian capture of Jerusalem in 597 B.C. These sources also supplied details of the events that took place between 626 and 594 B.C., including accounts of some hitherto unknown military engagements. From the new information provided by these texts it is now possible to assign the fall of Jerusalem with complete accuracy to the second day of the month Adar (March 15/16) in 597 B.C.

In addition the tablets make abundantly clear the shattering defeat the Babylonians inflicted upon the Egyptians at Carchemish in 605 B.C., one result of which was that the Babylonian armies were able to occupy "the whole area of Hatti."[12] A previously unrecorded battle between Egyptian and Babylonian forces occurred in 601 B.C., in which both sides lost large numbers of men. The Babylonians in particular were compelled to withdraw to their capital for a year in order to obtain new supplies and equipment before further conquests could be entertained. Once they had refitted, however, they spent the next year making exploratory raids in Syrian territory before reducing Jerusalem in 597 B.C. The evidence supplied by these cuneiform texts thus confirms the Biblical tradition that Jerusalem fell to the Babylonian forces in 597 B.C. and in 587 B.C.

The Second Captivity of Judah

After the attack of 597 B.C., Nebuchadnezzar established Zedekiah (Mattaniah), the uncle of Jehoiachin, as a puppet ruler in Judah. His influence was weak, however, and he was unable to prevent political contact with Egypt, despite an oath of allegiance to Babylon (II Chron. 36:13). The new ruling class urged Zedekiah to ally with Egypt, and the accession of the pharaoh Hophra (588 B.C.), who had political ambitions in Palestine, added impetus to this request, despite the most solemn warnings from Jeremiah (Jer. 37:6ff.; 38:14ff.). When Zedekiah decided to depend upon Egyptian support and revolted against Nebuchadnezzar, the Chaldean armies swept down on Judah in 587 B.C., bent on destruction. The small Syrian states collapsed before the Babylonian armies as Jeremiah had foretold (Jer. 25:9), and Nebuchadnezzar laid siege to Lachish and Azekah. When they fell he attacked Jerusalem, and a time of great hardship ensued (II Kings 25:3).

Jeremiah repeatedly predicted that the city would be burned by the Chaldeans, and he urged Zedekiah to submit to Nebuchadnezzar in the best interests of all concerned. When this advice was rejected he endeavored to leave the city, but was accused of deserting to the enemy and was thrown into prison. His life was spared by Zedekiah, but he remained incarcerated throughout the siege of Jerusalem. An Egyptian force marched to the relief of the city, and for a time the beleaguered defenders entertained hopes of resisting the Babylonian invaders.

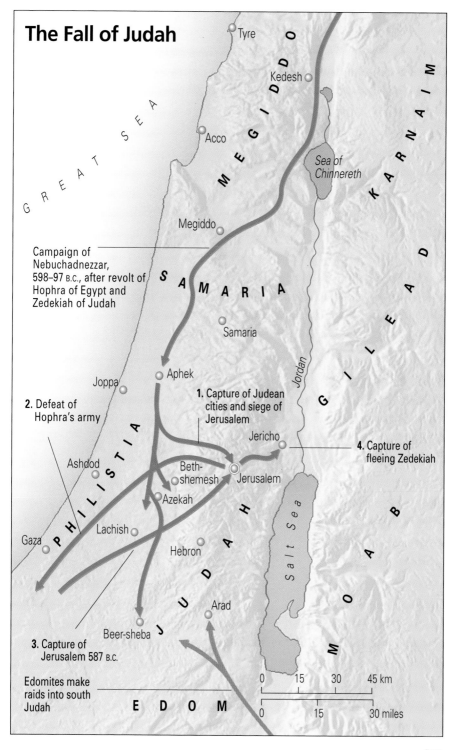

The Fall of Judah

Tyre

Kedesh

MEGIDDO

Acco

Sea of Chinnereth

GREAT SEA

Megiddo

Campaign of
Nebuchadnezzar,
598–97 B.C., after revolt of
Hophra of Egypt and
Zedekiah of Judah

S A M A R I A

K A R N A I M

G I L E A D

Samaria

Joppa

Aphek

Jordan

1. Capture of Judean
cities and siege of
Jerusalem

Jericho

G

2. Defeat of
Hophra's army

Ashdod

Beth-
shemesh

Jerusalem

4. Capture of
fleeing Zedekiah

P H I L I S T I A

Azekah

S a l t   S e a

Lachish

J U D A H

Gaza

Hebron

M O A B

Arad

Beer-sheba

3. Capture of
Jerusalem 587 B.C.

M

Edomites make
raids into south
Judah

E D O M

| 0 | 15 | 30 | 45 km |

| 0 | 15 | 30 miles |

But the city capitulated in 586 B.C., in the eleventh year of the reign of Zedekiah, and although the king tried to escape in the general confusion that followed, he was captured at Jericho, blinded, and carried off to Babylon, where he was imprisoned until his death. Jeremiah was removed from prison, and on the orders of Nebuchadnezzar was treated with great deference. But the horrors of captivity overtook the land of Judah once again. The Temple was pillaged and destroyed, the country was ravaged, and the potential leaders among the populace were deported to Mesopotamia.

The Lachish Letters

Archaeological discoveries at Lachish (Tell ed-Duweir), some twenty miles southwest of Jerusalem, have thrown new light on the last days of the southern kingdom. J. L. Starkey began to excavate the mound in 1932, and in clearing the ruins of a small guard-room outside the gate of the city three years later he uncovered eighteen potsherds, all of them about four inches in length, and inscribed in ink in the Phoenician script current in the time of Jeremiah. In 1938 three more ostraca were found at Lachish, making a total of twenty-one inscribed potsherds. A comparison of the levels indicated that the guard-room had been rebuilt after Nebuchadnezzar had partly destroyed Lachish in 598 B.C., and the ostraca formed part of the deposit resulting from the final overthrow of the city in 587 B.C.

A few of these potsherds contained name lists originating a little before the fall of Jerusalem in 586 B.C. Most of the ostraca, however, consisted of correspondence involving a prophet, and written by a certain Hoshaiah to Jaosh, who was perhaps a military commander at Lachish. The mention of intelligence reports and signal communications has led some scholars to think of the letters as military correspondence, since Letter IV confirms the statement of Jeremiah 34:7 concerning the fortified cities of Judah:

> . . . we are watching for the signals of Lachish, according to all the indications which my lord hath given, for we cannot see Azekah.[13]

The method of signaling by fire was very old, and as the Mari tablets have shown, it was an accepted means of communication in Mesopotamia at least twelve hundred years before Jeremiah was born.

Letter III, written also by Hoshaiah, made reference to a "prophet" as follows:

> . . . And it hath been reported to thy servant, saying, "The commander of the host, Coniah son of Elnathan, hath come down in order to go into Egypt; and unto Hodaviah son of Ahijah and his men hath he sent to obtain . . . from him." And as for the letter of Tobiah, servant of the king, which came to

Artist's impression of the assault on the city of Lachish.

Shallum son of Jaddua through the prophet saying, "Beware!" thy servant hath sent it to my lord.[14]

The proper names in this passage are characteristically Biblical, and this has led to speculation concerning the identity of the "prophet." Some scholars assumed that the reference was to Jeremiah himself, while others felt that an unknown contemporary prophet was being quoted when the letters were written. Since prophetic oracles were sought periodically in the conduct of military affairs, it would not be unusual for a prophet to be mentioned in military correspondence, particularly by his followers among the officers.

Professor H. Torczyner finally took the view that the ostraca were part of a group dealing with the fate of a prophet, whom he identified with Urijah (Uriah) of Kirjath-jearim. He had prophesied the destruction of Jerusalem and then fled to Egypt for refuge, but was extradited by order of Jehoiakim, and put to death in Jerusalem (Jer. 26:20ff.). Torczyner thought that Letter IV had actually been addressed to the prophet, but that the emergency of 598 B.C. had prevented it from being delivered. Whether it is possible to substantiate his contention that the "fire signals" were accompaniments of a Divine manifestation rather than being military communications (cf. Judg. 20:38ff.) is difficult to say. It is true, however, that the letters show at least as much concern for the fate of the prophet as for the crisis at Lachish, but in the last analysis it is very doubtful if the identity of the "prophet" will ever be established.

Letter VI contained passages strongly reminiscent of Jeremiah 38:2ff., where the prophet was accused of demoralizing the people when he recommended surrender to the Chaldeans. In this instance, the same royal officials who not long before had been clamoring for vengeance are themselves providing the discouragement:

> ... And behold the words of the (princes) are not good, (but) to weaken our hands ... my lord, wilt thou not write to them saying, "Why do ye thus (*even*) in Jerusalem? Behold unto the king and unto (*his house*) are ye doing this thing!". ... as the Lord thy God liveth, truly since thy servant read the letters there hath been no (*peace*) for (thy ser)vant. ... [15]

The Lachish ostraca represent one of the most significant archaeological discoveries in Palestine, and furnish striking confirmation of the political situation that obtained during the last days of the southern kingdom, as portrayed by Jeremiah.

After the Chaldeans had devastated Judah, Gedaliah, who had befriended Jeremiah (Jer. 39:14), was appointed governor over the "poor of the land." Remnants of the old royal house who had managed to escape to Egypt regarded him as a collaborationist, however, and Ishmael, a descendant of the royal Hebrew line, slew Gedaliah at Mizpah while he was endeavoring to resettle the scattered populace. Fearing Babylonian vengeance, Ishmael and his followers fled to Egypt, taking with them some of those who had survived the second captivity. Jeremiah, and Baruch his scribe, were also carried off to Egypt at this time, and were lost to subsequent history.

The Babylonian regime was determined to forestall any further uprisings in Palestine, and in 581 B.C. Chaldean forces undertook the third and final stage in the depopulation of Judah. No further resistance was possible, and with this last severe blow the power of the southern kingdom was at an end.

NOTES

1. L. Finkelstein (Ed.), *The Jews, Their History, Culture and Religion*, I, 43.

2. J. Finegan, *Light From the Ancient Past*, pl. 69.

3. G. A. Barton, *Archaeology and the Bible* (1946 ed.), p. 475.

4. D. D. Luckenbill, *Ancient Records of Assyria and Babylonia*, II, Sect. 240.

5. *Ibid.*, II, Sect. 690.

6. *Ibid.*, II, Sect. 646f.

7. L. Finkelstein, *op. cit.*, I, 44.

8. J. B. Pritchard, *Ancient Near Eastern Texts Relating to the Old Testament*, p. 295.

9. D. D. Luckenbill, *op. cit.*, II, Sect. 580.

10. J. Finegan, *op. cit.*, pp. 180f.

11. *Ibid.*, pp. 188f.

12. D. J. Wiseman, *Chronicles of Chaldean Kings (626–556 B.C.) in the British Museum* (1956), p. 25.

13. J. B. Pritchard, *op. cit.*, p. 322.

14. *Ibid.*

15. *Ibid.*

9. The Exile

CHRONOLOGY OF THIS CHAPTER

The New Babylonian Empire   612–539 B.C.

THE CALAMITY JEREMIAH HAD PREDICTED FOR SO LONG HAD finally overtaken the kingdom of Judah. The impregnable fortress of Jerusalem had capitulated, the Temple had been destroyed, and the nation had been led away into shameful captivity. This was to be the most severe test to which the Israelites had been subjected in their long and eventful history, and upon its outcome would hang the destiny of the Chosen People. But the fulfillment of Hebrew prophecy was a matter of little concern to the Babylonian conquerors, for in leading Judah into captivity they had other important considerations in view. First, they were anxious to insure the reduction of Palestinian military opposition to the Babylonian regime, so that the empire could consolidate its western holdings in preparation for a further attack upon Egypt. In the second place, the captivities provided Nebuchadnezzar with the gratuitous service of craftsmen and artisans for his ambitious building projects in Babylonia. By deporting potential leaders and skilled workmen alike, the Babylonians achieved at one blow the two main purposes of their conquests in Palestine.

The record in II Kings 24:14 places the number of captives carried away in 597 B.C. at ten thousand, describing them as royal officials and notables, craftsmen and smiths. A more accurate estimate of the number of people removed from Palestine in the three deportations has been preserved in Jeremiah 52:28ff., which records the total of deported Judeans as three thousand and twenty-three, eight hundred and thirty-two, and seven hundred and forty-five respectively for the three captivities. The discrepancy between the two sources may be due to the fact that the record in Kings preserves only a rough estimate of the number carried into captivity, or as Albright has suggested, the figures given in Jeremiah may constitute the actual number of those who survived the long journey to Babylon.[1] It is difficult to estimate the size of the population left behind in the land, but it is probable that about one hundred and twenty thousand were abandoned to the fate of eking out their existence in a desolated country. Recent archaeological excavations in Palestine have shown with what thoroughness the land was razed by the Chaldeans, although the Israelite settlements of the Negeb and Transjordan apparently escaped destruction.

The Reaction to Captivity

For those captives who were transported to Babylonia, the experience was as devastating as it had been sudden. For years they had been encouraged in their idolatrous ways by the soothing voice of false prophecy. Although men like Jeremiah had ventured to predict the failure of political alliances with foreign powers, there were others who had a far more comforting and reassuring message for the needs of the moment. The disillusionment that followed when the false prophets and the political opportunists were proved to be wrong dealt a crushing blow to the morale of the beleaguered Judeans, even though Jeremiah himself was present to share the tribulations of his fellow citizens. Previously there had been few among the inhabitants of Judah who were convinced that the same fate that had overtaken Israel nearly a century and a half earlier would also engulf the southern kingdom, despite the warnings contained in such passages as Isaiah 6:7ff.; 39:6; Micah 4:10; and Jeremiah 25:9ff. Now that it had happened, the proud Judeans were bewildered by their sudden humiliation, and angered by the obvious pleasure some of their traditional enemies such as the Edomites manifested at their downfall (Obad. 11ff.).

Quite distinct from the shame that attended the destruction of Judah and the captivity of the people was the psychological effect of deportation into a strange land, whose geographical characteristics were entirely the opposite of those to which the Judeans had been accustomed throughout their lives. To them the mountains of Judah had been the unquestioned assurance of security and support, and although they were probably familiar with the desert areas to the south and east, they could have had no concept whatever of the vastness that characterized the open spaces of Mesopotamia. For a hill-dwelling community to be transplanted forcibly into a land of enormous unending plains is a very serious matter, inviting the lurking terrors of agoraphobia as the least result of the ensuing psychological traumata. When such a people are led into shameful exile under the impression that they have been betrayed by their rulers and abandoned by their God, the emotional and spiritual crisis that is thereby precipitated is immeasurably more acute.

The reaction of some of the exiles to the idea of captivity was undoubtedly one of bitter hatred and resentment against God. According to the popular concept, He was the unfailing protector of those who stood in a covenant relationship with Him. The people of Judah still clung with pathetic earnestness to this idea, even when the prophets of the eighth and seventh centuries B.C. had demonstrated beyond reasonable doubt that God had rejected His people because of their idolatry and neglect of the covenant provisions. Although they had been warned that they would be punished by being taken in captivity to Babylon, they were loath to believe the serious nature of the prophetic pronouncements. When captivity finally overtook them, they felt that God had abandoned them in their hour of need, and their flimsy faith was completely shattered. All that remained for them was the memory of a sad past and the forbidding prospect of an embittered future. Henceforward they could have no delusions about the power of their God, for His obvious defeat at the hands of superior Assyrian forces told its own story.

But there were other exiles who took a less superficial view of the situation. All too late they had realized the urgency of the prophetic warnings, and were painfully aware of the fact that their own shortcomings had rebounded upon them in strength. Having sown the wind, they were reaping the whirlwind, and the self-consistency of the Divine nature could scarcely permit any other sequence to take place under the circumstances. For these people, the Exile constituted the long-heralded punishment for the violation of the covenant obligations, and as such it must be received in a spirit of penitent acceptance. If such a calamity had overtaken the nation after due warning by the servants of God, could it not be that the selfsame prophetic utterances might contain some message of consolation and hope for this sad occasion?

Whatever response was evoked at the spiritual level, it is certain that a fundamental reorientation of thought and outlook was demanded by the upheaval of captivity in Babylonia. Indeed, there are many who would assert that the Exile provided the necessary stimulus for an immense reassessment of spiritual values among the Judean captives, commencing the period of transition and development that culminated in the religious patterns of subsequent ages.

Settling Down in Babylonia

But the most immediate problem was that of adaptation to the new environment. The magnificent buildings and spacious cities of Mesopotamia made the Temple and the capital city of Jerusalem appear paltry and insignificant by comparison. The open plains and fertile soil stood in marked contrast to the rocky crags and indifferent arable land of Judah, while the general prosperity and opulence of contemporary Mesopotamia must have aroused many wistful recollections of the departed glory of Judah in the minds of the older captives. The Chaldean regime was at its height, and Nebuchadnezzar was busily engaged in building operations in order to beautify his empire.[2] Although he was renowned as a military strategist, Nebuchadnezzar appears to have been more interested in culture and the pursuit of peaceful arts than in extensive military conquests.

A reconstruction of the magnificent Ishtar Gate into the ancient city of Babylon. The gate was decorated with lions and other creatures in enameled brick.

The royal inscriptions that date from his reign depicted the splendor and magnificence of Babylonia during the New Empire period, and these accounts have been substantiated by the Greek historian Herodotus and other writers. Particular efforts were directed towards reconstructing and enlarging the capital city of Babylon, making it the most splendid city in the entire Near East. It was built on both sides of the River Euphrates, and surrounded by a double wall of defensive fortifications, which, according to Herodotus, enclosed an area of two hundred square miles. Of this, nearly nine-tenths consisted of parks, fields, and gardens, and the remainder was occupied by temples, public buildings, and private houses. The city walls were lofty, and were defended by two hundred and fifty towers placed at strategic intervals. Of the numerous gates that gave access to the city, one of the most famous was the huge double gate dedicated to Ishtar. It led to the wide processional street whose walls were elaborately decorated with enameled figures of bulls and dragons.

The two portions of the city were intersected in all directions by a network of navigable waterways and canals. To the east of a great bridge built to connect the two halves of Babylon was the magnificent palace of Nebuchadnezzar, which contained the celebrated "hanging gardens." These masonry terraces were regarded by the Greeks as constituting one of the seven wonders of the world, and although they cannot now be identified with any certainty, they were supposed to have been built in the form of a square whose sides were about four hundred feet in length, and raised on arches to a height of seventy-five feet. Of the *ziggurats* and temples Nebuchadnezzar restored, the most impressive was the enormous temple of Marduk, whose stepped tiers and lofty dimensions required an advanced degree of engineering and constructional skill.

It was for such enterprises as these that Nebuchadnezzar required skilled labor in abundance. While a great many specialized workmen were imported for the construction projects, the majority of those who helped to carry them out were slaves who had been brought as captives to Babylon. Among these were the Judean exiles who were settled in colonies in Babylonia, one of which was at Tel Abib near the River Chebar (Ezek. 3:15). Cuneiform sources indicate that the latter was the Kabar canal in central Babylonia, which ran between Babylon and Nippur.[3]

Although the Babylonians had taken Jehoiachin into captivity and had established his uncle Zedekiah as regent in the devastated southern kingdom, it is clear that they still regarded the exiled king as the rightful sovereign of Judah. Excavations at the Ishtar Gate in Babylon uncovered tablets, to which reference has already been made in the preceding chapter, showing that Jehoiachin ("Yaukin, king of the land of Yahud") and his household were recipients of royal bounty, as indicated in II Kings 25:27ff. But while the Babylonian captors showed deference to the exiled ruler and his family, they treated the remainder of the Judean captives in the same manner as other expatriate groups in Babylon. The inferior classes merely exchanged servility in Judah for enslavement in Mesopotamia, and while the Babylonians and Chaldeans were in general good-natured and tolerant, there is some reason for believing that the common people suffered harsh treatment while laboring to beautify the imperial cities, as Isaiah (47:6) had predicted. But those of the exiles who had enjoyed a higher social status in Judah were accorded a number of privileges, and were permitted limited freedom in choosing employment.[4] The thriving economy of the New Babylonian empire presented almost unlimited opportunities for enterprising individuals, and the Babylonians made no attempt to hinder any of the Judean exiles from rising in a proper manner to positions of prominence and responsibility. In consequence, men like Daniel (2:48) and Nehemiah (11:11) came to exercise important functions in government circles, while lesser individuals who lived near busy commercial centers such as Nippur had every opportunity for amassing wealth and property.

While, therefore, the Babylonian captivity cannot be compared for severity with the oppression in Egypt, there were certain features of a somber character that impressed themselves upon the minds of the exiled Judeans, or Jews, as they became known about this time.

The career of Daniel illustrates the extent to which the Babylonians were prepared to encourage talented foreigners to serve the interests of the New Empire. Although nothing is known of his life apart from the information contained in the book of Daniel, he appears to have been taken as a hostage to Babylon along with other Judean captives by Nebuchadnezzar in the third year of Jehoiakim of Judah. There he was trained along with certain other compatriots for the service of the royal court (Dan. 1:1–6), and was given the common Babylonian name of Belteshazzar. He soon gained a reputation for being able to interpret visions and recall forgotten dreams, and like Joseph of old he functioned as an adviser to the reigning king.

As his renown increased, he occupied high positions in the government under a succession of rulers, which included Nebuchadnezzar, Darius the Mede,[5] and Cyrus. During his lifetime he himself saw a number of visions, which he interpreted in terms of the future triumph of the Messianic kingdom. His last recorded experience of this kind took place at an advanced age on the banks of the River Tigris in the third year of Cyrus the Great. The activities of Daniel as a Hebrew statesman in a foreign court thus covered the period of the Babylonian exile completely, and represented an outstanding witness of fidelity to Hebrew covenantal faith in the highest circles of pagan Babylonia.

The Letter of Jeremiah

Although the colorful life of the New Babylonian empire had its attractions from a material point of view, there still remained the inescapable fact that the once proud inhabitants of the Promised Land were now exiles among a strange people. However well they might have been treated by the Babylonians, the Jews could never forget that they had been dealt a severe blow by the captivity. But just as the prophetic message had sounded dire warnings in earlier days, so now it provided a reminder of the status the captives were to occupy, and the prospects that would confront them during the next few decades. The prophet Jeremiah had written to the exiles from Jerusalem (Jer. 25), stating that God had delivered His people into the power of the Babylonians as a punishment for their iniquity. The sojourn in Babylon would last for some seventy years, after which God would bring the faithful Jews back to their native land. Because of these conditions, Jeremiah counseled the captives to accept the Divine sentence with the best grace they could muster, and attempt to learn the spiritual lessons it was intended to convey.

To this end he advised them to settle down in their unfamiliar surroundings, to marry, and to cultivate the land that had been assigned to them. They were to live peaceably with their pagan neighbors, and to work for the day when God would hear their prayers and restore them to their homeland. If there arose from among their number men who claimed to be prophets of the Lord, but who uttered words of dissension and discontent, they were false prophets, and were to be repudiated by the exiles. Any resistance to the idea of captivity would be construed as rebellion against the revealed will of God, and would only evoke further punishment.

The Outlook of the Captives

To those Judeans who interpreted the fall of Jerusalem and the destruction of the Temple in terms of the failure or inability of the God of Israel to protect His people, this letter must have had a bitter and ironic sound. In a time of dire emergency, their God, they felt, had been tried and found wanting, and this proclamation merely served to add insult to injury. For them, the future could only be one of religious agnosticism, and no utterance of priest or prophet, however piously or forcefully it was framed, could again have any real meaning for their existence. Material prosperity alone could temper the despair they were experiencing, and provide some solace for their disillusioned and bewildered minds.

Others, whose religious outlook was more enlightened, were still reeling from the shock of captivity when the letter of Jeremiah was made known to them. They found it hard to believe that God had punished His people in the severe manner long foretold by the prophets, and they were living in hopes of an early return to the homeland. For them, the letter must have been a profoundly depressing affair, since it dispelled once and for all any hopes the captives might have had of seeing the land of Judah in the near future.

Restored tiled depiction of a mythical creature from the Ishtar Gate, Babylon.

For those exiles whose faith in the justice and mercy of Jehovah had survived the grim ordeal of deportation to a foreign country, the letter of the prophet came as a further revelation of the Divine will, and as a challenge to belief and hope. Whereas formerly God had predicted punishment and doom for His people, He was now assuring them of forgiveness and restoration in due time. The bitter experience of exile was meant to induce a spirit of true penitence for the iniquity of earlier days, and to foster the growth of a religious outlook that was in harmony with the nature of God as revealed in the Mosaic covenant.

But not even an appreciation of the moral and spiritual implications of captivity could prevent those feelings of discouragement, sadness, and nostalgia which from time to time overtake all exiles in every age. The depths of pathos found their fullest expression, naturally enough, in the poetry of a sorrowing nation, and some of the most beautiful of the Hebrew Psalms emerged from this period.

The Work of Ezekiel

To these unhappy and discouraged people, a message of hope and deliverance was brought by the prophet Ezekiel. A younger contemporary of Jeremiah and Daniel, he was of priestly stock, and had been carried into captivity with King Jehoiachin in 597 B.C. He lived among the colony of Jews at Tel Abib on

271

the Kabar canal, and he began to prophesy some five years after his captivity (Ezek. 1:2). Recapturing something of the spirit of Jeremiah, he pointed out to the exiles the underlying causes of the disaster that had overtaken Judah, and roundly condemned the wickedness and idolatry of his fellow countrymen.

The versatility of Ezekiel made it possible for him to act as prophet, priest, and pastor to the exiled community. His consciousness of vocation is strongly reminiscent of the prophetic tradition of Jeremiah, by whose teachings he had been influenced prior to the fall of Jerusalem. Although his message seldom appealed to the majority of the exiles, his integrity and sincerity won for him the admiration of the Jewish elders (Ezek. 14:1; 20:1), and his eloquence carried his utterances far beyond the limited audience to which they were addressed. He surveyed in retrospect the history of the nation in order to discern the lessons the past could teach. Like Jeremiah, he insisted upon the sovereignty and omnipotence of the God of Israel, who in righteous indignation had delivered His people for a time into captivity. Like him he also taught that national renewal would only begin when integrity of character and motive became the supreme concern of all religious activity.

Ezekiel's priestly interests expressed themselves in his deep conviction that the future of the nation was bound up with the revival of the theocratic ideals of former days. Essential to this political structure was a Temple, whose worship would be carefully regulated by an organized priesthood, carrying out the ideals of a strict ritual law. The life of the community would be governed by the concept of holiness, and would draw its inspiration from the presence of God in the sanctuary. His emphasis on the correctness of ritual worship was intended as a safeguard against the recurrence of idolatrous practices, and was not to be regarded as an acceptable substitute for penitence, obedience, and faith.

As a pastor it was his duty to comfort the disconsolate and afflicted exiles, and encourage them to look in hope towards the time when God would restore them to their native land. He labored conscientiously to inculcate in his people a spirit of repentance, humility, and faith in the mercy of God, using visions, personal experiences, and symbolic acts to convey the truths implicit in his teachings. His particular concern was to impress his hearers with a sense of individual moral responsibility, and he expounded a folk saying to show that everyone would be punished for his own iniquity.

Ezekiel was not slow to realize that the changed conditions of the Exile would necessitate considerable modification of those forms of worship which had been in existence in Judah prior to the captivity. Because the Jews had been deported to a strange land against their will, they continued to regard their desolated capital city as the real center of national life in an almost defiant manner. With the passing of the decades, however, Jerusalem became invested with a mystical quality by which it embodied the best traditions and sentiments of the exiled nation. For the faithful Jews who awaited the return to Palestine, it was venerated in all its ruined glory as a symbol of hope and promise for the future, and the pious worshipers turned in its general direction as they prayed to God (Dan. 6:10).

Changes in Traditional Hebrew Worship

The restrictions their Babylonian captors placed upon them made it impossible for the Jews to offer sacrifices as in former days, and this paved the way for the development of that nonsacrificial type of worship earlier prophets had long desired. It was clear to Ezekiel that if the unity of the nation was to be preserved throughout the period of captivity, it could best be accomplished by the observance of those religious duties and ceremonies which could be pursued without causing offense to the captors. Because Ezekiel desired to stir up feelings of penitence among the exiles, he encouraged periods of fasting and prayer on anniversaries that commemorated the fall of Jerusalem. The feasts that had been so prominent a part of Hebrew worship in earlier days were replaced by memorial celebrations of a more somber character. With the departure of the feasts went the debased Canaanite polytheistic influence that had done so much to corrupt the life of the nation in previous generations.

From the beginning of the Exile, open-air meetings had been held by the mud flats of the Kabar canal, at which the law was read and opportunities for confession and prayer were provided. Because the absence of a Temple robbed the populace of a central meeting-place, it became necessary to improvise in this respect. As a result, house gatherings for instruction in the law (cf. Ezek. 20:1) came into being, and the sabbath assumed a position of particular prominence as the weekly day of worship. In a prophetic utterance Ezekiel advised the elders of the community to enforce the proper observance of the sabbath (Ezek. 20:20), and because it was impossible to indulge in animal sacrifices as part of the worship of that day, he stressed the place of prayer, confession, and instruction in the law. This became the basic pattern for that type of worship which took place in the synagogues of the postexilic period.

A number of Temple priests had accompanied the people of Judah into captivity (Jer. 29:1), and during this period they devoted considerable energy to interpreting the law and enforcing its demands. If the nation in exile was to remain a unit, it must be aroused to an awareness of its unique and distinct nature as contrasted with the Mesopotamian peoples. In consequence, much of the activity of the religious leaders was directed at emphasizing the distinguishing features of Jewish religious and national traditions. Circumcision took on a new meaning, since it gave the captive Jew a sense of moral superiority over his Babylonian neighbors, who did not observe the rite. Emphasis on the ancient Mosaic laws of purity directed the devotions of the exiles into new and unusual channels, and a number of distinctive exercises of piety such as formal acts of purification and the rejection of certain types of food came into being. An increasing awareness of the spiritual greatness implicit in the Hebrew tradition led the priests to emphasize the religious literature of the nation, and it is possible that a certain amount of collection of canonical material also took place at this time.

All these measures helped to awaken in the exiles the feeling that they were superior to their captors because their religion, their national identity, and ultimately their daily lives were inspired by more lofty ethical and spiritual concepts than were to be found in the cult worship of Marduk. When finally the Jews became conscious of the extent to which the sin of the nation had incurred Divine anger, a profound feeling of penitence and remorse arose among them, and expressed itself in an earnest desire for forgiveness.

The Remnant

The assurance that a righteous remnant would be restored to the land of their fathers had constituted an important part of the teaching of Ezekiel (cf. 20:41f.), and reflected the prophetic utterances of Isaiah (10:20f.) and Jeremiah (32:37). This minority who would survive the calamitous experience of deportation would be augmented by righteous individuals of other nations (Isa. 11:11), and as a result of obedience to the Divine laws would become a holy people. Isaiah had predicted that God would treat this minority graciously, and the symbolic name he gave to his son Shear-jashub proclaimed his conviction that the remnant would return to the land of Judah.

While Ezekiel continued to demand repentance for national sin from the exiled community, he was also aware of the fact that many of those who had been engulfed in the calamity of the Exile had had very little part in bringing about the actual disruption of national life. To them he preached a message of assurance and hope, proclaiming that God was able to quicken them by His Spirit, and weld them together into a living witness to His powers of redemption and restoration. In a dramatic vision, Ezekiel saw the nation as a heap of dried bones scattered throughout a remote valley, and devoid of every appearance of life. But when the desiccated bones listened to the divinely inspired prophetic messages, they came together in order, receiving flesh and sinews. Quickened by the breath of life, they arose and resembled an army in magnitude (Ezek. 37:1ff.).

The meaning of this vision was perfectly clear. The bones represented the forlorn, hopeless remains of the dismembered children of Israel. The only hope for their spiritual and national renewal lay in unquestioning obedience to the Divine injunctions, and an allegiance to the new covenant of the Spirit, long promised by Jeremiah (31:31ff.) and emphasized afresh by Ezekiel (37:26). Given these conditions, the nation would revive and return to its ancestral

The famous Cylinder of Cyrus, dating from 536 B.C. It records the fall of Babylon to Cyrus's forces and his proclamation that enabled exiled nationals to return home.

home, and there live as a holy people under the favor and protection of the Almighty.

As the decades passed, this ideal was accomplished to an increasing extent, and when the prospect of a return to Palestine became a distinct probability, the morale of the faithful remnant rose to new heights. Expectation of deliverance coincided with significant political developments in the Babylonian empire, with the rise to power of the Medes and Persians in Mesopotamia. For those Jews who had become captivated with the splendors of cosmopolitan Babylon, and had risen to positions of political and social prominence, the prospect of a return to desolation and poverty was far from attractive. So comparatively few of these shared the spiritual ideals of the righteous remnant, and being satisfied with their current state of material prosperity, they showed little indication of abandoning it for the doubtful privilege of rebuilding an impoverished nation in the ancestral homeland.

The worldly success to which some of the Jewish exiles had attained in the Babylonian empire encouraged a degree of assimilation with the Mesopotamian peoples, and an abandonment of those ideals which were implicit in the Mosaic covenant. In consequence, these Jews preferred to remain behind in Babylonia when the opportunity for a return to Palestine was given to the captive Jewish community. They formed a recognizable element of the population of Mesopotamia, and subsequently became known as the Eastern Dispersion. Some of their later literature included the Babylonian Talmud.

NOTES

1. Finkelstein (Ed.), *The Jews, Their History, Culture and Religion*, I, 47.

2. Cf. W. H. Lane, *Babylonian Problems* (1923), pp. 178ff.

3. G. A. Cooke, *A Critical and Exegetical Commentary on the Book of Ezekiel* (1936), pp. 4, 42.

4. H. M. Orlinsky, *Ancient Israel*, p. 121.

5. On the identity of Darius the Mede see J. C. Whitcomb, *Darius the Mede* (1959), pp. 5ff.

10. The Return and Restoration

THE GREAT WEALTH AND PROSPERITY OF THE NEW BABYLONIAN empire continued throughout the reign of Nebuchadnezzar II, and his proud boast as recorded in Daniel 4:30 was certainly in keeping with his ambitious building schemes. His interests also extended to some of the old Sumerian cities, and at Ur he restored the huge complex of the temple of Nanna, remodeling it and raising the level of the outer court. This work appears to have been undertaken in the spirit of religious reformation, which places the account of the image worship in Daniel 3:1ff. in a new perspective. Woolley discovered that the rooms the sacred hierodules and priestesses had occupied near the sanctuary had been removed completely during the restoration. A space had been cleared in front of the sanctuary, and an altar had been set up in full view of the worshipers, so that they could observe the priest as he made his offerings in public on the altar.

This was a distinct departure from earlier procedure, since the ritual acts of the ministrant were secrets known only to the priesthood. It seems clear that Nebuchadnezzar had initiated a program of religious reform that sought to modify the sensuous rituals of antiquity, and permit the worshiping public to participate as a group in the sacrificial offerings. This reform of ritual is reflected in the third chapter of Daniel, which recorded a decree ordering the populace to worship an image of the king. This monument had been set up in the plain of Dura, and all had ready access to it. As Woolley comments:

What was there new in the king's act? Not the setting up of a statue, because each king in turn had done the same; the novelty was the command for general worship by the public: for a ritual performed by priests the king is substituting a form of congregational worship which all his subjects are obliged to attend.[1]

The Illness of Nebuchadnezzar

As might be expected, contemporary Babylonian historical records made no mention of the mental affliction that according to the book of Daniel (4:16ff.) overtook Nebuchadnezzar towards the end of his life. The illness in question, which was a rare form of monomania known as boanthropy, must have been a source of perplexity and embarrassment to official circles. It was only after three centuries that a Babylonian priest, Berossus by name, recorded a tradition that said that Nebuchadnezzar was suddenly taken ill towards the end of his reign. Eusebius (fourth century A.D.) quoted a different account, which related that the king suddenly disappeared after predicting the downfall of his empire.[2] This tradition appears to be a garbled reflection of the narrative in Daniel (4:31), and may have been preserved in that form to conceal the presence of mental derangement, which was held in universal awe and dread in antiquity.[3]

The Decline of Babylonian Power

When Nebuchadnezzar died in 562 B.C., he was succeeded by his son Amel-Marduk, who is called Evil-merodach in II Kings 25:27. With his accession the power of the empire waned, and after two years he was murdered by his brother-in-law, Neriglisar, who reigned for four years. In 556 B.C. his son occupied the throne for a few months, but he, too, was killed in a conspiracy, and one of his murderers, Nabonidus, succeeded him. He reigned until 539 B.C., and was the last monarch of the New Babylonian empire. He was a man of considerable culture, who was particularly interested in archaeological pursuits. He dispatched his scribes throughout Mesopotamia to collect ancient inscriptions from widely divergent sources, and ordered names and dates of Mesopotamian kings to be compiled. There is some reason for thinking that his mother had been a priestess in the temple of the moon god at Haran, and this may have influenced Nabonidus to become a religious antiquary.

He was the last Babylonian ruler to attempt repairs to the *ziggurat* of the moon deity at Ur, and when his restorations were completed he installed his daughter there as high priestess.[4] She apparently collected a number of artifacts from an earlier period, and maintained a small museum of local antiquities, part of which was unearthed by Woolley.[5]

For most of his reign Nabonidus shared the rule of the empire with his eldest son Belshazzar, to whom in 553 B.C. he committed much of his regal authority before setting out on a campaign against Teima in Arabia. When he had conquered the city, he took up his residence there, and according to the Nabonidus Chronicle he erected lavish buildings comparable to those in Babylon.[6] Nabonidus lived in Arabia for a number of years, during which time Belshazzar was the sole ruler in Babylon. For this reason the latter was represented in the book of Daniel (5:30) as the last king of Babylon. The reference in Daniel 5:18 to Belshazzar as a son of Nebuchadnezzar is also correct according to Semitic usage, which, especially where royalty was concerned, was more interested in the succession than in the actual lineal relationship of individuals. Nitocris, the mother of Belshazzar, was apparently the daughter of Nebuchadnezzar,[7] and since the Semites often used the terms "son" and "grandson" interchangeably, it would still be correct to speak of Belshazzar as the "son" of Nebuchadnezzar.

The Rise of Cyrus

The declining power of the New Babylonian empire encouraged the rise of an energetic Persian ruler, Cyrus II, who succeeded his father Cambyses I about the year 559 B.C. as ruler of Anshan. He rapidly united the people of this vassal state of Media, and in 549 B.C. he revolted against Astyages his suzerain. After a short time he conquered him in battle, and thus Cyrus fell heir to the Medo-Persian empire. So great was his potential strength that an alliance was hurriedly formed against him.

Those who participated were Croesus, king of Lydia (Asia Minor), the fabulously wealthy king who is credited with having invented coinage; Nabonidus of Babylon; and Amasis, the pharaoh of Egypt (c. 569–525 B.C.).

In 546 B.C. Cyrus attacked the forces of Croesus and defeated him, thereby gaining control of the whole of Asia Minor. His next thrust was at Babylon itself, and the Cyrus cylinder recorded the way in which Marduk the patron deity assisted the subsequent victory:

> Marduk . . . to his city Babylon he caused him to go, he made him take the road to Babylon, going as a friend and companion at his side . . . without battle and conflict he permitted him to enter Babylon. He spared his city Babylon a calamity. . . .[8]

Cyrus is said to have diverted the course of the River Euphrates in his assault on the capital city, so that his troops entered Babylon along the bed of the river. At all events, Babylon fell to the Persian forces in 538 B.C., and the Chaldean army under Belshazzar was routed. With the conquest of Babylon Cyrus became the ruler of the largest empire the world had known, and during the reign of his son the influence of Persia was to extend as far west as Egypt. Cyrus regarded the fall of Babylon as a rebuke to Nabonidus for his neglect of Marduk, and for his unwarranted action in taking all the statues of the gods to Babylon when the Persian forces were invading the land. But to the exiled Jews, the fall of proud Babylon was the beginning of their own restoration, and they regarded Cyrus as the divinely appointed deliverer who would release them and permit them to return to the land of their fathers.

The Edict of Cyrus and the Return

This expectation was not unfounded, for immediately after the capture of Babylon, Cyrus ordered all the statues Nabonidus had brought to the capital to be restored to their native cities. This was followed by an act of clemency to all captives in Babylonia, which while being humanitarian in nature was also an astute political

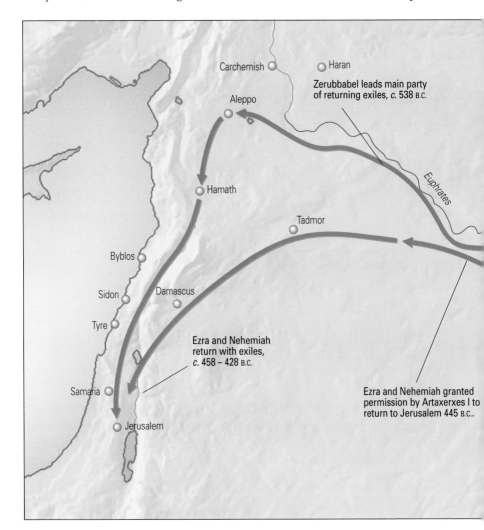

Carchemish

Haran

Zerubbabel leads main party
of returning exiles, c. 538 B.C.

Aleppo

Euphrates

Hamath

Tadmor

Byblos

Sidon   Damascus

Tyre

Ezra and Nehemiah
return with exiles,
c. 458 – 428 B.C.

Samaria

Ezra and Nehemiah granted
permission by Artaxerxes I to
return to Jerusalem 445 B.C.

Jerusalem

move. The Cyrus cylinder recorded the edict the new ruler proclaimed in 538 B.C., granting freedom to the enslaved peoples and permitting them to return to their homelands to take up the threads of their former existence once more:

> From . . . to Ashur and Susa, Agade, Ashnunnak, Zamban, Meturnu, Deri, with the territory of the land of Gutium, the cities on the other side of the Tigris . . . the gods, who dwelt in them, I brought back to their places . . . all their inhabitants I collected and restored them to their dwelling places. . . .[9]

The Biblical record of the proclamation of Cyrus (II Chron. 36:23; Ezra 1:2ff.) indicates that the exiles were given every encouragement by the Persian monarch to return to Judah and rebuild the Temple at Jerusalem. Cyrus even

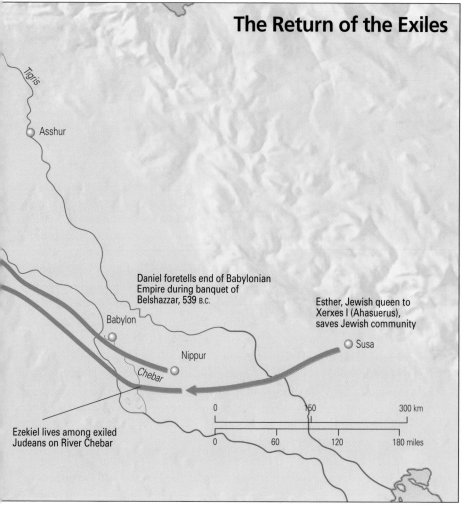

The Return of the Exiles

Tigris

Asshur

Daniel foretells end of Babylonian
Empire during banquet of
Belshazzar, 539 B.C.

Esther, Jewish queen to
Xerxes I (Ahasuerus),
saves Jewish community

Babylon

Susa

Nippur

Chebar

Ezekiel lives among exiled
Judeans on River Chebar

0   150   300 km

0   60   120   180 miles

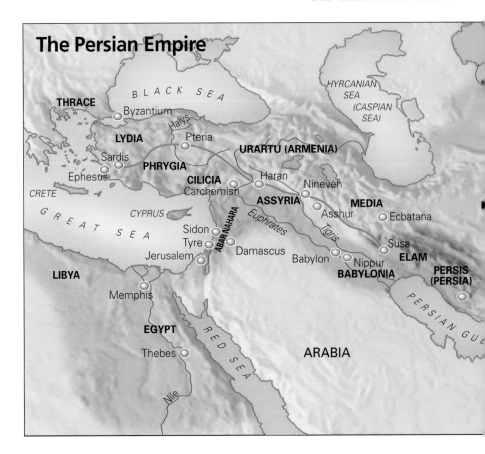

The Persian Empire

restored the vessels of gold and silver Nebuchadnezzar had brought to Babylon when Jerusalem fell to the Chaldeans, and appointed Sheshbazzar, a member of the royal family, as governor of Judah. These narratives are an accurate reflection of the policy Cyrus adopted towards all those who had been expatriated under the New Babylonian regime. By urging the captive peoples to return to their native lands and rebuild their religious shrines, Cyrus was at once relieving himself of responsibility for maintaining them in servility and promoting good will for his own regime in all parts of his newly-won empire.

But even with this form of encouragement, many of the Hebrew exiles were unwilling to return to their desolated homeland and work towards the reconstruction of national life. The more materially minded Jews had by now acquired considerable capital interests in Babylonia, and were not the least desirous of abandoning the comforts of life for the uncertainties and hardships of a pioneer existence in a desolated country.

By about 536 B.C. some of the former captives began the long and dangerous journey back to Judah, under the leadership of Sheshbazzar and Zerubbabel. They took their herds and flocks to their impoverished native country, and

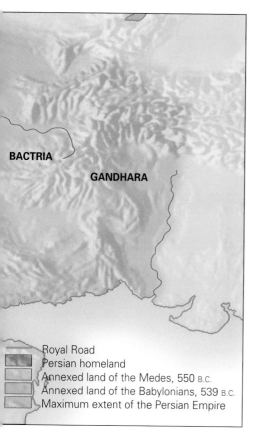

BACTRIA

GANDHARA

Royal Road
Persian homeland
Annexed land of the Medes, 550 B.C.
Annexed land of the Babylonians, 539 B.C.
Maximum extent of the Persian Empire

when they arrived in Jerusalem, they visited the site of the Temple and surveyed the desolate scene. Some of the more prominent heads of families contributed sums of money to the treasury for the restoration of the Temple, and Ezra described the donation of gold in terms of coinage, using the word *daric* (K.J.V. "dram"). It used to be argued that the drachma was not current in Palestine until after the conquests of Alexander the Great (c. 330 B.C.), but it is now known that the rising influence of the Greek empire contributed to the use of the Attic drachma as a standard coin in Palestine from the middle of the fifth century B.C.[10]

In the first year of the return, the altar of burnt offering was rebuilt, and some of the ancient rites were restored to public worship. Funds for the rebuilding of the Temple mounted steadily, and carpenters, masons, and other workmen were engaged to clear the site and commence the work of reconstruction. As in the days of Solomon, cedar trees from the Lebanon range were brought to Jerusalem, and in the second year of the return the foundations of the new Temple were laid, amidst scenes of considerable emotion (Ezra 3:8ff.).

Opposition to Reconstruction in Judea

But just when all seemed favorable for the rapid completion of the building, unexpected opposition arose from the people who had been living in the land during the Exile. These settlers were descendants of the Mesopotamians who had been deported to Palestine by Sargon, Esarhaddon, and Ashurbanipal, but in the main they comprised those who had populated Samaria when the northern kingdom collapsed. When the Samaritans volunteered to help in the work of building the Temple, their offer was rejected, probably because the Jews were afraid of becoming contaminated once again with idolatry. Smarting under this rebuff, the Samaritans indulged in political intrigue in order to hinder the rebuilding of the Temple, and obtained an injunction from Cambyses II (530–522 B.C.), the son of Cyrus, preventing further progress from being made.

283

The authentic nature of the Aramaic correspondence in Ezra 4:7ff. has been amply demonstrated by the famous Elephantine papyri. These documents were discovered in 1903, and consisted of letters written in Aramaic by Jews living in a military colony situated on the island of Elephantine near Aswan in Upper Egypt. Like the Biblical records, the papyri show that the Persian kings were interested in the religious and social welfare of their subjects.[11] During the Persian period (539–331 B.C.), Aramaic became the language of trade and diplomacy throughout the empire, and gradually replaced Hebrew as the spoken language among the Jews. In particular, the papyri show that the literary forms Ezra employed were characteristic of the fifth century B.C., and that the letter contained in the fourth chapter of his book is to be dated not later than that period. The spelling of the royal names in Ezra exhibits some variation from the usage current in the fifth and later centuries B.C., and it is probable that the Biblical forms were derived from earlier Persian renderings, which were subsequently modified.

Some thirteen years had elapsed from the laying of the foundations of the second Temple when a period of confusion arose in the Persian empire. Cambyses, who had included Egypt in the mighty dominions of Persia by defeating Psamtik III at Pelusium about the year 525 B.C., became mentally ill shortly afterwards, and committed suicide in 522 B.C. Some of the provinces that had been subjugated by Cyrus revolted and endeavored to break away from the empire, but order was finally restored by an Achaemenid prince, Darius the Great (522–486 B.C.). While he was regaining military control, the inhabitants of Judah experienced a measure of independence, and when Darius reestablished imperial rule, he maintained a policy of tolerance and benevolence towards them. When he encouraged them to finish the work of rebuilding the Temple at Jerusalem, further opposition was encountered, whereupon Darius ordered a search to be made for the original decree authorizing the work (Ezra 6:1ff.). When it was found, Darius forbade further interference with the rebuilding, and provided a large subsidy for the completion of the undertaking.

Haggai and Zechariah

It was at this point that the prophets Haggai and Zechariah furnished the necessary moral impetus for the culmination of a task that had begun some fifteen years earlier. In the summer of 520 B.C. Haggai castigated the Jews for their indifference, and rebuked them for building their own houses while the house of God was neglected. He assured the inhabitants of Jerusalem that the adversities they had been experiencing were punishments for their apathy. Zerubbabel was spurred on to give proper oversight to the work in hand, and when it appeared that the revolts in Babylonia might still be successful, he seems to have been regarded as the divinely anointed one who should lead Judah to independence.

Relief portrait of Darius I.

Zechariah, who prophesied in the late autumn of 520 B.C., also looked forward to the liberation of the nation from foreign domination, and confidently expected a restored people to be ruled over by a descendant of the house of David. He continued the work of Haggai in urging the completion of the second Temple, and in 515 B.C., some seventy years after the destruction of the first building, its successor was dedicated. Although the Persians had appointed Tattenai as the military governor of Judah (Ezra 6:13), they encouraged the state to function as a religious rather than a political community, with Josiah the high priest at its head. Whether Zerubbabel died, or was removed from office by the Persians as a precautionary measure, is unknown. At all events, the political situation in Judah appears to have been stabilized by the establishment of a theocratic system supported by Persian rule.

The book of Ezra passes over the period of fifty-seven years that followed the completion of the second Temple in silence. In the Persian empire, the death of Darius I in 486 B.C. was followed by the accession of his son Xerxes (486–465 B.C.). This ruler, who is probably the Ahasuerus of Ezra 4:6, maintained the scope and splendor of the empire, and kept some of his more restless subjects under rigid military control. An inscription from his reign that was found at Persepolis in 1939 attests to the vigor of his rule, and showed his enthusiasm for the worship of the Persian deity Ahuramazda.[12] He was succeeded in 465 B.C. by his second son, Artaxerxes I Longimanus, who is evidently the Artaxerxes mentioned by Ezra and Nehemiah.

During this period the Judean community struggled valiantly to overcome the poverty with which the land was beset, and tried hard to wring a measure of prosperity from the inhospitable soil. But the once proud capital city still bore the marks of its humiliation, and although the Temple had been completed, the city was still without walls. In consequence, the Samaritans and others who had settled in the vicinity had easy access to Jerusalem, and could pillage, rob, and destroy at will. When a prosperous state failed to materialize within a short time of the return from exile, the enthusiasm of the people waned. Although the glowing words of prophecy stirred them to action for the building of the Temple, it was not long before the inhabitants of Judah, or Judea, as the new state came to be known, succumbed to the opposition of their local enemies. For several decades the Jews eked out a precarious living around Jerusalem, and were at the mercy of anyone who chose to frustrate their humble designs.

The Work of Ezra and Nehemiah

But unexpected assistance was forthcoming from Jews in the Persian empire who, while being loyal to the Achaemenid regime, were also interested in the religious welfare of the struggling theocracy in Palestine. They brought pressure to bear upon the Persian government, and in 458 B.C. Artaxerxes I, who was sympathetic to their requests, appointed Ezra, a member of a Jewish priestly family, to go to Jerusalem as a royal commissioner to establish Jewish law there. He was accompanied by a number of Babylonian Jews and some Levites (Ezra 8:1ff.), and he brought with him a royal decree that required the Jews to obey his directions for the regulating of religious life in Judea.

When he arrived in Jerusalem, Ezra was distressed to see the way in which the Jews had intermarried with their heathen neighbors. Being conversant with the earlier history of the nation, he realized that such a course might well end in disaster, since it would probably bring about a renewal of the idolatrous practices for which the nation had been punished by exile. Accordingly he offered up prayers to God for the forgiveness of the people, and they in turn acknowledged their sin with penitence and grief. Relying on his authority as a royal commissioner, he then proposed drastic measures, which involved the dissolution of the mixed marriages that had already been contracted. This reform was particularly offensive to the Samaritans, who claimed to be descended from Jewish stock and resented any suggestion to the contrary.

Ezra saw that the position of the inhabitants of Jerusalem would continue to be insecure until the wall of the city was rebuilt. But when he prepared to undertake this task, his enemies allied with Rehum, the governor of Samaria, and persuaded Artaxerxes that once the walls of Jerusalem were rebuilt, Judea would revolt against Persian rule and become an autonomous state. About this time Ezra returned to Persia, probably to report on his mission to the central administration, and the Judeans were once more left to the mercy of their enemies.

Twelve years later, Nehemiah, a highly placed Jewish official in the Persian court, was informed of the privations that had overtaken the returned exiles. When he learned of the desolation and helplessness of Judea he was greatly distressed, and sought permission of Artaxerxes to go to Jerusalem and rebuild the ruined portions of the city. In keeping with the tolerance towards other religions that characterized the Persian rulers as a whole, Artaxerxes appointed Nehemiah as governor of Judea, and furnished him with the necessary documents establishing his authority. Whereas Ezra had shown more enthusiasm than discretion in prosecuting his work, Nehemiah realized that the utmost tact and diplomacy would be necessary if the Jewish state was to survive. He had already demonstrated his administrative abilities in the Persian court, and he now brought these talents to bear upon the discouraging situation that confronted him in Jerusalem in 445 B.C.

While Nehemiah shared with Ezra the conviction that the most urgent task was the reconstruction of the city walls, he was sufficiently practical in outlook to realize that it could only succeed if it received the enthusiastic support of the whole populace. He therefore called the leaders of the community together, and fired them with a desire to rebuild the city walls as a preliminary step towards restoring the economy of the city. Whereas Eliashib the high priest and others had opposed the reforming zeal of Ezra, probably because of professional jealousy, they were prepared to follow the energetic leadership of a competent layman.

The enthusiasm Nehemiah kindled among the people of Judea was timely. For some years the repatriated Jews had experienced great hardship, and the economy of the community was in a precarious state. The wealthier inhabitants were depriving the poorer ones of their holdings, while unscrupulous traders were profiting from the uncertain economic conditions. Intermarriage with the surrounding peoples was rife, and the resurgence of Canaanite idolatry was an ever-present threat to the spiritual life of the faithful Jews.

But Nehemiah was undismayed, and he began to organize the population for the task of rebuilding. When the foundations had been cleared and the projected course of the walls had been determined, Nehemiah divided up the people into groups and set them to work in such a manner that the entire reconstruction proceeded smoothly and without interruption. Those who were skilled artisans labored at their own trades, while others contributed in whatever way they could to assist the masons and builders.

Many of those who owned property near the city wall worked in the vicinity of their own homes, and Nehemiah discreetly enlisted the concern they felt for their own belongings and used it to kindle enthusiasm and a sense of responsibility among the whole populace. Almost immediately a great wave of patriotism

Persepolis—ruins of the royal city of the Achaemenid rulers of Persia. King Darius I commenced building the city in 518 B.C.

swept over the Jews in Jerusalem, and spread to neighboring towns such as Jericho, Gibeon, and Tekoa, bringing the inhabitants of those places away from the harvest fields to work on the walls of Jerusalem under the blazing summer sun. Nehemiah gained further popular support by controlling profiteering in foodstuffs and regulating the interest rates on mortgaged property (Neh. 5:1ff.). He set a fine example of behavior and moral rectitude by refusing to accept compensation for his own part in the task of reconstruction, and this magnificent gesture raised the morale of the people to new heights.

Renewed Local Opposition

But the enthusiasm with which the Jews were applying themselves to their long-neglected task alarmed Sanballat, one of the Samaritan leaders. From the beginning he had ridiculed the project, and had freely predicted its complete failure.

He had reckoned without the inspired leadership of Nehemiah, however, and now that the wall was rising steadily all around the city, he saw that his hopes for controlling Jerusalem were disappearing rapidly. He therefore conspired with Tobias the Ammonite and Geshem the Arab to attack the builders and demolish the walls. In anticipation of such an eventuality, however, Nehemiah had posted guards all around the city, and armed the workers so that they could beat off any attack in their vicinity.

The names of the two men who allied with Sanballat have been authenticated by recent archaeological discoveries. The Zeno Papyri found at Geraza in the Egyptian Fayyum contained a letter from "Tobias, the governor of Ammon" dealing with affairs in Palestine. This document came from the archives of an Egyptian official who lived in the reign of Ptolemy II Philadelphus (285–246 B.C.), and the author of the letter was without doubt a descendant of the man who opposed Nehemiah.[13] Ruins of the family castle of Tobias may still be seen just east of Amman in Transjordan, and his name is carved on the rock face near the ancestral tombs.[14] Geshem the Arab, whom Nehemiah also called

Gashmu (Neh. 6:6), is now known to have been the Persian governor of north-west Arabia.[15]

With the increasing progress of the building operation, the morale of the inhabitants of Jerusalem rose to new heights, and all those who were involved worked continuously to bring to completion that which they had begun so diffidently. When Sanballat saw that it was now impossible for him to succeed in a frontal attack upon the rapidly growing fortifications, he endeavored to lure Nehemiah to his death outside the city (Neh. 6:1ff.). But this plan was doomed to failure from the very start, and when Nehemiah refused to have any dealings with him, Sanballat sent him a letter that in effect accused him of disloyalty to the Persian regime (Neh. 6:5ff.). Even this threat was insufficient to deter Nehemiah from accomplishing his task, and such was his resolution and fortitude that the walls of Jerusalem were erected in the amazingly short period of fifty-two days, after which they were consecrated amid scenes of great splendor and rejoicing (Neh. 12:27ff.).

The Reforms of Ezra

Once the city was safe from attack, the inhabitants were free to build their own houses and cultivate their lands without fear of outside interference. Nehemiah saw that the right time had now arrived for the reorganization of community life along spiritual lines, and Ezra was summoned in 444 B.C. to proclaim the law to the people. This learned scribe revived the ancient Feast of the Booths, or Tabernacles (Neh. 8:14ff.), and when he was assured that the community would remain loyal to the precepts of the law, he approached once again the vexing question of Jewish intermarriage with foreigners. After a period of prayer and fasting on the twenty-fourth of Nisan in the year 444 B.C., the people made a covenant by which they undertook to abandon marriage with non-Jewish peoples, and observe the obligations of the law in communal living. In addition, they promised to keep the sabbath consistently as a holy day, to re-introduce the sabbatical year with its remission of debts (Deut. 15:1ff.), and to revive the principle of tithe offerings. The traditional enemies of Israel were also expelled from fellowship with the worshiping community (Neh. 13:1ff.), and a register of unsullied Israelite stock was compiled.

When the religious foundations of Judaism had thus been laid, Nehemiah placed his brother Hanani in charge of the city, along with Hananiah, the palace governor. Some authorities think that Nehemiah was recalled to Persia because of some dissatisfaction with his administration of affairs, but in any event he returned to Jerusalem in the thirty-second year of King Artaxerxes I (433–432 B.C.).[16] On his arrival he discovered that the high priest Eliashib had allowed Tobias the Ammonite, who had been allied with Sanballat, to live in one of the rooms of the Temple (Neh. 13:4f.). Nehemiah evicted Tobias promptly, and commenced a program of reform that resulted in better administrative machinery being established for the Temple, and also an assured income for the priests and Levites. In addition, he enforced the regulations regarding sabbath observance and intermarriage with pagans that had been promulgated by Ezra the scribe.

Perhaps the most significant result of these reforms was the worsening of relations between the Jews and Samaritans, which took place when Nehemiah discovered that one of the grandsons of Eliashib had married the daughter of Sanballat. The offending individual was speedily expelled from the community, and according to a tradition preserved by the Jewish historian Josephus, he became the first high priest of the Samaritans at Shechem. This event precipitated the rupture between the Jews and Samaritans that occurred during this period.

Chronological Problems of the Period

By the year 432 B.C., the foundations of traditional Judaism had been laid and the hieratic commonwealth firmly established. The reforming zeal of Ezra was supported by the realistic administration of the dynamic leader Nehemiah, without whose assistance Ezra would almost certainly have failed in his task. So closely interwoven are the activities of these two men that some scholars have reversed the Scriptural sequence of events, making Nehemiah precede Ezra, and placing both of them in the reign of Artaxerxes II (404–359 B.C.). This has been done in the belief that the reforms of Ezra would only be feasible against a background of powerful support from Nehemiah. Such a view merely substantiates the general impression left by the books of Ezra and Nehemiah as they now stand, and does not of itself necessitate any change in the traditional order of events.

Other scholars have found difficulty in interpreting the chronology of the fourth chapter of the book of Ezra, and many have adopted the view that the Artaxerxes mentioned in the narratives is Artaxerxes II.[17] Archaeology is unable at the present to throw specific light upon this perplexing matter, and a great many of the arguments from other standpoints are far from conclusive.[18] It has been alleged that there is a conflict between references in Ezra 9:9 and Nehemiah 12:23ff., where in the former Ezra is giving thanks for the restored walls of the city. This interpretation arises from an incorrect understanding of the text, which speaks of the hope of restoration rather than its actual accomplishment.

It would appear to the present writer that arguments for reversing the traditional order of events are inconclusive, and that the present problems of chronology are made even more complex by adopting such a procedure. As Gordon points out, it is important to realize that the presence of an able administrator such as Nehemiah would be a virtual necessity if the mistakes and failures of an overzealous and impractical scribe such as Ezra were to be rectified, and that the reverse situation would hardly be true to the facts of the case.[19]

Decline of the Persian Empire

Very little is known of what transpired in Judea between 432 B.C. and 411 B.C., when a Persian official named Bagoas was acting as military governor. At that time Johanan the high priest, grandson of Eliashib, occupied an important political position in the community. He fell into disfavor with Bagoas when he murdered his own brother in the Temple in 408 B.C., and shortly afterwards he was succeeded by his son Jedaiah.

The extent of the Persian empire Cyrus, Cambyses, and Darius had established "from India to Ethiopia" (Esth. 1:1) remained constant throughout the reigns of their successors. The Achaemenians treated their subjects with kindness and tolerance, and many provinces such as Judea enjoyed a considerable degree of autonomy. This occasionally incited malcontents in the empire to revolt, particularly if the satraps or provincial governors were behaving in a harsh or despotic manner. But while the empire was flourishing outwardly, the seeds of its own ruin were being sown quite inadvertently by the employment of foreign mercenary troops, particularly those from Greece, in the Achaemenian armies. Many of the Persian victories were won by Greek forces led by Greek generals, and it was only the suspicion and disunity that existed among the Greeks as a whole that enabled the Persians to utilize their services successfully. During the reign of Darius I (522–486 B.C.) and Xerxes I (486–465 B.C.), Greek influence spread quickly through the empire, due largely to the trade relations that existed between Persia and the countries of the Aegean. Darius I adopted the idea of monetary exchange current in Asia Minor and Phoenicia, and minted gold coins for the empire. His satraps throughout the Persian realm were given the privilege of minted coinage in silver.

The first signs of the decline of Persian power came in the reign of Artaxerxes II (404–359 B.C.), when revolts in different parts of the empire threatened to bring the regime to a close. For nearly forty years (378–340 B.C.) Egypt enjoyed independence from Persian rule while Artaxerxes III (358–338 B.C.) was struggling to regain the ground his predecessor had lost. Darius III, the last Persian king, who succeeded to the throne in 336 B.C., strengthened his control over the Greek cities, and reconquered Egypt in 334 B.C. To all appearances the stability of the Achaemenian regime was restored, and the Persians looked with confidence towards the continuance of their imperial power. But this state of affairs was not to last, for in 334 B.C. Alexander the Great set out to free the Greek cities from Persian control, and launched a military campaign against Persia in fulfillment of the ambition of his redoubtable father, Philip of Macedon.

NOTES

1. C. L. Woolley, *Ur of the Chaldees,* pp. 151f.

2. *Praep. Evang.* ix, 41.

3. Cf. R. K. Harrison, *Introduction to the Old Testament* (1969), pp. 1115ff.

4. C. L. Woolley, *op. cit.,* p. 153.

5. *Ibid.,* pp. 156f.

6. J. Finegan, *Light From the Ancient Past,* p. 190.

7. R. P. Dougherty, *Nabonidus and Belshazzar* (1929), pp. 59ff., 194.

8. J. Finegan, *op. cit.,* p. 191.

9. *Ibid.,* pp. 191f.

10. W. F. Albright in *Old Testament Commentary* (1948), p. 154.

11. J. Finegan, *op. cit.,* p. 201.

12. *Ibid.,* pp. 199f.

13. M. Burrows, *What Mean These Stones?,* p. 111.

14. *Ibid.,* p. 133.

15. W. F. Albright, *op. cit.,* p. 154.

16. H. M. Orlinsky, *Ancient Israel,* p. 139.

17. Cf. H. H. Rowley, *Bulletin of the John Rylands Library* (1955), XXXVII, No. 2, pp. 537ff.

18. Cf. J. Finegan, *op. cit.,* p. 200.

19. C. H. Gordon, *Introduction to Old Testament Times,* p. 270 *note.* For a survey of the chronological problems, see J. Bright, *A History of Israel* (1959), pp. 375ff.; R. K. Harrison, *op. cit.,* pp. 1145ff.

11. The Rise of Judaism

CHRONOLOGY OF THIS CHAPTER

THE GREEK PERIOD	331–65 B.C.

ALTHOUGH THE PEOPLES OF ISRAEL AND JUDAH HAD MET with exile at successive periods, and had been scattered among foreigners, they were never wholly absorbed by the communities in which they settled. For the most part, the Jews of the Dispersion, as these expatriate colonies were called, managed to survive through the exercise of their distinctive religious beliefs. During the Persian regime, they took advantage of the political tolerance that was displayed to subjugated peoples generally, and utilized their abilities in the political, business, and commercial life of the empire. Flourishing Jewish communities arose at widely separated points, and their loyalty to Achaemenian rule often caused them to be regarded with suspicion by their less prosperous neighbors, many of whom resented Persian domination bitterly.[1]

The Beginnings of Anti-Semitism

These conditions favored the rise of anti-Semitism, and one such outburst occurred in Egypt about 410 B.C., during the reign of Darius II, when the Jewish temple at Elephantine was sacked in an Egyptian uprising against the Persian conquerors. This attack on Jewish interests was mentioned in one of the Elephantine Papyri, and is the first recorded incident of its kind. The book of Esther reflects a similar situation at the other end of the empire, where a Jewish colony at Susa narrowly escaped extermination in a plot to destroy other Jewish colonies throughout the imperial domain.

294

The book of Esther is a valuable source of information about the Achaemenian regime, for its vocabulary has an unmistakably Persian flavor, and the narrative itself hails from a background of imperial administration. The author was familiar with the system by which a council of seven nobles (Ezra 7:14) advised the king on political matters (Esth. 1:14), and also knew that the laws of the Medes and Persians were immutable (Esth. 8:8). The court intrigue the book depicts was characteristic of the period, and the ease with which Esther calmly concealed her Jewish connections was in full accord with the concept Gordon has styled "dissimulation."[2] This principle permitted an individual to give the appearance of denying his normal religious affiliations and act as though he were a member of a different religious faith so as to avoid personal harm or danger. Thus Esther employed this defense when she was taken into the royal household (Esth. 2:10), and in the same way, when the scheming anti-Semite Haman met his end on the gallows he had prepared for Mordecai, the cousin of Esther, the Gentile population of Susa behaved as though they themselves were Jews (Esth. 8:17).

Excavations at Susa uncovered a quadrangular prism inscribed with numbers, similar to the die which Haman employed in setting a date for the annihilation of the Jews (Esth. 3:7), and which was known at that time as *pur*. The Feast of Purim, which was subsequently instituted to commemorate the deliverance of the Persian Jews from their enemies, took its name from the die that had providentially afforded them sufficient respite to employ counter-measures for their protection (Esth. 9:26).

In essence, the anti-Semitic attitudes of the Egyptians and Persians as exhibited in these incidents are characteristic of the hasty emotional judgments and consequent reactions of the unthinking majority when an expatriate minority achieves material success by dint of hard work. As Orlinsky properly points out, this situation could hardly fail to arise throughout the empire where communities of Jews were flourishing under the tolerant Persian regime.[3] It is quite probable that these and other factors contributed significantly to the rise of Jewish nationalism, which became a marked feature of this period. Despite the fact that the Jews were scattered throughout the empire, they acknowledged the Temple at Jerusalem as the center of Judaism proper, and the faithful Jew everywhere contributed his yearly half-shekel for the maintenance of Temple worship. The scattered Jewish colonies discovered that their ancestral faith proved to be a powerful cohesive factor in communal living, and its value in this respect was further stressed when the Persian empire collapsed under the attacks of Alexander the Great.

The Greek Period

The rise of Greek power commenced with Philip of Macedon, who united part of Greece before beginning an assault to recapture other Greek cities from Persian domination. He died in 336 B.C. before being able to accomplish his aim, and Alexander his son succeeded him. This vigorous ruler conquered Asia Minor in 333 B.C. marched through Syria, and annexed Egypt, which had been subdued by Darius III in 334 B.C. Alexander then led his forces beyond the Tigris to Gaugamela, where he inflicted a severe defeat upon Darius. Susa, Persepolis, and Ecbatana fell in quick succession, and after the power of the Persian regime had been broken, Alexander conquered India and returned to Babylon in 323 B.C., where he died at the age of thirty-three.

Although his effective military career was comparatively short, Alexander ushered in the Hellenic period, which brought about far-reaching changes in the cultural patterns of the Near East. Greek became the *lingua franca,* and the ancient cuneiform and hieroglyphic languages fell into gradual disuse. Hellenism dominated the old Persian empire, and the adoption of Greek traditions and customs brought about important changes in the fields of science, art, philosophy, and religion. Hellenistic culture was epitomized in such cities as Alexandria, a magnificent example of stately Greek architecture and design, which accommodated over a million inhabitants. Its seaport attracted the fleets of all maritime nations, and its reputation as an intellectual center was unparalleled in antiquity. From the third century B.C. the astronomical schools of Alexandria surpassed those of ancient Babylonia, while other academies of learning added to the already impressive intellectual reputation of the great city. The most renowned library of antiquity had been established there in the fourth century B.C. by Ptolemy I (323–285 B.C.) and was enlarged by Ptolemy II Philadelphus (285–247 B.C.), with the avowed aim of housing every significant literary work extant. Public gardens, zoos, and museums further contributed to the splendor of this cosmopolitan city, rivaling in their magnificence the glories of ancient Babylon.

The bustling activity of Alexandria was characteristic of the Greek period, which saw a greater interchange of commodities, traditions, and ideas than anything the world had known previously. This situation naturally presented a great many problems for the small state of Judea, which was struggling hard to retain its identity in the Greek world and preserve intact its traditional theocratic structure and ideals. The cultural changes that were taking place across the Greek empire were more pervasive than anything the Jews had experienced previously in their varied history. Even more important for the survival of Jewish cultural and religious life than the commercial activity of Greek traders, the social conflicts of Hellenic society, or the superstitions of pagan religion were the threats the various phases of Greek thought posed to traditional Judaism. The plain fact was that the gods of such Greek philosophers as Plato and Aristotle had little or nothing in common with the ancestral Deity of the Hebrew people.

Stoicism

One of the most important philosophical movements of the Hellenistic period owed its origin to a thinker of Phoenician stock named Zeno (336–264 B.C.). The philosophy he founded was named Stoicism, after the *Stoa Poikile,* the portico in Athens where Zeno taught his students. After his death his thought underwent some modification at the hands of his successors, particularly Chrysippus (c. 280–207 B.C.), and at a later time still it came under the influence of Platonism. Thus in the New Testament period, when Paul encountered Stoicism at Athens (Acts 17:18), he was dealing with a philosophy that had undergone considerable change at the hands of successive exponents.

While the main tenets of Stoicism do not lend themselves readily to consistent description, they followed the views of Socrates, Plato, and Aristotle in at least one respect, namely, that of thinking that the world was the product of an advanced degree of skill, and that it was guided by a beneficent providence so as to secure the greatest good for mankind.

But whereas Plato and Aristotle held to the general immateriality of reason, Stoicism employed the term "logos" or "word" to describe what was basically a principle of rationality that permeated all of nature. Zeno and his followers admitted to a belief in the survival of the human soul after death, but maintained that this state would only continue until the end of the particular world-phase to which it belonged. At this juncture, like everything else, it would be absorbed into the divine substance as the preface to an entirely new act of creativity. Since each new period was thought to constitute an exact repetition of the ones that had preceded it, some sort of concept of eternal life was able to be entertained.

Not merely were the Stoics pantheists, but they were also determinists and fatalists in the strictest sense. They believed that not even the divine will was really free, since in their view its course over the ages was determined by an inflexible logic that fixed all the manifold details of the successive cycles of existence long beforehand. Thus even God could not interfere in order to save a man from the consequences of his appointed fate.

Under Cleanthes and Chrysippus the rather pedantic ethic of Stoicism was modified until it assumed a more human and reasonable form. This trend was exemplified in the thought of the three great Stoic writers of the Roman empire, namely, Seneca, Epictetus, and Marcus Aurelius, to whom Stoicism as an ethical and philosophical system owes whatever popularity it has received in the Western world.[4]

Epicureanism

Epicurus (341–270 B.C.) was probably an even greater threat to the survival of

The Acropolis, Athens, surmounted by the Parthenon.

Judaism than either Plato or Aristotle. The founder of this influential philosophical movement was born in 341 B.C. on the island of Samos. He studied for a time under a disciple of Democritus, the atomistic philosopher, and his early career was marked by poverty and political disfavor. Gradually he attracted a circle of followers, and began to teach his characteristic doctrines. In 306 B.C. he established his school in Athens, and continued his activities there until his death in 270 B.C.

There can be little doubt that the experiences of his early life, coupled with the general uncertainty of existence in the period following the death of Alexander the Great, contributed materially to the distinct emphasis of his doctrine. Epicurus taught that the primary business of living was the pursuit of happiness by means of serene detachment from extremes of behavior. This attitude was held to be characteristic of that experienced by the gods, who were completely uninterested in human beings and their problems.

Epicurus followed Democritus in the belief that all phenomena were formed in a rather mechanical manner from a concourse of atomic quanta that apparently came together by accident. Because human beings were also constructed in this general way, it was maintained that there was no need for anyone to be concerned about the possibility of divine intervention in the affairs of everyday life. In the same manner the question of punishment after death for sins committed during this life did not really arise either, since death brought about a complete and irrevocable dispersion of the individual's constituent atoms.

The ruins of the Parthenon, Athens, devoted to Pallas Athena.

Epicurus counseled consistently against indulgences of any kind, and his more immediate followers professed to find contentment in a regulated existence that stressed the joys and comforts of friendship.[5]

Although his philosophical system was a valuable protest against the pantheism and fatalism of Zeno and his followers, his insistence that sensuality was incompatible with true pleasure or happiness was carefully overlooked by the majority of those in the Greek dominions who were influenced by his teachings. Hellenic society was notorious for its corruption, coarseness, and immorality, and the pursuit of pleasure for its own sake, combined with a lack of insistence on the authority of an absolute moral law, contained within itself the seeds of its own destruction.

Jewish Resistance to Greek Culture

The inhabitants of Judea struggled valiantly against the infiltration of these influences, and though they often found themselves hard pressed both from inside and outside by the onset of Hellenism, they manifested a consistent determination to maintain their distinctive religious character, as their forbears had done during the period of the Exile. It cannot be denied that, to the casual observer, the culture of the Greeks had a pervasive, even seductive charm, and it was only on closer examination that the intelligence and refinement Hellenism presented to the world were seen to be accompanied by factors that were of the most debasing and demoralizing kind.

While the majority of the Jews resisted the impact of Greek thought without undue strain, the upper classes appeared to be most susceptible to its attractions. Its insidious nature enabled it to penetrate into the strongholds of Judaism, despite the best efforts of the religious authorities to forestall it. Nevertheless, vigorous counter-measures were employed in an attempt to preserve the characteristic beliefs and customs of the Jews. The basis of traditional Judaism that had been laid in the Exile was strengthened and widened by the development of the theocratic ideal. The high-priesthood played an important part in this process, representing as it did the most advanced levels of administration in the religious community. During the postexilic period, the office of high priest appears to have undergone some degree of restoration, since there is no mention of such an individual in the ideal constitution envisaged in the book of Ezekiel. In developing Judaism, the high priest was in effect the spiritual head and representative of the state, controlling a spiritual hierarchy of priests, Levites, and Temple officers. The high priest epitomized the holiness of the state, and as such he claimed special privileges in the worship of the Temple.

The Scribes and the Synagogue

The early postexilic period in Judea saw the rise of an important group known as the scribes, who were influential in the development of traditional Jewish law. While Ezra the scribe had established the returned community on the basis of Pentateuchal law, it became evident that interpreters were needed to expound the tenets of that law to the people (Neh. 8:8), and to instruct them in its requirements. The same tradition of priestly scholarship that had brought Ezra to the forefront also supplied students, interpreters, and copyists of the law, who replaced the "sages" or "wise men" of the times prior to the days of Ezra. The office these men occupied was a responsible one, and brought to the scribes an increasing measure of public esteem. When many of the priests succumbed to the attraction of Hellenism, the scribes succeeded them as guardians and vindicators of the law.

As Aramaic came into vogue in Judea and replaced Hebrew as the common tongue, the scribes maintained their familiarity with the language of their forefathers, and established themselves as professional students of the law. They investigated the entire corpus of the Hebrew religious writings, and expounded them in relation to the problems of living that arose in the community. In course of time the interpretations they placed upon the law acquired an authority of their own, and in this way there arose a body of inferential teaching that sup-

Opposite: A view of part of the Herodian north palace at Masada. The graceful columns are executed in the popular Hellenistic Corinthian style.

plemented the dogmatic statements of the law. During the Greek period the scribes became accepted as the real instructors of the faithful Jews, and at a later time they were dignified by the title of "rabbi."

Because of their special position in the community as interpreters of the law, the scribes used the synagogues as their principal sphere of influence. Independence from the sacrificial worship of the Temple had been forced upon the Jews during the Exile, and the devotional form of worship Jeremiah, Ezekiel, and other prophets had envisaged became the established pattern of regular religious activity. In Judea, the synagogue met this need by providing a place where the law could be read and studied, so that the custom of attending the synagogue on the sabbath day for instruction in the law and for prayer grew with considerable rapidity. Archaeological excavations in Palestine have yielded no traces of the earlier "house synagogues" to date, and the oldest surviving indication of such a building is contained in an inscription at Jerusalem dating from the end of the second century B.C. Splendid examples of synagogues dating from the Christian era have been uncovered at Capernaum in Galilee, and elsewhere.[6]

Besides being the center of religious instruction for children and adults, the synagogue served as a focal point for community activity. In the main, the scribes were well versed in the ways of contemporary society, and so were in a position to offer sound advice on the various problems that affected the individual in his environment. Legal business of a local nature was often transacted in the synagogue, and in times of political disquiet the opinions of the faithful Jews were frequently crystallized by means of synagogue discussion groups.

The Pharisees

What has been seen as a reaction on the part of normative Judaism to the culture of the Greek empire[7] took place in the second century B.C. in the form of another group of zealous teachers of the law. Historically they were the successors of Ezra and the early scribes, and were known as Pharisees or "separatists," because they aimed at a higher degree of religious sanctity and moral strictness than the average Jew. In actual fact this separation consisted mainly of certain scruples respecting food and religious ceremonies, and the degree of outward show that was often involved brought charges of hypocrisy against the Pharisees as a whole. There can be no doubt, however, that they were sincere in their convictions, though it is equally true that their religion lacked depth.

They saw no incompatibility between an overruling divine providence and the free operation of human will, rejecting entirely the fatalism of Stoic philosophy. The general tradition of the Pharisees was based on the acceptance of oral law as of equal authority with the Pentateuch. If a man observed the injunctions of the written law of Moses, and also carried out the traditional teachings

The reconstructed third-century A.D. synagogue at Capernaum, on the Sea of Galilee. The synagogue served as a focal point for community activity.

that had arisen from the exposition of that law, he could obtain justification with God. They taught that atonement for sin could be obtained by fasting, confessions, ceremonial ablutions, and the giving of alms. While they agreed with the Stoics to some extent in their doctrine of predestination, the Pharisees also believed in the immortality of the soul, in angels, demons, and spirits, and in the resurrection of the body.

In addition, they encouraged the baptism of proselytes to Judaism, indulged in speculation about wisdom, and fostered the doctrine of the Messiah. This latter had both religious and political implications, for while the Pharisees expected the coming of a "Son of David" who would fulfill the law and elevate the theocracy to an unprecedented level, they also looked to Him to achieve permanent deliverance from foreign domination for the state of Judea, and make all nations subject to a restored and victorious Israel.

The shallowness of Pharisaic doctrine may perhaps be seen best of all in their thought concerning the state of future felicity after death. To say the least, these ideas were gross and materialistic in nature, conveying the impression that in the next world men would live in luxury, eating, drinking, and enjoying carnal relations with their earthly wives. It may have been for this as well as for other reasons that the Pharisees soon obtained the esteem and support of the populace, and so great was the influence they wielded that they left the impress of their doctrines on all subsequent forms of Judaism. In the second century B.C. they challenged the authority and prestige of the priestly scribes, and began to train their own lay scribes to instruct the people in the traditional law. While they undoubtedly placed great emphasis upon the legalistic and ritualistic aspects of religious life, they brought a degree of strength and stability to traditional Judaism that enabled it to survive the disaster that overtook the theocracy in the first century A.D.[8]

The Sadducees

A further religious group that arose in Jewish society at the end of the second century B.C. went under the name of Sadducees. The origin of this title is uncertain, and some authorities hold that it was derived from a Hebrew word meaning "righteous ones." Other scholars feel, however, that the party was named after Zadok, who was either the high priest under David (I Kings 1:8) and Solomon (I Chron. 29:22), or some early unidentified leader of the party. Ezekiel (44:15f.) had a high regard for the descendants of Zadok on account of their long-standing fidelity, and in his vision of the restored Temple the Zadokites were assigned special privileges, making them in effect the only legitimate priesthood. In the postexilic period, descendants of Zadok were found among the priestly class, and it is possible that the Sadducean party of later times originated with them.

Their importance in the Jewish state was out of all proportion to their limited numbers, for they consisted mainly of wealthy and educated individuals who kept aloof from the mass of the people generally. They were a conservative priestly aristocracy, who exercised a good deal of control over Temple ritual and worship, monopolizing the office of high priest. Despite the fact that they were in intellectual contact with Hellenism at an earlier period than the Pharisees, the Sadducees were more successful in resisting its attractions. This was probably the result of their insistence on confining their doctrines to what was found in the written law of Moses. They rejected entirely the validity of the oral tradition so dear to the Pharisees, and denied the authority of the unwritten Torah that the scribes and Pharisees alike expounded.

Only those doctrines which could claim a basis in the Mosaic law were acceptable to the Sadducees, for they regarded the Pentateuch alone of the Hebrew writings as authoritative in matters of faith. In consequence they denied the existence of angels, spirits, and demons, because they claimed that such spiritual beings had no real place in the events recorded in the Pentateuch. In the same manner they rejected the current theories of immortality, teaching instead that the soul died with the body. Probably the unpopularity of the Sadducees arose in part from their denial of so much that appeared to constitute an important part of Old Testament life and thought. Certainly their general aloofness and their connections with vested interests in Jerusalem did little to endear them to the common man.[9]

The Samaritans

These differing elements in Jewish society experienced a considerable measure of unity in the resistance they offered to the influence of the Samaritans. When the latter broke away from postexilic Judaism as a result of the reforms of Nehemiah, they established their own temple on Mount Gerizim, and formed a flourishing community in nearby Shechem at the beginning of the fourth century B.C. When Alexander swept victoriously across the Near East, the Samaritans revolted but were quickly crushed and driven out of Samaria. They were replaced by loyal Macedonians, and in an astute political move Alexander placed the province of Samaria under Jewish control. The Samaritans were required to comply with a number of exacting demands that were aimed at emphasizing the distinction between Jew and Samaritan. These circumstances greatly augmented the suspicion and animosity that already existed between the two peoples, and made it virtually impossible for them to have normal dealings with one another.

While the Jews regarded the Samaritans as the descendants of Mesopotamian expatriates whom Sargon had settled in Samaria at the time when the northern kingdom collapsed, the Samaritans themselves held quite a different theory of their origin. They traced their descent from the Israelites who remained loyal to Jehovah when the Ark of the Covenant was deposited at Shiloh (Judg. 18:1) instead of on Mount Gerizim, which they held to be its true location. As Gordon has pointed out, there is considerable evidence for the priority of the shrine in traditional Samaritan territory.[10] The book of Joshua (8:30ff.) records that after the fall of Ai, Joshua built a shrine in Mount Ebal, and at its consecration one half of the people assembled near the shrine while the other half gathered on Mount Gerizim, which stood at the other side of a narrow pass.

It is important to realize that the shrine Joshua built on Mount Ebal was the only one to be erected in accordance with the specific instructions of Moses (Deut. 27:4). The importance of the site may be judged from the orders Moses gave that the law should be inscribed upon the stones of the altar there (Deut. 27:8), and that the penalties that would follow breaches of the law should be proclaimed solemnly from the slopes of Mount Ebal (Deut. 11:29; 27:13; Josh. 8:33f.). It seems probable that Moses intended the center of Hebrew worship to be located on Mount Gerizim as the Samaritans insisted, and not at Jerusalem, which is never mentioned by name in the Pentateuch and which was a Jebusite stronghold in the time of Joshua.

The Samaritans had their own versions of the Hebrew Pentateuch, which they held to be as old as the sect itself. Their text was independent of Jewish

Artist's impression of the Jewish High Priest in his priestly robes and wearing his breastplate.

tradition, and is thought to have originated with the return of a deported priest to instruct the newly established inhabitants of Samaria in the law of Jehovah, after a plague of lions had terrorized them (II Kings 17:26ff.). If the Samaritan Pentateuch did arise in this manner, it would appear that the books of Moses were in existence by the time of Esarhaddon in a form similar to that which the Samaritans accepted as canonical. The text of the Samaritan Pentateuch has undergone considerable alteration at the hands of Samaritan scribes, but the canon is the same as that of the Hebrew Pentateuch. Like the Sadducees, the Samaritans rejected all other Hebrew religious writings, basing their faith and practice upon Pentateuchal doctrines alone. During the Greek period the Samaritans became attracted to the worldly materialism of Hellenic culture, but continued their religious interest in the provisions of the Mosaic covenant.[11]

Accurate scale model of Herod's Temple, Jerusalem.

The Jerusalem Temple

Probably the most symbolic feature of all Judaism was the Temple at Jerusalem.[12] In preexilic times the Temple had functioned in part as a royal chapel, but after the return to Judea it became the center of national religious life. Sacrificial worship was revived, and became the external mark of Jewish obedience to the Divine law. This important function of Temple life was controlled entirely by the priesthood, and since sacrifice could only be offered at Jerusalem, the Temple priests soon came to enjoy considerable prestige in the nation. Traditionally the priests exercised other functions in the community besides mediating between men and God, and these included the regulation of ritual, the enforcement of sanitary and medical laws, and the ordering of life in the state in a semi-judicial capacity.

Probably the work of Ezra included the revival of the preexilic system by which the priesthood had been divided into twenty-four sections. In the restored community each of these divisions ministered regularly in the Temple according to rota, and was attended by the Levites, who were organized on a similar basis. It was the task of the Levites to act as servants to the priests, but they also carried out other duties as overseers, doorkeepers, and singers. The Temple personnel were maintained by regular contributions of firstfruits, tithes, and other payments, which included the annual half-shekel contributed by every faithful adult Jew. This last donation was used to defray the expenses incurred in connection with the daily burnt offering and other communal sacrifices. The generosity of Jews who lived outside Palestine helped to swell Temple revenues, and towards the end of the Greek period the treasury housed great sums of money.

The offering of the daily sacrifice on behalf of the nation was the chief duty of the priests. This act of worship involved the sacrifice of a yearling lamb in the evening and at dawn, and was accompanied by cereal and drink offerings. The high priest generally officiated in worship on the sabbath day and at important religious festivals. The Temple was the place where public and private sacrifices took place under the direction of the priesthood, and was quite distinct from the synagogue, which was under the control of the scribes and Pharisees and provided a place for prayer, the reading of Scripture, and the exposition of the law. At a later period, the whole Jewish community was divided up into groups similar to those of the priesthood. Each group successively represented the entire nation at the sacrifice, making the daily offering on behalf of the populace. This practice continued until the destruction of the Jewish state in the first century A.D.

Although Judaism was established with the avowed purpose of exemplifying holiness, it proved to be subject to the temptations that overtake every authoritarian regime sooner or later. The esteem the priests commanded in the state was utilized to foist intolerable and oppressive religious and ceremonial burdens upon the nation. The worldliness of Hellenic culture proved very attractive to many members of the priesthood, and their attitude towards their duties and responsibilities became decidedly materialistic as a result. The high priest frequently used his spiritual position in the community to political advantage, and the later history of the Temple saw a great deal of intrigue taking place in the spheres of secular and religious power. But in spite of these adverse factors, the priesthood exerted a predominantly stabilizing influence in the lives of the people, and no other class in the entire history of the nation wielded more consistent control over individual and communal affairs alike.

NOTES

1. C. H. Gordon, *Introduction to Old Testament Times*, p. 274.

2. *Ibid.*, pp. 278f.

3. H. M. Orlinsky, *Ancient Israel*, p. 134.

4. E. Bréhier, *The History of Philosophy*, II: *The Hellenistic and Roman Age* (1965), pp. 31ff.

5. N. DeWitt, *Epicurus and His Philosophy* (1954), pp. 121ff.

6. J. Finegan, *Light From the Ancient Past*, pp. 226ff.

7. W. F. Albright, *From the Stone Age to Christianity*, p. 273.

8. M. C. Tenney, *New Testament Times* (1965), pp. 91ff.

9. *Ibid.*, pp. 94f.; J. Klausner, *Jesus of Nazareth* (1923), pp. 219ff.

10. C. H. Gordon, *op. cit.*, pp. 132f.

11. M. Gaster, *The Samaritans* (1923), pp. 10ff,

12. A. Parrot, *The Temple of Jerusalem* (1957), pp. 12ff.

12. The Period of the Maccabees

WHEN ALEXANDER THE GREAT DIED IN 323 B.C., THE EMPIRE he had established was robbed of leadership, and in an attempt to solve the impasse his generals divided up the conquered territory among themselves. As a result of this procedure five separate provinces were formed. Egypt was placed under the control of Ptolemy, who acted as regent for some years before actually becoming supreme ruler. Babylonia became the seat of the Seleucid regime while Macedonia was allotted to Antipater. Two others, Thrace and Phrygia, were governed by Lysimachus and Antigonus respectively. At a subsequent time further divisions occurred within the empire, and ultimately there emerged the three dynasties of Egypt, Syria, and Macedonia.

The Ptolemies

The Ptolemaic dynasty that succeeded to power in Egypt lasted for almost three centuries, and terminated only when Egypt became a Roman province in 30 B.C. Ptolemy I began his rule as regent for the mentally unstable half-brother of Alexander the Great, an arrangement that continued for six years. When his protégé was killed in 317 B.C., Ptolemy I continued as regent for the young son of Alexander, who succeeded to nominal power in Egypt. In the meantime Ptolemy was consolidating his position, and after a rule of only seven years, the descendant of Alexander the Great met an untimely end.

During the three years following the death of Alexander, Judea had formed part of the Syrian territory over which Seleucus I Nicator ruled, but in 320

B.C. Ptolemy I invaded Syria and annexed it to his own possessions. He then marched to Jerusalem, and taking advantage of Jewish unwillingness to desecrate the sabbath, he occupied the city without meeting any resistance and deported a number of the inhabitants to Egypt. The primary concern of Ptolemy was to gain military control over Judea, and once this was achieved he pursued the liberal and tolerant policy of Alexander. He encouraged the growth of Jewish settlements in Egypt, and won the confidence of the Jews to such an extent that many left Palestine and made Egypt their home. Ptolemy found the Jews to be loyal and reliable subjects, and under his successors the province of Judea enjoyed a long period of prosperity.

The Seleucids

A similar desire for friendship with the Jews characterized the earlier Seleucids. Nicator, who acquired a large portion of Babylonia and Syria at the death of Alexander, encouraged the Jews to migrate to Asia Minor, and offered them the privileges of citizenship in his domains. Later rulers of the Seleucid empire (312–64 B.C.) did not display the tolerance of the brilliant military strategist who established the dynasty, however, and a great many of the tribulations through which the Jews subsequently passed were caused by the tyrannical rule of the Seleucids who followed Antiochus III (223–187 B.C.), the sixth king of the dynasty.

The enlightened Ptolemy II (285–247 B.C.) is of importance for the interest he took in the history and culture of his Jewish subjects. It was during his reign that the great work of translating the sacred Hebrew Scriptures into the Greek language was begun. This version became known as the Septuagint, a name derived from the seventy scholars whom Ptolemy was supposed to have summoned from Jerusalem on the advice of his librarian to undertake the work of translation. It is probable that only the Pentateuch was rendered into Greek during the lifetime of Ptolemy II, since the entire version took until about the middle of the second century B.C. to be completed. The Septuagint proved to be the principal means by which Hebrew thought was conveyed to the Jews who lived outside Palestine, and being written in the *lingua franca* it brought before the pagan world also the treasures of the Old Testament. Prior to the Christian era the Hebrew Scriptures were frequently quoted from the Septuagint version, a practice that survived into the New Testament writings.

The political activities of Ptolemy II were directed at conciliating the people of Palestine, who were by this time firmly under the control of Egypt. To this end he built a number of cities that served as centers of influence for the Ptolemaic dynasty, among which were Philotera, south of the Sea of Galilee, and Ptolemais near Mount Carmel, founded on the site of the ancient Canaanite port of Accho. Under Ptolemy III (247–222 B.C.), a fresh wave of migrations to Egypt took place, with a resultant increase in the size of Jewish communities located in Alexandria and other Egyptian cities. The Ptolemaic dynasty was at its height during this period, and the benevolence of Egyptian rule, combined with the material prosperity of the age, proved very attractive to those Jews who were contemplating the prospect of life in Hellenized Egypt.

The Idumeans

During this period the inhabitants of Judea came into periodic contact with their Edomite enemies of preexilic days, whose descendants had become known as Idumeans. Archaeological discoveries in Transjordan have shown that the Edomites were overwhelmed by Arab groups before the end of the fifth century B.C.[1] Ostraca recovered from contemporary levels at Elath contained names that were clearly Arabic in character, indicating that Edomite power was already in eclipse during the period of Nehemiah.[2] Shortly thereafter many Edomites moved to Judea, where they settled in the south and received their name of Idumeans.[3]

After about a century the Arab group that had replaced the Edomites was itself ousted by the Nabateans, who were first mentioned in 612 B.C. when Antigonus the Greek launched an attack on their capital city of Petra.[4] Although he managed to capture the rocky plateau behind the city, his victory was short-lived because his troops were ambushed and wiped out as they returned home. The Nabateans adopted Aramaic as their spoken language instead of their native Arabic, and they set about restoring the economic fortunes of the former Edomite territory.

They commenced the formidable task of carving out their homes and temples from the red sandstone cliffs of the valley, and the ruins of these buildings can be seen at the present time. Of particular interest at Nabatean sites are the remains of the high places where sacrifices were offered to Nabatean gods, since they may throw some light on preexilic Israelite sacrificial practices. Other excavations have shown the extent to which the Nabateans constructed fortresses at strategic locations along their frontier in order to protect their kingdom from invasion.[5]

Religion and Politics in Judah

Comparatively little is known of the internal conditions of Judea under the Ptolemies, except that the Jews paid tribute to the Egyptians at regular

The Nabatean temple of El-khazne, cut into the rock face in Petra. The figures give some indication of the temple's dimensions.

intervals, and for their loyalty to the regime were rewarded with a degree of autonomy in local matters. There can be little doubt that the authority of the high priest was gradually increasing, and it is probably at this time that the judicial council, which was to become known as the Sanhedrin, began to exercise an influence over communal affairs. The origins of this Jewish supreme court are obscure, and at first it may have consisted of an assembly of elders. King Jehoshaphat appears to have bestowed a degree of legal authority on some such group (II Chron. 19:8ff.), and the basis of postexilic development may have been laid during the Exile, when elders in the community appear to have exercised a local magistracy. But the earliest reliable mention of such an assembly in Jerusalem occurs in the time of the Seleucid ruler Antiochus the Great (223–187 B.C.), when it was known by the Greek title *Gerousia*. At this period it consisted of the heads of leading Jewish families, and was imperialistic and priestly in nature.

During the reign of Ptolemy I, the office of high priest was greatly enhanced by the dignity and graciousness of the imposing figure of Simon I (c. 300–287 B.C.), whom Josephus styled "the Just." He was credited with the renovation of the Temple and the repair of the fortifications that surrounded Jerusalem. His virtues were lauded in the apocryphal book of Ecclesiasticus, and his influence was such that during his lifetime the government of the nation by the high priest assumed its most attractive form. This pleasing example was soon disregarded, however, for a successor, Onias II, who was of an avaricious nature, determined to withhold the tribute paid annually to his suzerain Ptolemy III. Josephus, the nephew of Onias, managed to thwart this scheme, and was rewarded by Ptolemy with the office of tax controller in Judea. He held this position for over twenty years, and during his period of administration he was able to effect considerable improvement in the financial condition of his country.

But a good deal of political intrigue was taking place in Jerusalem during his tenure of office. About 225 B.C. a small group of reactionaries arose, who began to influence the Jews against the continuance of the current Egyptian domination. When Antiochus III (the Great) succeeded to the throne of Syria in 223 B.C., this political party clamored for allegiance to his regime instead of to Egyptian rule. Relations between Egypt and Syria deteriorated in consequence of this reaction, and when Antiochus attempted to extend his influence into Palestine, Ptolemy IV (222–205 B.C.) was compelled to send an expedition against him, and defeated him in battle near Raphia. On his return, Ptolemy marched into Jerusalem, and after attempting to desecrate the Temple, he continued his journey to Alexandria, where he deprived the resident Jews of some of their privileges as a punishment for the disloyalty of their compatriots in Judea.

Another view of the rock-cut Nabatean structures at Petra.

Syria Annexes Judea

When Ptolemy IV died suddenly in 205 B.C., a period of political confusion ensued, during which his infant son Ptolemy V was placed on the throne. Antiochus III saw that the time was ripe for another invasion of Judea, and he appears to have been welcomed as a liberator by some segments of the populace. An Egyptian army marched into northern Palestine to check his advance, but it was defeated near Sidon in 198 B.C. Antiochus then occupied Judea, making it a part of the province of Syria, and when Jerusalem capitulated without a struggle the incorporation of Palestine into the Seleucid kingdom was complete.

Antiochus III continued the policy of tolerance towards the Jews that Seleucus I had initiated, and the people of Judea looked forward to a further period of prosperity under the Seleucid dynasty. Antiochus appointed Syrian military governors to office in Judea and imposed regular taxes upon the populace. While he guaranteed the sanctity of the Temple and gave ample grants to subsidize the priesthood, he exercised a degree of control over Judea that soon showed the Jews that they had actually gained nothing by their change of overlords. The political situation was complicated by the growing strength of Rome, and the internal civil strife so characteristic of the Greek period furnished the Romans with an excuse for intervention and the restoration of peace to the old Greek empire.[6]

315

Intervention of Rome

When the Roman legions invaded Asia Minor about the year 197 B.C., Antiochus was forced to abandon any plans he might have had for the complete subjugation of Egypt. He sent an expedition against the Romans, and after a protracted campaign the Syrian forces suffered heavy losses at the hands of Scipio Africanus at Magnesia in 190 B.C. Three years later Antiochus the Great was killed in an uprising at Elymais, and was succeeded by his son Seleucus IV (187–175 B.C.).

During the reign of Seleucus IV an incident took place that was to have a bearing upon subsequent political and religious factions in Judea. The reigning high priest Onias III was involved in a dispute with Simon, the commander of the Temple guard, over the vexing question of the collection of revenues by a civil official instead of by the high priest. In a fit of pique, Simon informed the viceroy of Seleucus that vast treasures were stored in the coffers of the Temple. Seleucus was anxious to pay off some of the debts Antiochus the Great had incurred in his struggle against the Roman empire, and accordingly he sent an envoy, Heliodorus, to plunder the Temple. This wicked intent was frustrated by a miracle (II Macc. 3:23ff.), and the situation was saved for the moment.

This incident accentuated the tension that existed in Judea between the more orthodox Jews and those who had succumbed to Hellenism. The latter were endeavoring to end the separation between Jews and Gentiles, and were using the language, habits, and traditions of the Greeks as means to this end. These Hellenized Jews were strongly in favor of Seleucid ideals, and were led by Simon and his brother Menelaus. The more orthodox section of Jewry remained loyal to Onias, and favored the leadership of Egypt. They resisted the encroachments of Hellenism with great vigor, in the realization that their traditional religious beliefs had nothing in common with the scepticism, irreligion, and moral degeneration of Hellenic culture.

Role of Antiochus IV

In 175 B.C. Seleucus IV was succeeded by Antiochus IV Epiphanes, who reigned for eleven years. His avowed policy was the dissemination of Greek culture throughout his realm, so as to unify the various races of his heterogeneous empire and insure the stability of the Seleucid regime.[7] Antiochus was a proud, extravagant ruler, and the popular assessment of his character was reflected in the cynical play on words that altered his royal title from

A view of Cave 4 in the cliffs of the Wadi Qumran.
The steep rock-face makes access extremely difficult.

The reconstructed watch-tower at the Qumran settlement.

Epiphanes ("illustrious") to Epimanes ("madman"). With his accession the policy of severity towards Judaism that Seleucus IV had considered became an actuality, boding ill for the inhabitants of Judea. Almost immediately after his accession, Antiochus was involved in a dispute between the Hellenizing faction and the orthodox Jews in Jerusalem. Probably as the result of intrigue, a difference of opinion had arisen between the high priest Onias III and his younger brother Joshua. The latter was the leader of the Hellenizing party in Jerusalem, and had gone so far as to reject his Semitic name for the Greek form Jason.

True to his policy of forcing Hellenic culture upon his subjects, Antiochus decided in favor of Jason, and removed the patriotic and loyal Onias from office. In return for a large bribe he installed Jason as high priest in 174 B.C., on condition that the Hellenizing of Jerusalem would be accomplished as expeditiously as possible. Accordingly Jason received permission to establish a gymnasium in the city, and he set about encouraging the spread of Greek fashions in a manner that caused dismay among the loyalists, or Hasidim, as they became known. A number of serious conflicts broke out between the Hellenist Jews and the Hasidim, and involved the Temple priesthood. After three years Jason was supplanted by Menelaus, who gave an even larger bribe to Antiochus for the privilege of becoming high priest. But Jason was not to be outdone, and a period of bitter conflict ensued, which ultimately forced Antiochus himself to intervene.

At this time he had virtually completed his second military campaign against

Egypt when a rumor that he had been killed in battle reached Jerusalem. This report encouraged Jason to reassert himself, and further turmoil ensued in Jerusalem. On hearing of what had transpired in Judea, Antiochus brought his campaign to a close and marched angrily on Jerusalem. He pillaged the Temple and put many thousands of people to death as an act of reprisal. To suppress any further revolts he installed a Phrygian of barbaric disposition as military governor, while he himself went to Antioch.

Reprisals Against Jerusalem

In 168 B.C. Antiochus prepared for another military expedition against Egypt, and was within sight of Alexandria when word of his intentions reached the senate in Rome. An envoy was dispatched to Antiochus, who told him bluntly to abandon any plans he might have for the conquest of Egypt. Antiochus was wise enough to see that disobedience would involve him in war with Rome, a situation he wished to avoid at all costs. But the rebuff stung his pride, and he marched in anger once more on Jerusalem, on which he determined to vent his rage.

It was his intention to eradicate Judaism and colonize the territory with people of Hellenic sympathies, and with this in mind he sent Apollonius in

A view of the remains of the community buildings at Qumran, with the cliffs of Wadi Qumran beyond. The sect seems to have originated in the Maccabean period. See p. 328ff.

168 B.C. with a detachment of twenty thousand men to the city. This army took advantage of the sabbath day to enter the city and begin their work of destruction. A royal decree ordered all that was characteristic of Judaism to be removed. The Temple was profaned and the sacred books of the law were burned. A Greek altar was erected in the Temple courts and the sacrificial worship of Judaism was prohibited. Pagan religious rites were introduced and the people were compelled to participate in them on pain of death. The city walls, which had been built by Nehemiah, were destroyed and the old city of David was refortified and garrisoned by Syrian soldiery.

In 167 B.C. a further decree forbade circumcision, sabbath observance, and the reading of the law. Indecent orgies were encouraged in Temple buildings, and the Jews were forced to take part in pagan worship and eat unclean food. Resistance to these measures took various forms. Some of the Hasidim perished in the massacres while others fled to the wilderness. Some adopted the principle of passive resistance whereas others embraced the new order with an outward show of acceptance if not of enthusiasm.

The Maccabean Revolt

Active resistance to the Syrian regime flared up at Modin (I Macc. 2:14ff.), not far from Jerusalem, where the priest, Mattathias, who belonged to the Hasmonean family, killed an apostate Jew and a Greek officer who were attempting to make him sacrifice to idols. Mattathias immediately fled to the hills, accompanied by a group of loyalists, and there commenced a guerrilla campaign against the forces of Antiochus (I Macc. 2:45). He succeeded in persuading his followers that the law of sabbath observance must not interfere with self-preservation, and thereafter the guerrilla tactics of his armed bands proved surprisingly successful in harassing the Syrian forces.

When Mattathias died in 167 B.C., he was succeeded by his son Judas Maccabaeus (I Macc. 2:49ff.), who, emboldened by success, began systematic military campaigns against the enemy. So well trained and equipped were the Jewish forces that they defeated the Syrians in battle at Beth-horon in 166 B.C., and in the following year at Bethzur, where the Syrian regent Lysias was in command. Lysias retreated to Antioch, being unable to call upon Antiochus for military assistance, since the latter was already engaged in crushing an uprising in Parthia and Armenia. Judas Maccabaeus took advantage of the opportunity to reconsecrate the polluted sanctuary at Jerusalem and restore the daily sacrifice. For the next two years Judas was in virtual control

Observant Jews pray at the so-called "Wailing Wall", Jerusalem. Now usually known as the Western Wall, some of the masonry in the wall dates from the time of Herod the Great and formed part of the outer wall of the Temple area.

of Judea, and he began to regroup and strengthen his forces in anticipation of a further Syrian invasion.

Antiochus died in 163 B.C., and was succeeded by his nine-year-old son Antiochus V, who reigned for two years. In 163 B.C. Judas mustered his forces in an attempt to expel the Syrian garrison from the old city in Jerusalem, and at the same time Lysias set out with a large army and joined with other troops, which had been sent by the young Antiochus to regain control of Judea (II Macc. 9:1ff.). A fierce battle was fought near Bethlehem, and Judas suffered a decisive defeat. But Lysias had received news that the person whom Antiochus Epiphanes had appointed as guardian for his young son, and whose functions had been taken over by Lysias, was marching towards Antioch. In view of these circumstances, Lysias hurriedly concluded a treaty with Judas by which the religious liberties of the Jews were restored, and then he withdrew to Antioch.

Further trouble in Jerusalem followed the nomination of the Hellenist Alcimus (Eliakim) as high priest. When the Maccabees opposed his appointment, Alcimus appealed to Demetrius I (162–150 B.C.), the successor of Antiochus V, for his assistance, and a Syrian force led by Nicanor was sent to Jerusalem. Nicanor was killed in battle in 161 B.C. near Beth-horon, and with his passing it appeared that the long-desired independence from the Seleucid regime was at last in sight. But heavy reinforcements had already been dispatched to aid Nicanor, and although they arrived too late to serve their original purpose, they were thrown into the battle against the forces of Judas, who were overwhelmed by superior numbers. Judas himself was killed and his followers had to flee for their lives. According to the narrative in I Maccabees 8:31, Judas had endeavored to secure the protection of Rome, but instructions from the senate to Demetrius requesting him not to oppress the friends and confederates of the republic arrived too late to prevent the attack on Judas that resulted in his death.

End of the Revolt

The religious war Mattathias had commenced really came to an end with the treaty by which Lysias guaranteed the restoration of Jewish liberties (I Macc. 6:59). While a strong Hellenizing party still remained in Judea, the majority of the people gave solid support to the Maccabeans, who are often known by their family name of Hasmoneans. Jonathan succeeded his brother Judas as leader of the loyalist movement, and he attempted to remove Alcimus from the office of high priest, on which he himself had designs. His activities took a different turn, however, after Alcimus died in 159 B.C., and he began a series of military operations against Syria that resulted in the withdrawal of Syrian forces from Judea in 153 B.C. Jonathan became military governor of

Excavations in the Negeb have disclosed the ruins of Avdat, a town built by the Nabateans. It may have been in the vicinity of this place that Ezra was supposed to have received a vision (II Esdras 9:26).

Judea, and he increased his control of the country to such an extent that Demetrius sought his friendship. Alexander Balas, who succeeded Demetrius in 150 B.C., helped Jonathan to achieve his ambition by appointing him as high priest of the nation (I Macc. 10:20), and this was confirmed by Demetrius II, who succeeded Balas as king of Syria in 145 B.C.

Independence from Syria

Jonathan might have brought the nation to independent sovereignty had he not become involved with the internal dissensions of the Syrian empire. An ambitious general who had supported the claims of Antiochus VI, the son of Balas, to the Syrian throne plotted against Jonathan, and put him to death in 142 B.C. Simon, the last surviving son of Mattathias, succeeded Jonathan, and took advantage of internal strife in Syria to win freedom from tribute for his people (I Macc. 13:41) in 142 B.C. That same year the Syrian garrison in the old city of Jerusalem capitulated, and the triumph of the Hasmoneans was complete.

A formal decree was issued in 141 B.C. which recognized Simon as hereditary high priest and governor of the Jews (I Macc. 14:41). Being now independent of Syrian control, the nation enjoyed a period of peace and prosperity, during which Simon enforced the traditional customs and beliefs of the Jews, and established the supremacy of the law. He paid considerable attention to the economy of the kingdom, and developed the natural resources of the country. Because foreign trade was important to the stability of the national life, he encouraged the development of a brisk import and export business based on the seaport of Joppa.

Rule of John Hyrcanus

Only seven years after he had assumed leadership in Judea, Simon was treacherously murdered, along with two of his sons, by his son-in-law Ptolemy. In 135 B.C. John Hyrcanus, the one surviving son, succeeded Simon, and he began to consolidate his position in Judea. But the independence of the nation was soon challenged by a new Syrian king, Antiochus VII Sidetes (139–129 B.C.), who demanded payment of tribute from Judea. When this request was ignored, he invaded the country and laid siege to Jerusalem. Hyrcanus was forced to come to terms, and he agreed to become tributary once again to the Seleucid regime.

But when Antiochus VII was killed in an expedition against Parthia in 129 B.C., Hyrcanus repudiated the agreement and capitalized on the internal weakness of the Syrian empire to extend the borders of his own realm. He fought a number of battles in Transjordan, and then attacked Shechem, the chief center of the schismatic Samaritans, in 128 B.C. After subjugating the Edomites, he laid siege to Samaria, which fell after a protracted struggle. Hyrcanus was a brilliant administrator and a forceful leader, whose chief aim appears to have been the territorial expansion of his kingdom to the proportions of the monarchy during the Solomonic era. He was less distinctive as a religious figure, however, and during his reign he withdrew from the religious party which by then was known as the Pharisees, and which had become heir to the ideals of the Hasidim.[8] Towards the end of his life his antipathy to Pharisaic doctrines drove him into the camp of the Sadducees, whose aims were secular and political rather than religious.

Unrest in Judea

The death of Hyrcanus in 105 B.C. was followed by the short reigns of his three sons, Aristobulus, Antigonus, and Alexander Jannaeus. The latter, who reigned from 104 B.C. to 78 B.C., was a weak, dissolute individual, whose military policies provoked a good deal of resentment among those who cherished the ideals of Judaism. He endeavored to enlarge the territory over which his father had ruled, and after a number of attempts he conquered most of the large towns on the Philistine coast as well as securing large areas of

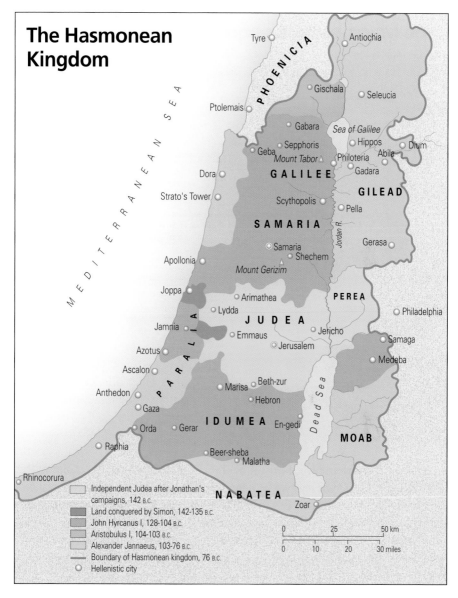

The Hasmonean Kingdom

Tyre

PHOENICIA

Antiochia

MEDITERRANEAN SEA

Gischala

Seleucia

Ptolemais

Gabara

Sea of Galilee

Sepphoris

Hippos

Dium

Geba

Mount Tabor

Philoteria

Abila

Dora

GALILEE

Gadara

GILEAD

Strato's Tower

Scythopolis

Pella

SAMARIA

Jordan R.

Samaria

Shechem

Gerasa

Apollonia

Mount Gerizim

Joppa

Arimathea

PEREA

Lydda

Philadelphia

Jamnia

PARALIA

JUDEA

Jericho

Emmaus

Samaga

Azotus

Jerusalem

Ascalon

Medeba

Marisa

Beth-zur

Anthedon

Hebron

Dead Sea

Gaza

IDUMEA

En-gedi

MOAB

Orda

Gerar

Raphia

Beer-sheba

Malatha

Rhinocorura

Independent Judea after Jonathan's campaigns, 142 B.C.

NABATEA

Zoar

Land conquered by Simon, 142-135 B.C.

John Hyrcanus I, 128-104 B.C.

Aristobulus I, 104-103 B.C.

Alexander Jannaeus, 103-76 B.C.

Boundary of Hasmonean kingdom, 76 B.C.

O Hellenistic city

0   25   50 km

0   10   20   30 miles

Transjordan. But domestically his reign was marked by the increase of civil strife and discontent, for Jannaeus was a fervent supporter of Hellenism. In consequence he came into increasing conflict with the Pharisees, who mustered bitter opposition to his attempts to secularize the high-priesthood.[9]

Civil war finally broke out, and for six years Jannaeus used mercenary troops against the people of Judea in an attempt to regain control of the situation. After this the Pharisees enlisted the aid of Syria, and forced Jannaeus to flee. He made a desperate appeal to national sentiment, and secured pop-

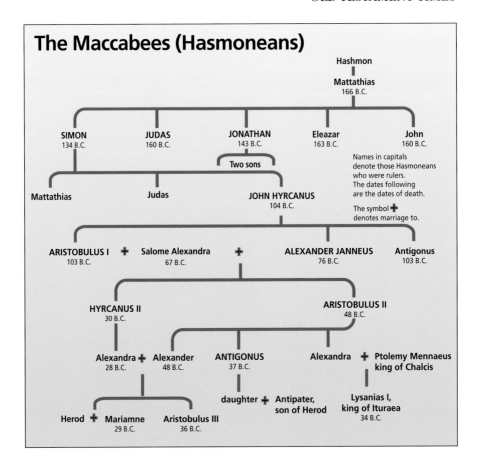

The Maccabees (Hasmoneans)

Hashmon

Mattathias
166 B.C.

SIMON
134 B.C.

JUDAS
160 B.C.

JONATHAN
143 B.C.

Two sons

Eleazar
163 B.C.

John
160 B.C.

Names in capitals
denote those Hasmoneans
who were rulers.
The dates following
are the dates of death.

The symbol ✚
denotes marriage to.

Mattathias

Judas

JOHN HYRCANUS
104 B.C.

ARISTOBULUS I ✚ Salome Alexandra ✚ ALEXANDER JANNEUS Antigonus
103 B.C. 67 B.C. 76 B.C. 103 B.C.

HYRCANUS II
30 B.C.

ARISTOBULUS II
48 B.C.

Alexandra ✚ Alexander
28 B.C. 48 B.C.

ANTIGONUS
37 B.C.

Alexandra ✚ Ptolemy Mennaeus
king of Chalcis

daughter ✚ Antipater,
son of Herod

Lysanias I,
king of Ituraea
34 B.C.

Herod ✚ Mariamne
29 B.C.

Aristobulus III
36 B.C.

ular support by depicting himself as the successor of the Maccabees. The opposition of the Pharisees was crushed, and Jannaeus exacted cruel reprisal by having eight hundred of the chief Pharisees crucified and their dependents slaughtered. When he died in 78 B.C., his widow Alexandra became queen, and came to terms with the Pharisees to such a degree that they assumed the real rule in Judea. Hyrcanus II, the elder son of Alexandra, was installed as high priest, but he was weak in character and submitted readily to Pharisaic manipulation.

Hyrcanus II had a younger brother, Aristobulus, a shrewd and able individual who disliked the political machinations of the Pharisees intensely. During the reign of Alexandra he was kept from contact with public affairs, but when she died in 69 B.C., Aristobulus compelled his brother to abdicate in his favor.[10] With his accession, the influence of the Hasmonean family began to decline, and he had barely become established in office with the assistance of the Sadducees when events took an unexpected turn.

A limestone ossuary from Palestine, c. first century B.C. Chests of this kind were used to store bones from previous burials to make room for later burials at the same site.

Rule of Aristobulus

Antipater, governor of Idumea, sided with Hyrcanus II, and, after weakening the position of Aristobulus by means of intrigue, he encouraged Hyrcanus to attempt the repossession of his throne. In this exploit Hyrcanus was supported by Arabian forces supplied by the king, to whom he had fled for refuge at an earlier time. Aristobulus was defeated in battle, and when most of his army deserted, he and his supporters took refuge in a citadel near the Temple, which Hyrcanus also besieged. At this juncture Rome intervened, but in 65 B.C. one of the staff officers of Pompey accepted a bribe to support Aristobulus and order the withdrawal of Hyrcanus. The following year Pompey himself marched into Syria and deposed Antiochus XIII, the last of the Seleucid dynasty, making Syria and Phoenicia into a Roman province. Pompey then prepared to act as arbitrator in the dispute, but after an appeal from the Pharisees for the abolition of Hasmonean rule, he suspended judgment temporarily.

Aristobulus took advantage of the lull to occupy the fortress of Alexandrium, whereupon Pompey marched against him and ordered him to capitulate. But fanatical elements in the Jewish ranks rejected this appeal to reason, and, fleeing to the Temple mount, they resisted the Roman forces for three months. When an assault on the Temple finally succeeded, a wholesale slaughter of the resurgents took place, in which twelve thousand people perished. Priests were killed as they conducted the sacrifices in the Temple, and Pompey himself marched with sword in hand into the Holy Place and inspected the Holy of Holies. He did not pillage the Temple, however, and when the fighting had ceased he ordered the sanctuary to be purified and the sacrifices to be resumed.

The leaders of the insurrection were promptly executed, and Aristobulus himself was taken in chains to Rome. Although Hyrcanus was allowed to retain the title of high priest and ethnarch, he was not permitted to rule as king. The sphere of his authority was severely restricted, so that in actual fact his jurisdiction extended over Judea alone. Jerusalem was garrisoned by Roman troops, while the districts outside Judea were incorporated into the newly formed province of Syria, Judea was compelled to pay tribute to Rome, and with this imposition the sovereignty of the Jewish state came to an end. Hyrcanus fell under the control of Antipater, father of Herod the Great, and although the Hasmoneans made several abortive attempts to regain power between 57 B.C. and 54 B.C., they were unable to overthrow the Herodian dynasty. Before Antipater was murdered in 43 B.C. he gained firm control over Judea by installing his eldest son as governor of Jerusalem and his younger son Herod the Great as governor of Galilee.[11]

Herod was a brilliant if ruthless individual, and his political astuteness enabled him to gain the support of Antony after the battle of Philippi in 42 B.C. But the son of Aristobulus II launched an attack against him with Parthian support, and though Herod was victorious, he had to flee to Rome, where Augustus recognized him as the rightful king of Judea in 40 B.C. The following year Herod returned to Ptolemais with an army and conquered Idumea, Samaria, and Galilee in quick succession. After a siege that lasted three months he took Jerusalem in 37 B.C., beheaded the son of Aristobulus II at Antioch, and regained full control of Judea.

Just before Jerusalem fell, Herod had married Mariamne, who as a descendant of both Aristobulus and Hyrcanus II represented the two opposing sections of the Hasmonean dynasty. But the temperamental and unscrupulous ruler did not feel secure as king of the Jews until he had murdered Mariamne

A view of Mount Tabor, easy to recognize by its unusual profile.

View of Herod the Great's palace (foreground) and stronghold (background) at Herodium.

and her surviving relatives. When this was accomplished in the first decade of his reign, the Hasmonean dynasty was at an end. Although Herod catered to the religious feelings of the Jews by enlarging the Temple, his acts of brutality and violence during the thirty-three years of his reign (37–4 B.C.) earned him the hatred of his subjects generally.

The hopes of independence for the nation that the Hasmoneans had entertained were no more. The Herodian dynasty controlled the political life of Judea under Roman supervision from this time. The Sanhedrin was already dominated by the Pharisees, who used their position to impose a wide variety of restrictions upon the religious life of the nation in an attempt to resist the incursions of Hellenism. While their political and economic ideals differed considerably from those of the Sadducees, they were determined to maintain their controlling interest in the life of the nation and at the same time show due deference to Roman overlordship. But the mass of the people longed for freedom from external restraint, and began to look increasingly to the mysterious personage of the Messiah, long promised by prophecy, as the one who would come in due time to restore an independent theocratic state in Judea, and rid the land once and for all of its burdensome oppressors.

The cistern of the community settlement at Qumran.

The Qumran Sect

This revival of the Messianic vision was but one indication of the religious ferment that had been a conspicuous feature of second-century-B.C. life in Judea. There was a good deal of dissatisfaction on the part of the general populace with the way in which the Sadducees and Pharisees were competing for power in the Jewish state. Some groups became so disillusioned with what they regarded as the blatant misuse of priestly functions that they broke away from the mainstream of Judaism and formed their own religious communities. In the century before the birth of Christ there were a number of baptizing Jewish sects in Judea, the remains of the most notable of these being discovered in 1947 in some caves high up the cliffs of the Wadi Qumran, and also at a nearby ruin. By chance some Bedouin Arabs discovered jars and manuscripts in the Qumran caves, and thus brought to the attention of the world the celebrated Dead Sea scrolls.[12]

The largest of these manuscripts was a copy of the book of Isaiah, which on examination proved to be nearly one thousand years older than any previously known copy. From the same cave were recovered a commentary on Habakkuk, a Community Rule that regulated the conduct of the sect from which the manuscripts had come, and another scroll which was in poor condition and which was later found to be a paraphrase of portions of Genesis. Other manuscripts that belonged to the same collection had been removed earlier by Arab tribesmen and subsequently came into the possession of the Hebrew University of Jerusalem. These scrolls included a smaller, fragmentary copy of the book of Isaiah, some thanksgiving hymns, and an allegorical document entitled "The War of the Sons of Light and the Sons of Darkness."

Further exploration of the general area revealed the presence of some other caves in the Wadi Qumran, which were found to contain additional manuscripts or fragments, while an adjacent ruin known as Khirbet Qumran attracted the attention of archaeologists from Jerusalem and Jordan. When the mound was partly excavated, it was found to have been the locale of the community, whose origins were subsequently placed in the Maccabean period. From the ruins emerged the remains of a community room, a dining hall, aqueducts and cisterns used for collecting rain water, workshops, and a scriptorium in which the manuscripts of the community had been copied out.

Excavations at the site from 1953 showed that there had been three principal periods of occupancy, the first of which, marked by the presence of coins from the time of John Hyrcanus (135–104 B.C.), extended to about 39 B.C. Perhaps an earthquake that damaged the community center caused the site to be abandoned for a time,[13] but at all events the second phase of occupancy began with the reign of Archelaus (4 B.C.–A.D. 6), as indicated by a cache of coins from that period. The center seems to have been abandoned again about A.D. 70, when it was perhaps occupied by Roman soldiers, if a few contemporary coins recovered from the site are any indication. The final stage of occupancy, marked by coins from the time of Hadrian (A.D. 117–138) shows that the settlement was probably used for a time by Jewish guerrillas during the period of the Second Jewish Revolt.[14]

The literature of the Qumran sectaries makes it evident that early in the second century B.C. the religious brotherhood had separated itself from what it regarded as the apostate priesthood of the Pharisees and Sadducees. In the desolation of the Judean wilderness the sectaries had established a baptizing community of a rigorous and exclusive character which was based firmly on the principles of the Mosaic law, and which regarded itself as being the only true forerunner of the Jewish Messiah.

The nature of their Messianic thought was indicated by the discovery of a collection of proof texts from the Old Testament on the subject, and also by the way in which their sacramental meal anticipated the triumphal banquet that would supposedly take place at the dawn of the Messianic age. It is one of the numerous ironies of Jewish history that this profoundly religious community, which was seeking in all earnestness to recapture that which was of abiding spiritual value in the tradition of the Hebrew people, was prevented by its very exclusiveness from ushering in the Messiah of Israel for whose coming it was striving so resolutely.

This expectation was realized shortly before Herod the Great died by the birth of Jesus Christ, the Messiah of God, whose coming fulfilled the hopes of the prophets. What was tragic about the situation was that the Jews failed to recognize in His person and work that larger deliverance of the human spirit which by its very nature transcended purely political or territorial considerations. The freedom Jesus was to win for men was of a spiritual order, liberating them from bondage to purely human institutions and claiming their loyalty to a kingdom that was not of this world. The atonement Jesus achieved on the cross emancipated men from subservience to sin and attained a redemptive goal that was utterly beyond the scope of the ancient law. It brought His sincere followers into a fellowship of spiritual liberty, transcending barriers of race and locale, and establishing upon earth a new and lasting Israel of God.

NOTES

1. N. Glueck, *Bulletin of the American Schools of Oriental Research* (1938), No. 72, pp. 11f.

2. *Ibid.* (1940), No. 80, pp. 3ff.

3. W. F. Albright, *The Archaeology of Palestine,* p. 149; *Archaeology and the Religion of Israel,* pp. 144ff.

4. J. Starcky, *The Biblical Archaeologist,* XVIII (1955), No. 4, p. 84.

5. W. H. Morton, *The Biblical Archaeologist,* XIX (1956), No. 2, pp. 26ff.

6. P. K. Hitti, *History of Syria* (1957), p. 243.

7. A. H. M. Jones, *The Herods of Judaea* (1938), pp. 7f.

8. Cf. Josephus, *Antiquities of the Jews,* XIII, 10, 5f.

9. Cf. H. Loewe in *Judaism and Christianity,* I (1931), pp. 123ff.

10. Josephus, *Antiquities of the Jews,* XIV, 1, 1ff.; *A History of the Jewish People in the Time of Christ* (1899 ed.), 11, 2, pp. 313ff.

11. A. H. M. Jones, *op. cit.,* pp. 62ff.

12. For early accounts see M. Burrows, *The Dead Sea Scrolls* (1955); J. M. Allegro, *The Dead Sea Scrolls* (1956). The first decade of discovery is discussed in R. K. Harrison, *The Dead Sea Scrolls* (1961).

13. Cf. Josephus, *Wars of the Jews,* I, 19, 3.

14. M. Burrows, *op. cit.,* pp. 65f.

Indexes

Index

Page numbers in *italics*
represent pages with illustrations

irrigation 38, 41, 42
Isaac 73, 84, 88–89, 90
Isaiah 219, 234, 240, 241, 244
Ishbi–Irra 54–55
Ishbosheth 191
Ishmael 84, 262
Ishtar Gate *267, 271*
Isin *55*
Israel: as Chosen People 24–26; in Egypt
    110–111, 119–122, 126; nationhood
    136; new name for Jacob 90
Israel (northern kingdom) 212–213;
    Assyrian captivity 234, 236; maps 215,
    227, 233; and other nations 9–10
Ithet–Tawy 108
ivory 228–229

Jabesh–gilead 180–181
Jabin 170, 175
Jacob 88–90; and birthright 74; death 111;
    enters Egypt 110–111; and Laban
    89–90; map 91; meets Esau 90; name
    69
Jael 176
Jaosh 260
Jashar, Book of 24
Jason (high priest) 318–319
Jebel Musa 134
Jebel Serbal 134
Jeconiah 257
Jehoahaz I 226
Jehoahaz II 256
Jehoash 224, 226, 228
Jehoiada 224
Jehoiachin 257, 268
Jehoiakim 256–257, 261
Jehoram 217, 222–223
Jehoshaphat 222, 223, 314
Jehu 224, 226
Jemdet Nasr 40
Jephthah 177
Jeremiah 255, 256, 258, 262, 265,
    269–270
Jericho *21,* 167–*169;* excavations 22, 36,
    122, 124, 126, *151*–152; Hyksos period
    94; significance 152
Jeroboam I 212
Jeroboam II 228, 229, 232
Jerusalem: in David's time *192–193,*
    194–195; falls to Babylon 257–258;

foundation 110; garrisoned by Rome
    328; invaded by Antiochus 320;
    Solomon's building program 208–*211;*
    walls 287–290, 320, *321; see also under*
    temples
Jesus Christ 333
Jethro 134
Jezebel 217, 218, 224
Jirku, A. 80
Joab 191, 198–200, 201
Joash 224, 226, 228
Jonathan Maccabeus 322–323
Joppa 324
Joram 217, 222–223
Jordan (river), crossed by Israelites 167
Joseph 90–94; death 111; and Egypt 24,
    110; inheritance rights 76; length of
    life 26
Josephus 314
Joshua 134, 150–152; builds shrine 305;
    length of life 26
Josiah 248–252, 256
Jotham 234
Judah (kingdom), and other nations 9–10
Judah (southern kingdom) 212–213;
    captivity in Babylon 257–260,
    264–275; fall 239–262; maps 215, 259;
    tributary to Babylon 257
Judas Maccabaeus 320–322
Judea 286; annexed by Syria 315; and
    other nations 10; tributary to Rome
    328; under Herod 328–330
judges 175–176

Kadesh-barnea 142
Kahun papyri 15
Karnak Temple *14*
Kenites 134
Kenyon, Kathleen 21, 22, 126, 151, 168
Khafre 103
Khamosis 111
Kharkar 221
Khatti 86
Khattusas 88
Khufu 102
Kibroth–hattaavah 142
king lists 15–16, 26–27, 44–45, 214–216
King's Highway 81, 142
kingship, Sumerian 43
Kiriath-sepher 171–172

INDEX

Index of Bible References

Maps and Plans